Recent progress towards economic and monetary union in Western Europe has highlighted the importance of regional policies, while events in Eastern Europe have focused attention on the role of finance in development and may lead to a substantial diversion of international capital flows. Research on endogenous growth has considered the relationships among growth, convergence and capital market imperfections, focusing on the contribution of capital markets to the real economy and the effects on developing countries of increased access to international capital markets.

This volume, derived from a conference on 'Finance and Development in Europe', held by the Centre for Economic Policy Research in Santiago de Compostela on 13–15 December 1991, with financial support from the Regional Government of Galicia, addresses many of these issues. Theoretical papers shed light on the debates over the role of financial structure in economic development and the scope for government intervention to promote regional development. A number of highly topical empirical papers examine the relationship between international lending and economic development in a historical perspective, the recent experience of regional policies in the European Community and its member states and of financial liberalization in the high-growth East Asian economies, and the development of financial markets in the transforming economies of Eastern Europe.

Finance and development: issues and experience

Centre for Economic Policy Research

The Centre for Economic Policy Research is a network of more than 170 Research Fellows, based primarily in European universities. The Centre coordinates its Fellows' research activities and communicates their results to the public and private sectors. CEPR is an entrepreneur, developing research initiatives with the producers, consumers and sponsors of research. Established in 1983, CEPR is already a European economics research organization with uniquely wide-ranging scope and activities.

CEPR is a registered educational charity. Grants from the Leverhulme Trust, the Esmée Fairbairn Charitable Trust, the Baring Foundation, the Bank of England and Citibank provide institutional finance. The ESRC supports the Centre's dissemination programme and, with the Nuffield Foundation, its programme of research workshops. None of these organizations gives prior review to the Centre's publications nor necessarily endorses the views expressed therein.

The Centre is pluralist and non-partisan, bringing economic research to bear on the analysis of medium- and long-run policy questions. CEPR research may include views on policy, but the Executive Committee of the Centre does not give prior review to its publications and the Centre takes no institutional policy positions. The opinions expressed in this volume are those of the authors and not those of the Centre for Economic Policy Research.

17 August 1992

Finance and development: issues and experience

Edited by
ALBERTO GIOVANNINI

CAMBRIDGE
UNIVERSITY PRESS

CAMBRIDGE UNIVERSITY PRESS
Cambridge, New York, Melbourne, Madrid, Cape Town, Singapore, São Paulo

Cambridge University Press
The Edinburgh Building, Cambridge CB2 8RU, UK

Published in the United States of America by Cambridge University Press, New York

www.cambridge.org
Information on this title: www.cambridge.org/9780521440172

First published 1993
This digitally printed version 2008

A catalogue record for this publication is available from the British Library

Library of Congress Cataloguing in Publication data
Finance and development: issues and experience / edited by Alberto Giovannini
    p.   cm.
  'A selection from the papers presented at the conference on "Finance and
Development in Europe", jointly sponsored by the Centre for Economic
Policy Research and the Xunta de Galicia . . . [and held] in Santiago de
Compostela on 13–15 December 1991' – Pref.
  Includes index.
  ISBN 0 521 44017 3 (hc)
  1. Economic development – Finance – Congresses.
2. Regional planning – Congresses. 3. Economic development – Finance –
Case studies – Congresses. 4. Regional planning – Case studies – Congresses.
I. Giovannini, Albert. II. Centre for Economic Policy Research (Great Britain).
III. Galicia (Spain: Region). Xunta.
HD75.F56 1993
338.9 – dc20 92–38166 CIP

ISBN 978-0-521-44017-2 hardback
ISBN 978-0-521-05756-1 paperback

Contents

Figures

Tables

Preface

This volume contains a selection from the papers presented at the conference on 'Finance and Development in Europe', jointly sponsored by the Centre for Economic Policy Research and the Xunta de Galicia. The conference was part of the CEPR research programme in International Macroeconomics, and was hosted by the Xunta de Galicia in Santiago de Compostela on 13–15 December 1991. We gratefully acknowledge the Xunta's impeccable hospitality and financial support.

I would like to thank a number of individuals who have contributed to the success of this project. First and foremost is Guillermo de la Dehesa, a member of the Centre's Executive Committee, who encouraged me in the pursuit of the project, organized the conference with me, and put CEPR in contact with the sponsors. Guilllermo's enthusiasm is a powerful engine of CEPR activities. David Guthrie and Kate Millward have pushed this volume through the various production stages with unfailing energy and determination. John Black of the University of Exeter, as Production Editor, has helped maintain the high standard of CEPR publications.

Alberto Giovannini

Conference participants

Philippe Aghion *European Bank for Reconstruction and Development and CEPR*
Richard Baldwin *Institut Universitaire des Hautes Etudes Internationales, Genève and CEPR*
David Begg *Birkbeck College, London, and CEPR*
William Branson *Princeton University and CEPR*
Robin Burgess *European Bank for Reconstruction and Development*
Guillermo Calvo *IMF*
Daniel Cohen *Université de Paris I, Ecole Normal Supérieure, CEPREMAP, Paris, and CEPR*
Susan Collins *Harvard University*
Juan Ramón Cuadrado *Universidad de Madrid*
Guillermo de la Dehesa *Banco Pastor and CEPR*
Angel de la Fuente *Universidad Autónoma de Barcelona*
Riccardo Faini *Università degli Studi di Brescia and CEPR*
John Flemming *European Bank for Reconstruction and Development*
Giampaolo Galli *Banca d'Italia*
Curzio Giannini *Banca d'Italia*
Alberto Giovannini *Columbia University and CEPR*
Bruce Greenwald *Columbia University*
Patrick Honohan *The Economic and Social Research Institute, Dublin*
Thomas Huertas *Citibank*
Paul Krugman *MIT and CEPR*
Ramon Marimon *Universitat Pompeu Fabra, Barcelona*
Colin Mayer *City University Business School, London, and CEPR*
Antonio Mello *Banco de Portugal*
Stefano Micossi *Confindustria*
Ronald McKinnon *Stanford University*
Yung Chul Park *Korea University*
Joan Pearce *Commission of the European Communities*

xvi

Richard Portes *CEPR and Birkbeck College, London*
Andrés Precedo *Universidad de Santiago de Compostela*
Helmut Reisen *OECD*
Rafael Repullo *Banco de España and CEPR*
André Sapir *Commission of the European Communities and CEPR*
Luigi Spaventa *Università degli Studi di Roma, 'La Sapienza', and CEPR*
Joseph Stiglitz *Stanford University*
Oren Sussman *Hebrew University of Jerusalem*
Susie Symes *Commission of the European Communities*
Xavier Vives *Universitat Autònoma de Barcelona and CEPR*
David Webb *LSE*
Stephen Yeo *CEPR*
Antonio Zabalza Marti *Ministerio de Economia y Hacienda, Madrid*

1 Introduction

ALBERTO GIOVANNINI

The creation of the Single European Market and Economic and Monetary Union (EMU) are likely to change in a profound way the economic landscape of Europe. These processes are effectively taking away from national governments their ability to regulate the economy, both directly – by imposing pan-European regulatory standards, or giving regulatory authority to EC institutions – and indirectly – by allowing greater mobility to factors of production, thereby facilitating regulatory avoidance.

What would be the effects of the single market and EMU? Suppose that non-tariff barriers have persisted until 1992, and will be largely eliminated in 1993 or soon after. Standard international trade models would suggest that the elimination of the last barriers to trade would produce, in every country, greater specialization, by causing the progressive shrinkage and elimination of entire sectors located in individual countries, and – correspondingly – the booming of other sectors. Less standard models, emphasizing external economies and the gains from geographical proximity, would predict that increased international factor mobility would create new pockets of poverty, possibly exacerbate the problems of existing underdeveloped areas, and at the same time bolster richer areas.

These phenomena, coupled with the reduced effectiveness of government policies, will – according to some – signficantly increase the exposure of the standard of living of individuals in every European country to economic disturbances, by decreasing the ability of governments to provide insurance against income fluctuations.

It is this interpretation of the effects of the single market and EMU that has prompted many EC countries to bargain for greater 'structural funds', that is greater transfers of resources from the richer to the poorer countries. Such a response, however, meets a naturally sceptical reaction from the economics profession, which regards the system of transfers as being particularly vulnerable to political influences and to downright

1

corruption, and unable to allocate funds where they are needed most (that is, where they are most productive).

What do economists regard as the preferred response to the changes brought about by market integration, for the purpose of minimizing the creation of pockets of poverty? On this question there are, perhaps not surprisingly, two views. The first view emphasizes the efficiency of financial markets and intermediaries in allocating funds across different regions. According to this view, the right response to increased market integration is a thorough removal of all barriers to financial markets and intermediaries in Europe. Only if financial integration is truly complete will financial markets be able to bring funds where they are needed most, and perform the income-smoothing functions that economics textbooks assign to them. In this world, an area of poverty is an area where investment is too low, and therefore the productivity of capital is high. An area of poverty is a profit opportunity for financial intermediaries. Thus, the systematic pursuit of profit opportunities would, in the long run, eliminate pockets of underdevelopment.

The alternative view recognizes the presence of market and informational failures, and attempts to strike a balance between good efficiency criteria and the reality and imperfections of financial intermediation. Macroeconomic evidence seems to support the view that international financial integration is limited, or at any rate does not provide much income-smoothing. The correlation of per capita consumption across industrial countries is small, and savings and investment are highly correlated, even among industrial countries.

While a majority of economists would agree on the presence of financial market imperfections, the issue of their practical importance and their implications is much more controversial. Is it enough to encourage financial activities? What should be the appropriate forms of regulation? For example, some economists indicate, as a solution to the problem of pockets of poverty, the possibility of increasing the activity of development financing institutions. They claim that government-sponsored financial intermediaries identify, promote and monitor investment projects in less developed areas better than private intermediaries, and, like the World Bank, provide the right mixture of private and public finance (with governments essentially offering a capital commitment to bolster the creditworthiness of the institution). This solution, however, is by no means universally regarded as the answer to the problems raised above. Indeed, it is fair to say that there is to date no general theory of second best that, accounting for the informational and market failures in finance, indicates the optimal nature and extent of government intervention.

The papers in this volume provide a rather complete discussion of the theoretical and empirical questions surrounding the role of finance in economic development. Since the work of McKinnon (1973) and Shaw (1973) a whole branch of development economics has studied financial issues in developing countries. The questions raised by McKinnon, Shaw and their followers are not only classic questions for economic research, but also pressing issues in policy-making. They include the desirability of financial liberalization in developing countries, as well as the appropriate sequencing of liberalization, the role of foreign capital in economic development and the connections between monetary policy, financial markets, and financial capital flows.

Such essentially 'macro' questions are now receiving increased attention from micro finance theorists, who are reviving the research started by McKinnon and Shaw. The papers in this volume are an example of this renewed interest in development finance. The volume is divided into three parts. Part I contains four theoretical discussions on the role of financial markets in economic development. Part II presents a number of case studies, with those in Part IIA concentrating on financial markets, and those in Part IIB concentrating on government policies. The paper in Part III discusses the problems of financial intermediaries devoted to development financing, and in particular the European Bank for Reconstruction and Development. The volume is closed by an overview chapter.

In Part I, Paul Krugman reviews several theoretical strands on the role of international capital flows in economic development. Starting from the neoclassical growth model, he points out that traditional growth accounting assigns a very limited role to capital inflows in the generation of economic growth, under the standard assumptions about the aggregate production function. He suggests that the traditional two-gap theory of development might be more useful to identify the productivity of foreign capital, for example, in the former socialist economies now liberalizing. The new growth theory provides an even more dismal picture on the role of capital in economic development. Indeed, it is possible to construct cases where capital mobility might actually exacerbate the problems of underdevelopment, rather than alleviate them.

The problem of capital mobility is tackled more directly in the paper by Bruce Greenwald, Alec Levinson and Joseph Stiglitz. These authors explore the implications of a given informational structure, whereby local (regional) banks have better information about the value of local investment projects than banks located outside the region, but worse information than the entrepreneurs undertaking the investments. This model implies, as an extension of the standard credit rational results, that extra-regional lenders are bound to attract lower-quality borrowers, and thus they are bound to charge higher rates of interest. The paper also highlights the role of financial linkages among the regional markets. If regional banks cannot fully insure against region-specific shocks using national financial markets, it is possible that fluctuations in investment opportunities will give rise to externalities within regions, with multiplier effects on local economies. Greenwald, Levinson and Stiglitz provide evidence on the determinants of employment growth in US industries which they deem consistent with the presence of such externalities.

The role of capital flows is also the focus of the paper by Daniel Cohen. He asks whether opening a country to international borrowing and lending affects its growth performance. He shows that 'regions' (which are by definition financially integrated) and 'nations' (which are defined as less financially integrated with the rest of the world) in the steady state should grow at approximately the same rate, given the parameters in the model he uses. However, the liberalization of international capital flows can affect capital accumulation and growth significantly. Cohen finds that capital-poor countries that gain sudden access to the world capital markets should experience a fast and large increase in capital accumulation. Hence their growth rate peaks on impact, to gradually reach the steady state (which is approximately the same in open and closed economies). Despite these theoretical predictions, Cohen finds that, for a group of 34 developing countries that have benefited from renewed access to the world financial markets in the seventies, capital accumulation was actually less than for other developing countries. This evidence is against the predictions of growth models presented by Cohen. It could be due to data problems in the empirical implementation of the models or, more likely, to the presence of factors affecting capital accumulation and international capital flows that are not present in the models, and are not necessarily orthogonal to the variables included in the models.

Among the factors affecting capital accumulation one of the most important is financial intermediation. The financial industry displays – across countries – widely different degrees of development not only because of different regulatory constraints, but also because the profitability of such industry depends, possibly in a complex way, on the degree of development in each country. The paper by Oren Sussman examines these questions. Sussman studies a model of monopolistically competitive banking firms, whose costs of monitoring are affected by their 'proximity' to the borrowers (proximity is here to be interpreted in an informational sense). Hence each bank becomes more efficient the more specialized it is (that is, the smaller its market share). Increased specialization lowers the cost of financial intermediation. Having established a positive relationship between the aggregate capital stock and the efficiency of the banking industry, the author also finds that an increase in the capital stock of a country decreases the share of the financial system in GNP.

Sussman also provides some empirical evidence, along two lines. First, he examines the correlation between a standardized measure of markup in financial intermediation and GNP per capita over a cross-section of 81 countries for which data is available. He finds a weak negative relation between the markup and GNP per capita. In addition, he updates an early analysis by Kuznets on the relationship between the share of the financial sector in GDP and GDP per capita. He finds, contrary to the prediction of the theory but strengthening the results of Kuznets, that higher per-capita GDP is associated with a larger share of the financial sector. Like Cohen, Sussman concludes that straightforward predictions of simple economic models of the financial system are difficult to reconcile with the data.

The second part of this volume contains four case studies. Part IIA concentrates on the role of financial markets in economic development, and looks at the experience of Southern Italy, Korea and Taiwan. The paper by Riccardo Faini, Giampaolo Galli and Curzio Giannini provides a very thorough analysis of the relation between underdevelopment and the financial system, using a variety of datasets on the South of Italy. They start by observing a very marked negative correlation between loan rates and GDP per capita across Italian provinces. Looking at a dataset of 35,711 loan contracts between 76 banks and 9,127 firms they are able to conclude that, although firms in the South are generally riskier than in the rest of the country, the differential between loan rates in the South and the rest of the country has also to be attributed to higher costs of banks and less competition in financial intermediation. Local banks have measurable informational advantages, so much so that outside banks rely on various types of rationing practices. Finally, the authors find that the efficiency of the financial intermediation system appears to be lower in the South of Italy, as reflected by the fact that high-risk, high-return firms tend to be excluded from external finance and must rely more heavily on retained earnings. Faini, Galli and Giannini conclude their study by observing that the system of special credit institutions charging subsidized rates on their loans carries serious distortions, because it cuts out high-risk, high-return projects from long-term financing.

Discussing the experience in South Korea and Taiwan, Yung Chul Park questions the traditional view that the liberalization of financial markets is the main motor of development in the financial sector, and removes a major bottleneck in economic development. He argues that the deregulation of the 1980s has not appreciably affected the behaviour of financial intermediaries, and that financial growth – whether originating from deregulation or, as he finds more plausible, from output growth – is not associated with a higher average productivity of investment. Park concludes that, while the financial system clearly plays a crucial role in development, building a financial infrastructure beyond a certain level might not be as productive as often it is claimed to be.

Part IIB of this volume contains two case studies of the effects of government policies in the field of finance and development. The first, by Ronald McKinnon, surveys the problems of communist economies in their transition to a free market. The two central features of the macro financial system in a socialist economy are the implicit nature of taxation and the passive nature of money and credit allocation to enterprises. Taxes are implicit in the system of state-determined prices, which in communist countries has ended up extracting surpluses from agriculture through the building up of 'monopoly' profits in industrial enterprises. Money and credit allocation to enterprises is passive because the liquidity needs of enterprises are readily and freely matched, and liquidity hoardings are accumulated until either expropriated or spent. Given these initial conditions, two phenomena, according to McKinnon, are often observed when socialist economies liberalize. First, serious scarcity of government funds is experienced, due to the inability to set up a well-working tax system which is based on market incentives. This leads to monetization of fiscal deficits, and adds to the reluctance of firms to maintain liquid balances. As a result, and this is the second noteworthy phenomenon, firms end up carrying excess inventories of either goods or productive capital, leading to a misallocation of productive resources.

The second case study on government policies, by Juan Ramón Cuadrado, Guillermo de la Dehesa and Andrés Precedo, discusses the experience of regional subsidies in Spain. Their main conclusion is that regional policies in that country, rather than aiming at stimulating economic activity, have tried to compensate, ex-post, income differentials. They have, perhaps for this reason, failed to close the gap between poor and rich regions. The problem of 'compensatory' transfers in Spain has been that they protected backward regions from increased competition and, by reducing labour mobility, they have avoided migration from backward to prosperous regions, and the attendant adjustment of wage rates.

Part III of the volume, on the role of government-sponsored development financing contains one paper, by Philippe Aghion and Robin Burgess, on the areas of activity of the European Bank for Reconstruction and Development (EBRD). While the *prima facie* case for government intervention in development financing in the transition of socialist economies to free markets is obvious, much less obvious is the design of appropriate forms of intervention. The paper by Aghion and Burgess nicely complements the discussion of macroeconomic issues of McKinnon, by listing the microeconomic problems facing restructuring socialist economies, especially in the area of privatization. The authors suggest that an international agency like EBRD could provide a useful intermediary role between privatizing companies and potential foreign partners, could coordinate large scale privatization projects by providing its own expertise, and could bolster restructuring for those firms that cannot be privatized immediately, because of obsolescence in technological processes, in their trade structure (relying heavily on the Comecon command system), and in their management systems and culture.

Thus, Aghion and Burgess seem to conceive development banks as providers of expertise on a wide range of issues, which they deem to be inter-related in an important way. In the conception of Aghion and Burgess, the provision of financial resources has more of a subsidiary role in the activities of a development bank than traditionally envisaged.

The overview essay by Joseph Stiglitz, which closes this volume, further explores the implications of the pervasiveness of market failures and non-convexities in developing countries. Stiglitz questions the hypothesis that freer and more competitive financial markets necessarily allocate resources more efficiently. He claims that much of the literature on finance and development has focussed, mistakenly, on secondary capital markets, while the function of raising capital and allocating it efficiently is usually performed by primary capital markets.

Overall, the papers in this volume offer a rather sceptical assessment of the role of financial markets in economic development. In particular the papers have indicated that, first, simple growth models and models of the role of financial intermediation in the economy do not work very well, and even if they did, capital cannot play a central role in the process of growth. Second, informational problems are pervasive, and their presence is what prevents financial markets from fully performing the risk-sharing and income-smoothing functions which make them desirable in developing countries or regions. Third, government policies aimed at financial market liberalization have had limited success even in those countries whose economic performance has been much superior to the average. As Stiglitz points out, these findings suggest that a well-working financial system should only be an element of a much broader array of government policies to encourage development. These policies should include the creation of infrastructure, the enforcement of contracts, the fight against corruption and local organized crime, and the raising of skill levels and in general of human capital.

REFERENCES

McKinnon, R. (1973). *Money and Capital in Economic Development*, Washington: Brookings Institution.

Shaw, E.S. (1973). *Financial Deepening in Economic Development*, New York: Oxford University Press.

Part I
The role of finance in economic development

2 International finance and economic development

PAUL KRUGMAN

Although the 1980s was a decade of enormous activity in international financial markets, little of this activity translated into net resource transfers from capital-rich to capital-scarce countries. Indeed, as a result of the debt crisis resource transfers generally went from South to North. As the 1990s begin, however, the prospects for substantial external finance for development seems brighter, at least in some areas. In Europe, Portugal and Spain have recently attracted substantial inflows of external capital; it is widely believed, although some are sceptical, that reforming Eastern European nations may also be able to attract considerable external finance. In North America, Mexican economic reforms and the prospect of a free trade agreement have enabled that nation to resume voluntary access to the world capital market, with large inflows of direct investment in particular. In both the European and North American context, capital inflows have been widely seen both as a vote of confidence in the future economic growth of the recipients and as a key force propelling those growth prospects.

Some observers (e.g. Hale, 1991) have gone further and suggested that with the victory of the West in the Cold War, the stage is now set for a second golden age of capitalism. In this new golden age, the optimists suggest, international net capital flows may again rise to levels as a share of world product comparable to those in the pre-World War I era, and a worldwide convergence of per capita income will be the result.

Yet the key importance that many observers place on international financial markets as a driver of development, and their optimism that integrated capital markets will lead to economic convergence, are not solidly grounded either in economic theory or in the evidence of the past. Conventional analysis of growth puts relatively little weight on capital in general, let alone imported capital, as a source of growth, and thus offers little reason to suppose that capital flows will do much to promote economic convergence unless they are extremely large. Nor does recent

11

experience give us reason to expect very large capital flows to materialize. In the postwar period, no developing country has financed more than a small part of its investment from capital inflows.

Can the integration of international financial markets, and the external finance this integration permits, play an important role in the economic growth of developing nations and regions? This is really a two-part question. First, we need to ask whether developing regions can really expect to attract large inflows of capital. Second, we need to ask whether such inflows of capital, if they happen, will make a large contribution to economic growth.

The purpose of this paper is to pull together some of the existing theory and evidence that bears on these two questions. The questions are, of course, interrelated: both hinge on one's view of the process of economic growth, and of the role of capital in that process. However, it is possible to believe that fairly sizeable international capital movements will occur in the 1990s, while doubting whether they will promote much in the way of economic growth.

The basic conclusion of this paper is somewhat depressing. I argue that in spite of hopes that a new integration of world financial markets will bring a new era of development, not much will happen. Large-scale movements of capital from North to South have never happened before, and will probably not happen now; such capital flows as do occur will help growth in their recipients, but not in any dramatic way. Basically, international capital markets as an engine of development have been oversold.

The paper is in five sections. Section 1 summarizes the reasons why standard neoclassical analysis makes one sceptical about the importance of financial integration for development. Section 2 summarizes two theoretical views that explicitly or implicitly underly many arguments that capital flows can play a key role in economic growth. Section 3 briefly reviews the experience of international capital mobility, asking how large one might expect capital flows to be, based on past experience. Section 4 then turns to the direct evidence on the role of capital formation in economic growth. A final section suggests some general conclusions.

1   External capital and economic growth: neoclassical scepticism

At first sight it appears obvious that capital formation is a key engine of economic growth, and that export of capital from advanced to developing countries must therefore be a key to economic convergence. Workers in advanced countries evidently have much better, newer equipment to work with than workers in developing countries, and it is natural to suppose that in an integrated world capital market (or an integrated European or North American capital market) capital would flow south to work with cheaper labour, and by doing so produce a strong tendency to an equalization of wages and output per worker.

Yet the basic neoclassical analysis of economic growth suggests, even on the basis of first-cut empirical work, that capital in general plays a limited role in explaining international differences in levels and rates of growth of output, and that even fairly large capital flows would not make a large difference in these rates of growth. In this section of the paper I will review briefly this neoclassical analysis, before turning to two attempts (one traditional, one more recent) to find a greater role for external capital in economic development.

There are two kinds of evidence suggesting the relative unimportance of capital for economic development. First is the evident failure of international trade to equalize factor prices. Second is the evidence of growth accounting, in which capital formation generally plays a surprisingly modest role in explaining growth and in which capital inflows at rates that would widely be regarded as substantial would make only modest differences in growth rates.

The absence of factor price equalization has not, perhaps, received as much attention as it should. Yet the idea that what countries need to develop is basically more capital rests implicitly on the view that countries are essentially using the same production functions. If they were, however, standard trade theory predicts that a good deal of capital mobility could occur implicitly, as it were, via an export of labour-intensive products by capital-scarce nations in return for capital-intensive goods exported by capital-abundant nations. Admittedly, there are barriers to trade; but these seem fairly low relative to the observed differences in factor prices. For example, the average US tariff against imports from Mexico is only about 4 per cent; even allowing for harassment of Mexican exports by anti-dumping and unfair-practice suits, and the remaining red-tape barriers to such items as fruits and vegetables, it is hard to see this rate of protection as the main factor supporting a wage differential of six to one.

The fact that developing countries do not take advantage of what would appear to be the possibility of large embodied imports of capital services casts doubt on the view that large direct import of capital would be highly productive. In fact, most economists looking at the realities of trade and factor prices have concluded that poorer countries simply have worse production functions, and hence that the marginal product of capital is not in fact as high as their low capital-labour ratios would suggest.

Over the years, a number of economists have suggested that other factors besides capital – or perhaps a wider definition of capital that includes human capital – may allow us to explain international differences in output without invoking differences in production functions. We will turn to some of these explanations below. However, we may immediately note that the disappointing results of efforts to explain international trade flows on the basis of a fairly long list of factor endowments (Bowen *et al.*, 1987) further casts doubt on the idea that countries can be viewed as essentially using the same production functions, even if these production functions include a sizeable vector of inputs.

The absence of any strong tendency toward factor price equalization is an indirect piece of evidence that international income differentials are unlikely to be largely due to capital. It plays only a supporting role, however, to the more direct evidence that comes from growth accounting.

The basic growth accounting framework, of course, uses observed factor shares in income to estimate elasticities of output with respect to each factor. In the simplest version, one might write output growth as a weighted average of capital and labour growth, plus a residual factor:

$$\hat{Y} = a\hat{K} + (1 - a)\hat{L} + R \tag{1}$$

where the 'hats' represent growth rates, a is the share of capital in national income, and R is Solow's 'measure of our ignorance'. Since Solow's classic (1957) analysis, it has been a familiar point that growth in output per worker ends up being mostly explained by the residual rather than by increases in the capital-labour ratio. More directly to the point, however, growth accounting together with even a back-of-the-envelope calculation immediately suggests that the payoff to increases in the rate of capital formation, including those due to capital inflows, is pretty disappointing.

Consider, for example, a country with a capital-output ratio of 3 and a capital share a of 1/3. Suppose that such a country were to institute a package of political and economic reforms that made it a very attractive place for foreign investment, and that as a result capital flowed in to finance a current account deficit of 5 per cent of GNP (these numbers are on the order of the 'Mexican miracle' of the last two years). The increase in the rate of growth of capital would be only 1.67 per cent; the increase in the growth rate, even in the short run, predicted by the neoclassical model would be only 0.56 per cent. This is not a negligible sum, but it falls far short of the crucial importance that attracting capital flows is generally given in much current discussion.

The standard neoclassical approach, then, suggests that integration of capital markets will not play a crucial role in development. Many economists may simply accept this. Other economists, and probably most non-economist observers, feel that external capital is more important than this rather low-key story suggests. Our next step is to ask what kinds of models might explicitly or implicitly underly this view.

2   Why external capital might matter more

In this section of the paper I review two arguments about why external capital might matter more than the neoclassical approach suggests. One argument is very out of fashion, yet is used implicitly and perhaps unconsciously by many analysts. The other is trendier, but more problematic than widely realized.

2.1   Financing gaps and growth

Sometimes practical men are the slaves of defunct economists; more often, probably, they unconsciously reprise themes sounded a generation before by economists whose work has fallen since out of fashion. Since fashion and truth are not always perfectly correlated in economics, this is not always a bad thing.

Much of the recent discussion of the role of external capital in developing country growth is, in effect, a replay of old development issues from the 1950s and early 1960s. Consider, for example, the case of Mexico, widely touted as an economic miracle. Mexican real growth has so far not been very impressive; per capita output has risen for the past several years after an extended decline, but the turnaround is very modest. The main piece of visible good news is the emergence of large inward investment. Suppose that one asks an enthusiast about the Mexican recovery why these capital inflows are so important, given the rather disappointing algebra sketched out above. He is likely to reply in one of two ways. First, he may argue that the key thing is that capital inflows relax Mexico's foreign exchange constraint, permitting the economy to grow without running into a balance of payments crisis. Wittingly or not, this answer is essentially the same as that proposed by the long-rejected (but not necessarily wrong) 'two-gap' theory of Chenery and Bruno (1962) and McKinnon (1964). Alternatively, he may speak of dynamic effects – which brings in the 'new growth theory' issues raised below.

Two-gap theory consisted of the following: a developing country's growth was held to be limited by two constraints. First, growth was limited by the country's ability to save and invest. Second, however, there was an additional constraint, that of foreign exchange: with limited export revenues, too rapid a growth of the economy would cause imports to exceed what could be financed.

Capital inflows from abroad would relax both constraints. The proponents of two-gap theory argued, however, that for at least some developing countries it was the foreign exchange rather than the saving constraint that was binding. For such countries each dollar of foreign capital attracted would free the economy to raise domestic investment by several dollars, so that there would be an impact on growth several times as large as the marginal product of capital. (Two-gap theory was sometimes used as a theory of 'needs' for external capital. The point was that external capital would be highly productive as long as it was relaxing a binding foreign exchange constraint, much less productive once capital inflows were large enough so that the foreign exchange constraint was no longer binding; so the kink in the constraint set provided an estimate of financing needs. This now sounds somewhat silly, until one turns to the extensive post-1982 literature estimating the financing 'needs' of Latin America and the similar post-1989 literature asking the same question for Eastern Europe).

Two-gap theory fell into disrepute during the later 1960s and 1970s, and has by now been virtually forgotten. The basic critique of the theory was that the whole notion of separate constraints on growth made no sense in the context of a market economy. With prices moving to clear markets, the marginal product of each input – be it foreign exchange or domestic capital – should be set equal to its price, and there will be a margin of substitution between any two inputs at a rate equal to their relative prices. Or to translate, a dollar of capital is a dollar of capital, foreign or domestic.

And yet the current discussion of growth prospects echoes strongly the two-gap approach. This suggests that two-gap theory, like many other concepts from the heyday of development economics (e.g. backward and forward linkages), is an idea that actually does make sense under some circumstances, but became discredited because it was under-formalized and over-applied.

What conditions are necessary for two-gap theory to make sense? The basic situation that the two-constraints view seems to envision is one in which both the labour and foreign exchange markets fail to clear. The labour market is characterized by excess supply – there is a pool of surplus or unemployed labour that can be employed if investment is increased.[1] The foreign exchange market is characterized by excess demand: hard currency is in scarce supply. Thus capital in general is more productive than its market return because an increase in capital allows one to increase employment, and external capital is even more productive because it allows the country to increase imports too.

The neoclassical economist would ask why these markets do not clear. Why does the real wage rate not fall to clear the labour market? Why does the central bank not devalue the currency (or the real exchange rate get depreciated via deflation) to the point where foreign exchange no longer needs to be rationed?

Traditional development economics, which viewed such gaps as long-term issues, had no good answers. In the context of medium-term adjustment, however, it is not unreasonable to argue that both a non-clearing labour market and a foreign exchange shortage could persist for an extended period. Consider a Latin American debtor, which has still not emerged from the deep recession of the 1980s, and which is still coping with an inflationary threat. It is not unreasonable to suppose that such a country might (i) still have a large pool of unemployed who would be willing to work at the current real wage and (ii) feel compelled to peg its currency at a level that leaves foreign exchange scarce as part of an anti-inflation programme. Similarly, an Eastern European country in transition may have large numbers of workers laid off from bankrupt state enterprises and again be using the exchange rate to control inflation. In both cases the argument that in the medium term external finance is much more productive than the growth accounting exercise might suggest is pretty reasonable.

I would argue that something like this resurrected two-gap case is in fact the underlying implicit theoretical premise behind most assessments that external capital is a key factor in the development of either Latin America or Eastern Europe – including the fast-fading idea of a Grand Bargain for the Soviet Union.

The foreign exchange gap idea is, however, at some basic level more about adjustment than development. To make external capital play a crucial role in long-term development, one needs to turn to yet another possible deviation from the neoclassical approach.

2.2   Increasing returns and long-run growth

Since the influential paper by Romer (1986) and the Marshall lectures of Lucas (1988) there has been an explosion of theoretical work on models in which long-term growth can be explained entirely by growth in capital, without any appeal to a Solow residual. The basic idea of this literature, which goes back to the classic paper of Arrow (1962), is that there may be external economies to capital accumulation, so that the true elasticity of output with respect to capital greatly exceeds its share of GNP at market prices. Romer has argued in particular that in order to explain sustained growth via capital accumulation alone one must presume that the true relationship between factor and output growth is approximately

$$\hat{Y} = \hat{K} + (1 - a)\hat{L} \tag{2}$$

I will turn to the evidence, such as it is, on the actual role of capital in growth below. (It does not on the face of it support the idea that the social return to capital is much higher than the private return). For now, however, let us ask whether strong external economies in growth create a presumption that an integrated capital market would in fact strongly favour development of currently undeveloped regions.

At first sight it might seem that it must. If the social return to capital is much higher than the private rate of return, then any given capital inflow to a developing nation will raise its growth rate by much more than the pessimistic calculations of the neoclassical approach suggest. In particular, if something like the Romer equation is actually valid, then capital inflows at a rate of 1 per cent of GNP should raise output growth by 0.33 rather than 0.11 per cent.

There is, however, a logical problem. If returns to capital are constant or nearly so, then the rate of return on capital will not be decreasing in the capital-labour ratio – and so there will be no incentive to move capital from rich to poor countries! Or to put it differently, if (2) rather than (1) is the right growth equation, capital will tend to move to large economies rather than poor ones.

It is even possible to make straightforward arguments suggesting that international financial integration will promote greater inequality rather than greater convergence in per capita income. Consider, for example, a hypothetical two-factor, two-sector world in which the capital-intensive industry is also characterized by external economies. Imagine that two countries with equal labour forces trade in this world, and that one of them for some reason has a slightly larger initial capital stock than the other. The country with larger capital will then have a comparative advantage in the capital-intensive sector. Higher output in this sector, however, yields higher productivity; as a result, the rate of return on capital in the capital-abundant country will actually be *higher* than in the capital-scarce country.

Now imagine integrating financial markets. Capital will not flow from capital-abundant North to capital-scarce South; it will flow in the opposite direction, reinforcing the asymmetry until all capital-intensive production is concentrated in the high-income North.

This is an extreme (though remarkably easy to construct) example.[2] The basic point, however, is milder: the new growth theory does not offer any comfort to those who think that international financial integration is very good for development. The conventional neoclassical view does suggest that capital will tend to flow from capital-rich to capital-poor countries, but since it does not give capital *per se* a very large role, it cannot place much weight on the effects of these capital inflows. The new growth theory gives capital much more importance, but the same assumptions that make the social product of capital larger make it seem less likely that capital will flow in the 'right' direction.

3 Prospects of capital for development

International capital movements in the postwar period have been generally limited. Although Germany and Japan ran current surpluses in excess of 4 per cent of GNP for a few years in the 1980s, their average surpluses over the past 20 years have been less than 2 per cent of GNP, and industrial countries as a group have exported capital at a rate of less than 1 per cent of GNP. Meanwhile, inflows to developing countries have been modest as well. The period 1972–81 is generally regarded as a period of large-scale borrowing leading to excessive debt in the Third World. The IMF's group of 15 HICs (highly indebted countries), however, on average ran current deficits over that period of only 3 per cent of GNP, financing less than 15 per cent of their domestic investment. And this period of borrowing was, of course, followed by a devastating collapse of financing that forced net resource transfers to run in reverse for the following decade.

As many economic historians have noted, the pre-World War I period was marked by much larger capital flows relative to income. The United Kingdom ran an *average* annual current surplus of 4 per cent of GNP, about 30 per cent of domestic savings, over a 30-year period before the War. Current account deficits among some countries were well beyond any recent levels. For example, Canada ran deficits in excess of 10 per cent of GNP in the years just before World War I. Arguably, these large capital flows were made possible by a political climate in which expropriation was unlikely, a world economic order enforced by the dominant capitalist powers.

It seems natural to speculate that with the collapse of the major Marxist powers and the new attractiveness of foreign capital, the stage is finally set for large-scale development financing. Unfortunately, even a slightly closer examination of the pre-1914 experience raises serious doubts. Although the golden age of capitalism was marked by large international capital movements, very little of this capital movement reflected North-South transfers from rich to poor countries. Essentially, there has never been a period in history in which capital-abundant countries have invested heavily in the development of labour-abundant countries.

The nature of pre-1914 global financial integration was neatly summarized by Nurkse (1954). Very little capital flowed from North to South; essentially it flowed from East to West, from Europe to the rapidly growing but already high-income 'regions of recent settlement' where European immigration was producing rapid population growth. The figures reported by Feis (1964) are fairly startling. More than 53 per cent of Britain's overseas investments in 1913 were in Canada, New Zealand, Australia, Argentina, and the United States; these were all nations which at that time had per capita incomes that were comparable to or higher than those in Britain itself. Nurkse argued that white South Africa, Uruguay, and southern Brazil were at the time viewed as similar regions; this raises the share of regions of recent settlement to 67 per cent. These regions comprised a very small share of world population. Canada, New Zealand, and Australia combined had only about 5 per cent of the population of India; all four were British territory, with Indian independence still a remote prospect, and thus presumably offered considerable security of property rights; yet the three Europeanized nations had attracted 2.4 times as much British capital as India.

In other words, during the high tide of international capital market integration, European investors were in effect willing to supply capital to meet the needs of rapidly growing, high-wage European immigrant populations overseas, but not willing to invest except to a very limited extent in low-wage economies.[3]

It is conceivable that the current situation will be different, that (say) Eastern European nations will be able to persuade international investors that they have so much growth potential that in spite of their slow growth in population they can still productively absorb large quantities of foreign capital. All that we can say is that contrary to what many economists believe, large capital movements from high to low wage countries have never happened in the world economy before, even during periods when the political conditions for such movements seemed highly favourable.

4   The effect of capital inflows

Suppose that in spite of my pessimism about the re-emergence of pre-1914 level international capital flows some developing countries do succeed in financing substantial amounts of investment from abroad. Will this investment have a large positive impact on growth?

I will leave on one side the financing gap issue. It seems reasonable to believe that moderate capital inflows could make the transition in Eastern Europe considerably easier, although over the past 9 years economists have become increasingly sceptical of the view that external finance is the key constraint on Latin American growth. The more fundamental issue is whether the social rate of return on investment is sufficiently high relative to the private rate to lead to very high payoffs to increased foreign investment.

A number of authors, including in particular Barro and Sala-i-Martín (1990) and Romer (1990) have recently tried to examine the question of returns to capital accumulation using cross-sectional data. This is a difficult literature to interpret. For one thing, it can be seen as in effect testing the null hypothesis that increasing returns in the economy are so strong that there are constant or increasing returns to capital alone. What we are really interested in, unfortunately, is the opposite null hypothesis: is there evidence that the social return to capital significantly exceeds the private return?

In any case, the literature seems to be in conflict in its conclusions. Romer finds that long-run differences in investment shares in output are correlated with long-run growth rates; since in Solow-type models with diminishing returns to capital differences in savings rates should have no effect on long-run growth rates, he interprets this as evidence of constant returns to capital. Unfortunately the coefficient is too small to be consistent with this interpretation; and the results could be explained as the result of reverse causation, from high growth to high savings rates. Barro and Sala-i-Martín, on the other hand, find evidence of convergence in per capita incomes, which they take as a demonstration of diminishing returns to capital – although it could also reflect technological diffusion.

Perhaps the closest analysis to a test of the divergence between social and private returns is Mankiw *et al.* (1990), which shows that a regression with rates of investment, rates of accumulation of human capital, and population growth not only explains much of the variation in *levels* of income between countries, but yields estimated elasticities consistent with market returns. This work, on the other hand, conflicts with the many direct attempts to compare production functions that seem to show large international differences in both levels and rates of growth total factor productivity.

On the whole, one may argue that the international cross-sectional testing has not made a very convincing case either for or against the proposition of substantially higher payoff to investment than the market return.

What about other evidence? Urban economists have long accepted as a basic insight that increasing returns are necessary to explain the very existence of cities. The size of cities is, however, limited by land and congestion; a nation that supports a system of cities will be characterized by increasing returns at a micro level but constant returns at the aggregate level (see Henderson, 1974). I have argued that regional concentration of population reflects increasing returns; when both labour and capital are mobile, however, quite mild increasing returns can give rise to cumulative processes of concentration. Thus one can accept an increasing returns view of cities and even regional concentration while doubting whether capital inflows will lead to very large growth payoffs.

On the whole, we have to say that the case is not proven. Many businessmen and economists now have a strong intuition that inflows of capital, especially in the form of direct investment, will act as catalysts of growth through their 'dynamic' effects – this is the generic sense of 'dynamic', meaning 'things you don't know how to put in the formal model'. This may be true, although only a dozen years ago many observers had an equally strong intuition that foreign capital, especially in the form of direct investment, had a strongly negative effect because it created economic dependency. What we can say is that there is really no convincing evidence for such effects.

5   Conclusions

This paper has briefly surveyed some theoretical and empirical issues on the role of international financial integration in development. The basic question is whether external finance is likely to be a major engine of development in the new world economic order.

My answer, depressingly, is no. There is nothing in past historical experience to suggest that developing countries will be the recipients of large capital flows; there is no convincing evidence that rather low neoclassical estimates of the impact of capital on growth are wrong.

This does not mean that international financial integration is an unimportant issue. It is a potentially mutually beneficial form of international exchange, like trade in goods and services. It is simply one that has been somewhat overrated.

NOTES

1 There is a sloppiness here about stocks versus flows. Is there excess capacity, which can be brought into play via Keynesian expansion, or is the capital stock fully utilized, so that one can grow only by adding capacity? Related to this question is whether the axis in the diagram should have the level or the rate of growth of output on it. I avoid these questions by not drawing a diagram, and focussing on the general features of the approach.
2 In general, models with increasing returns can quite easily give rise to processes of regional divergence rather than convergence. Somewhat surprisingly, divergence generally tends to be more likely the better integrated markets are – i.e., the lower are transportation costs or the larger the share of mobile factors in income. See Krugman (1991) for some examples.

3 Although figures are not available, I would suspect that the same is true for interregional capital movements within the US. It has almost surely been true that for much of the 20th century the old industrial regions of the Northeast have been exporting large amounts of capital. Some of this capital has gone to the low-wage Old South, whose income has gradually converged on the national average. Almost surely, however, the really large capital-importing regions have been in the West, where wages have been consistently *above* the national average but where the population has been growing rapidly through immigration.

REFERENCES

Arrow, K. (1962) 'The economic implications of learning by doing', *Review of Economic Studies* **29**, 155–73.

Barro, R. and X. Sala-i-Martín (1991) 'Convergence across states and regions', *Brookings Papers on Economic Activity*, 107–82.

Bowen, H., E. Leamer and L. Sveikauskas (1987) 'Multicountry, multifactor tests of the factor abundance theory', *American Economic Review* **77**, 791–809.

Chenery, H.B. and M. Bruno (1962) 'Development alternatives in an open economy: the case of Israel', *Economic Journal* **57**, 79–103.

Feis, H. (1964) *Europe, the World's Banker 1870–1914*, New York: Kelley.

Hale, D. (1991) 'Why the 1990s could be the second great age of capitalism since the 19th century', presented at the G7C meeting, Tokyo, October 1991.

Henderson, J.V. (1974) 'The sizes and types of cities', *American Economic Review* **64**, 640–56.

Krugman, P. (1991) *Geography and Trade*, Cambridge, MA: MIT Press.

Lucas, R.E. (1988) 'On the mechanics of economic development', *Journal of Monetary Economics* **22**, 3–42.

McKinnon, R. (1964) 'Foreign exchange constraints in economic development and efficient aid allocation', *Economic Journal* **74**, 388–409.

Mankiw, G., D. Romer and D. Weil (1990) 'A contribution to the empirics of economic growth', mimeo, Harvard University.

Nurkse, R. (1954) 'International investment today in the light of 19th century experience', *Economic Journal* **64**, 134–50.

Romer, P. (1986) 'Increasing returns and long-run growth, *Journal of Political Economy* **94**, S71–102.

(1990) 'Capital, labor, and productivity', *Brookings Papers on Economic Activity: Microeconomics 1990*.

Solow, R. (1957) 'Technical change and the aggregate production function', *Review of Economics and Statistics* **39**, 312–20.

Discussion

RICHARD E. BALDWIN

Paul Krugman has written a very stimulating paper that addresses the importance of external capital to the development process. His basic thesis is that capital flows do not boost GDP by much and in any case they have historically always been small between developed and developing countries. I agree with the basic implication of his thesis – capital inflows are not a magic solution to the problem of development. However I would like to point out a few aspects of international capital flows that Paul did not cover. Having oversimplified Paul's argument, I think it only fair to oversimplify my own. Development is a difficult process, yet in so far as capital inflows can make development somewhat easier and quicker, they may permit policy-makers to undertake reforms that would not otherwise be politically feasible. In this sense, capital flows may be thought of as playing a linchpin role in development.

In setting out the view that he latter demolishes, Paul states, 'in both the European and North American context, capital inflows have been widely seen both as a vote of confidence in the future economic growth of the recipients and as a key force propelling these growth prospects'. Summing up his own rebuttal, he writes, 'large scale movements of capital from North to South have never happened and will probably not happen now; such capital flows as do occur will help growth in their recipients, but not in any dramatic way'. I will undertake to argue that these two statements are not at odds with each other.

The first component of the Krugman argument is that capital does not boost output by much. This is based on a simple calculation that a capital inflow equal to one per cent of GDP would boost domestic output by only one-ninth of one per cent. This small number comes from two reasonable assumptions: the capital-output ratio is 3 and the capital-output elasticity is one-third. These assumptions mean that the capital inflow raises the capital stock by a third of one per cent and the output elasticity implies that this extra capital raises output by one-third of one-third of a per cent. Taking the Mexican case where capital inflows were about 5 per cent of GDP, we get that external capital raised the growth rate by five-ninths of a percentage point. The growth effect is inevitably small since it is a product of two fractions. Consequently the main conclusion from this rough calculation is quite robust.

This reckoning however leaves aside a number of important issues. First consider the timing of the extra capital formation and output growth. Introduction of a reform package is very costly and very risky from the point of view of the policy-makers implementing it. Indeed although I am not a political historian, it seems to me that introducing a radical economic reform package has not historically proved to be the best way for a politician to extend his tenure in power. A quick boost of output – even a modest one – can be crucial to sustaining a politically difficult reform. Clearly in this light external capital may be a key force propelling growth prospects. It is critical not for its ability to boost output but rather due to its ability to permit a quick output response that suggests that there may be a light at the end of the tunnel.

It is worthwhile taking this point one step further. That is, although it is conceivable that the same quick output response could come from domestic capital formation, this would require foregoing current consumption. For instance if the extra five-ninths of one per cent output growth were internally instead of externally financed, Mexican consumption would have had to drop an extra 5 per cent in the short run. Obviously this would substantially dampen the luminosity of the light at the end of the tunnel and thereby lessen the prospects of the reform being sustained. External capital means that both domestic consumption and domestic output can rise quickly in response to a reform package. In anticipation of such problems, policy-makers in countries without access to external capital may quite rationally put off reforms that would lead to long-term growth.

My second point leads me to wade into the murky waters of psycho-political economics. Paul refers to the 'vote of confidence' aspect of capital inflows, but does not follow up on it. My guess is that this aspect is actually rather important in the real world, although I immediately admit that I cannot marshall empirical evidence or even a simple, intuitive model to back up this guess. Countries that need to be developed typically have governments that have not historically followed sound economic policies. Even worse, workers, farmers and industrialists in such countries may suspect that every new policy package is simply another scheme to lower their incomes for the benefit of one of the other groups. Plainly in countries where the population may not have historically trusted their government to pursue good policies, a sizable inflow of capital may play a critical role in convincing citizens that this reform is 'for real'. That is, a vote of confidence from objective observers that put money behind their votes, may have a disproportionately large impact on expectations. Expectations are important in at least two ways. First, as is well known, the cost of anti-inflation policies depends on the extent to which workers and firms believe they will work. Second, as Paul himself showed in a simple, rigorous model, the eventual outcome of a particular policy can depend on agents' expectations about the outcome. This sort of 'history versus expectations' framework may indeed be important in the context of development.

My last point is that Paul has viewed foreign capital as a perfect substitute for domestic capital. In fact external capital flows, especially those involving foreign direct investment or substantially equity participation, typically bring along foreign technology. In such cases external capital boosts output directly by boosting the capital stock and indirectly by boosting the domestic technology.

In conclusion, I agree with Paul's main contention: the international capital market as an engine of long-term growth has been oversold. Nevertheless, I would say that the fundamental reforms that are required for development are unlikely to occur in the absence of external capital flows. Perhaps then we should think of the international capital as the signalman rather than the locomotive.

WILLIAM H. BRANSON

This interesting paper by Paul Krugman explores the potential for international investment flows to play an important role in development in the 1990s. Paul comes to the somewhat 'depressing' conclusion that they will not, both because the evidence for the importance of investment for output growth is weak, and because the potential for international investment is small. In this comment I will argue that the case is not as grim and unclear as Paul suggests. I also want to make the point that financial opening in developing countries can have important growth effects via the introduction of competition to the economy, separate from effects through capital flows. I will begin with comments on Paul's case.

In the first substantive section of the paper two kinds of evidence supporting the '. . . relative unimportance of capital for economic development . . .' are presented. The first is the lack of factor price equalization in a two-factor model. If production functions are the same across countries, this would imply that there are already large foregone gains

from not embodying capital movements in trade. Since these are foregone, it would not be clear why explicit trade in capital would be any
more important. If production functions are not the same, we cannot
expect capital to flow toward the areas with inferior productions. Paul
dismisses the possibility that a many-factor model might do better on
factor price equalization with the same production function. I read the
evidence differently. In reviewing the evidence, Colin Bradford and I
(1987a, p. xv; see also 1987b, p. 10) concluded that it provides '. . .
support for a general factor endowment HO view of sources of comparative advantage and growth'. If production functions are not the same,
it may be possible that foreign investment carries with it new technology,
creating an externality as it shifts the production function. I do not
consider the evidence on the basis of the failure of factor price equalization persuasive on the unimportance of capital.

The second kind of evidence on the unimportance of capital is the
standard Solow growth accounting arithmetic. With a capital share of 1/3
and a capital-output ratio of 3, a 5 per cent of GDP increase in investment
would increase the growth rate by about 0.5 percentage points. This is
consistent with growth regressions estimated across countries by Stephen
Schwartz and myself (1992), where the coefficient of the investment ratio
is about 0.1. However, if capital embodies technical progress, these
estimates of the effects of investment themselves can increase by 50 per
cent (from 0.5 to 0.75). In addition, as the paper points out in the second
section, if investment absorbs surplus labour, the effect can increase. If
investment attracts labour at the pre-existing capital-labour ratio, in the
example in the paper the effect of a 5 per cent of GDP increase in
investment would increase to 1.67 percentage points on the growth rate.
Thus the effects of embodiment of technology and the presence of surplus
labour can brighten the conclusion on the importance of capital substantially. This would provide the higher social payoff than the market
return discussed toward the end of the fourth section of the paper.

The third section discusses the prospects for large-scale international
investment flows. Here I agree with Paul. Even borrowing at the rate of
the highly-indebted developing countries achieved an average of only 3
per cent of GDP in the early 1980s. Suppose all of that were an increment
to domestic investment. From the previous high case in which a 5 per cent
of GDP added 1.67 points to the growth rate, 3 per cent would add 1 point
to the growth rate. Thus at this point I conclude that capital is more
important than Paul thinks, but foreign investment as such is not, in
general, going to be the engine for growth.

However, we do not have to end with this pessimistic note. Paul
Krugman can cheer up! The title of the paper is 'International finance and

economic development'. Developing countries integrate into the international financial system by opening their financial markets. If this is done correctly, it is part of a programme of structural adjustment, to use a World Bank term, that is generally moving the economy in the direction of considered use of market mechanisms.

In this context, the financial sector is the brain of the economy. If it is working properly, it allocates resources efficiently, and stimulates domestic saving and investment. For example, a structural adjustment programme of this sort in Indonesia beginning in 1986, including an open financial system, resulted in an annual growth rate of non-oil GDP of nearly 8 per cent from 1987 to 1990. This was achieved not via a massive current account deficit and investment inflow, but rather by shifting to a more efficient structure, including an open financial system. Thus I would say that financial market integration is not so important because it generates net capital flows. It is an essential part of bringing the economy out of a low-level equilibrium and placing it on an actual growth path.

REFERENCES

Bradford, Colin I. and William H. Branson (1987a) 'Overview', in C.I. Bradford and W.H. Branson (eds), *Trade and Structural Change in Pacific Asia*, Chicago: University of Chicago Press, pp. xi–xix.
(1987b) 'Patterns of trade and structural change', in C.I. Bradford and W.H. Branson (eds.), *Trade and Structural Change in Pacific Asia*, pp. 1–24.
Branson, William H. and Stephen Schwartz (1992) 'Financial markets and economic efficiency', forthcoming, *Greek Economic Review*.

3   A theory of financial development

OREN SUSSMAN

1   Introduction

That financial structure and economic development are interrelated is a well known hypothesis (see Goldsmith, 1969, McKinnon, 1973, Shaw, 1973, Kuznets, 1971, Cameron, 1967 and Townsend, 1983; see also Gertler, 1988, for an excellent survey of the background and Greenwood and Jovanovic, 1989, for a recent contribution). In the present paper, we utilize some recent developments in the theory of contracts and the organization of financial markets (most notably Diamond, 1984, and Gale and Hellwig, 1985), in order to reformulate the financial development hypothesis in a way which is both theoretically comprehensible, and empirically testable. We focus on the 'gross markup' of the banking system, roughly the gap between the (real) rate at which banks borrow and lend money. This gap reflects (in addition to the more conventional default-premium component), the cost of financial intermediation. In the theoretical part we construct a spatial model of a monopolistically competitive banking system. When the capital stock increases, the market for financial intermediation grows, and the number of banks increases (due to entry). Each bank becomes more specialized, and thus efficient, over a smaller market share. Also, the industry becomes more competitive. As a result the cost of intermediation falls and the markup decreases. In the empirical part we present some evidence showing that the markup is lower in high-income countries relative to low-income countries. The results can be summarized as follows: when GNP per capita increases by $1,000 (1980 prices), the markup falls by about one-fifth of a percentage point.

The model is fully micro-founded. We use the *ex post* asymmetric information costly state verification formalization suggested by Townsend (1979) (and extended by Gale and Hellwig, 1985). Banks are created endogenously in this framework: when a borrower claims bankruptcy, he must be monitored (otherwise he will always default). The information revealed in this process is relevant to all lenders and should be considered a public good. Hence there are efficiency reasons to delegate the power of monitoring to the hands of a single lender, who becomes a financial intermediary (see Diamond, 1984).

We assume a constant returns to scale technology in monitoring, so that when the banking system is perfectly competitive growth is balanced.[1] More accurately, when the capital stock grows, the markup (and the share of the banking system in national income), is not affected. Thus the financial development hypothesis is reduced to the simple (more operational) question whether growth is balanced in those indicators of the financial system.

To get away from the balanced growth result we turn to a spatial model of banking and finance with a monopolistically competitive banking system. We assume that the borrowing firms are distributed on the circumference of a circle. A central assumption is that monitoring costs are increasing in the distance between the bank and the firm. This assumption captures a specialization effect:[2] a bank can reduce the cost of monitoring a firm by locating closer to it. Thus when the number of banks increases, each bank specializes in a smaller geographical region, where it is (on average) more cost efficient.

In a credit market of the type discussed above, banks have some market power. Moreover, a borrower is identified by its location so that banks price-discriminate across firms. The bank's market power is constrained by the cost advantage it has over its competitors, namely the neighbouring banks (to the left and to the right). Under our assumption about the cost function, this cost advantage is a function of the distance between the banks. As banks get closer together, monopolistic rents decrease. Thus, when the capital stock increases the market for financial intermediation grows and new banks enter the industry. Each bank serves a smaller market share and gets closer to its competitors. As a result, the markup falls both via the specialization effect, and the decrease in market power.

In order to get a result which can be applied to macro data, we have to go explicitly into the business of aggregation. This is somewhat tedious because firms differ in both the interest rate they pay to the bank (due to price discrimination), and the amount they borrow. Yet we are able to construct a price index of the markup, and perform comparative statics on the aggregate to show the financial development effect.

It should be noted that the approach sketched above deviates from the main line of research in this area. Previous work tended to stress the role of the banks as providers of liquidity and clearing services.[3] As a result, empirical analysis usually focused on money-GNP ratios (c.f. McKinnon, 1973). Our analysis focuses on the allocation of capital (under asymmetric information), and has the advantage of being more closely related to standard growth theory, where capital accumulation still plays a central role. It should be pointed out however that our analysis goes only half way to a complete analysis of growth with imperfect capital markets: we show how changes in capital stock affect the structure and conduct of financial markets. The investigation of the effect back into the capital stock (i.e. capital dynamics) is left to future work.

The paper is organized as follows: Section 2 analyses the bench-mark case of perfect competition with balanced growth; Sections 3 and 4 extend the analysis to the case of monopolistic competition; Section 5 performs the aggregation and Section 6 the empirical analysis. Concluding remarks can be found in Section 7.

2 Balanced growth

The basic assumptions of our one-period model are

A.1 A real economy: we assume an economy with no money and one good only.

A.2 Technology: each firm (entrepreneur) is endowed with a *gross* production technology $y = \omega f(k)$, $f(k) = k^a$, where y is gross output and k capital stock. $\omega \in [0, \infty)$ is a multiplicative productivity shock to be realized at the end of the production period. The technological shock has a density function $h(\omega)$ with $E(\omega) = 1$, and a cumulative distribution function $H(\chi) = \int_0^\chi h(\omega) d\omega$. We use the exponential distribution $h(\omega) = e^{-\omega}$, so that at any point χ the hazard rate $h(\chi)/[1 - H(\chi)]$ equals one.

A.3 Credit and information: firms have no resources of their own and turn to the 'bank' to finance their investment. We assume *ex post* asymmetric information, namely that the firm knows the level of ω for free, while the bank can produce this information only by monitoring the first at a cost of $c_1 f(k)$, $c_1 < 1$ (which is distributed to some primary factors of production). This functional form is later interpreted as a constant returns to scale technology.

A.4 Attitude towards risk: both the 'bank' and the firm are risk-neutral (later on in the paper it turns out that the bank is fully diversified, so only the assumption about the firm's risk-neutrality is binding).

A.5 No aggregate risk: there is a continuum of identical firms on $[0, 1]$, and the productivity shock ω is uncorrelated among them.

The debt contract is endogenously determined. It determines the amount of capital invested in the firm, a state-contingent payment scheme from the firm to the bank, and a state-contingent monitoring strategy by the bank.[4] The contract is efficiently designed, which means that there does not exist any Pareto-improving relocation of income (across states of nature). It should also give the firm an incentive to reveal information truthfully, especially in those states where it is not monitored (incentive compatibility).

The design of such a contract is usually quite complicated. It can be shown however that the solution for our case is actually the standard debt contract. By this we mean that monitoring is interpreted as bankruptcy and the optimal contract satisfies three properties: whenever solvent the firm has to pay a fixed repayment x to the bank;[5] bankruptcy takes place under states of nature in which the firm cannot meet the fixed repayment; once bankruptcy takes place, the bank takes all it can recover from the firm (maximum recovery).

The proof is very similar to that provided by Townsend (1979), Diamond (1984), Gale and Hellwig (1985) and Williamson (1987), and is omitted for the sake of brevity.[6] It can be explained intuitively with the aid of Figure 3.1. The optimal contract (for a given k) is described by the bold line, and χ is the cut-off point (in terms of ω) between the bankruptcy and the solvency states. Clearly the payments scheme for the solvency states is flat: if not the firm would always declare the state with the lowest payment (among the solvency states). Payments for all bankruptcy states must be lower than in the solvency states otherwise the firm would have an incentive to pay the fixed repayment and avoid monitoring. Also, since monitoring is costly, efficiency requires that the number of the bankruptcy states is brought to the minimum. Any deviation from maximum recovery (like T' in Figure 3.1) would force the bank to increase the fixed repayment (to recover costs) which would increase the number of the bankruptcy states.

A remarkable property of the above model is that it can easily provide a rationale for financial intermediation. Diamond (1984) has pointed out the fact that monitoring reveals information which is a public good. Efficiency considerations require that only one lender (denoted as the financial intermediary or the bank) will perform the monitoring, on behalf of all other lenders (denoted as depositors).[7] This, however, raises the agency problems at the level of the intermediary and its creditors. But then, under assumption A.5 the bank can (perfectly) diversify and eliminate the possibility of bankruptcy, which removes the above problem. We call the bank's debt time deposits,[8] and denote their gross rate of return (which is risk-free) by r.

It may be useful to summarize the structure of the model by a description of the balance sheets of the economy's three sectors.

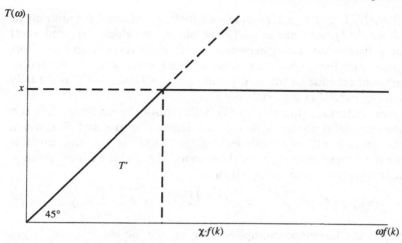

Figure 3.1 The optimal contract

Firms		Banks		Households	
capital	loans from banks	loans to firms	time deposits	time deposits	net worth

The (exogenous) amount of resources supplied by households will determine the quantity of capital invested by firms.

The optimal contract is thus a combination of a fixed repayment x, and a capital stock k, that maximizes the firm's profit subject to the bank's zero-profit constraint

$$\underset{x,k}{\text{Max}}\, f(k)\, \Pi\left[\frac{x}{f(k)}\right] \tag{1}$$

s.t.

$$f(k)\, V\left[\frac{x}{f(k)}, c_1\right] = rk$$

where

$$\Pi\left[\frac{x}{f(k)}\right] \equiv \left\{\int_x^\infty \omega h(\omega)\, d\omega - \left[\frac{x}{f(k)}\right]\left\{1 - H\left[\frac{x}{f(k)}\right]\right\}\right\}$$

$$V\left[\frac{x}{f(k)}, c_1\right] \equiv \left\{\int_0^x \omega h(\omega)\, d\omega + \left[\frac{x}{f(k)}\right]\left\{1 - H\left[\frac{x}{f(k)}\right]\right\} - c_1 H\left[\frac{x}{f(k)}\right]\right\}$$

Note that Π, V and $C(\chi,c_1) = c_1 H(\cdot)$, satisfy an adding-up requirement $(\Pi + V + C = 1)$, and are actually the shares in which expected (net) output is distributed among expected profits, bank revenue and monitoring costs respectively. Note also that all bank revenue is distributed to primary lenders (due to the zero-profit constraint), so that V is actually the share of capital in the firm's output.

Another important property of (1) is that both the objective function and the constraint are homogeneous of degree one in x and $f(k)$, which reflects constant returns to scale technology in lending. It is thus possible to state the programing problem (1) in terms of k and the cut-off point χ. The first-order condition (FOC) is thus

$$f'(k) \cdot F(\chi,c_1) = r, \qquad F \equiv \frac{\Pi + \lambda V}{\lambda}, \qquad \lambda \equiv -\frac{\Pi'}{V_1} > 0 \qquad (2)$$

where λ is the Lagrange multiplier.[9] We denote the solution by (k_1,χ_1). The fixed repayment is $x_1 = \chi_1 f(k_1)$. The probability of bankruptcy and the expected shares of profit, capital and monitoring costs in output are

$$B \equiv H(\chi_1), \qquad S_\pi \equiv \Pi(\chi_1), \qquad S_k \equiv V(\chi_1,c_1), \qquad S_c \equiv C(\chi_1,c_1) \qquad (3)$$

respectively (clearly $S_\pi + S_k + S_c = 1$).

We can now define the gross markup of the banking system as (approximately) gap between the credit rate x/k and the time deposit (riskless) rate

$$t = \frac{x/k}{r} - 1 \qquad (4)$$

It is gross in the sense that it can be decomposed into a default-premium, and an element that reflects agency costs. That can be done by solving for x from the zero-profit constraint

$$x_1 = \frac{[rk_1 - f(k_1)\int_0^{\chi_1} \omega h(\omega)\,d\omega]}{1-B} + \frac{c_1 f(k_1) B}{1-B} \qquad (5)$$

The first right hand side argument has to do with default risk: because the repayment of x is uncertain, it must be increased above rk to compensate the bank against the loss of revenue in the bankruptcy states. Thus, even if monitoring costs vanish the gross markup is still positive.[10] The second right hand side argument captures the effect of expected monitoring costs on x. Using (4) and the fact that $S_k = rk_1/f(k_1)$, we can decompose the markup into the default and agency premia (t_r, t_a) respectively

$$t = \left[\frac{1}{(1-B)} - \frac{\int_0^{\chi_1} \omega h(\omega)\,d\omega}{(1-B)S_k} - 1 \right] + \left[\frac{S_c}{(1-B)S_k} \right] \qquad (6)$$

We turn now the balanced growth result. We show first that

Lemma 1: The optimal contract has the following property: the probability of bankruptcy, the expected shares of profit capital and monitoring costs in output, and the gross markup of the bank, are all independent of the interest rate.

Proof: The optimal contract is derived from the FOC and the zero-profit constraint in (1). Using the iso-elastic specification for $f(k)$ these two yield

$$aF(\chi, c_1) = V(\chi) \tag{7}$$

Thus, χ_1 is independent of the interest rate. But B, S_π, S_k, S_c, $\int_0^{\chi_1} \omega h(\omega) \, d\omega$ and thus t_r and t_a, depend on χ_1 (and maybe c_1) only. ‖

Assume now that the aggregate capital stock K is given exogenously.

Proposition 1. When the aggregate capital stock changes, the markup of the banking system, and its share in gross national income, are not affected.

Proof: Substituting χ_1 into the FOC we get the economy's demand schedule for capital which is decreasing in the time deposit rate. Thus, a unique market-clearing equilibrium exists for any K. Changes in the aggregate capital stock lead to changes in the interest rate, but due to Lemma 1, the gross markup is not affected.

The share of the banking industry in national income is simply S_c, which is also independent of the interest rate. ‖

The basic question of our paper is how to get away from the balanced growth result. One possibility is to assume efficiency gains in intermediation as a result of growth. This means dropping the constant returns to scale assumption. In a sense this is done in the next sections, only the efficiency gains are not coming from the scale of the individual debt contract, but from the scale of the banking industry and the changes in organization that follow.

In order to extend the model in that direction, closed-form solutions are needed. We use the exponential distribution assumption to derive the following results

Lemma 2. The optimal contract has the following properties: the probability of bankruptcy is independent of c_1; the expected shares of profit, capital and monitoring costs in are $S_\pi = (1 - a)$, $S_k = a(1 - c_1)$, $S_c = ac_1$ respectively.

Proof: Using the assumption of a unit hazard rate we get

$$\Pi' = -(1 - H) < 0, \qquad V_1 = 1 - H - c_1 h > 0$$

Integrating and remembering that $\Pi(0) = 1$, and $V(0) = 0$, we get

$$\Pi(\chi) = 1 - H(\chi), \qquad V(\chi, c_1) = (1 - c_1) H(\chi) \tag{8}$$

Substituting (8) into (2) reveals that $F(\cdot) = (1 - c_1)$. Thus capital stock can be calculated from the FOC only (without the zero-profit constraint in (1)) to be

$$f'(k) = \frac{r}{1 - c_1} \tag{9}$$

Substituting (8) and (9) into the zero-profit constraint we get

$$H(\chi_1) = a$$

so in the optimum, the probability of bankruptcy is constant and equal to a. Using (8) again, we get the shares as stated above. $\parallel$

Note also that the reduced form for the capital stock can be expressed as a product of two functions

$$k(r, c_1) \equiv k_r(r) \cdot k_c(c_1), \qquad k_r' < 0, \qquad k_c' < 0 \tag{10}$$

This property is carried into the reduced-form profit function where

$$\pi(r, c_1) \equiv (1 - a) \cdot f[k_r(r)] \cdot f[k_c(c_1)], \qquad \pi_r' < 0, \qquad \pi_c' < 0 \tag{11}$$

3   Market power

To study the interrelations between growth and the organization of financial markets we turn to a standard spatial model usually used to study monopolistically competitive markets (see Tirole, 1988, ch. 7). The following assumptions are added

A.6 Space: the continuum of firms assumed in A.5 is uniformly distributed on the circumference of a circle with length one. A point can be interpreted as either a physical location, or as one of the economy's sectors. We assume that a firm cannot change its location, probably because the entrepreneurial skill of its owner is specific. We denote the number of banks by n and assume free entry into the banking industry. We assume further that whatever the number of banks turns out to be, they locate at equal distances one from the other. Monitoring costs for bank i, $c_i f(k)$, are increasing and convex in the distance z between the bank and the firm so that $c_i = c(z)$, $c'(z) > 0$, $c''(z) > 0$ and $c(1/2) < 1$, so that whenever there are more than two banks $c_i < 1$ (like in Section 2); operating a bank requires E units of (non-depreciating) capital.[11]

Our assumptions about space are summarized in Figure 3.2. The distance between one bank (bank 1) and its nearby competitor (bank 2) is $1/n$. Because banks have the same cost functions, bank 1 has a cost

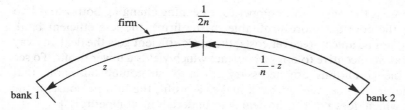

Figure 3.2   Organization in space

advantage over bank 2 with respect to all firms located to the left of $1/(2n)$ (namely $c_1 < c_2$).

Our assumptions give banks the opportunity to price-discriminate across firms. This is because banks take into consideration the heterogeneity (by location) among firms. Moreover, since the bank knows the location of the firm, and knows the location of its competitor, it can calculate the terms of the contract offered by the other bank, and respond with a contract that is attractive to the firm but still leaves it with a monopolistic rent. Thus, each firm gets a contract which depends on its location relative to the two banks. We assume

A.7 Bertrand competition: trade takes place in two stages. At stage one the competing banks state a contract (simultaneously). At stage two the firm chooses the best offer.

The main point in A.7 is that banks make a take-it-or-leave-it offer to the firm, while the latter is not allowed to respond with a counter offer (which would have started a process of bargaining). Thus, A.7 allocates all the bargaining power in the lender-borrower game (and thus all the gains from the bank-firm trade) to the more efficient bank. In that sense, the assumption is somewhat arbitrary. We choose it because it simplifies the analysis. Also, a different allocation of the gains from trade would not change the spirit of our results. Unlike the usual Bertrand case (see Tirole, ch. 5), the two banks compete on all of the clauses in the contract [in our case the vector (χ, k)], and not just the price. Still, the result is similar.

Proposition 2. A pair of contracts is a Nash equilibrium if and only if (a) the contracts are bilaterally Pareto-efficient; (b) the firm's profit is determined by the contract that would give the less efficient bank a zero profit (we assume that if the firm is indifferent between the two contracts, it is financed by the more efficient bank).

Proof: the first point is immediate: no bank would offer a contract which is not bilaterally Pareto-efficient. To see that the above conditions are sufficient for a Nash equilibrium note that no bank finds that its best response is to undercut its competitor (meaning changing both χ and k to make the contract more profitable to the firm): the less efficient bank would not be able to recover costs, the more efficient gets the deal anyway and has no incentive to offer a contract which yields a lower profit. To see that the conditions are necessary for a Nash equilibrium note that whenever the less efficient bank makes a profit, the best response of the bank which does not get the deal is to undercut its competitor. ‖

It follows that the equilibrium contract is the solution to the programming problem

$$\text{Max}_{\chi,k} f(k) V[\chi, c_1] - rk \tag{12}$$

s.t.

$$f(k) \Pi[\chi] = \pi(r, c_2)$$

where $\pi(r, c_2)$ is the reduced-form firm's profit compatible with zero profit to bank 2, as calculated in the previous section.

Denote by (k^*, χ^*) the solution for the programming problem in (12). We characterize the solution with the aid of two other contracts: (k_2, χ_2) is the best contract bank 2 can offer [which determines $\pi(r, c_2)$], and (k_1, χ_1) is the contract bank 1 would have offered had it behaved competitively (i.e. is the same contract denoted by this symbol in section 2).

FOC to (12) is still given by equation (2). For the exponential distribution assumption, capital stock can be solved from the FOC only. Thus $k^* = k_1$, which can still be solved from (9). Clearly $k^* > k_2$: because bank 1 is more efficient, investment is less affected by the agency problem.

It is easy to see that the contract offered by bank 1 has a higher probability of bankruptcy relative to the contract offered by bank 2. Writing the constraint in (12) as

$$f(k^*) \cdot \Pi(\chi^*) = f(k_2) \cdot \Pi(\chi_2)$$

and remembering that $\Pi' < 0$, it is clear that $\chi_2 < \chi^*$. Thus, the probability of bankruptcy is

$$B(c_1, c_2) = H(\chi^*) = 1 - (1 - a) \cdot \frac{f(k_2)}{f(k^*)} > a \tag{13}$$

To calculate the bank's rent, we substitute (k^*, χ^*) into the objective function in (12), apply the adding-up properties of the functions V, Π, and C, use $k^* = k_1$ and the constraint in (12). We get

$$\pi_b = f(k_1) - rk_1 - c_1 f(k_1) H(\chi^*) - f(k_2) \Pi(\chi_2)$$

where π_b is the expected profit of the bank. Using the solution for (1) we get

$$\pi_b = [f(k_1)\Pi(\chi_1) - f(k_2)\Pi(\chi_2)] - c_1 f(k_1)[H(\chi^*) - H(\chi_1)] \qquad (14)$$

Equation (14) carries the main intuition of this section. Bank 1 is more cost-efficient, which increases investment by the firm. Had bank 1 behaved competitively (like in section 2), the firm would have enjoyed higher expected profits. But as assumption A.7 gives bank 1 such a strong bargaining position, all this profit is extracted by the bank, which yields the first right hand side element in (14). Extracting monopolistic rent, however, is a costly business in our framework: the fixed repayment has to be increased, which increases the probability of bankruptcy. Thus, monitoring has to be performed at a higher probability and expected monitoring costs are higher, which eats up some of the monopolistic rent. This effect is captured by the second right hand side element in (14). A more compact statement of this result can be obtained by using Lemma 2, (11) and (14) yields

$$\pi_b(r, c_1, c_2) = (1 - c_1)(1 - a)f[k_r(r)]\{f[k_c(c_1)] - f[k_c(c_2)]\} \qquad (15)$$

$$\pi_{b1} < 0, \qquad \pi_{b2} < 0, \qquad \pi_{b3} > 0$$

The signs of the partial derivatives follow immediately. Note also that when $c_1 = c_2$, the bank has no cost advantage over its competitor and monopolistic rents go to zero.

The firm's output is distributed to primary factors (capital), profits, monitoring costs, and to an additional component which is bank's profit. Those expected shares (respectively) are calculated in (16), and it can be checked that they add up to 1

(a) $\quad S_k(c_1) = \dfrac{rk^*}{f(k^*)} = \dfrac{rk_1}{f(k_1)} = V(\chi_1) = a(1 - c_1)$

(b) $\quad S_\pi(c_1, c_2) = \Pi(\chi^*) = \Pi(\chi_2)\dfrac{f(k_2)}{f(k_1)} = (1 - a)\dfrac{f(k_2)}{f(k_1)} = 1 - B$

$$(16)$$

(c) $\quad S_c(c_1, c_2) = C(\chi^*) = c_1 H(\chi^*) = c_1 B$

(d) $\quad S_b(c_1, c_2) = \dfrac{\pi_b}{f(k^*)} = (1 - c_1)(B - a)$

We conclude this section by re-calculating the gross markup of the bank

$$t(c_1, c_2) = \left[\frac{1}{1 - B} - \frac{\int_0^{\chi^*} \omega h(\omega)\, d\omega}{(1 - B)S_k} - 1\right]$$

$$+ \left[\frac{S_c}{(1 - B)S_k}\right] + \left[\frac{S_b}{(1 - B)S_k}\right] \qquad (17)$$

A new element, resulting from the bank's market power, is added to the markup. We denote it as the monopoly premium (t_m).

4   General equilibrium

Substituting $c_1 = c(z)$ and $c_2 = c[(1/n) - z]$ into the equations derived in the previous section we get a complete space-dependent specification of our endogenous variables. Based on this specification we can define

D.1 General equilibrium: A general equilibrium is a combination of the time deposit rate and the number of banks (r, n), such that

$$P(r,n) \equiv 2 \int_0^{1/2n} \pi_b \left[r, c(z), c\left(\frac{1}{n} - z\right) \right] dz = rE \tag{18}$$

$$D(r,n) \equiv n \left\{ 2 \int_0^{1/2n} k \left[r, c(z) \right] dz + E \right\} = K \tag{19}$$

We refer to (18) and (19) as the free entry and clearing conditions respectively.

Free entry implies that pure profits vanish in equilibrium. Equation (18) thus sums all monopoly profits over the bank's market share ($1/2n$ to the left and right of the bank's location). The sum is equated to the opportunity cost of the bank's capital, which is determined by the yield on time deposits. Equation (19) derives the economy's demand for capital by both firms and banks.

Comparative statics depends on the partial derivatives of the $P(\cdot)$ and $D(\cdot)$ functions. Clearly

$$\text{a.} \quad P_r < 0 \qquad \text{b.} \quad D_r < 0 \tag{20}$$

Increasing the interest rate (holding the number of banks constant) would decrease the amount of rent extracted from each firm in the bank's market share, and its demand for capital (see (15) and (10)).

Next we calculate[12]

$$P_n = S'(n) \cdot 2 \left\{ \pi_b \left[r, c\left(\frac{1}{2n}\right), c\left(\frac{1}{2n}\right) \right] + 2 \cdot \int_0^{1/2n} \pi_{b3} \, dz \right\}, \quad S(n) = \frac{1}{2n} \tag{21}$$

Increasing the number of banks (holding the interest rate constant) would decrease the bank's market share (the negative S' term). The bank would lose the firm on the margin of its market share from which it extracts a rent of $\pi_b(\cdot)$. But then, rent is zero on the marginal firm because the bank has no cost advantage over its competitor. It follows that this term vanishes. Also, the neighbouring bank gets closer and its cost of monitoring the firms on the existing market share falls, which has a negative effect on the bank's rent (through the positive π_{b3} term; see (15)). Thus

$$P_n < 0 \tag{21a}$$

Finally we calculate

$$D_n = \left\{ 2 \int_0^{1/2n} k[r, c(z)]\,dz + E \right\} + 2n \cdot S'(n) \cdot k\left[r, c\left(\frac{1}{2n}\right) \right] \tag{22}$$

Adding one bank would affect the demand for capital in two ways. First, the new bank would need capital to finance itself (the E term) and the firms in its market share (the left hand side argument). Second, the market share of all existing banks and thus their demand for capital would decrease (the right hand side argument). The two effects operate in opposite directions. (22) can be re-written, however, as

$$D_n = (1/n) \left\{ \frac{\int_0^{1/2n} k[r, c(z)]\,dz}{1/2n} - k\left[r, c\left(\frac{1}{2n}\right) \right] \right\} + E$$

The left hand side element (in brackets) is the average investment (per firm) in the bank's market share, while the right hand side element is the investment level by the marginal firm. Because $k(\cdot)$ is decreasing in z the average firm invests more than the marginal firm, and hence

$$D_n > 0 \tag{22a}$$

The main result of this section can now be proved immediately:

Proposition 3. When the aggregate quantity of capital increases, the interest rate falls, while the number of banks increases.

Proof: Comparative statics is solved from

$$\begin{pmatrix} P_r - E & P_n \\ D_r & D_n \end{pmatrix} \begin{pmatrix} dr \\ dn \end{pmatrix} = \begin{pmatrix} 0 \\ dK \end{pmatrix}$$

from which it can be verified that

$$\frac{dn}{dK} > 0, \qquad \frac{dr}{dK} < 0. \;\|$$

Thus growth leads to entry into banking system. Intuitively, the markup should fall via both the agency and the monopoly premia. The exact result is derived in section 5.

5   Aggregation

Agents in our model portray a great deal of heterogeneity: each firm holds a different amount of capital and pays a different rate of interest. Real world data, however, usually appear at a high level of aggregation. In order to state our results in a testable way, we turn now to the somewhat tedious task of aggregation. We calculate a price index of the gross markup, national income, and the share of the banking system in national income. The main problem is to derive comparative statics of those aggregates with respect to changes in the aggregate level of capital accumulation. We start with the following definition

D.2 A price index of the gross markup is

$$\bar{t} = \frac{\int_0^{1/2n} t\left[c(z), c\left(\frac{1}{n} - z\right)\right] \cdot k[r, c(z)]\,dz}{\int_0^{1/2n} k[r, c(z)]\,dz} \tag{23}$$

(price indexes for the agency and monopoly premia are defined in a similar way).

The index is simply a weighted average of all individual firms' markups, where individual capital stocks are used as weights. In the discussion below, the word average is always used in this particular sense.

The comparative statics calculations are facilitated by the following result

Lemma 3. The gross markup index is independent of the riskless interest rate.

Proof: it is easy to see that the probability of bankruptcy is independent of the interest rate (see also equation (24) below). As a result, all the shares in (16) and the gross markup in (17) are independent of the interest rate. Using the product property of the $k(\cdot)$ function stated in (10), $k_r(\cdot)$ can be taken out of the integration sign in both the numerator and denominator of (23), and cancelled. $\parallel$

For the sake of brevity we use the following notation for the rest of this section

$$k_c[c(z)] \equiv k(z), \qquad k'(z) < 0$$

It follows from lemma 3 that $\bar{t} = \bar{t}(1/2n)$. Our goal is to calculate the sign of

$$\frac{d\bar{t}}{dK} = \frac{d\bar{t}}{d(1/2n)} \frac{d(1/2n)}{dK}$$

Note that the sign of $d(1/2n)/dK$ is given by proposition 3.

In order to understand the problem raised by aggregation, we describe in some detail the calculations related to the index of the monopoly premium. From (16) and (17) we get

$$t_m(c_1, c_2) = \frac{1}{a} \cdot \frac{[B(c_1, c_2) - a]}{[1 - B(c_1, c_2)]}, \qquad \frac{dt_m}{dB} > 0$$

The probability of bankruptcy is calculated from (9) and (13)

$$B(c_1, c_2) = 1 - (1 - a) \left\{ \frac{1 - c_2}{1 - c_1} \right\}^{a/(1-a)} \tag{24}$$

It follows that

$$B_1 = -\frac{a}{(1-a)} \frac{(1 - B)}{(1 - c_1)} < 0, \qquad B_2 = \frac{a}{(1-a)} \frac{(1 - B)}{(1 - c_2)} > 0 \tag{25}$$

and

$$\frac{dB}{dz} = B_1 c'(z) - B_2 c'\left(\frac{1}{n} - z \right) < 0$$

Also,

$$1 < B < a, \qquad \text{and} \qquad B\left[c\left(\frac{1}{2n} \right), c\left(\frac{1}{2n} \right) \right] = a$$

As a result

$$t_{m1} < 0, \qquad t_{m2} > 0, \qquad \frac{dt_m}{dz} < 0, \qquad t_m\left[c\left(\frac{1}{2n} \right), c\left(\frac{1}{2n} \right) \right] = 0$$

Figure 3.3 shows how the monopoly premium varies over space. It is high close to the bank where competition is soft, and zero on the margin of the market share when the bank has no cost advantage relative to its competitor. The whole curve shifts to the right when the number of banks falls from n to n'.

Calculating the derivative of aggregate index of the monopoly premium reveals two contradicting effects

$$\bar{t}_m\left(\frac{1}{2n} \right) = \frac{1}{\int_0^{1/2n} k(z)\, dz} \left\{ 2 \int_0^{1/2n} t_{m2}\left[c(z), c\left(\frac{1}{n} - z \right) \right] \cdot c'\left(\frac{1}{n} - z \right) \cdot k(z)\, dz \right.$$

$$\left. + k\left(\frac{1}{2n} \right) \left[t_m\left[c\left(\frac{1}{2n} \right), c\left(\frac{1}{2n} \right) \right] - \bar{t}_m \right] \right\} \tag{26}$$

On the one hand, when market share increases, banks become further apart and competition weakens. As a result, more rent is extracted from each firm on the market share. On the other hand, when market share increases, the bank finances some additional firms. Those firms are located on the margins of the market share where the monopoly premium is zero. Adding those low value observations tends to decrease the index of the monopoly premium. Lemmas 5 and 6 below derive sufficient conditions for the first effect to dominate the second. The conditions are

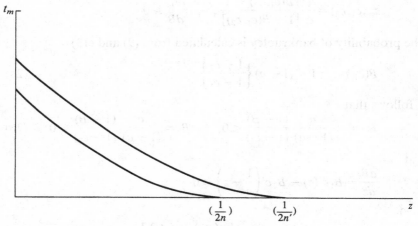

Figure 3.3 **The monopoly premium and market share**

stated for some general function m and are used repeatedly in the proceedings.

We first point out that the whole problem is a result of the fact that the probability of bankruptcy is decreasing in z.

Lemma 4. Assume $m(c_1, c_2) > 0$ is some general function with $m_2 > 0$ and $dm/dz > 0$. $\bar{m}(1/2n)$ is defined as in D.2. Then $\bar{m}'(1/2n) > 0$.

Proof: $\bar{m}'(1/2n)$ is similar to (26). $m_2 > 0$ by assumption. Because m is increasing in z, $m[c(1/2n), c(1/2n)]$ is greater than $\bar{m}$. So $\bar{m}'(1/2n) > 0$. ||

For the case of a decreasing function, the following sufficient condition is derived.

Lemma 5. Assume $m_2 > 0$, $m_1 < 0$. A sufficient condition for $\bar{m}'(1/2n) > 0$ is that for any z, $m_2 > (-m_1)$.

For proof see Appendix A.

An immediate implication of lemma 5 is that

Proposition 4. An increase the aggregate capital stock decreases the aggregate index of the monopoly premium.

Proof: $c_2 > c_1$, so using (25) $t_{m2} > (-t_{m1})$ for any z, the sufficient condition in lemma 5 is satisfied and $\bar{t}_m(1/2n) > 0$. Next, apply proposition 3. ||

Another useful sufficient condition is the following

Lemma 6. Assume $mg(c_1, c_2) = g(c_1) \cdot m(c_1, c_2)$, where $g \geq 0$, $g' > 0$, m satisfies the sufficient conditions stated in Lemma 5, and $\overline{gm}$ is defined as in D.2. Then, $\overline{gm}'(1/2n) > 0$.

For proof see Appendix A.

We can now show that

Proposition 5. An increase in the aggregate capital stock decreases the aggregate index of the agency premium $\bar{t}_a$.

Proof: Using equations (16.a) and (17), we can express the agency premium as a product of two functions

$$t_a = \frac{c_1}{a(1 - c_1)} \cdot \frac{B}{(1 - B)}$$

The function on the left hand side is increasing in c_1, while the function on the right hand side satisfies the sufficient conditions in Lemma 5. We can now use Lemma 6 to show that $t_a'(1/2n) > 0$. ∥

Unfortunately, it is impossible to show that growth decreases the default premium. It is possible to show, however, that the effect of the agency and monopoly premia is strong enough to assure that

Proposition 6: An increase in the aggregate capital stock decreases the gross markup of the banking system.

For proof see Appendix A.

We turn now to value of the product generated by the financial sector. We start with the following definition

D.3 Gross National Product (GNP) is the sum of income received by all primary factors of production:

entrepreneurship
$$2n \int_0^{1/2n} S_\pi f\left[k_r(r) \cdot k(z)\right] dz$$

capital (invested in the real sector)
$$2n \int_0^{1/2n} S_k f\left[k_r(r) \cdot k(z)\right] dz$$

capital (invested in the financial sector) $n \cdot rE$

factors employed in monitoring
$$2n \int_0^{1/2n} S_c f\left[k_r(r) \cdot k(z)\right] dz$$

The first two flows are income generated by the real sector, the last two by the financial sector. We thus refer to these as the product of the real and financial sector respectively.

We can now substitute the free entry condition (18) for the third line, and the adding-up property of S_k, S_π, S_c, and S_b to show that national income equals

$$2n \int_0^{1/2n} f\,[k_r(r) \cdot k(z)]\,dz \tag{27}$$

which is GNP. We now turn to the share of the financial sector in national income

Proposition 7: The share of the financial sector in national output is the weighted average of $(S_c + S_b)$ where output (rather than capital stock) is used as weights.

Proof: Divide the sum of the last two lines in D.3 by (27). ‖

It follows that

Proposition 8: An increase in the aggregate capital stock reduces the share of the banking industry in GNP.

Proof: Note that lemmas 3, 4 and 5, can be extended for the case of weighted average in terms of output. Note that

$$S_c + S_b = B + ac_1 - a$$

So (the extended) lemma 5 can be applied for the first element and lemma 4 for the second one. ‖

Proposition 8 states that the more capital a certain economy accumulates, the smaller is the fraction of resources used in the process of financial intermediation. In that aggregate sense, the economy becomes more efficient at intermediation.

6   Some evidence

Our model generates two testable hypotheses; that the markup and the share of the financial sector in GNP both fall when capital stock is accumulated. In this section we shall examine some cross-section country data to test these hypotheses.

Denote by i_l and i_d the *nominal* lending and time deposit rates (respectively) as usually reported in the statistics, and by π the expected rate of inflation. Since, $(1 + i_l)/(1 + \pi) = x/k$ and $(1 + i_d)/(1 + \pi) = r$

$$t = \frac{(1 + i_l)}{(1 + i_d)} - 1 \tag{28}$$

Note that inflationary expectations in the numerator and the denominator cancel, so that measuring the markup does not require their estimation.

The markups for eighty-one countries are calculated in Table 3.1, (all countries for which the International Monetary Fund (IMF) makes the data available, except some very small ones; for more detail on the data see Appendix B). Unfortunately, the quality of the data is quite poor, especially among low income countries. This is evident from the fact that about a quarter of the countries in that group report negative markups. A negative markup can result from measurement errors (in the statistical sense), but more likely from structural reasons. It is possible that the data come from 'official' credit markets, where favoured borrowers get highly subsidized credit, while intermediation in the sense of the present paper takes place in 'grey' or 'kerb' markets and is not captured by the data.

The (positive) markups are plotted against (purchasing power-adjusted) GNP per capita in Figure 3.4 (see again Appendix B for a few technical comments). The data seem to point at a weak negative correlation between the two variables. This negative correlation can be verified by some least-squares calculations. In estimation (1) (see Table 3.2), we estimate the average markup in the three income groups defined in Table 3.1. The markup in the high income countries is about two points lower relative to the middle income countries. But then, the markup in the low income countries is also (about) two points lower relative to the middle income countries. We attribute this result to the low quality of the data among low income countries. Estimation (2) checks whether lack of uniformity in the measurement of the riskless rate is a source of concern. The answer to that question is no.

Estimations (3) to (5) estimate the markup-GNP line, taking into consideration the large negative errors among low income countries discussed above. In estimation (3) all negative markups are omitted. The problem with such a truncation of the data set is that it may create an upward bias in the estimation of the slope. In estimation (4) all low income countries are omitted. Estimation (5) again checks for the lack of uniformity problem in the measurement of the riskless rate. Though significance levels are marginal and the fit of the estimation is quite poor, it seems to be a reasonable conclusion that when GNP/capital increases by one thousand dollars (1980 prices), the gross markup falls by about one-fifth of a point, at least among middle and high income countries.

Some factors which are irrelevant to the testing of our theory affect the measured markup. Note that surprisingly large differences exist among high income countries. Thus for example, the UK has a markup of just above half a point, while France has a markup of more than seven points! Germany lies in the middle with a markup of about four points. The common wisdom is that those countries differ greatly in terms of their regulatory systems.[13,14,15] In principle, one can add another component

Table 3.1. *Gross markup, GNP/capita and share of the financial sector in GNP in 1985*

Country	Abbre-viation	Gross[1,2] markup (%)	GNP/capita[3] US$ (1980 prices)	Share of finance in GDP (%)[4]
Low Income Countries				
Chad	CH	2.29 D	254	n.a.
Tanzania	TZ	7.71 D	295	n.a.
Ethiopia	ET	5.34 T	304	5.49
Niger	NG	− 0.48 M	311	6.71
Burundi	BR	4.67 D	331	1.26
Mali	MA	− 0.78 M	337	5.12
Uganda	UG	1.64 T	347	9.55 3C
Somalia	SM	6.25 D	348	4.29
Burkina Faso	BF	− 0.48 M	359	3.40
Ghana	GN	3.48 T	361	2.26
Rwanda	RW	4.48 D	373	7.63
Malawi	ML	5.41 T	374	6.54 C
Central African Repub	CA	3.21 D	441	3.47
Sierra Leone	SL	4.46 T	474	5.85
Togo	TG	− 0.48 M	486	5.86 1
Mauritania	MR	5.16 D	526	n.a.
Nepal	NP	11.43 T	526	7.70
Benin	BN	− 0.48 M	552	7.66 A
Liberia	LB	9.15 P	588	10.31
Nigeria	NR	− 0.52 D	590	3.07 3
Kenya	KN	0.09 T	592	13.26
Zambia	ZB	4.76 T	629	9.67
Bangladesh	BD	0.67 D	646	8.75
India	IN	5.91 M	755	7.57
Senegal	SN	− 0.48 M	756	37.69 A
Lesotho	LS	1.79 T	795	13.29
Honduras	HN	− 6.21 D	915	13.17
Cote d'Ivoire	CV	− 0.48 M	919	11.90 2
Zimbabwe	ZM	8.01 T	990	5.86
Cameroon	CM	5.05 D	1,138	11.86 4
Congo	CG	2.75 D	1,189	7.85 A
Morocco	MC	− 2.00 T	1,218	2.98
Guyana	GN	2.00 T	1,222	6.72
Bolivia	BV	− 11.37 D4	1,236	12.33
Indonesia	ID	7.51 M6	1,279	6.49
Philippines	PH	1.48 T	1,360	6.10
Papua N.G.	PP	1.03 T	1,414	6.87
Sri Lanka	SL	0.01 T	1,446	5.85
Guatemala	GT	2.75 D	1,597	8.96 C
Mauritius	MT	2.37 M	1,676	14.72
Jamaica	JM	2.41 T	1,728	14.66
Thailand	TH	7.19 T	1,879	8.02
Botswana	BT	2.29 D	1,987	6.71
Tunisia	TS	− 0.59 M	2,064	3.85
Peru	PR	0.00 D4	2,124	10.14
Ecuador	EC	8.29 D4	2,361	7.56
Turkey	TK	0.99 D	2,532	5.54
Costa Rica	CR	− 5.53 D	2,663	8.99

Table 3.1. (*cont.*)

Country	Abbre-viation	Gross[1,2] markup (%)	GNP/capita[3] US$ (1980 prices)	Share of finance in GDP (%)[4]
Middle Income Countries				
Korea	KR	0.55 M	3,082	11.76
Gabon	GB	3.37 D	3,313	n.a.
Malaysia	MS	3.69 M	3,426	8.91 C
Chile	CL	6.91 P	3,511	15.43 3
Venezuela	VZ	1.23 D	3,604	13.42
Portugal	PR	3.88 T	3,769	10.14
Mexico	MX	3.52 T4	3,987	7.72
South Africa	SA	3.35 T	3,990	12.65
Greece	GC	2.99 T6	4,499	6.83
Poland	PO	7.69 D	4,910	n.a.
Yugoslavia	YG	10.98 M6	5,060	3.51
Trinidad and Tobago	TR	8.91 T	5.087	12.27
Ireland	IR	0.59 T	5,226	5.28
Hungary	HG	1.36 D	5,762	5.18
High Income Countries				
Spain	SP	2.36 T	6,339	13.14
Italy	IT	3.78 T	7,552	21.87 A
New Zealand	NZ	3.36 T3	8,083	17.81
United Kingdom	UK	0.65 T	8,717	18.53
Australia	AU	0.54 T	9,030	18.61
Netherlands	NT	2.84 T	9,257	15.74
Finland	FN	− 2.69 M	9,296	14.15
Japan	JP	0.06 M	9,569	15.44
Belgium	BL	2.83 T	9,716	15.68
Singapore	SG	2.42 M	9,791	27.04
Sweden	SW	2.23 T	9,961	15.96
France	FR	7.13 M	9,976	17.46
Switzerland	SS	1.23 T	10,638	16.23
Germany	GR	4.27 T	10,712	12.34
Denmark	DM	4.30 M	10,947	14.63
Canada	CD	1.05 T	12,189	16.55
United States	US	2.27 T	12,526	23.07
Norway	NW	1.04 M	12,829	11.27
Kuwait	KT	1.05 T	15,709	12.54

Source: See Appendix B.

[1] Real percentage points.

[3] T, M, D and P on the right indicates the source of the riskless rate: the treasury bill, the money market, the discount rate or the deposit rate (respectively) (see Appendix B). A number after type letter (say 4), indicates that the markup was calculated for a year other than 1985 (in this case 1984), because the data for 1985 are not available.

[4] A number on the right (say 3) indicates that the share was calculated for a year other than 1985 (in this case 1983). C indicates that the share was calculated from constant price data (Table 1.11 instead of 1.10, see Appendix B). A indicates that the share includes other activities (items 8 + 9, see Appendix B).

Table 3.2. *Explaining the financial markup.* (*Ordinary least squares. Dependent variable is markup*)

Estimation Data set: Table 1, Excluding observations	No. of obs.	R^2	Intercept	GNP per capita (000 US dollars)	Income dummies		Type dummies	
					Low	High	M	D
(1)	81	0.04	4.22* (4.38)		−1.88* (−1.72)	−2.07† (−1.63)		
(2) type p	79	0.06	4.64* (4.28)		−1.70† (−1.52)	−2.14† (−1.64)	−1.11 (−1.12)	−1.21 (−1.19)
(3) type p negative	64	0.07	4.28* (9.19)	−0.17* (−2.13)				
(4) type p low inc.	32	0.08	4.69* (3.94)	−0.23† (−1.63)				
(5) type p low inc.	32	0.09	4.73* (3.27)	−0.24† (−1.54)			0.32 (0.29)	−0.25 (−0.15)

Note: Number in parenthesis below coefficient is the *t*-statistic.
* Significant at a 10% level.
† Significant at a 15% level.

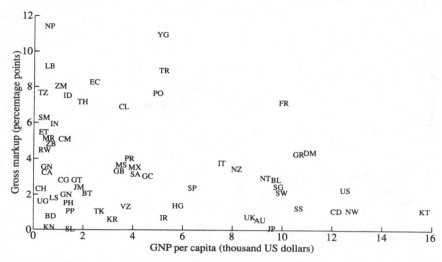

Figure 3.4 Gross markup and GNP per capita (positive values only)

(the regulation premium) into our decomposition formula (17), which will include the effect of regulation on the markup. We leave such decomposition to future research.

The omission of the regulation factor from the analysis not only adds 'noise'; it can bias the estimation. If, for example, markets tend to be less regulated when the countries are more developed, then it is possible that growth decreases the amount of regulation, and this rather than some efficiency gains is the cause of the lower markup.

Other possible sources of bias operate in the opposite direction and strengthen our argument. Intermediation, like most service industries, is a non-tradable. The relative price of non-tradables is strongly and very significantly correlated with GNP/capital (see Kravis and Lipsey, 1983). Thus, higher labour cost should increase the cost of intermediation (which is probably labour-intensive) in high income countries. Our results imply that the financial development effect is strong enough to dominate the Kravis-Lipsey effect.

For the same countries, data about the share of the financial sector in GDP appear on the last column of Table 3.1. These are the United Nations data, which is the same source as that used by Kuznets (1971). The observations are plotted against GNP/capita in Figure 3.5, and they show a clear positive correlation, much stronger than that observed by Kuznets. Indeed, calculating a least-squares line yields a positive slope (with a t statistic of 7.63) and an R^2 of 0.45.

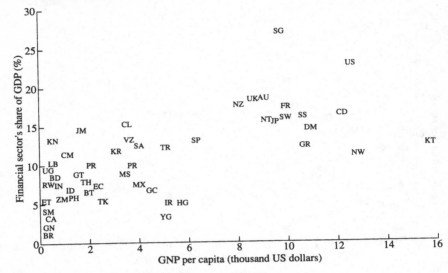

Figure 3.5   Size of the financial sector and GNP per capita

This finding seems to contradict the predictions of our model. A more careful examination of the results reveals, however, that this is not necessarily so. To understand why, note that the data which appear in Table 3.1 are based on a very broad definition of the financial sector, which includes – in addition to banking – insurance, real-estate and other financial services.

The process of financial development, especially when defined in such a broad way, is characterized by a substantial increase in types of activities which are financed (or insured) by the financial system. It is matched by an increase in the number of people (or firms) who have access to organized financial markets, and who can benefit from trading in these markets. Thus, for example, consumer, small business or new venture finance evolve (sometimes using new contracts or instruments which are inno-vated along the development process). These new markets substitute some other old forms of finance like within-family or unorganized credit markets. The same thing, maybe even in a more dramatic way, happens in insurance. This increase in scope will lead to a relatively larger financial sector.

This process is not described by our theoretical model, where only 'corporate' finance exists, and it is executed with a single contract which does not change along the growth path. Also, all capital is financed by saving and intermediated by the banking system. It is the reduction in cost of this single activity which relatively decreases the value of services produced by the banking system.

Obviously, the two processes discussed above complement and feed each other: because intermediation becomes cheaper, it can expand in scope and scale, finance more activities and prove useful to more individuals and firms.

7   Concluding remarks

One set of issues which has been totally ignored up to this point has to do with social welfare considerations and policy implications. While leaving a complete analysis to future work, a few simple points can be made at present. Specifically, we would like to warn against the following erroneous interpretation of the results: if intermediation and growth are indeed related, then banking is a 'key sector' and its subsidization can be used as a lever for growth. This argument, which may be supported within other models, cannot be supported by the present one.

Indeed, in some sense our model has too much rather than too little intermediation. Suppose that the goal of the social planner is to increase national income (relative to the equilibrium discussed in the paper). He can abolish the banking system, and allocate all the capital in the economy evenly among firms, at a zero rate of interest. This re-allocation economizes on the resources which are used by the banking system, and increases national output. No inefficiencies would result from the fact that information on firms' output is not produced, because this information is irrelevant for allocative efficiency, only for the distribution of output.

It is clear, however, that unlike in the case of complete markets, maximizing national output is a problematic goal for the social planner. In the complete markets case, output can be distributed in a way which is independent of the allocation of productive resources. In our model, if the social planner wants to reallocate income, he will have to tax firms. But then, any firm has the incentive to claim a zero gross output, and to evade the tax. Thus, the planner would face the same information problem the banks had, and would have to allocate resources for the purpose of monitoring the firms, just like the banks did.

Appendix A: Proofs of lemmas 5 and 6 and proposition 6

Proof of Lemma 5: Note first that m is indeed falling in z

$$\frac{dm}{dz} = m_1 c'(z) - m_2 c'\left(\frac{1}{n} - z\right) < 0$$

If $m_2 > (-m_1)$, and because of the convexity of $c(\cdot)$ assumed in A.6,

$$-\frac{dm}{dz} < 2m_2 c'\left(\frac{1}{n} - z\right)$$

Referring to equation (26)

$$2\int_0^{1/2n} B_2[\cdot]c'(\cdot)k(\cdot)dz > \int_0^{1/2n} -\frac{dm}{dz}\cdot k(z)dz$$

But k is falling in z so

$$\int_0^{1/2n}\frac{dm}{dz}\cdot k(z)dz > k\left(\frac{1}{2n}\right)\int_0^{1/2n} -\frac{dm}{dz}\,dz$$

$$= k\left(\frac{1}{2n}\right)\left\{m\left[c(0), c\left(\frac{1}{n}\right)\right] - m\left[c\left(\frac{1}{2n}\right), c\left(\frac{1}{2n}\right)\right]\right\}$$

Using equation (26) again we get

$$\bar{m}'\left(\frac{1}{2n}\right) > \frac{1}{\int_0^{1/2n}k(z)dz}\,k\left(\frac{1}{2n}\right)\left\{m\left[c(0), c\left(\frac{1}{n}\right)\right] - \bar{m}\right\} > 0. \parallel$$

Proof of Lemma 6: It can be calculated that

$$mg_1 = g'm + m_1 g, \qquad mg_2 = gm_2 > 0$$

The sign of mg_1 is not clear. There are three possibilities:

(a) $mg_1 < 0$. In that case $mg_2 > (-mg_1)$, and the above is proved by reference to Lemma 5.

(b) $mg_1 > 0$ and $dmg/dz > 0$. In that case the above is proved by reference to Lemma 4.

(c) $mg_1 > 0$ but $dmg/dz < 0$. Still

$$\left(-\frac{dmg}{dz}\right) < 2mg_2 c'\left(\frac{1}{n} - z\right)$$

and the proof can be completed following the same steps as the proof of Lemma 5. $\parallel$

Proof of proposition 6: Under the exponential distribution assumption, $H(\chi) = 1 - e^{-\chi}$. Equating to B we can solve for χ^*, and thus for

$$\int_0^{\chi^*} \omega h(\omega)d\omega = B + (1 - B)\cdot\log(1 - B)$$

Substituting into (17) we get

$$t = \frac{1}{a(1 - c_1)}[-\log(1 - B)] - 1$$

The proof can now be completed along the lines of the proof of proposition 5. $\parallel$

Appendix B: Sources and methods for Table 3.1 and Figure 3.4

The markup is calculated using equation (28). The source of the data is *International Financial Statistics* (*IFS*) year book for 1989. The table reports the markup for all *IFS* countries (for which the data is available), except for the very small ones (with population of under one million).

The calculation of the markup requires two variables: the lending rate, and the riskless rate. The *Lending Rate* is taken from line 60p on the country pages, which accounts for the 'short- and medium-term financing needs of the private sector'.[16]

Our analysis suggests that the riskless rate should be identified with the time deposit rate. Unfortunately, the *IFS* provides a *Deposit Rate* (line 60l, the rate 'offered to resident customers for demand, time and saving deposits'), which does not make a clear enough distinction between time and demand deposits. We thus prefer the *Treasury Bill Rate* (line 60c, 'the rate at which short-term government debt is issued or traded'), usually the closest substitute to time deposits, whenever available. If 60c is not available, the *Money Market Rate* (line 60b, 'the rate at which short-term borrowings are effected between financial institutions') is used, or, failing this, the *Discount Rate* (line 60, 'the rate at which the monetary authorities lend or discount eligible paper for deposit money banks'). The source of the riskless rate is indicated in column type in Table 3.1.

The source for GNP per capita is Summers and Heston (1988). We used an updated magnetic tape tape received from the authors.

Due to congestion in Figure 3.4, the following observations are omitted: MT, ML, SL and BR (overlapping JM, ET and RW respectively). Due to similar reasons, some observations had to be slightly relocated.

The last column (to the right) in Table 3.1 is taken from the United Nations volume of *National Accounts Statistics* (for 1988). Unless otherwise stated (in the notes to Table 1) it is the product in *Finance, Insurance, Real-estate, and Business services* (item 8 of Table 1.10), divided by GDP (same table) – both in current prices. Item 9 (same table) which was used in some cases is *Community, Social and Personal services*.

Due to congestion in Figure 3.5, the following observations are omitted: BL, MA, ML, TG, ZB, LS, CV, PP, SL, GN, BF and NP. Due to similar reasons, some observations had to be slightly relocated.

NOTES

This paper was written when I was visiting the University of Pennsylvania. The main ideas have been crystallized in a series of extensive discussions with Rafael Rob. I would also like to thank Costas Azariadis, Allan Drazen, William English, Joseph Haubrich, Fumio Hayashi and Joseph Zeira for fruitful discussions and helpful comments on an earlier draft, and Bob Summers and Alan Heston for providing some of the data used in the empirical section. I would also like to thank David Begg, John Black, Alberto Giovannini and Rafael Repullo, whose comments during and after the Santiago conference have improved this version, and Yoel Naveh who provided technical assistance.

1 We apply the term perfect competition to an environment with no market power. Information may still be incomplete.
2 This part of the analysis is stimulated by Romer (1986).
3 Banks have three roles: allocating capital (intermediation), providing liquidity via demand deposits (a type of insurance according to Diamond and Dybvig, 1983), and the operation of the clearing and payment system (see Fama, 1980, on this multiple role of the banking system). See Repullo also (1990) for a model of a liquidity-oriented (imperfectly competitive) banking system.
4 We ignore the possibility of mixed strategies, and assume the bank can pre-commit to follow its monitoring strategy.
5 As y is gross output, x is gross repayment, and should be interpreted as both interest and principal.
6 We assume that monitoring costs are linear in expected output, and thus concave in k, unlike Gale and Hellwig (1985) who assume that monitoring costs are convex in k. As a result we have to put stronger restrictions on the distribution of ω.
7 We implicitly assume that no one lender has enough resources to finance a whole firm by himself.
8 This is to stress that deposits do not provide any liquidity services of the type discussed by Diamond and Dybvig (1983).
9 Under the exponential distribution assumption the solution is unique (see below), and satisfies the second-order condition.
10 The exact proof is immediate: when monitoring costs are zero $x_1 = rk_1 + \int_0^{\bar{\omega}_1}[x_1 - \omega f(k_1)]h(\omega)\,d\omega$, but x is greater than $\omega f(k)$ for all bankruptcy states, so $x > rk$.
11 It will appear on the balance sheets of the banking system as fixed assets.
12 We ignore integer constraints.
13 For this 'common wisdom' see for example 'A Survey of European Capital Markets', *The Economist*, December 16, 1989.
14 For a detailed analysis of the relations between a regulatory system, high markups, and government finance, see Sussman (1991).
15 Allan Drazen pointed out to me that there is some correlation between reserve requirements and the markup, at least for Western Europe.
16 Description of data taken from *IFS* year book 1989 pp. 8.

REFERENCES

Cameron, Rondo (1967) *Banking in the Early Stages of Industrialization*, New York: Oxford University Press.
Diamond, Douglas (1984) 'Financial Intermediation and Delegated Monitoring', *Review of Economic Studies* 51, 393–414.
Diamond, Douglas and Philip Dybvig (1983) 'Bank Runs, Deposit Insurance, and Liquidity', *Journal of Political Economy* 91, 401–19.

Fama, F. Eugene (1980) 'Banking in the Theory of Finance', *Journal of Monetary Economics* **6**, 39–57.

Gale, Douglas and Martin Hellwig (1985) 'Incentive Compatible Debt Contracts: The One-Period Problem', *Review of Economic Studies* **52**, 647–64.

Gertler, Mark (1988) 'Financial Structure and Aggregate Economic Activity: An Overview', *Journal of Money Credit and Banking* **20**, 559–88.

Goldsmith, Raymond (1969) *Financial Structure and Development*, New Haven: Yale University Press.

Greenwood, Jeremy and Boyan Jovanovic (1989) 'Financial Development, Growth, and the Distribution of Income', NBER Working Paper No. 3189.

International Monetary Fund (1989) *International Financial Statistics, Yearbook*, Washington DC: IMF.

Kravis, Irving B. and Robert E. Lipsey (1983) 'Toward an Explanation of National Price Levels', Princeton Studies in International Finance No. 52.

Kuznets, Simon (1971) *Economic Growth of Nations: Total Output and Production Structure*, Cambridge: Harvard University Press.

McKinnon, Ronald (1973) *Money and Capital in Economic Development*, Washington D.C.: The Brookings Institution.

Repullo, Rafael (1990) 'A Model of Imperfect Competition in Banking' (mimeo).

Romer, M. Paul (1986) 'Increasing Returns, Specialization, and External Economies: Growth as Described by Allyn Young', Rochester Center for Economic Research Working Paper No. 64.

Shaw, Edward (1974) *Financial Deepening in Economic Development*, Oxford: Oxford University Press.

Summers, Robert, and Alan Heston (1988) 'A New Set of International Comparisons of Real Product and Price Levels Estimates for 130 Countries, 1950–1985', *Review of Income and Wealth*, Ser. 34, No. 1, 1–25.

Sussman, Oren (1991) 'The Macroeconomic Effects of a Tax on Bonds Interest Rate', *Journal of Money Credit and Banking* **23**, 352–66.

Tirole, Jean (1988) *The Theory of Industrial Organization*, Cambridge: MIT Press.

Townsend, M. Robert (1979) 'Optimal Contracts and Competitive Markets with Costly State Verification', *Journal of Economic Theory* **21**, 265–93.

Townsend, M. Robert (1983) 'Financial Structure and Economic Activity', *American Economic Review* **73**, 895–911.

United Nations (1990) *National Accounts Statistics: Main Aggregates and Detailed Tables, 1988*, New York: United Nations.

Williamson, D. Stephen (1987) 'Costly Monitoring, Optimal Contracts, and Equilibrium Credit Rationing', *Quarterly Journal of Economics* **102**, 135–45.

Discussion

DAVID BEGG

Oren Sussman's paper gives an elegant account of one particular aspect of the relationship between finance and development. It is a merit of the paper that its theoretical analysis yields sharp, testable predictions, which the author then confronts with evidence from a very large number of countries. I begin by summarising the model and its principal results. Then I discuss their robustness and the light they shed on financial development. Finally, I comment on the empirical testing.

In this paper, finance does not mean money or liquidity, but rather corporate borrowing from banks to finance investment. Given *ex post* asymmetric information, the standard debt contract is the efficient contract when monitoring is costly. Banks specialize in such monitoring and intermediate the exogenous amount of household net worth available for lending to firms for investment. Sussman shows that it is possible to devise a set up in which there is balanced growth, in the sense that the profit margins of banks (the cost of intermediation) is independent of the size or wealth of the economy.

Such a model does not have a very interesting role for a link between finance and development. To allow such a possibility, some kind of scale economies must matter. To introduce these, the author develops a spatial model of monopolistic competition between banks. Customer-firms are exogenously located, monitoring costs increase with the distance between the bank and the firm, and banks can locate endogenously. There is free entry to the banking industry. General equilibrium determines a lending rate and a deposit rate of interest and a number of banks such that (i) banks make zero profit, (ii) exogenous household wealth is fully invested, and (iii) the demand and supply of bank loans are equal.

Within this framework, Sussman develops two basic results. An increase in wealth and capital lead to a reduction in margins in the banking industry, for two reasons. First, the number of banks increases, thereby increasing competition and reducing the degree of local monopoly power enjoyed by banks. Second, with each bank more spatially specialized, its monitoring costs fall. The second result is that this fall in profit margins will also be associated with a lower share of banking in GDP.

Before turning to the empirical evidence, let me consider how useful this theoretical framework can be in helping us understand links between finance and development. Although the model is neat, it is special in several respects. First, it is an explicit assumption that there is no aggregate risk for banks, who can completely diversify credit risk; in turn this means that there is no need to monitor banks themselves. Yet this assumption sits rather uneasily on the model of spatial competition, in which each bank specializes in a particular locality (which stands more broadly for a group of customer characteristics). Such specialization, whether by geographical locality or product characteristics, surely has the implication that a bank's customers are likely to face highly correlated risks which cannot be diversified fully by the bank. In turn this reintroduces the agency problem for banks and the need to monitor banks themselves.

The second aspect of the theoretical framework about which I have reservations is the assumption of free entry into banking. Even within highly developed economies, substantial deregulation of banking is a relatively recent phenomenon; historically, whatever determined the successful growth of today's rich countries did so against a background in which their banking systems were highly regulated. My suspicion would be that in poorer countries banks tend to be very regulated indeed, and there are some good reasons why this should be the case. One reason is essentially macroeconomic rather than microeconomic: governments need money. When fiscal administration is relatively rudimentary, the government will often be under enormous pressure to raise revenues through seigniorage. Strictly regulated banks, including requirements to hold massive amounts of cash against deposits, provide a nice base for the inflation tax. A highly regulated banking system is unlikely to be a banking system in which free entry occurs. Regulation may well play a key role in financial development, and causation may run in both directions. By neglecting such regulatory issues, Sussman's model risks omitting one of the key aspects of the analysis.

My third remark refers to the nature of finance on which the analysis is focused. In the paper, banks lend to firms for investment. In the real world, much the largest part of corporate investment is financed by retained earnings. The role of bank-financed investment may be less as a source of cash than as a device for corporate control: managers know that if they screw up, the banks will intervene and are likely to restructure the management. This may be an important pressure on managers, but it is not one Sussman's model can address, since output depends on capital input and random shocks but not, for example, on managerial effort.

These three qualifications do, it seems to me, lead one to question whether Sussman has got the whole story, or even sufficient of the story that one would expect it to stand out in the data. He shows that there is weak evidence in the data that richer countries on average have a lower cost of intermediation as his theory predicts. On the other hand, the data alerts us to some of the other missing influences. For example, in 1985 the cost of intermediation was 14 times higher in France than the UK even though, in terms of the huge disparity of wealth in the data sample, these were essentially countries of comparable wealth and capital. Clearly, part of the answer lies in different regulatory regimes: London was well on the way to deregulation, Paris much less so at that time. Empirical analysis is unlikely to be very convincing until the regulatory regime is explicitly included.

RAFAEL REPULLO

The purpose of this paper is to analyse how capital accumulation might affect the gross markup of the banking system, defined (roughly) by the ratio between average lending and deposit interest rates. The paper first presents a competitive model of banking under asymmetric information and costly state verification, which yields the 'balanced growth' result that the intermediation markup is independent of the capital stock. Since this result does not appear to be consistent with the evidence, the paper then proposes a monopolistic competition model of banking based on Salop's circular road model. In this model, as the capital stock increases the banking system becomes more competitive and, as a result, the intermediation markup decreases, which seems to accord with the empirical evidence.

This is a very interesting although somewhat misguided paper. Also, it is unnecessarily obscure. For this reason, in what follows I will give an alternative presentation of the two models, commenting on the results as I go along.

1   The perfect competition model

In the competitive model there is a representative risk-neutral bank which can raise deposits at a given gross rate of return r, and a continuum of identical risk-neutral firms with a gross production technology $\tilde{\omega}f(k)$, where k is the amount of capital borrowed from the bank and $\tilde{\omega}$ is an exponentially distributed iid productivity shock with unit mean. There is *ex post* asymmetric information about the realization of the shock, although the bank can observe ω at a cost of $cf(k)$. In this setting, the optimal contract between the bank and the firm is a standard debt contract where $\chi f(k)$ is the fixed promised repayment and χ is the cut-off point between the bankruptcy and the solvency states. Using the properties of the exponential distribution, the expected payoff to the firm can be simplified to:

$$\int_{\chi}^{\infty} (\omega - \chi) f(k) \, dH(\omega) = f(k) h(\chi) \tag{1}$$

whereas the expected payoff to the bank can be written as:

$$\int_{0}^{\chi} (\omega - c) f(k) \, dH(\omega) + \int_{\chi}^{\infty} \chi f(k) \, dH(\omega) = (1 - c) f(k) H(\chi)$$

where $h(\omega)$ and $H(\omega)$ denote, respectively, the exponential density and cumulative distribution functions.

The optimal contract is the solution to the maximization of the firm's expected payoff (1) subject to the bank's zero expected profit constraint:

$$(1 - c) f(k) H(\chi) = rk \tag{2}$$

But since $h(\chi) = 1 - H(\chi)$, one can substitute the constraint into the firm's objective, to get:

$$\underset{k}{\text{Max}} \left[f(k) - \frac{rk}{1 - c} \right] \tag{3}$$

Under standard assumptions about the production function $f(k)$, solving (3) gives the bank's demand for funds (deposits) $k(r)$, which would be decreasing in the deposit rate r. Moreover, for the case where $f(k) = k^a$, $0 < a < 1$, one can substitute $k(r)$ into (2) to get $\chi = -\log(1 - a)$, a constant independent of r. Since the gross intermediation markup, defined by

$$1 + t = \frac{\chi f(k)}{rk}$$

is by equation (2) equal to:

$$1 + t = \frac{\chi}{(1 - c) H(\chi)} \tag{4}$$

it follows that the markup is also constant.

Finally, given the aggregate capital stock K, one can solve the equation $k(r) = K$ to obtain the equilibrium deposit rate r. But since the intermediation markup is independent of r, the balanced growth result (Proposition 1) follows.

Is this result consistent with the empirical evidence? To check this, Sussman regresses the value of t for a large cross-section of countries on their GNP per capita (taken as a proxy for K), which yields the results in Table 3.2. Although the coefficient of GNP per capita is barely significant, the author states that 'it seems to be a reasonable conclusion that when GNP per capita increases by one thousand dollars (1980 prices), the gross markup falls by about one-fifth of a point, at least among middle and high income countries'.

Thus the competitive model is taken to be rejected by the data, and so the author turns to the monopolistic competition model. But before I discuss this model, I want to illustrate how in the context of the first model it is quite straightforward to obtain a negative relationship between the intermediation markup and the capital stock.

2   *Two variations on the competive model*

First, let us suppose that the production function is modified to $f(k) = k + k^a$. In this case, solving the programme (3) gives a new deposit demand function $k(r)$, which is also decreasing in the deposit rate r. However, it can be shown that the bankruptcy point χ is now an increasing function of r. Since for an exponential distribution $\chi/H(\chi)$ is increasing in χ, it follows by (4) that an increase in the deposit rate r increases the intermediation markup t. Hence, an increase in the aggregate capital stock K not only reduces the equilibrium deposit rate but also the markup.

Second, let us now suppose that monitoring costs, as a proportion of expected output, decrease with k. In particular, assume that we have the monitoring cost function $c(k)f(k)$, where $c(k) = 1 - k^{1-\beta}$ and $f(k) = k^a$, $0 < a < \beta < 1$. Solving the programme (3) with $c(k)$ instead of c gives a new deposit demand function $k(r)$, which is decreasing in the deposit rate r. Substituting $k(r)$ into (2) one gets $\chi = -\log(1 - (a/\beta))$, a constant independent of r, so that by equation (4) one concludes that in this case the gross intermediation markup t is also an increasing function of r (since $1 - c(k(r))$ is a decreasing function of r). Hence, as in the case above, an increase in the aggregate capital stock K reduces both the equilibrium deposit rate and the intermediation markup.

Thus, to get a negative relationship between the intermediation markup and the capital stock one does not need to go beyond the competitive model. But let us now turn to the core of the paper, which is the monopolistic competition model.

3 The monopolistic competition model

In this model, there is a continuum of firms uniformly distributed around a circle, and a finite number n of banks distribution symmetrically around the circle. Monitoring costs for any bank are assumed to be increasing and convex in the distance z between the bank and the firm, and this is the (informational) source of banks' market power. For each location in the circle, (neighbouring) banks compete by offering contracts (k, χ), where k is the capital provided and $\chi f(k)$ is the promised repayment in solvency states. (Incidentally, I do not think that this should be called Bertrand competition.)

The (symmetric) Nash equilibrium *for each location* is found by maximizing the expected profits of the bank which is closer to the firm (say bank 1):

$$(1 - c_1) f(k_1) H(\chi_1) - rk_1$$

where $c_1 = c(z)$ and z is the distance between the firm and this bank, subject to the constraint that the firm is indifferent between the contract (k_1, χ_1) and the best contract that the other bank (bank 2) can offer and make zero profits:

$$f(k_1) h(\chi_1) = f(k_2) h(\chi_2)$$

where (k_2, χ_2) is the optimal contract derived from the competitive model with monitoring costs $c_2 f(k)$, with $c_2 = c((1/n) - z)$.

Given that $H(\chi) = 1 - h(\chi)$, one can substitute the constraint into the bank's objective, to get:

$$\underset{k_1}{\text{Max}} (1 - c_1) \left[f(k_1) - \frac{rk_1}{1 - c_1} - f(k_2) h(\chi_2) \right] \tag{5}$$

Clearly, the solution for k_1 in (5) is the same as the solution for k in (3) when $c = c_1$. Hence the firm is going to borrow the *same* amount of capital as in the competitive model with monitoring costs $c_1 f(k)$, but is going to pay back more (except, of course, in the case where the firm is located at the mid-point between the two banks).

Once the optimal contract for each location is derived, Sussman introduces a capital requirement E for operating a bank, and defines a free entry equilibrium in the standard way. Finally, given the aggregate capital stock K, the equilibrium deposit rate r is endogenously determined by the capital market clearing condition (equation (19) of the paper).

The main results of this model are Propositions 3 and 6. The former states that as the capital stock increases, the equilibrium deposit rate falls and the number of banks increases. Proposition 6 shows that there is a negative relationship between the weighted average $\bar{t}$ of the individual gross intermediation markups and the capital stock.

Thus, we get the desired result. However, is this *really* consistent with the empirical evidence?

4   *The empirical evidence reconsidered*

Looking again at the evidence presented by Sussman in support of this result, one may worry (among other things) about the heterogeneity of banking institutions and regulations across the different countries. Moreover, if we restrict attention to a more homogeneous subset of countries the result does not appear to hold. In particular, if we regress the value of t for the 19 OECD countries in the sample on their GNP per capita, we get the following result:

$$t = 3.04 - 0.06\,GNP/cap$$
$$(-0.37) \qquad\qquad\qquad (R^2 = 0.008)$$

Even if we were to drop France (which is an outlier in this regression), the result would not improve:

$$t = 3.13 - 0.10\,GNP/cap$$
$$(-0.78) \qquad\qquad\qquad (R^2 = 0.04)$$

Hence, one cannot conclude that the empirical evidence supports the key result of the paper.

5   *Final remark*

Summing up my discussion, I have shown that in order to get a negative relationship between the intermediation markup and the capital stock one does not need to go beyond the competitive model. On the other hand, it is the model of imperfect competition that I regard as the main contribution of the paper. To the best of my knowledge, this is one of the first models of banking in which banks' market power is derived from informational advantages. I believe that it is here, rather than in the particular result about the effect of growth on the cost of intermediation, that the value added of this paper lies.

4　Capital market imperfections and regional economic development

BRUCE C. GREENWALD, ALEC LEVINSON
and JOSEPH E. STIGLITZ

The role of monetary and, more broadly, financial market interventions in promoting regional growth is an increasingly important economic issue. It has been a commonplace of traditional economic theory that national monetary policy is an important tool for promoting macro-economic stability and growth. Yet little attention has been paid to the impact of monetary and financial policy on the pattern of economic activity across regions of a particular national economy. In traditional models, the reason for this seems clear, if rarely stated explicitly. Within any national economy, free capital mobility and a common currency will ensure that interest rates are equal across regions. Since monetary policy has traditionally been viewed as operating through interest rates, common interest rates mean that monetary policy should be neutral in its regional impact. Indeed, with nationally integrated financial markets, arbitrage should maintain equality of local interest rates even in the face of deliberate efforts to subsidize local capital investment;[1] thus defeating the purpose of the original subsidies. Consequently, monetary and currency integration in Europe (and elsewhere) which reduces existing national economies to regional status should, in this view of the world, all but eliminate the possibility of local monetary stimulation of formerly national economies. Regional monetary changes would simply be translated into attenuated movements in transnational interest rates. Whether the resulting loss in policy flexibility is desirable depends largely on one's view of the likely efficacy of government interventions in general. However, under any circumstances, it is important to know how far this basic argument applies in practice.[2]

In a world with imperfect and asymmetrically distributed information, the traditional theory no longer applies. If, for example, local investors and financial institutions have superior information about investment opportunities in their region than outside investors, this will inhibit capital mobility and interregional arbitrage for two reasons. First, local institutions and investors will have incentives to invest locally to take advantage of their superior local information. Second, investment opportunities passed up by local investors will tend to be adversely selected and, thus, those available to outside investors will have abnormally low rates of returns, inhibiting outside investment. In principle, national fundraising by local financial institutions might overcome these problems. However, to the extent that asymmetric information regarding the prospects of these institutions themselves reduces their ability to raise funds – particularly equity capital – the problems of capital mobility are unlikely to be completely eliminated.[3] These informational imperfections, by sustaining varying returns on capital across regions, lead to suboptimal allocations of capital and other resources. However, at the same time they create the possibility that monetary and other financial market interventions may positively affect regional development and compensate, at least partially, for any original misdistribution of capital. This paper is, therefore, devoted to assessing the importance of and modelling the effects of regional information-based capital market imperfections.

Such a model is also useful as a basis for evaluating the possible effectiveness of regional finance-based development policies. A widely recognized difficulty with direct government investments in local economies is that to be successful the government must be able to identify firms and industries which are economic 'winners'. Yet the original justification for government intervention is the inability of private investors to identify such firms and it seems unlikely that government functionaries will be better at doing so than private investors. An alternative to direct investment is to support local financial institutions which, based on their access to local information, would then lend to firms. Assuming subsidies are properly structured (e.g., do not penalize successful investment relative to unsuccessful investment by financial institutions) these financial institutions would invest in local firms based on their superior local information. The problem of picking 'winners' would then be reduced to that of selecting successful local financial institutions, each of which would presumably have a diversified portfolio of loans within the region. However, if these financial institutions were merely to recycle local subsidies back into national financial markets, the effect of government policy would be negligible. It is important, therefore, to understand how and why local financial institutions might be prevented from doing so.

In order to examine these questions as practically as possible, we begin with a model of a prototypical financial institution, a bank, with access both to local investment opportunities, about which it has imperfect information, and a national market for government securities. We will assume that its information about projects is superior to that of banks outside its region, but inferior to that of the local entrepreneurs seeking financing.[4] We then examine the likely efficacy of government financial market interventions, when interest rates in the national government bond market are held fixed.[5] The interventions that we consider include both direct subsidies to local banks and more traditional expansion of reserves held by regional banks (and hence of the regional money supply). The implications of the model depend on matters of institutional structure – in particular the levels of seigniorage realized by banks on money creation and government deposit guarantees – which have been largely ignored in considering the local impacts of financial policy. They point to an important potential role for government policy in fostering regional development only when the underlying structure of financial institutions is appropriate.

Next, we develop a set of empirical implications of this imperfect capital market model for fluctuations in employment across regions and industries which we test using data for the different states of the United States. In particular, we look at manufacturing industries which, within the United States, trade their goods in single national markets. For traditional models, local employment in any particular industry (e.g., office equipment) should fluctuate with national, not local conditions. Thus, aggregate local activity should vary with the national activity of the industries which constitute the local economy. Automobile manufacturers in Michigan should do badly and, thus Michigan as a whole should do badly (if its economy is heavily concentrated in automobile manufacturing), if the automobile industry does badly. But other industries in Michigan should not do badly because Michigan as a whole does badly.[6] In contrast, with informationally segmented capital markets, deterioration in local conditions as a whole will impair the financial health of local banks (through loan defaults, etc.) which will reduce capital availability to and activity in other local industries. This second pattern is, in fact, the one we find in the United States data.

The paper itself consists beyond this introduction of four parts. Section 1 develops the model of financial institutions in a world of imperfect information. Section 2 then develops the empirical implications of that model. Section 3 applies the model to data for individual states within the United States. Section 4 concludes with a brief discussion of policy conclusions.

1 Lending institutions with imperfect information

Following Stiglitz and Weiss (1981), we assume that each bank faces a group of borrowers who look identical and undertake projects which require a fixed investment B. Since issues of equity and collateral do not fundamentally alter the nature of the analysis,[7] we assume for simplicity that borrowers must obtain the full cost of the project from their banks and that they post no collateral. However, we will assume that for each project undertaken the borrower pays a cost, C, which represents the cost of his time and administrative overhead.[8] Thus, B will also denote the common amount sought by each borrower. The uncertain returns to a borrower's investment will be denoted R with a distribution function $F(R,\theta)$, a density $f(R,\theta)$ and a common expected return $\bar{R}$. The index θ will denote the riskiness of a borrower's project, with higher levels of θ corresponding to greater risk in the sense of Rothschild and Stiglitz (1970). Finally, we will assume that project returns are correlated across borrowers and that the correlation coefficient of project returns is μ for all projects. The random return $\tilde{R}_j$ on the jth project can be thought of, therefore, as being written

$$\tilde{R}_j = \theta_j^{1/2}(\tilde{R}_0 + \tilde{R}_1)k + \bar{R}$$

where $\tilde{R}_0$ is a random variable common across projects with mean zero and variance μ, $\tilde{R}_1$ is an independent random variable across projects (and independent of R_0) with variance $(1 - \mu)$ and mean zero and k is a constant term.

If a bank charges its borrowers a contractual rate of interest, r, on loans, then the returns to the borrower and bank respectively, when the project return is R, are

$$\pi(R,r) = \begin{cases} R - (1-r)B - C & \text{if } R \geq (1+r)B \\ -C & \text{otherwise} \end{cases}$$

and

$$\rho(R,r) = \begin{cases} (1+r)B & \text{if } R \geq (1+r)B \\ R & \text{otherwise} \end{cases}$$

where π is the return to the borrower and ρ is the return to the bank. If we assume further that borrowers are risk-neutral, then the following results follow immediately (see Stiglitz and Weiss, 1981).

(1)   For any given contractual rate of interest r, there is a critical value of $\theta, \hat{\theta}$, such that the expected value of firm profits is positive – and the firm borrows from the bank – if and only if $\theta \geq \hat{\theta}$.

(2)   As r increases the criticial value, $\hat{\theta}$, below which firms do not apply for loans increases, and

(3)   The expected return to the bank on any loan, $\bar{\rho}$, is a decreasing function of θ which reflects the riskiness of the loan.

The second of these conditions suggests that as the level of r increases the riskiness of a bank's loan portfolio increases, since higher levels of r lead to higher levels of θ in the borrower population and, hence, more risky loans. In fact, matters are not quite so simple. On the one hand the direct impact of changes in r is to increase the riskiness of a loan to any particular θ level of borrowers. That is

$$\frac{dV_\rho}{dr} = 2[(1 + r)B - \bar{p}]B \int_{(1+r)B}^{\infty} dF(R,\theta) > 0$$

where $\bar{p}$ is the expected return to the bank of the loan and V_ρ denotes the variance of the bank's loan returns. However, increases in θ do not always lead to increases in the variance of a bank's loan return. Consider, for example, a mean-preserving spread that consists of (1) a shift in probability mass upward for some $R \geq \bar{R}$ where the mean of the R distribution $\bar{R} > (1 + r)B$ and (2) a shift in probability mass downward from $\bar{R} > R \geq (1 + R)B$ to $\bar{p}$. This mean-preserving spread in the distribution of R actually reduces the variance of the ρ distribution. Nevertheless, if loan default is a relatively rare event and thus $\bar{p}$ is close to $(1 + R)B$, it can be shown that for most increases in θ, the variance of ρ also increases.[9] Consequently, assuming such conditions hold, it will be true that (3) increases in r, the contractual rate of interest, will be associated with increases in the riskiness of a bank's loan portfolio.[10]

As a result, if as Stiglitz and Weiss demonstrate, condition (3) implies that under reasonable circumstances increases in r beyond a certain point will lead to decreases in $\bar{p}$, then the risk-return trade-off available to imperfectly informed bank lenders may take the form illustrated in Figure 3.1, which has been drawn with B set equal to unity (a convention that will continue for the remainder of this paper). At low levels of the contractual rate of interest, higher interest rates lead to higher expected loan portfolio returns, but at the same time to a higher variance on the bank's loan portfolio return. As the contractual rate of interest rises, safe borrowers, who are also characterized by high expected loan returns, are discouraged and the pool of borrowers deteriorates. This deterioration tends to offset the direct impact of the higher contractual rate of interest and ultimately drives $\bar{p}$ down. At the same time, increasing levels of r are likely to lead to a steadily increasing level of loan portfolio variance. Thus the risk-return trade-off facing banks in their loan portfolios may first increase and then decrease as shown in Figure 4.1.

In analysing the behaviour of banks in the face of such a trade-off, Stiglitz and Weiss considered that the loans involved represented the only outlet for a bank's loanable funds and that the bank's decision-makers were risk-neutral. This led them to focus on a rationing equilibrium in

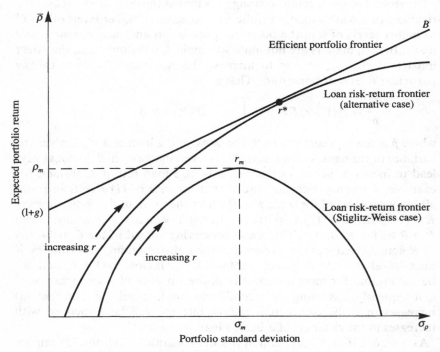

Figure 4.1   Risk-return frontiers available to lenders

which at the return-maximizing rate of interest, r_m (see Figure 4.1), there is an under-supply of loanable funds; that is the demands by borrowers exceed the amount of loans supplied by bankers at the expected pay-off ρ_m. In practice, banks typically have access to and take advantage of alternative investments, most notably government bonds. Also bank-managements appear to be concerned with both the risks and the returns of their loan portfolios. To remedy these omissions, we will assume that banks may invest any amount in government securities which provide a safe rate of return $(1 + g)$. And, we will ultimately assume that bank managers are risk-averse.

Let W denote the wealth of a single representative bank, and let a denote the share of that wealth that the bank devotes to government bonds. Then at any given level of the interest rate, g, in the government bond market the fraction of wealth devoted to government bonds will depend on the investor's optimal portfolio allocation, which is illustrated in Figure 4.2. An efficient portfolio frontier can be defined by the tangency of a ray from the safe government bond return at $(1 + g)$ on the vertical axis (government

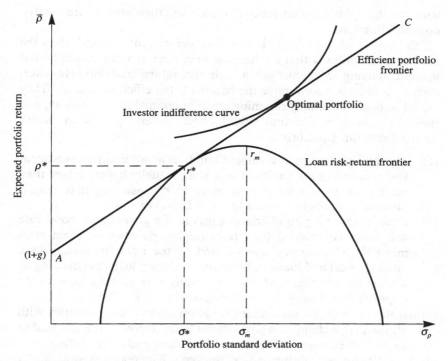

Figure 4.2 Optimal lender portfolio with credit rationing

bond risk is assumed to be zero) to the loan return trade-off curve. This tangency necessarily occurs to the left of r_m, the contractual loan rate which maximizes the expected loan return. (At points beyond the tangency point, r^*, on the loan return trade-off curve, the bank is essentially short-selling government bonds in order to make loans.)[11] The optimal level of a is determined as in any portfolio problem by the tangency of the efficient frontier with the investors' (in this case banks') risk-return indifference curves.

The question is then one of equilibrium in the loan market. The level r^* on the loan return trade-off curve represents the corresponding contractual interest rate charged by banks. At this contractual rate of interest the universe of potential borrowers will generate a loan demand $L^D(r^*)$. In general, the lower r^*, the higher loan demand will be. At the same time, banks, which face expected loan returns ρ^* at risk levels σ^*, will offer an amount of loanable funds

$$L^s = (1 - a)W \tag{1}$$

where to the right of the tangency at r^*, a is less than zero. There are two possible situations.

If the supply of loan funds is less than the current demand, then the natural assumption is that contractual loan interest rates would be bid upward, moving the banks along their risk-return trade-off. However, such a movement would move the banks off the efficient frontier. They would be better off simply rationing credit at optimal interest rate r^*, and thus a rationing equilibrium would occur. Several points are worth noting about this equilibrium:

(1)   The introduction of government bonds as an alternative investment and accounting for bank risk-aversion, actually lowers rather than increases loan interest rates from r_m to r^* (assuming that at r_m a rationing equilibrium with $L^s = W < L^D(r_m)$ exists).

(2)   Even in rationing equilibria changes in the government bond rate will affect contractual loan rates (higher government bond rates move the r^* tangency upward and to the right, increasing loan interest rates) and loans outstanding (reducing loans outstanding as a rises) but the degree of credit rationing may actually move in the opposite direction (if L^D falls by more than L^s).

(3)   If the slope of the loan return trade-off curve changes rapidly with r^*, then large changes in government bond interest rates may lead to only small changes in contractual loan rates and total lending.

(4)   A rationing equilibrium may exist even if $\bar{p}$ increases monotonically with r as long as the loan return curve is sufficiently convex (this is shown for the frontier $r^* - B$ in Figure 4.1).

A second possibility is that at r^*,

$$L^D(r^*) < (1 - a) W$$

In this situation, there will be an excess supply of loans and competition will bid down contractual interest rates since each bank can satisfy its loan supply by an infinitesimal reduction in contractual loan rates. In effect, competition among banks will constrain investors to a single point on the loan return trade-off curve, below and to the left of r^*. This point is shown at r^{**} in Figure 4.3. Then the loan market equilibrium will be determined by the full interaction of the loan supply and demand equations. Formally

$$(1 - a(g, \rho(r), \sigma(r))) W = L^D(r)$$

where we will assume in the regional spirit of the analysis that g is determined exogenously. Given the relative complexity of the interactions involved, it is difficult to describe any definitive characteristics of the

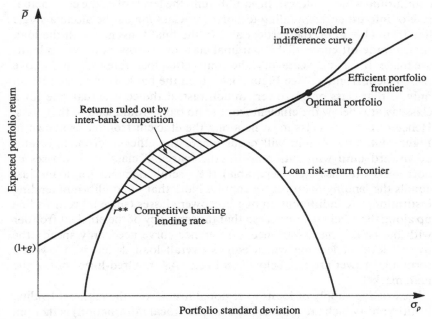

Figure 4.3 Optimal lender portfolio with no credit rationing

resulting equilibrium beyond the obvious ones. Lower government bond rates will reduce contractual loan interest rates and increase the amount of lending, and an increase in W, bank wealth, will increase lending and reduce interest rates.

The analysis so far applies to any lending institution. There is nothing particular to the notion of a bank. Indeed the only bank-like attribute of lenders is embodied in the assumption that at equilibria to the right of the loan risk-return curve on the efficient frontier (i.e., $a < 0$), lenders can themselves borrow at the government bond rate. Thus, the analysis applies to any government-insured financial institution (whether the insurance is explicit or implicit).[12]

In the competitive analysis of Figure 4.3 we do however assume that all lenders have essentially the same information for selecting the class of borrowers to whom they make loans. If there are several observable classes of borrowers, then the efficient frontier will consist, as in Figure 4.4, of a combination of points from the loan return trade-off curves for each of the borrower classes. For simplicity we have assumed in Figure 4.4 that borrower categories can be strictly ranked by the attractiveness of their loan return trade-off curves (this is not critical to the nature of the equilibrium which follows). In equilibrium, the levels of r_j, the contractual rate of interest corresponding to borrower class j, must lie along a single line from $(1 + g)$ on the vertical axis to the final tangency with the loan return trade-off curve of the marginal class of borrowers to whom loans are made. If for some category, the contractual loan rate were at $\bar{r}_j$ above the efficient frontier – see Figure 4.4 – then the bank would seek to lend only to that class of borrower. In contrast, if the contractual rate for a class lay at r_j below the efficient frontier no bank would lend to that class. Hence r_j^* for each class must lie along the efficient frontier as shown in Figure 4.4. Equilibrium will occur where the efficient frontier rotates downward until with rationing for the marginal class r_k^* (if classes of borrowers are discretely separable) the overall demand for loans just equals the lending institution's supply. Note that in equilibrium lending institutions are indifferent among borrower classes (since all returns line up along the efficient frontier) so that the tangency of the efficient frontier with the bank's mean-variance indifference curve need only specify the overall level of lending which equals overall loan demands. However, certain borrower groups, below k in Figure 4.4, are 'red-lined' out of the loan market.

The existing supply of loans to regional firms from the regional lending institutions (which are assumed to share identical information) is the sum of loans to the classes of borrowers above r_k. In the terms of the single lender case of equation (1) total loan supply will be the sum of loans supplied by the regional lenders

$$L_s = \Sigma L_s^i = \Sigma(1 - a^i) W^i \tag{2}$$

where L_s^i is the loan level of the ith lender, a^i is his optimal government bond allocation (which may be less than zero) and W is the lender's wealth.

If we assume that outside lenders cannot distinguish among the various j borrower classes, then they will attract all borrowers including those below class k who are 'red-lined' (or cut off from loans) by well-informed regional lenders. Moreover, because they attract these lower quality borrowers extra-regional lenders must charge higher contractual rates of interest than local banks to obtain returns that justify lending. However, in doing so, the extra-regional banks will lose all the 'good' borrowers above class k to the regional lenders. The loan populations for extra-regional banks will, therefore, consist entirely of high risk borrowers and the rates that they must charge will be correspondingly high. Indeed under reasonable circumstances, extra-regional lenders may face a situation like that in Figure 4.5 in which their optimal portfolio includes no loans within the region. The regional supply of loans, especially of reasonably priced loans, will therefore consist primarily of those provided

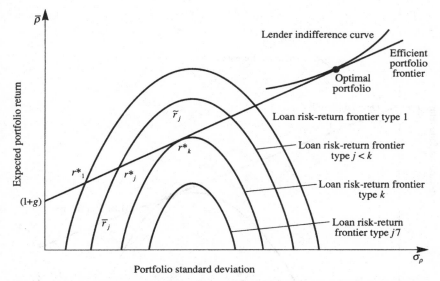

Figure 4.4 Optimal lender portfolio – multiple borrower types (higher j = worse borrowers)

by regional lenders and these too will depend on the wealth of regional financial institutions (i.e., W^i). Thus, a primary determinant of regional investment will, under these circumstances, be the aggregate wealth (for firms, the equity) of regional lenders.

A possible strategy of regional development is, therefore, one of subsidizing regional lending institutions. And, if the impact of such subsidies on lending are to be maximized, then these subsidies should be directed towards lending institutions with good information about borrowers and hence high levels of a^i. The set of natural candidates for such lenders given their access to payment and cash flow information is, of course, local banks. Therefore, in the analysis which follows we will focus on local banks and the channels of subsidy that may already exist.

However, before doing so one final point should be made. In the absence of effective markets for selling bank equity (for reasons described elsewhere[13]), the wealth of banks for portfolio purposes will be added to (or subtracted from) largely by current and safely anticipated future earnings. Thus,

$$W_t^i = \pi_t^i + W_{t-1}^i$$

where π_t^i stands for period t retained gains. In the event of a regional recession (due for example to adverse effects on an industry of

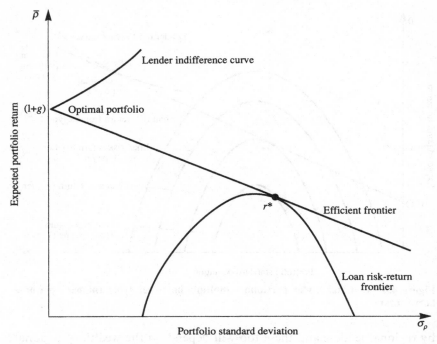

Figure 4.5   Optimal portfolio – external lender

disproportionate regional importance), operating gains may be negative as loan defaults generate losses. Bank wealth will then be impaired, lending will decline and the original recession will be exacerbated. Thus, active mechanisms for stabilizing regional economic disturbances (like those experienced in the United States) by means of countervailing regional bank subsidies are a significant potential source of local benefit.

We will assume that banks which have access to the loan opportunities described above have access to two basic sources of funds – bank deposits, D, and the bank's own equity capital, A. The return paid to bank depositors will be assumed initially to be set exogenously by the monetary authorities at a rate of interest, i. This can be thought of as occurring in two ways. Most straightforwardly, i may simply be set by fiat of the monetary authorities. An example of this is the zero interest rate on demand deposits mandated by the United States Federal Reserve System from the middle 1930s to the early 1970s. Alternatively i can be thought of as being set implicitly through limits on the extent to which banks and other institutions may compete in offering interest on demand deposits. This is what actually happened in the United States as banks competed by offering depositor services instead of officially proscribed interest on demand deposits. In other countries competition is limited by restricting the level of total deposits that banks may offer and limiting the competition to banks in offering money-type assets that other financial institutions may provide. We will assume throughout that

$$i \leq g$$

the rate of interest on safe government bonds. This condition will hold in any regime in which central banks effectively guarantee bank depositors against loss so that demand deposits in banks are at least as safe as government bonds.

The assets in which bank funds may be deposited are three – loans to a single type of firm,[14] required reserves (assumed for simplicity to pay no interest) and government securities. We will consider initially a situation in which the contractual rate of interest on bank loans is given exogenously (by market forces in the bank loan market) to each individual bank. Thus, r will denote the contractual rate of return on loans that each bank may charge and r may or may not involve credit rationing (in which case r will equal r^*). Assuming that no dividends are paid and that for informational reasons banks may not sell additional equity capital,[15] the end-of-period equity position of a bank is

$$\tilde{A} = G(1 + g) + L(\tilde{p}) - (1 + i)D + H$$

where G is the bank's initial holding of government bonds, L is its level of loans, $\tilde{p}$, the random return on its business loan portfolio, has a mean $\bar{p}(r)$ and a variance $\sigma^2(r)$ (and to the extent that the central limit theorem applies an approximately normal distribution), H is the bank's reserve holdings and D is the level of demand deposits at the bank. Assuming further that the bank must keep a fraction, β, of its deposits as reserves this can be rewritten as

$$\tilde{A}_1 = G(1 + g) + L(\tilde{p}) - (1 + i)D + \beta D$$

where

$$G + L = (1 - \beta)D + A$$

We will assume that bank decision-makers maximize a utility function whose argument is this terminal equity position of the bank and which is characterized by decreasing absolute risk-aversion.[16]

Under these assumptions a representative bank maximizes

$$E[u(Y + L(\tilde{p} - (1 + g)))]$$

subject to the constraint that[17]

$$Y = A(1 + g) + D[(1 + g(1 - \beta)) - (1 + i)]$$
$$= A(1 + g) + D(g(1 - \beta) - i)$$

where Y represents the 'wealth' of the bank.

Finally, in order to simplify matters, we will assume that banks are initially identical and thus that total deposits are constrained by the established supply of banking system reserves. In particular, if $\bar{H}$ denotes the available reserves per bank, then

$$0 \leq D \leq \bar{H}/\beta \tag{3}$$

Then the Lagrangian for the bank's decision problem is

$$E[u(Y + L(\tilde{p} - (1 + g)))] + \lambda_1 L + \lambda_3 D + \lambda_2(\bar{H}/\beta - D)$$

The first-order conditions describing banking deposit and lending behaviour are

$$E[\tilde{u}' \, \tilde{p}] - (1 + g)E[\tilde{u}'] + \lambda_1 = 0 \tag{4}$$

and

$$E[u'][g(1 + \beta) - i] - \lambda_2 + \lambda_3 = 0 \tag{5}$$

where λ_1 is the Lagrange multiplier associated with the non-negativity constraint on loans, λ_2 is the multiplier of the reserve availability constraint of equation (3) and λ_3 is the multiplier associated with the non-negativity constraint on demand deposits.

Finally, maximizing with respect to r, the contractual rate of interest, and assuming that other banks offer the same rate (and hence any single bank draws its loans randomly from the universe which characterizes the loan return trade-off curve),

$$\frac{d}{dr} E[\tilde{u}] = 0$$

The nature of the solution to the bank's decision problem depends critically on equation (5). If $g(1 - \beta) - i > 0$, then the condition of equation (5) can only be satisfied by having the reserve availability constraint bind (i.e. $\lambda_2 > 0$) in which case $\lambda_3 = 0$ (demand deposits are strictly positive). If $g(1 - \beta) - i > 0$, then banks can always increase their profits by accepting deposits and investing the proceeds in government bonds. Thus, deposits will expand until they reach their limit $\bar{H}/\beta$. In contrast, if $g(1 - \beta) - i < 0$, then the solution to equation (5) implies that the non-negativity constraint on demand deposits binds ($\lambda_3 > 0$) and the deposit reserve constraint does not bind ($\lambda_2 = 0$). Under these circumstances it is always cheaper to raise funds for loans from direct borrowing (at a cost g) than by means of demand deposits (at a cost $i/(1 + \beta)$).[18] Demand deposits will always, therefore, be zero (i.e., banks will simply not accept such deposits and increases in H will appear as increases in non-bank cash holdings). In the analysis that follows we will assume that

(A1) Banks enjoy a positive seigniorage return from holding deposits and, thus, that $m \equiv g(1 - \beta) - i > 0$.

In this case, the 'initial wealth' of the representative bank is

$$Y = A(1 + g) + m(\bar{H}/\beta) \tag{6}$$

If, in addition, we assume that the distribution of loan portfolio returns is approximately normal, the bank's maximization problem can be analysed in two steps. First, we can examine choices of r and L which minimize the variance of the bank's terminal equity subject to the condition that the expected terminal equity exceed an established level, $\bar{E}$. These will define an efficient portfolio frontier for the bank's investment loan problem. Then we can investigate levels of lending that maximize bank utility along the efficient frontier.

Formally, the first-stage problem can be written

min. σ_A

subject to: $\bar{A} \leq \bar{E}$

where

$$\sigma_A = L(\sigma_\rho), \quad \bar{A} = Y + (\bar{\rho} - (1 + g))L$$

Since, at the optimum, the expected terminal equity constraint must be binding, the first-order conditions with respect to L and r respectively are

$$\sigma_\rho - \lambda(\bar{\rho} - (1 + g)) = 0$$

and

$$L\frac{d\sigma_\rho}{dr} - \lambda L\frac{d\bar{\rho}}{dr} = 0$$

These can be combined and rewritten to yield

$$\frac{1}{\lambda} = \frac{(\bar{\rho} - (1 + g))}{\sigma_\rho} = \frac{d\bar{\rho}/dr}{d\sigma_\rho/dr}$$

Since the right-hand side of this expression represents the slope of the loan return frontier, the efficient level of the unconstrained contractual interest rate, r^*, occurs where a line from a level $(1 + g)$ on the vertical axis in Figure 4.2 to the loan return frontier (such a line has a slope $(\bar{\rho} - (1 + g))/\sigma_\rho$) is just tangent to the loan return frontier. The corresponding efficient bank portfolios consist of combinations of the loan portfolio at r^* and government bonds which trace out an efficient risk-return trade-off Ar^*C in Figure 4.2 Points to the left of r^* on this frontier involve net positive holdings of government bonds. Points to the right of r^* involve net bank borrowings at the government bond rate (banks short government bonds or equivalently borrow at the government bond rate).

If a bank's loan returns are approximately normally distributed, then the terminal value of the bank's equity – being a linear function of the loan portfolio return – will also be approximately normally distributed with

$$\bar{A} = Y + (\bar{\rho} - (1 + g))L = \left(\frac{Y}{1 + g} - L\right)(1 + g) + L\bar{\rho}$$

and

$$\sigma_A = L\sigma_\rho$$

The bank's objective function $Eu(\tilde{A})$ can then be rewritten in terms of the mean and standard deviation of the distribution of $\tilde{A}$ as

$$Eu(\tilde{A}) = V\left\{\left[\left(\frac{Y}{1 + g}\right) - L\right](1 + g) + L\bar{\rho}, L\sigma_\rho\right\}$$

Changes in L that move the firm along its efficient frontier lead to a first-order condition

$$\bar{V}_A(\bar{\rho} - (1 + g)) + V_{\sigma_A}\sigma_\rho = 0$$

or

$$\left(\frac{\bar{\rho} - (1 + g)}{\sigma_\rho}\right) = -\frac{V_{\sigma_A}}{\bar{V}_A}$$

where the right-hand side of this final expression is the slope of the mean-variance indifference curve of the bank and the left-hand side is the slope of the efficient mean-variance frontier. Thus, the optimal loan level is determined by the tangency of the efficient frontier and the bank's risk-return indifference curves as described qualitatively in Figure 4.6. The horizontal intercept, when the bank is entirely invested in government bonds, yields an expected terminal bank equity of

$$Y = A(1 + g) + (H/\beta)(g(1 - \beta) - i)$$

The point r^*, at which the bank neither holds government bonds nor borrows at the government bond rate, corresponds to a level of lending

$$L = A + (H/\beta)(1 - \beta)$$

which leads, in turn, to expected terminal equity level

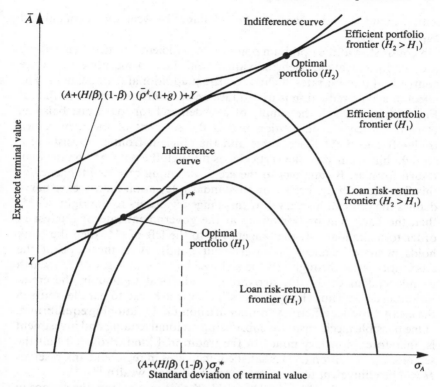

Figure 4.6 Optimal bank portfolio determination

$$\bar{A} = (A + (H/\beta)(1 - \beta))(\bar{\rho}^* - (1 + g)) + Y$$

and a standard deviation of terminal quality

$$\sigma_A = (A + (H/\beta)(1 - \beta))\sigma_\rho^*$$

Thus, changes in H leave the slope of the efficient frontier unchanged, but shift the frontier upward by an amount $(H/\beta)(g(1 - \beta) - i)$ equal to the present value of seigniorage. This is shown in Figure 4.6.

The actual supply of loans at the optimal point along the efficient frontier may either exceed or fall short of the corresponding loan demand at a contractual rate of interest r^* and a government bond rate $(1 + g)$. If the supply is less than demand, then a rationing equilibrium occurs. Raising contractual interest rates would move banks along the loan return frontier below the efficient frontier and, therefore, they have no incentive to do so. Reducing contractual interest rates would similarly move banks below the efficient frontier and at the same time, by increasing loan demand, would exacerbate the imbalance between loan demand and supply.

In contrast, if at the optimum point on the efficient frontier, loan supply exceeds loan demand each individual bank has an incentive to reduce contractual interest rates slightly to attract additional loan demand. The effect of such a reduction is to produce an equilibrium, similar to that of Figure 4.3, at which the supply of and demand for loans just balance. Here the force of competition makes the segment of the loan return trade-off above r^{**} inaccessible and the efficient frontier consists of a straight line from Y on the vertical axis through the point r^{**} on the loan return frontier. By analogy to the credit rationing case, the tangency of this frontier with the bank's mean-standard deviation indifference curve defines the optimal loan level. If this tangency occurs to the right of r^{**}, then the bank will be borrowing at the government rate of interest in order to make loans. If the tangency is to the left of r^{**}, then the bank holds positive balances of government bonds. Also the slope of the efficient frontier through r^{**} has a slope $[\rho(r^{**}) - (1 + g)]/\sigma(r^{**})$ which is independent of Y (this derivation is identical to that in the credit rationing case). Thus changes in H which affect Y lead to parallel shifts in the mean-variance efficiency frontier in a non-credit rationing equilibrium.

One possible mechanism for subsidizing regional lending and investment is, therefore, monetary policy of the traditional kind. Provided that the seigniorage condition (A1) is satisfied, increases in regional bank reserves H will be equivalent to increases in regional bank wealth.[19]

An increase in a bank's initial 'wealth', Y, that results from the change in $(\bar{H}/\beta)$ will, at constant interest rates (i.e., fixed g), move the bank's efficiency frontier vertically upwards. This effect is identical to that of an increase in bank equity. As the efficient frontier moves upward decreasing absolute risk-aversion will flatten the indifference curves and shift the bank's portfolio choice toward more loans away from government bond holdings. The magnitude of this 'seigniorage' or 'wealth' effect can be quite substantial.[20] Indeed in some simple models, the bank's loan supply increases proportionately with increases in the initial 'wealth'. Since the equity base embodied in Y is typically small relative to the level of loans, a dollar increase in such seigniorage may induce many additional dollars of business loans and hence substantial new business investment.

If loan supply is more than the new $L^D(r^*)$ so that there is no rationing, then competition among banks for loan customers will drive down the contractual loan interest rate. This will reduce both the expected return to and the risk of business loans, but on the whole the efficient frontier (now recognizing the constraints of bank competition) becomes flatter. This will shift the bank's optimal portfolio toward government bond holdings, reducing the supply of loan funds. At the same time, reductions in r increase the demand for loan funds until supply and demand just balance. In this instance, there is no credit rationing.

Note, however, that the efficacy of traditional monetary policy for regional development depends on the existence of the seigniorage effect. To the extent that this is eliminated by competitive banking reforms, the overall effectiveness of monetary interventions for regional development will suffer.[21] The situation without seigniorage arises when

$$m = g(1 - \beta) - i < 0$$

In this case, the behaviour of the banking system is quite different. For, if $m < 0$, then banks will not at the same time hold government securities and accept demand deposits. Moreover, if we continue to assume that banks can effectively borrow all they want at the government bond interest rates (without meeting the reserve requirements associated with deposits), then deposits – being a more expensive source of funds than shorting government bonds – will always be zero. Seigniorage will consequently also be zero. Thus, if in addition the rate of interest on government bonds is fixed exogenously at the national level, then open market operations will have no effect on loan supply and economic activity.

If a bank cannot borrow external funds, then even with g fixed and no seigniorage, traditional monetary policy may still be an effective tool of regional development. Now

$$L \equiv \text{Loans Outstanding} = D(1 - \beta) + A$$

and the bank's decision problem can be simplified to maximize

$$E[u((D(1 - \beta) + A)\tilde{p} - (1 + i)D + \beta D)]$$

subject to

$$D \leq \bar{H}/\beta$$

Now the first-order condition takes the form

$$E[\tilde{u}' \tilde{p}](1 - \beta) - (1 + i)E[\tilde{u}'] + \beta E[\tilde{u}'] - \lambda_1 + \lambda_2 = 0 \tag{7}$$

where λ_1 is the Lagrange multiplier associated with the maximum deposit constraint and λ_2 is the multiplier of the bank deposit non-negativity constraint. This has three possible solutions. If for $D \leq \bar{H}/\beta$ the returns to loans are sufficiently large (because investment opportunities are good), that the right-hand side of equation (7) is positive, then bankers will still generate deposits and make loans[22] up to the point where $D = \bar{H}/\beta$. As a result monetary policy, and especially open market operations, will still affect regional bank lending (with or without credit rationing).

In contrast, if loan returns are relatively poor so that, at $D = 0$, the right-hand side of (7) is negative, then banks will not find it worth accepting deposits. Indeed in this case, bankers will divide their portfolios in the usual way between government bonds and loans. However, because banks do not accept deposits the only effect of open market operations will be through changes in the government debt market equilibrium and as a result the effectiveness of monetary policy for regional development will be eliminated.

Finally, at intermediate levels of loan returns, banks may accept deposits but only in amounts below the ceiling set by reserve availability. In this case, the right-hand side of (7) reaches zero at a level of $D < \bar{H}/\beta$. Under these circumstances changing reserve requirements will again affect bank behaviour only through its effect on government bond interest rates and again the impact of monetary interventions will be national rather than regional.

2   Empirical implications

In the models developed in the previous section of this paper, local lending activity depends on (1) the position of the risk-return trade-off curve on loans which is traced out as the contractual rate of interest r varies and (2) the effective equity 'wealth' of the local banks,

$$W_j \equiv A_j(1 + g) + D_j(g(1 - \beta) - i)$$

where A_j now denotes local bank equity and D_j denotes local deposits which may or may not be constrained by the monetary authorities.

If local borrowers can be identified by their industry segments then the position of the loan return trade-off curve for each industry will depend on industry conditions facing each borrower as long as unfettered interregional trade makes it appropriate to speak of 'national industry' conditions. This will interact with the wealth position of regional banks to yield a local industry contractual rate of return

$$R_{kj} = F(S_k, A_j)$$

where S_k denotes the state of the kth industry and A_j the wealth of financial institutions in the jth region. In traditional competitive models, the term A_j will not appear. In the absence of regionally segmented financial markets only national wealth levels should affect lending terms. Moreover, in traditional models wealth distributions between firms and households (and among firms) do not affect economic activity since firms can obtain as much equity as they wish through sales of new equity to households.

The quantity supplied by firms in industry k from region j, should be defined by an equation of the form

$$Q^s_{jk} = Q(P_k, R_{kj}, E_j) = Q(P_k, S_k, A_j, E_j) \tag{8}$$

where P_k is the 'national' price level in industry k and E_j is the prevailing wage level in region j. Traditional Keynesian variables like the demand in region j for the output of industry k should not matter as long as markets in traded goods are national (e.g., where transport costs are relatively small). The perfect information version of equation (8) takes the form

$$Q^s_{jk} = S(P_k, R, E_j) \tag{9}$$

since for reasons outlined above, local wealth distribution should not affect the terms on which local capital is available.

The demand for labour in industry k in region j should vary, like output, with national prices, capital availability (and interest rates) and local wages. Thus

$$L^D_{jk} = M_k(P_k, R_{kj}, E_j) = M_k(P_k, S_k, A_j, E_j)$$

Overall labour demand should depend on the same variables, and equilibrium local wages should be determined by an equation of the form

$$L^s_j = \sum_k M_k(P_k, S_k, A_j, E_j) + N_j$$

where N_j is the demand for non-manufacturing employment in region j. Solving for E_j, local wage levels can be written

$$E_j = N(\bar{P}, \bar{S}, A_j, L^s_j, N_j) \tag{10}$$

where $\bar{P}$ and $\bar{S}$ are vectors of national prices and other conditions across industries. The function N is increasing in N_j and A_j but decreasing in L^s_j; higher non-manufacturing demand for labour raises wages, higher local bank lending stimulates activity and raises wages and increases in local labour supply reduce wages.

Substitution from the reduced form equation (10) into equation (8) yields a quasi-reduced form for supply in region j for industry k

$$Q^s_{jk} = Q(P_k, S_k, \bar{P}, \bar{S}, A_j, N_j, L^s_j) \tag{11}$$

The variables on the right-hand side of equation (11) can be separated into national variables $(\bar{P}, \bar{S})$, industry variables (P_k, S_k) and local variables $(A_j, N_j$ and $L^s_j)$. In looking at regional variations over time, the national variables will disappear as long as regional levels are measured as variations from national averages. They will, therefore, be suppressed in what follows. The national industry variables, which fluctuate over time, will be represented by national dummies for the relevant industries.

The three local variables fall into two categories. The first is labour supply conditions which should affect all industries but should be relatively stable over time. Thus, if local supply and other variables are measured as deviations from local trends, the impact of these variables should also disappear since they should be absorbed by the local trends. The second are local 'demand' and financial variables (N_j, A_j). These may vary quite rapidly, particularly with local business cycles, for several reasons. First, poor local economic conditions should lead to a deterioration of local bank equity positions (e.g., as loan defaults rise) and to a decline in lending, either directly or through higher interest rates.

Banks are not likely to be able to protect themselves against these losses by using national financial markets. The natural way of doing so would be by spreading the risks through equity sales. However, standard problems of adverse selection (see above) make this difficult to do and, in practice, equity markets are severely limited. The alternative is to try to arrange contingent rewards based on aggregate local conditions not particular to a single bank itself. But, here again, the bank's superior knowledge of local conditions will militate against the purchase of such instruments by outside investors. Also the banks themselves are protected to some extent by their ability to benefit from joint weakness. If all banks in a region do badly, then all bank lending will be curtailed and interest rates will rise to restore bank earnings. Unfortunately, this comes at the expense of local firms.

Second, a decline in overall local economic activity should affect the local demand for service workers, N_j. However, this should have an opposite effect on local manufacturing. Lower local service employment demand should reduce local wages and stimulate manufacturing output and employment; in contrast to the deterioration in local bank positions, which decreases loan availability and lowers manufacturing output and employment. Thus, positive local effects on local manufacturing employment in particular industries argues for either financial feedback of the type described in this paper or for Keynesian demand effects. And since the industries involved produce manufactured goods with national markets, local Keynesian demand effects should be small.

Thus, estimation of a model

$$(N_{jkt} - \bar{N}_t) = a + b(N_{ki} - \bar{N}_t) + c(N_{jt} - \bar{N}_j) \tag{12}$$

should discriminate between a model of information-based, regional capital market segmentation and a more traditional competitive model, where

$N_{jkt} \equiv$ Employment in industry k in region j in time t
(which we use as a surrogate for output),
$\bar{N}_t \equiv$ Total national employment in period t,
$N_{kt} \equiv$ National employment in industry k in period t,
$\bar{N}_j \equiv$ Average local employment in region j,
$N_{jt} \equiv$ Local employment in region j in period t
(used as a surrogate for local economic activity).

In a traditional model, the coefficient on regional employment, c, should be negative since the only feedbacks should be through the labour market and hence negative for reasons outlined above (that on national industry conditions should be positive). Only in an imperfect information model or due to some other Keynesian effect should the local employment coefficient be positive. Hence, in order to test the appropriateness of the theoretical model of the previous section we have estimated a variant of equation (12).

3   Estimation

The variant of equation (12) that we estimated used log-differences as the basic variables, essentially regressing percentage employment growth in industry k in region j on national percentage employment growth, dummies for industry k and percentage employment growth in region j. The data used are for the United States, with each region corresponding to a particular state. Industries were identified by 2-digit SIC-code with only manufacturing industries used to minimize Keynesian demand effects, and the effects of industry conditions were allowed to differ by industry. The data are for the years from 1972 to 1982. The results are presented in Table 4.1.

The coefficients of the industry variables are generally positive (as expected) and where negative (in two cases) are insignificant. The national economic activity coefficient is strongly positive, suggesting that positive capital market (or traditional Keynesian) effects of the national market are large and significant (both statistically and economically). More importantly, the local activity coefficient is also strongly positive and statistically significant, suggesting that there are strong local economic spillovers among industries and that, since these are positive, some form of the capital market imperfections model or local Keynesian model should apply.

The only disturbing element in the regression is the relatively small magnitude of the industry effects but this may well be attributable to definitional problems in allocating firms to SIC-codes and the resulting

Table 4.1. *Determinants of growth in employment*
(Dependent variable: industry percentage growth in employment by state in each year)

Variable	Coefficient	t-Statistic
National growth rate of employment	0.885	32.01
State growth rate of employment	0.673	17.39
National growth rate of employment		
SIC22	− 0.034	0.27
SIC23	− 0.019	0.71
SIC24	0.005	0.26
SIC25	0.024	1.20
SIC26	0.005	0.20
SIC27	0.045	2.02
SIC28	0.068	3.26
SIC29	0.039	1.62
SIC210	0.017	0.37
SIC211	0.113	2.58
SIC212	0.054	1.31
SIC213	0.020	0.94
SIC214	0.029	1.15
SIC215	0.032	1.80
SIC216	0.049	2.60
SIC217	0.046	1.93
SIC218	0.106	2.70
SIC219	0.067	2.26
$R^2 = 0.0876$		

errors in variables. Nevertheless the empirical results provide relatively strong support for the basic hypothesis of capital market imperfections and are consistent with the results of Stockman (1988) at the national level.

4   Policy implications

The specific empirical evidence of the previous section ought not to be surprising. There is widespread, albeit informal, evidence that regional recessions – beyond the effects of fluctuations in industries which happen to be regional – are a significant economic phenomenon. Moreover, the nature of persistent regional imbalances in development (over periods of as much as fifty years) suggest that there are significant barriers to capital mobility. In theory, capital ought to be a more mobile factor of production than labour. Yet, in practice, adjustment to such imbalances (e.g., Northern vs. Southern Italy, Northern vs. Southern England) seems to consist more of labour migration out of depressed regions than of inward capital migration. Informal barriers to capital mobility are one clear explanation for such phenomena. Moreover, there is now substantial evidence that capital markets are imperfect and that it is difficult for firms to raise certain kinds of capital (notably equity in public markets).

It is equally widely recognized that access to external sources of funding is essential for economic development, whether at the regional or national level. Thus, capital market barriers of the kind discussed in this paper are likely (especially if they are the primary source of regional fluctuations like those found in the United States data) to impair seriously efforts at regional development whether in Eastern Europe, within an integrated Common Market or within existing national boundaries. Especially in situations like that of Eastern Europe, shortages of investment capital are likely to be far more significant than shortages of labour or materials. Development of appropriate mechanisms for allocating capital is, therefore, critical, and providing subsidies to the institutions involved can certainly be justified in terms of the kinds of informational failures to which this paper is addressed.

In simple welfare terms, lending in these models is always suboptimal. It is constrained, on the one hand, by imperfect information concerning borrowers and, on the other hand, by the reluctance of banks to lend when they cannot diversify the risks of that lending by selling new equity. It is the second difficulty that is most easily addressed. Providing financial institutions with equity capital (especially if all institutions are forced to accept the funds so that they do not individually suffer from the adverse signal of doing so) on a subsidized basis should yield a net welfare gain.[23] The question that then arises is what form such subsidies might most effectively take.

Here history suggests that the seigniorage associated with the power to issue money (on favourable interest rate terms) is a valuable subsidy mechanism. Money creation has almost universally been associated in developed economies with lending institutions that support critical social institutions (government debt issue in the early days of banking and commercial and industry lending more recently). The advantages of the central banking arrangements that achieve this are several. First, the subsidy directly passes to the institutions (i.e., banks) with the information to use it effectively as a basis for greatly amplified amounts of lending activity. Second, where there are constraints on bank interest payments (either formal or informal), the seigniorage effectively takes the form of equity capital which is the form most difficult to raise in financial markets. To see the importance of just these two factors, consider first the likely impact on economic activity of a $25 billion increase in household wealth (say, for example, at the expense of foreign dollar holders). In a $5,000 billion economy this is likely to be trivial. However, an equal increase in bank capital would represent a substantial subsidy (i.e., an increase of perhaps 10%) which could well provide a significant stimulus to economic activity. The latter is, of course, approximately what (ignoring reserve requirements) a $25 billion increase in the money supply represents when interest on bank deposits is constrained to be zero.

Furthermore, seigniorage subsidies can be supplied more or less continuously (as opposied to tax subsidies which are usually constrained by annual budget cycles) and highly flexibly. For example, central banking authorities may directly subsidize regional banks by cutting their reserve requirements either directly or by lending through the discount window against reserves at very low rates of interest. Comparable flexibility in fiscal programmes (free of direct political intervention) is rare. Broadly, therefore, the model of this paper argues for the maintenance of traditional central banking structures and against the kind of institutional deregulation of bank interest rates that has gone a long way to eliminating seigniorage profits in the United States.

More generally, the models involved argue for the efficacy of institutional (e.g., banks, insurance companies, venture capital firms) rather than public market mechanisms for allocating capital (e.g. The New York Stock Exchange). Among these, industrial companies are perhaps the most important through their power to direct both retained earnings and depreciation recoveries. The greater mobility of within-firm (as opposed to public financial market capital or even institutional funding) capital suggests that investment decisions of large multinational or national corporations are an efficient means of funding regional development. Similarly, the existence of national as opposed to regional financial institutions should in principle help to offset regional imbalances in capital availability.

However, there may be limits to the flow of information and hence capital within both financial and non-financial firms. If the individuals within a national firm or bank who are responsible for investment decisions are located in and, thus, well-informed about one region of a national economy, then investment funds will tend to be concentrated in that region. The resulting imbalance in the allocation of funds will be more severe than that under a regime of local banks or firms. Local firms in the favoured region would be constrained in their access to funds (particularly equity) and this would limit any bias in favour of that region. National banks or firms would, in contrast, have access to national sources of funds and the investment imbalance would then not be limited by barriers to capital mobility. Mechanisms of this kind may account for relative lack of success in regional development in the United Kingdom, France and Italy as opposed to the striking success of the locally-based banking system in the United States in promoting growth in the formerly depressed Southeastern United States. The emphasis in developing financial institutions should, therefore, be on the national collection of investment opportunity information rather than just on pooling national funds.

NOTES

1 Local recipients of capital should have many means of transferring these capital funds back into national pools that are largely immune to detection. The only effective mechanisms for subsidizing capital accumulation in a particular region are, therefore, likely to be direct subsidies paid for physical capital investment and these have many familiar drawbacks.

2 Especially since regional fluctuations seem to be an increasingly important phenomenon in the United States.

3 The basic situation involved here is one in which the managers of individual financial institutions are better informed about the prospects of their institutions than investors at large. The fact that they are willing, under these circumstances, to sell stock in their companies at prevailing market prices suggest that the market price certainly does not undervalue the company and on average, therefore, is in some sense too high. This is a classic 'lemons' problem (see Akerlof, 1970), and investors should in general resist such equity offers (see Greenwald *et al.*, 1984).

4 Thus, it faces informational problems of that sort that lead to credit rationing and other borrowing constraints (see Stiglitz and Weiss, 1981).

5 This clearly corresponds to the situation of a regional monetary authority (assuming the region is small) or a national authority in a world of fixed exchange rates and free capital market flows (assuming also that the nation is also small).

6 Indeed, to the extent that unemployment of auto workers eases labour market conditions, other industries should do well.

7 See Stiglitz and Weiss (1981) and subsequent papers.

8 Alternatively we could assume that C represents the cost of developing a bank loan application. However, in this case, the existence of credit rationing would reduce the demand for loans since borrowers would be uncertain of profiting from a loan application. The resulting analysis would be more complicated without being fundamentally different from that presented here.

9 The precise condition involves shifts in probability mass into the range $\bar{p} \pm ((1 + r)B - \bar{p})$ and is relatively tedious and unenlightening to derive.

10 This also depends on the existence of systematic risk across the loans in a bank's portfolio.

11 If bank liabilities are government insured, then banks ought to be able to borrow on terms equivalent to those of the government.

12 If lenders must themselves borrow at above the government bond rate then the efficient frontier runs from the vertical axis to r^* as shown in Figure 4.2. It then runs along the loan-portfolio-risk-return frontier until a point r^{**} at which a

ray from the vertical axis at $(1 + g)$ is tangent to the frontier where L is the rate of interest the lending institution pays on its loans. The efficient frontier then runs along this ray. Their net effect is to reduce the amount of lending done.

13 See Greenwald *et al.* (1984) or Myers and Majluf (1984).

14 It should be clear from the multiple firm type analysis that this simplifying assumption will not significantly alter the conclusions of the model.

15 Consider the consequences of a situation in which the owner/managers of firms are better informed about their firms' future prospects than participants in financial markets at large. Under these circumstances, as demonstrated by Leland and Pyle (1976), Stiglitz (1982), Myers and Majluf (1984) and Greenwald *et al.* (1984), markets for the sale of equity shares in firms will function only imperfectly and firms will be constrained in the amounts of equity capital that they can raise. Since these results are familiar, the focus of the paper is on how such finance constraints are likely to affect productivity growth. Consequently no attempt will be made to describe explicitly the informational underpinnings of the failure of equity markets. Instead, with the aim of simplifying the analysis as far as possible, we will assume that firms are unable to raise equity in external financial markets.

16 Such a specification is generally consistent with an agency model in which bank managers can be offered only pay-off functions which are linear in the terminal 'wealth' of the bank and where those managers have individual preferences characterized by decreasing absolute risk aversion. An alternative formulation yielding essentially similar results is one in which firms maximize expected profits less an expected cost of bankruptcy which is increasing in the scale of bank lending (see Greenwald and Stiglitz, 1990, for a model of this phenomenon).

17 An additional constraint that L be less than $(1 - \beta)D + A$ would apply if short sales of government bonds are not permitted. However, we will assume that banks may borrow on terms essentially equivalent to those of the government so that $G \geq 0$ is not a constraint on the bank portfolio.

18 Note that this need not be the case if the bank cannot borrow at the government rate of interest.

19 An open market purchase of securities from a regional bank will lead that bank to increase its supply of deposits and loans by an appropriate multiple amount. Leakage of the resulting reserves out of the regional banks will only occur as the region in question runs a deficit in its balance of payments with other regions (and like all deficits this one can always be neutralized by the monetary authorities).

20 Note that if $g(1 - \beta) - i = 0$, then Y does not change with $\bar{H}/\beta$ and, since the slope of the efficient frontier is unchanged (g is fixed), the efficient frontier does not change either. This effect should be distinguished from the wealth effect of Pesek and Saving (1967) in that the latter operates through consumption demand (a small effect at best) and the former operates through reducing the risk-aversion of bank decision-makers.

21 As noted above, increases and decreases in bank equity A act very much like changes in deposits. Indeed, not being modified by $g(1 - \beta) - i$, which may be near zero, changes in bank equity should have an especially strong effect on bank lending. Thus, extensive loan losses will in this model lead to precisely the kind of regional credit crunches that are subject of much current concern in the United States.

22 Although they might do better to borrow with instruments that do not have reserve requirements.
23 See Greenwald and Stiglitz (1986) for a general welfare analysis of models with imperfect information. In many ways equity funding is superior to loans which (a) attract a population of borrowers prone to default (as in the case of Savings and Loan institutions in the United States) and (b) may induce uneconomic risk-taking behaviour whenever the equity base of firm decision-makers becomes negative or near negative.

REFERENCES

Akerlof, G. (1970) 'The Market for Lemons: Qualitative Uncertainty and the Market Mechanism', *Quarterly Journal of Economics* **84**, 288–300.

Greenwald, B. and J.E. Stiglitz (1986) 'Externalities in Economies with Imperfect Information and Incomplete Markets', *Quarterly Journal of Economics* **100**, 229–64.

(1990) 'Macroeconomic Models with Equity and Credit Rationing' in R.G. Hubbard (ed.), *Information, Capital Markets and Investment*, Chicago: University of Chicago Press.

Greenwald, B., J.E. Stiglitz and A.M. Weiss (1984) 'Informational Imperfections and Macroeconomic Fluctuations', *American Economic Review, Papers and Proceedings* **74**, 194–99.

Leland, H.E. and D.H. Pyle (1977) 'Information Asymmetries, Financial Structure and Financial Intermediation', *Journal of Finance* **32**, 371–87.

Myers, S.C. and N.S. Majluf (1984) 'Corporate Financing and Investment Decisions When Firms Have Information That Investors Do Not', *Journal of Financial Economics* **11**, 187–221.

Pesek, B.D. and T.R. Saving (1967) *Money, Wealth and Economic Theory*, New York: MacMillan.

Rothschild, M. and J.E. Stiglitz (1970) 'Increasing Risk, A Definition', *Journal of Economic Theory* **2**, 225–43.

Stiglitz, J.E. (1982) 'Information and Capital Markets', in W.F. Sharpe and C. Cootner (eds), *Financial Economics: Essays in Honor of Paul Cootner*, Englewood Cliffs, NJ: Prentice Hall.

Stiglitz, J.E. and A.M. Weiss (1981) 'Credit Rationing in Markets With Imperfect Information', *American Economic Review* **71**, 393–410.

Stockman, A. (1988) 'Sectoral and National Aggregate Disturbances to Industrial Output in Seven European Countries', *Journal of Monetary Economics* **12**, 387–409.

Discussion

XAVIER VIVES

This paper discusses the implications of capital market imperfections for the availability of credit in regional markets and the potential effects of monetary policy instruments on the allocation of capital. It is argued that while in the traditional theory monetary policy should have a neutral regional impact (since capital moves freely and interest rates are equalized), in the presence of asymmetric information with local investors and banks having superior information, outsiders to the region suffer from an adverse selection problem which impairs capital mobility. Local financial institutions, because of similar information problems, have a difficult time raising funds in national markets. The result is that there is a suboptimal allocation of capital: too little lending in short. The thesis of the authors is that monetary policy can and should be used to subsidize capital on a regional basis.

The analysis builds on the Stiglitz-Weiss model of credit rationing under asymmetric information. In essence, given limited liability of entrepreneurs, an increase in the loan rate of a bank may increase the riskiness of the pool of applicants for loans and may end up decreasing the expected return to the bank. In the paper it is further assumed that there is a fixed number of risk-averse banks displaying decreasing absolute risk aversion (DARA) and which, due to adverse selection reasons, can not raise outside equity. Banks can invest in risky loans or safe government bonds and have to hold a certain fraction β of reserves. The deposit rate (i) is exogenous, say regulated, and deposit supply is not modelled. Assuming (approximately) normal returns banks face a mean-variance portfolio choice problem. The market equilibrium may or may not display rationing.

Monetary policy can work through open market operations and/or through influencing the 'wealth' or 'capital' position of banks. A change in the government bond rate g will move the efficient frontier and affect portfolio choice. It is assessed that a decrease in g will tend to increase the volume of loans made. The wealth position of a bank depends on the net margin $g(1 - \beta) - i$ (given a certain amount of deposits) and on the initial equity position of the bank. The government can increase the capital of the bank by decreasing the implicit tax on deposits β, by lowering the deposit rate i, or by injecting capital directly. The effect of an increase in the wealth position of a bank is an increase in the supply of loans since due to DARA the bank wants then to invest more in the risky loan asset. The consequence of this is that deregulation, by narrowing the net margin, may have undesirable effects on the supply of loans.

I would like to mention three potential criticisms of the model:

(1) The mechanism by which an increase in capital increases the amount of risky loans provided does not seem robust. If banks are not risk-averse but risk-neutral and face bankruptcy costs it may well happen (it indeed happens for low enough levels of capital) that their behaviour is of the risk-loving type and by increasing capital banks will in fact take *less* and not more risk. It is an empirical issue to determine the level of net worth at which banks turn risk-lovers and follow strategies of the 'go-for-broke' variety, as in the case of the S&L crisis, for example.

(2) The supply of deposits is not modelled. For example, a decrease in the deposit rate i will induce in general a decrease in the supply of deposits and, for a given i, a decrease in the wealth position of the bank. The total effect depends as usual on the elasticity of deposit supply. General equilibrium type effects are not considered either.

(3) Competition among banks is not modelled explicitly.

The empirical implications of the model are developed by the authors in a regional context and a test shows support for the hypothesis of capital market imperfections. Without getting into the details of the analysis I would like to point out that the fact that in the regressions the coefficient of regional employment turns out to be positive seems to be consistent also with explanations other than the one presented, like the presence of demand externalities for example.

What then can a 'regional' monetary policy be? Not open market operations, evidently. Nevertheless the wealth position of banks can be influenced with regionally-based reserve requirements, rate regulation, discriminating discount window or direct subsidies. What is not considered in the paper is the effectiveness of these tools or the potential side effects they may produce. Indeed, the measures mentioned open the door to arbitrage opportunities which need the presence of important frictions in the market to prevent institutions which benefit from positive discrimination from using it to obtain a more favourable competitive position in the national market, without affecting in a significant way the target regional market. Further, potential side-effects of the proposed measures arise from regulatory capture, investment or allocation distortions, and moral hazard. Rate regulation is a good example of the first two effects. Subsidies on the other hand have well-known moral hazard implications.

For example, a bank receives a bad shock, its net worth position deteriorates and it turns to a high risk strategy. A subsidy in these conditions, like flat premium deposit insurance, will most probably finance the assumption of too much risk instead of discouraging it. Another moral hazard possibility is plain fraud.

In conclusion:

(i)   The paper makes a nice contribution by (1) isolating a mechanism by which shocks (regional perhaps) may be persistent: a decrease in the wealth position of banks generates a credit crunch (in the presence of decreasing absolute risk aversion) which is amplified via multiplier effects; and (2) indicating the possible ways in which monetary policy may have a stabilization role in this context. Nevertheless the mechanism isolated is not the only possible and might not be the most relevant one, and the policy interventions proposed may have undesirable side effects.

(ii) I believe the model is more appropriate to study stabilization than regional development issues. The latter would need a general equilibrium formulation and in particular an explicit consideration of saving behaviour.

(iii) I am in sympathy with the quest for financial intermediary mechanisms which, in the presence of asymmetric information, explain fluctuations and other macroeconomic phenomena, including the potential role of monetary policy. However, and as usual, it seems that there is still a lot more work to do.

NOTE

I am grateful to Angel de la Fuente for a very useful discussion.

DAVID C. WEBB

In this thought-provoking paper Greenwald, Levinson and Stiglitz (GLS) argue that regional information-based capital market imperfections may yield a prima facie case for regional monetary and financial policies. The idea is that local financial institutions may have superior information about their local borrowers than non-local banks and that policy should be directed at subsidising these institutions or aiding them in expanding regional credit by increasing their reserves, thereby allowing them to finance winners.

GLS argue that because of informational problems capital markets may be regionally segmented, so that if a region does badly local bank portfolios may suffer, which reduces capital available to local industries. Good firms cannot issue equity at fair prices because of a 'lemons problem' in the equity market à la Myers and Majluf (1984).

If a region suffers a negative shock and some loans fail, then regional banks find themselves short of capital. Because of the 'lemons problem' in the equity market they too may not be able to raise equity capital at prices which make financing loans to good borrowers profitable. This leaves banks the option of reducing holdings of government bonds or expanding deposits. However, the banks' ability to do this may be limited because of shortage of reserves. Hence, although regional banks have a comparative advantage in lending to local firms, they do not, and consequently local recessions are exaggerated.

Much of the paper is devoted to understanding the regional banking equilibrium which is modelled along the lines of Greenwald and Stiglitz (1986) generalization of the Stiglitz-Weiss (1981) model. In this model project returns depend upon idiosyncratic and common risk with projects ranked by second-order stochastic dominance. The regional capital market equilibrium is characterized by sub-optimal lending and possibly credit rationing. Shocks which cause some firms to fail and weaken banks' balance sheets add to capital shortages and raise interest rates and result in the loss of profitability of marginal projects, which are good projects. The key point of the paper is that in the absence of perfect capital markets local capital policy should be used to reduce locally higher interest rates or subsidize bank capital.

The authors do not model the global economy so that the argument about the failure of a global capital market to develop institutional arrangements to mitigate regional capital shortages is essentially heuristic. This makes it difficult to understand exactly why global institutions for risk sharing or markets for bank capital do not evolve.

Whilst the paper provides an interesting and stimulating model, it leaves too many issues unresolved. In general, with discretion of bank managers over their portfolios, different banks will have different quality balance sheets and it is not clear how they establish the quality of their loan portfolios. Some mechanism for revealing this must be necessary if the government is to direct finance in the direction of winners. However, many mechanisms for revealing this information would be linked to the development of private global banking institutions for capturing the value of good projects. It is not established that the government will be any better at picking winners than the private sector. Incomplete modelling means that the market failure is not established as robust.

In arguing that the government should intervene through directed monetary policy or subsidies to banks the need for financial disclosure by banks is not examined. Moreover, the moral hazard problems which such schemes engender are not discussed. I think this would make an interesting generalization of the model.

The lesson of the paper is that because of informational problems regional capital markets will not be fully integrated, which increases the magnitude of regional recessions. I accept the general methodology of the paper is a good one but am a little worried that the failure to develop integrated institutional arrangements is based on fairly ad hoc reasoning. This makes it easier than it should be to develop a role for targeted policy.

REFERENCES

Greenwald, B. and J.E. Stiglitz (1986) 'Externalities in Economies with Imperfect Information and Incomplete Markets', *Quarterly Journal of Economics* **100**, 229–64.
Myers, S.C. and N.S. Majluf (1984) 'Corporate Financing and Investment Decisions When Firms have Information That Investors do Not', *Journal of Financial Economics* **11**, 187–221.
Stiglitz, J.E. and A.M. Weiss (1981) 'Credit Rationing in Markets With Imperfect Information', *American Economic Review* **71**, 393–410.

5 Convergence in the closed and in the open economy

DANIEL COHEN

1 Introduction

To what extent may regional integration help a poor country to speed up its capital accumulation and its growth rate and, perhaps, catch up with the rich? In a couple of recent papers, Barro and Sala-i-Martín (1990, 1991) (henceforth BS) have challenged the conventional wisdom according to which regional integration may speed up 'convergence'. They show indeed that the pattern of growth of regions is not significantly different from the pattern of growth of nations. In both cases, they show that regions or nations appear to converge towards their steady state at the same speed of about 2% a year. In conclusion of their latest paper (1991) they go as far as suggesting that regional integration such as that (spectacularly) undertaken in Germany will proceed at this quite universal speed of 2% a year, implying that about 25 years will be needed before *half* the gap between the two parts of Germany is closed. How can this be? What if West Germany were to devote *all* its resources to merging with its Eastern counterpart?

In order to address these questions, I present in the first part of the paper a simple theoretical model in which I examine the effects of free access to world financial markets on the pattern of growth of a (small) country. In the model that I examine, the conditions for convergence (towards a steady state) are the *same* in the closed and in the open ecnomy. (One should consequently *not* expect access to the world financial market to turn an economy that is converging towards a steady state into one that is 'taking off' on an endogenous pattern of growth). As I show in the simple example that I examine, the dynamics of the closed end of the open economy actually look quite similar and the reason why is simple: in both cases, growth is asymptotically driven by the accumulation of human capital.

If we take 'regions' to be open economics and 'nations' to be closed economies, then we replicate, theoretically, BS's results according to which regions and nations appear to exhibit the same pattern of growth. Yet, this does *not* imply (in our model) that a nation which suddenly becomes a region should converge towards its *new* steady state at the same speed. It may very well be instead that the stock of capital (and the level of income) is first (rapidly) lifted up to a *new* level before it starts converging, say at '2% a year', to its *new* steady state (at the same speed as the other regions or nations).

There are few examples – other than Germany – of one-off discrete shifts of regime. In this paper, we take as a potential example the case of the sub-group of developing countries which gained, in the 1970s, renewed access to world financial markets. We shall focus on capital accumulation, which is the channel through which, one would guess, the access to the world financial markets should operate quickly. Did the large debtors accelerate their speed of capital accumulation with respect to the other developing countries? We find that they did *not*. Capital accumulation actually appears to be *lower* in the group of large debtors than in the other developing countries. Interestingly, we shall see that this is due to *exogeneous* rather than to endogeneous reasons. The group of large debtors do not look like a sub-group of open economies but rather like a sub-group of closed economies with a low saving rate. To that extent our controlled experiment failed and we are not able to refute – empirically – BS's claim that a change of regional status has no implication for growth. We may learn, however, that regional integration – in order to make a difference – may have to imply much larger transfer of resources than those observed in the seventies toward the developing countries.

2   A model

Consider an overlapping generations model in which the production function is:

$$Y_t = K_t^\alpha H_t^\beta L_t^\gamma; \qquad \alpha + \beta + \gamma = 1 \qquad (1)$$

in which H_t is human capital (see below) and L_t is the total number of hours worked. Each agent lives for two periods: during the first period he gets trained and works: during the second he consumes whatever wealth he has accumulated.

During the first period of his life, a young agent is endowed with a given number of hours, N_t^i, that he can allocate freely between training and working. (Leisure is not taken into account). There are N_t number of hours of work which are originally available.

2.1   The training technology

To simplify the analysis we shall proceed as follows. We assume that a young agent must divert $\theta_t^i N_t^i$ hours from working in order to get trained so that his offer of 'raw labour' is $L_t^i = (1 - \theta_t^i) N_t^i$ hours. Out of these θ_t^i hours he gets a training $e_t^i = f(\theta_t^i) z_t$ in which f is a concave function and z_t is a measure of the 'knowledge' that is freely transmissible from one generation to the next. The agent then supplies $H_t^i = e_t^i L_t^i$ units of 'human capital'. We assume that z_t is a combination of 'learning by doing' and the formal training that has been accumulated by the previous generation. Formally, we postulate:

$$z_t = g(\bar{H}_{t-1}, \bar{K}_{t-1}) \tag{2}$$

in which $\bar{H}_{t-1}$ is the average level of education of the (preceding) working population

$$\left(= \frac{\Sigma_i H_{t-1}^i}{L_{t-1}} \right) \quad \text{and} \quad \bar{K}_{t-1} = \frac{K_{t-1}}{L_{t-1}}$$

is the previous capital-per-worker ratio which represents the 'learning-by-doing' form of knowledge).

The decision to obtain θ_t^i hours of training is consequently the result of the following maximization problem:

$$\text{Max}[w_h e_t^i + w_1](1 - \theta_t^i) N_t^i$$

in which w_h is the price of education and w_1 is the price of a raw unit of time. This yields

$$w_h[(1 - \theta_t^i) f'(\theta_t^i) - f(\theta_t^i)] z_t = w_1$$

which yields an identical choice $\theta_t^i = \theta_t$ for all young agents.

Assuming that w_1 and w_h are respectively paid to the marginal product of raw labour and education, one gets:

$$\frac{w_1}{w_h} = \frac{\gamma}{\beta} \frac{H_t}{L_t} = \frac{\gamma}{\beta} f(\theta_t) z_t$$

Thus the choice of getting θ hours of training is a solution to $f'(\theta)(1 - \theta) = [1 + (\gamma/\beta)] f(\theta)$. The left hand side is a decreasing function of θ and the right hand side is an increasing one. Assuming $f'(0) > [1 + (\gamma/\beta)] f(\theta)$, we get the existence and the uniqueness of the solution. We call such a solution θ^*.

This result will dramatically simplify the analysis since we can now take the law of motion of education to be

$$H_t^i = f^* \cdot g(\bar{H}_{t-1}, \bar{K}_{t-1}) \cdot N_t^i$$

in which $f^* = f(\theta^*)(1 - \theta^*)$.

We can aggregate this relation across young agents and get:

$$\frac{H_t}{N_t} = f^* g\left(\frac{H_{t-1}}{N_{t-1}}, \frac{K_{t-1}}{N_{t-1}}\right)$$

Production, on the other hand is:

$$Y_t = (1 - \theta^*)^\gamma K_t^\alpha H_t^\beta N_t^{1-\alpha-\beta} \equiv A K_t^\alpha H_t^\beta N_t^{1-\alpha-\beta} \tag{3}$$

while the income which is received by the young people is simply $(1 - a) Y_t$. We consequently see that all variables can now be written in per capita terms. From now on, to simplify the analysis, we shall simply assume $N_t = 1$.

2.2   The intertemporal allocation of consumption

We assume that each agent is maximizing

$$U[C_t(t), C_t(t + 1)] = \log C_t(t) + \beta \log C_t(t + 1)$$

in which $[C_t(t), C_t(t + 1)]$ is the pattern of consumption of an agent born at time t at times t and $t + 1$ respectively. Each young agent saves

$$S_t = \frac{\beta(1 - a)}{1 + \beta} Y_t \quad \text{and consumes} \quad C_t(t) = \frac{1 - a}{1 + \beta} Y_t$$

Let $s = \dfrac{\beta}{1 + \beta}(1 - a)$.

We simply have

$$K_{t+1} = s A K_t^\alpha H_t^\beta \tag{4}$$

3   Convergence in the closed and in the open economy

The dynamics of the economy are obtained by specifying the law of motion of education:

$$H_t = f^* g(H_{t-1}, K_{t-1})$$

Let us postulate: $H_t = B H_{t-1}^\lambda K_{t-1}^\gamma$

3.1   The closed economy

Let small letters denote the logs of large letters. The dynamics of the economy can be log-linearized as:

$$\left.\begin{array}{l} k_{t+1} = \log s + a + ak_t + \beta h_t \\ h_{t+1} = b + vk_t + \lambda h_t \end{array}\right\} \tag{5}$$

or equivalently:

$$\left.\begin{array}{l} k_{t+1} - k_t = a + \log s + (a-1)k_t + \beta h_t \\ h_{t+1} - h_t = b + vk_t + (\lambda - 1)h_t \end{array}\right\} \tag{6}$$

We assume that $\lambda \leq 1$ so that the trace of the system (6) is necessarily negative.

The system is consequently convergent if and only if:

$$\Delta \equiv (1-a)(1-\lambda) - \beta v > 0$$

3.2 Convergence in the open economy

Let us now assume that the country has free access to world financial markets on which, we assume, a constant interest rate r prevails. Let us assume full depreciation of capital. Investors at any time t always invest in the country so as to close the gap between the marginal productivity of capital and the world interest rate. We have:

$$a A K_{t+1}^{a-1} H_{t+1}^{\beta} = 1 + r, \qquad \forall t \geq 0 \tag{7}$$

The dynamics of the open economy are therefore:

$$\left.\begin{array}{l} k_{t+1} = \dfrac{\beta}{1-a} h_{t+1} + \dfrac{1}{1-a} \log \dfrac{a}{1+r} + \dfrac{1}{1-a} a \\ h_{t+1} = b + vk_t + \lambda h_t \end{array}\right\} \tag{8}$$

One can write

$$h_{t+1} = b + \frac{v}{1-a} \log \frac{a}{1+r} + \frac{v}{1-a} a + \left(\frac{v\beta}{1-a} + \lambda\right) h_t$$

The system is consequently stable if and only if:

$$\frac{v\beta}{1-a} + \lambda - 1 < 0$$

which is the same condition as that which was obtained in the closed economy: In this model, *the conditions for convergence in the closed and in the open economy are equivalent.*

The intuition behind this result is quite simple. Define $\hat{K}_t$ as the solution to:

$$\hat{K}_t = s A \hat{K}_t^a H_t^{\beta}$$

$\hat{K}_t$ is the level of capital that the economy would converge to if the level of human capital were to stay constant. In log terms, one can write:

$$\hat{k}_t = \theta_c + \frac{\beta}{1-a}h_t$$

with this notation, the law of motion of capital can simply be written as:

$$\frac{d}{dt}k_t = (1-a)(\hat{k}_t - k_t)$$

In the open economy, the stock of capital instantaneously reaches a level for which

$$a\hat{K}_t^{a-1}H_t^{\beta} = 1 + r$$

In log terms:

$$k_t = \theta_0 + \frac{\beta}{1-a}h_t$$

One consequently sees that the closed economy is running after a moving target $\hat{k}_t$ which is (up, perhaps, to a constant) the same as the one that the open economy immediately reaches. (While the law of motion of human capital is the same). If there is 'convergence' (the economy eventually stops growing endogenously) this must occur for both systems.

3.3   An example

As a simple benchmark, let us consider the case when $v = 0$, $\lambda < 1$. The dynamics of human capital are then simply given by:

$$h_{t+1} = b + \lambda h_t$$

Call $h_\infty = [b/(1-\lambda)]$, one has (in the closed as well as in the open economy):

$$h_t = h_\infty + \lambda^t(h_0 - h_\infty)$$

3.3.1 In the open economy case, one has:

$$k_t = k_\infty + \frac{\beta}{1-a}\lambda^t(h_0 - h_\infty)$$

in which

$$k_\infty \equiv \frac{1}{1-a}\log\frac{a}{1-r} + \frac{1}{1-a}a + \frac{\beta}{1-a}$$

So that y_t can be written:

$$y_t = y_\infty + \lambda^t(y_0 - y_\infty)$$

in which $y_\infty \equiv a + ak_\infty + \beta h_\infty$

3.3.2 In the closed economy case, one has:

$$k_t = k_\infty + a^t(k_0 - k_\infty) + \beta \frac{\lambda^t - a^t}{\lambda - a}(h_0 - h_\infty)$$

in which

$$k_\infty = \frac{1}{1 - a}[\log s + a + \beta h_\infty]$$

One can then write:

$$y_t = y_\infty + \beta \lambda^t(h_0 - h_\infty) + a^{t+1}(k_0 - k_\infty) + \beta \frac{\lambda^t - a^t}{\lambda - a}(h_0 - h_\infty)$$

3.3.3 Closed and open economy dynamics

In order to compare the dynamics in the closed and in the open economy cases, one needs to distinguish two cases:

(1) *If $\lambda < a$*, one has, asymptotically, in the closed economy:

$$k_t = k_\infty + a^t[(k_0 - k_\infty) - \frac{\beta}{\lambda - a}(h_0 - h_\infty)]$$

and $h_t = h_\infty + \lambda^t[h_0 - h_\infty]$.

In that case, the dynamics of the system are equivalent to:

$$y_t = a + ak_\infty + \beta h_\infty + a^{t+1}[(k_0 - k_\infty) + \frac{\beta}{a - \lambda}(h_0 - h_\infty)]$$

i.e.

$$y_t = y_\infty + a(k_t - k_\infty)$$

while the open economy is characterized by $y_t - y_\infty = \lambda^t(y_0 - y_\infty)$.

In that case, growth in the closed economy is driven by the (slow) process of capital accumulation while the open economy case is driven by the (fast) process of human capital accumulation.

(2) *If $\lambda > a$*, then the asymptotic properties of the system are:

$$k_t = k_\infty + \beta \frac{\lambda^t(h_0 - h_\infty)}{\lambda - a}, \text{ in the closed economy and}$$

$$k_t = k_\infty + \beta \frac{\lambda^t(h_0 - h_\infty)}{1 - \lambda}, \text{ in the open economy.}$$

As one sees, in this case, a one-dimensional analysis of income growth would deliver a law of motion that would asymptotically look like:

$$y_t - y_\infty = \lambda^t(y_0 - y_\infty)$$

both in the closed and in the open economy. (However, a two-dimensional analysis of the system (h, k) should reveal a difference between (5) and (8)).

To summarize the results so far obtained, we see that two cases emerge. In one $(\lambda > a)$, growth parallels human capital both in the closed and in the open economy and convergence goes (asymptotically) at the same speed in both instances. (In the closed economy, physical capital 'rapidly' follows human capital, while in the open economy it joins human capital instantaneously). In the other case $(\lambda < a)$, growth parallels physical capital accumulation in the closed economy and human capital in the open economy. Only in this latter case would a one-dimensional analysis of growth differentiate the dynamics of a closed economy from the dynamics of an open economy.

3.4   The general case

Let us now briefly analyse the general case of the systems depicted, in the closed economy, by equations (5) and, in the open economy, by equations (8).

The system (5) has two eigenvalues which are, respectively,

$$\lambda_1 = \frac{a + \lambda - \sqrt{(a - \lambda)^2 + 4\beta v}}{2}$$

$$\lambda_2 = \frac{a + \lambda + \sqrt{(a - \lambda)^2 + 4\beta v}}{2}$$

and the system (8) is one-dimensional system with a unique eigenvalue which is $\lambda_0 = \lambda + (\beta v/1 - a)$. Asymptotically, the closed economy system is driven by the largest eigenvalue, λ_2.

As in the example that was examined in the previous section, one needs to distinguish two cases:

(A) $\lambda > a$

In that case, using the fact that $\sqrt{1 + x} < 1 + \frac{1}{2}x, \forall x \neq 0$. One can show that:

$$\lambda_2 < \lambda + \beta v < \lambda + \frac{\beta v}{1 - a} = \lambda_0$$

In the case when the system is converging ($\lambda_0 < 1$), convergence is now faster in the *closed* economy than in the open economy (rather than the same as in the previous section). This (perhaps paradoxical) result is due to the fact that the dynamics of convergence of capital is fast (when $a < \lambda$) in the closed economy and spills over onto the accumulation of human capital, albeit convergence may be towards a *low* level of income when saving is low).

(B) $\lambda < a$

Let us take βv to be a small number. We can then approximate λ_2 as:

$$\lambda_2 \approx \frac{a + \lambda + (a - \lambda)\left[1 + 2\dfrac{\beta v}{a - \lambda}\right]}{2} \approx a + \beta v$$

While λ_0 (the open economy eigenvalue) is:

$$\lambda_0 = \lambda + \frac{\beta v}{1 - a}$$

When λ is small, then $\lambda_0 < \lambda_2$; when a is big, then $\lambda_0 > \lambda_2$. One sees, here, that there is no unambiguous result: convergence may be faster or slower in the closed economy than in the open economy.

3.5   Conclusions

The model should help seeing why Barro and Sala-i-Martín's conclusion about the effect of turning a nation (East Germany) into a region (Eastern Germany) is misleading. It may very well be that both regions and nations appear to converge towards their (own) steady state at about the same speed and yet when a nation becomes a region (by being integrated to a larger nation) its capital stock may well be lifted up (rapidly) to a new point, from which it will resume converging (at perhaps '2% a year') towards its new steady state).

4   Empirical applications

4.1   General background

In analysing the pattern of growth of a nation and of a region, Barro and Sala-i-Martín have shown that the growth rate of an economy is negatively correlated to the initial income of a country, provided that the level of 'education' of the countries is controlled for. 'Education' is proxied by the initial level of school enrollment in primary and secondary school. Focusing here on secondary school enrollment a typical regression that they obtain comes as follows:

$$g = 0.05 + 0.012 \log (Enrol2)_0 - 0.85.10^{-2} y_0 \qquad (9)$$
$$ (6.35) (-2.91)$$

$R^2 = 0.37$
(t-statistic in parenthesis)

(in which $(Enrol2)_0$ is the initial value of secondary school enrollment).

Interpreted as a speed of convergence towards a steady state, this regression can be written as

$$g = g_0 + \lambda(y_\infty - y_0)$$

in which λ is interpreted as the speed of convergence towards a steady state which can be written $y_\infty = C + 1.41 \log (Enrol2)_0$. (Obviously, because of the exogenous trend, income-per-capita must be corrected by the exogenous trend of labour productivity.)

The key question that such an interpretation leaves unanswered is: why is it that initial enrollment in secondary school proxies the steady state towards which the economy is converging? The answer to this question is the (implicit) purpose of the work by Mankiw, Romer and Weil (1990), (henceforth MRW).

MRW generalize the Solow model in order to account for the accumulation of both human and physical capital. They assume that production can be written as:

$$Q_y = K_t^a H_t^\beta (A_t N_t)^a \qquad (10)$$

and they extend the Solow version of capital accumulation to two-dimensional dynamic system:

$$\left. \begin{array}{l} \dot{K}_t = -dK_t + s_1 Q_t \\ \dot{H}_t = -dH_t + s_2 Q_t \end{array} \right\} \qquad (11)$$

in which s_1 and s_2 are the saving rates that respectively apply to physical and human accumulation.

This extended Solow model displays dynamics that can be written as:

$$g = g_0 + \lambda(\hat{y} - y_0) \qquad (12)$$

in which

$$\hat{y} = C + \frac{a}{1-a-\beta} \log s_1 + \frac{\beta}{1-a-\beta} \log s_2$$

is the steady state towards which the economy is converging and $\lambda = (1 - a - \beta)(d + v + \mu)$ is the speed at which the economy is going towards it. s_1 is taken to be the *observed* value of I_t/Q_t, the investment ratio, and s_2 is taken – up to a non-essential transformation – to be the current (rather than the initial) value of *secondary-school enrollment*. With such an interpretation, one then finds that the BS's proxy is indeed consistent with an equation such as (12).

A typical result to be found in MRW comes as follows.

$$g = -0.5.10^{-2} + 0.013 \log (Enrol2)_t + 0.012 \log \frac{I_t}{Q_t} - 0.011 \, y_0 \qquad (13)$$
$$\qquad\qquad\quad (4.77) \qquad\qquad\qquad (3.7) \qquad\qquad (-3.87)$$

$R^2 = 0.47$ (*t* statistics in parenthesis)

Out of such an equation one can interpret (12) as delivering $a = 0.32$; $\beta = 0.36$, which is in line with MRW's general conclusion that production should be written $Q_t = K_t^{1/3} H_t^{1/3} (A_t N_t)^{1/3}$. The difference between BS and MRW therefore amounts to essentially two things. First, BS take initial rather than average values of secondary school enrollment, and – second – they do not control for investment. Each of those two discrepancies is minor. When one runs (9) while controlling for average secondary school enrollment, one gets:

$$g = -0.028 + 0.017 \log (Enrol2)_t - 0.86.10^{-2} y_0 \qquad (14)$$
$$\qquad\quad (6.80) \qquad\qquad (-3.09)$$

$R^2 = 0.40$

The fit is better than in (9) but the coefficients are essentially identical. Interestingly (14) can be interpreted as a version of (12) in which $a = 0$ and $\beta = 0.66$. It is therefore plainly consistent with the results obtained in (13), when one assumes that human and physical capital are collinear. It is therefore also plainly consistent with the view (displayed for instance in Section 3.3) that human capital is the underlying process whose growth drives the economy.

4.2   Capital accumulation in the group of large debtors and in other developing countries in the 1970s

These results are obviously very compelling and strongly point to the idea that the Solow model must be extended to a two-dimensional setting such as the one examined in Section 3. Let me then simply characterize an economy as a two-dimensional vector which represents the country's initial endowment in human and physical capital. So as to keep things

simple, assume that a universal production function such as that postu-
lated in (10) exists. It is then equivalent to represent a country as a
two-dimensional vector whose coordinates measure respectively the
initial per-capita *income* of the country and the per-capita physical
capital stock of the country. (Data on physical capital as available in
Summers and Heston, 1991; see Appendix A on how we reconstructed
the missing data). We restrict our analysis to the sub-group of 48
developing countries which belong to the population of 75 in MRW
(characterized by good income data, a population over one million and
non-oil producers) and for which we had enough data to reconstruct a
meaningful capital stock series within this subgroup. We then distinguish
another sub-sample of 34 countries which are characterized in the *World
Debt Tables* (1990) as large debtors. These countries form a sub-group of
countries which have benefitted from the renewed access to the world
financial markets in the seventies. (Actually, the *only* country in the 75
group of MRW which was a large debtor in the early eighties and was
not one in the late eighties was Korea, which does not belong to our
sample for lack of data).

The question that we now want to investigate is the following: did the
group of large debtors benefit from its new access to the world financial
market to raise its physical capital accumulation (along the lines which
are suggested by Figure 5.1? To answer this question we simply regressed
the rate of growth of physical capital (dk) on its initial value (k_0) and on
the initial value of income-per-capita (y_0) and controlled for a dummy
variable (DSM) representing the group of large debtors.

We get the following results:

$$dk = -0.10 - 0.026\,DSM + 0.82\,y_0 - 0.061\,k_0 \qquad (15)$$
$$(-2.25) \qquad\qquad (6.71)\;(-9.07)$$

$$R^2 = 0.66 \quad (\text{number of observations} = 48)$$

This regression is interesting in its own right. Capital accumulation
appears to be positively correlated with initial income and negatively
correlated with the initial stock of physical capital. Actually, one gets that
the speed of capital accumulation is positively correlated both with the
initial income per capita (y_0) and with the initial (log of) output–capital
ratio ($y_0 - k_0$). But the result of interest to us is the fact that the group of
large debtors accumulated *less* physical capital (in the seventies) than the
other developing countries (at a lower rate of about 2.6% a year).

In order to investigate the origin of this discrepancy, we ran the same
regression for the group of large debtors only. We find the following
result:

$$dk = -0.148 + 0.083\,y_0 - 0.0589\,k_0 \qquad (16)$$
$$R^2 = 0.64 \quad \text{(number of observations} = 34)$$

We see that there is a striking similarity between the coefficient obtained in this regression and in the nil obtained before. A Chow test (shown in Appendix B) shows that the coefficients are indeed *not* statistically different. This points to the idea that capital accumulation was lower in the group of large debtors, but for *exogeneous* rather than for endogeneous reasons. Compared to the other developing countries, it does not appear that the access to the world financial markets has implied a change of regime for capital accumulation.

5   Conclusions

While the analysis of the large debtors in the seventies fails to refute BS's view that regional integration would make no difference (for growth) we are now left to wonder why this is so. There are two competing explanations. One is that the rates of returns across countries are *already* equalized (so that capital mobility makes little difference). This is the view expressed in Lucas (1990) (see also Krugman, 1993). Another view (cf., e.g., Cohen, 1991) is that however large the financial flows to the developing countries may have been, there is a lot of leakage towards consumption which leaves only a marginal amount (about 1% of GDP) to contribute to capital accumulation. Sovereign risk, rather than low returns, is then what explains why capital accumulation failed to increase significantly in those countries (where saving rates are presumably lower). If this latter view is valid, then this is good news for regional integration. But to the extent that consumption leakages are not likely to disappear when a nation is integrated into a larger (group of) nation(s), it also means that it takes a lot of resources to make any difference.

Appendix A: The case of endogenous growth

(a)   Analysis of the example in Section 3.3

We have limited our attention in the text to the case when $\lambda < 1$, so that the economy was always converging towards a steady state. Let us here consider instead the case when $\lambda = 1$ (maintaining the assumption that $v = 0$). One then writes:

$$h_t = h_0 + b \cdot t$$

1 – *In the open economy*
One gets $k_t = \theta_0 + (\beta/1 - a)h_t$ so that the growth rate of physical capital is simply:

$$k_{t+1} - k_t = \frac{\beta}{1-a}b$$

The economy grows at a rate which is

$$g = a\left[\frac{\beta}{1-a}b\right] + \beta b = \frac{\beta}{1-a}b$$

the same as physical capital.

2 – *In the closed economy*
One gets $k_{t+1} = \theta_0 + ak_t + \beta h_t$. Taking first differences and looking for a steady-state growth rate, one then finds again that asymptotically:

$$k_{t+1} - k_t = \frac{\beta}{1-a}b$$

and that the economy grows at a similar rate.

We therefore see that the case $\lambda = 1$ is not different from the case $\lambda > a$ that we examined before: *When $\lambda > a$ the asymptotic properties of the growth rate of GDP are the same in the closed and in the open economies.*

(b) *The general case*

When the open economy system is not converging ($\lambda_0 = 1$), we know that the closed economy system is *not* converging either. In the open economy, human capital grows at a rate:

$$g_h = b + v\theta_0$$

while the economy and physical capital grow at an identical rate:

$$g = \frac{\beta}{1-a}g_h$$

In the closed economy, one can similarly check that the rate of growth of physical capital coincides with the rate of growth of the economy and depends upon the growth rate of human capital as in the open economy. In order to find the growth rate of human capital one can write the law of notion of physical capital as:

$$k_{t+1} = (1-a)\theta_C + ak_t + \beta\lambda_t$$

and write that, asymptotically, $k_{t+1} - k_t = g_k$ so that:

$$k_t = \theta_C + \frac{\beta}{1-a}h_t - \frac{1}{1-a}g_k$$

One can then substitute this value of k_t into the law of motion of human capital and get:

$$g_h = \frac{b + v\theta_C}{1 + \dfrac{v\beta}{(1-a)^2}}$$

When $\theta_C \leq \theta_0$ (the long-run productivity of capital in the closed economy is asymptotically lower than or equal to its open economy value), one sees that growth is always lower in the closed economy than in the open economy. For small values of v, however, one also sees that they need not be far apart.

Appendix B: Capital stock data

The Summers and Heston (1991) estimates include data on the capital stock for a sub-group of 29 countries for the years 1980–88 (in most cases). We take an aggregate measure of capital (inclusive of residential capital, for lack of data on the decomposition of investment), and we reconstructed for the period 1970–88 capital stock data by an inventory formula:

$$K_t = \sum_{s=0}^{t} I_s(1 - \delta)^{(t-s)} + K_0(1 - \delta)^{t-s}$$

We took $\delta = 12\%$, the value that fitted best Summers and Heston's capital stock series after 1980. We had to drop, however, five countries (Zimbabwe, Korea, Philippines, Thailand and Austria) for which the 1970 data made no sense.

In order to extrapolate these data to the larger sub-group of 75 countries analysed in MRW (and consisting of non-oil countries with a population larger than one million), we have run the following regression:

$$\log K_{1970} = a + b \log\left[\sum_{s=1960}^{1970} I_s(1 - \delta)^{(1970-s)} \right] + c \log Y_{60}$$

for the sub-group of 24 countries and use the prediction of the regression for the 51 other countries. For lack of data we had to drop 9 additional countries: Zimbabwe, Bangladesh, Burma, Indonesia, Korea, Philippines, Singapore, Thailand and Austria. We are therefore left with 66 countries.

Appendix C: Test of stability

We get the following statistics:

(1) Equation (16) SSR_1 (sum of squared residuals) = 0.064901 (48 observations)

(2) When running the same regression for the *other* developing countries, we get:

$$SSR_2 = 0.016214 \quad (14 \text{ observations})$$

(3) For equation (17) in the text, we get:

$$SSR_3 = 0.041083 \quad (34 \text{ observations})$$

We then calculate the following F statistic:

$$F = \frac{(SSR_1 - SSR_2 - SSR_3)/3}{(SSR_1 + SSR_3)/42} = 1.85$$

which is below the threshold level of confidence, $F(3,42) = 32.9$, so that we can reject the hypothesis that the coefficients are different.

NOTES

I thank J.F. Nivet for his invaluable research assistance.

REFERENCES

Barro, R. (1991) 'Economic Growth in a Cross-Section of Countries', *Quarterly Journal of Economics*, **56**, 369–406.

Barro, R. and X. Sala-i-Martín (1990) 'Economic Growth and Convergence Across the United States', NBER Working Paper No. 3419.

(1991) 'Convergence Across States and Regions', *Brookings Papers on Economic Activity*, no. 1.

Cohen, D. (1991) 'Test of the Convergence Hypothesis: A Critical Note', CEPREMAP.

Krugman, P. (1993) 'International Finance and Economic Development', (this volume).

Lucas, R. (1988) 'On the Mechanics of Economic Development', *Journal of Monetary Economics*, **22**, 3–42.

Mankiw, G., D. Romer and D. Weil (1990) 'A Contribution to the Empirics of Economic Growth', mimeo, Harvard University.

Summers, R. and A. Heston (1991) 'The Penn World Table (Mark 5): An Expanded set of International Comparisons, 1950–88', *Quarterly Journal of Economics* **56**, 327–68.

Discussion

THOMAS F. HUERTAS

Convergence is central to the debate on development. How quickly can countries with low per capita incomes catch up to ones with high incomes? Is there anything that can be done to accelerate the process? Does it matter whether the economy is open or closed?

An economy is 'open' in two senses. It may be open to foreign investment, and/or it may be open to foreign competition. Daniel Cohen's paper sets a framework by which one can judge whether opening a poor economy to foreign investment is likely to accelerate convergence. He posits a one-sector, three-factor growth model, where growth is a function of human and physical capital accumulation. In this model, the economy approaches its steady state at the same rate, regardless of whether the economy is open or closed.

This implies that foreign aid or foreign capital can only make a difference, if it lifts the economy to a significantly higher starting condition, or if it changes economy's production function.

Figure 5A.1 illustrates the two alternatives. It is phrased in terms of gross domestic product, as is the model in the paper. (A fuller version of the model would discuss the evolution of gross national product, allowing for payments to the owners of foreign capital. It would also discuss the equalization of wage rates for unskilled labour and for returns on training.)

The time to convergence (t) is a function of the initial ratio (R) of poor country to rich country GDP and the differential (D) between the poor country and the rich country growth rate:

$$t = - (\ln R)/D$$

An inflow of foreign capital raises the initial starting ratio of poor country GDP to rich country from R_0 to R_1, and reduces the time needed for convergence (for a given rate of growth) from t_0 to t_1. However, to raise R by 1% (e.g. from 0.5 to 0.505) requires an inflow of foreign capital equal to $(1/r)$% of the poor country's GDP, where r is the marginal productivity of capital (assumed equal to the world real interest rate). Even if r and D are high, quite large inflows of foreign capital produce only small reductions in the time to convergence. For example, if R_0 is 0.5, r is 15%, and D is 5%, an inflow of foreign capital equal to 10% of the poor

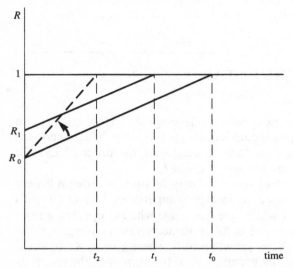

Figure 5A.1   Convergence depends on initial starting position and growth rate differential. R = ratio of poor country per capita income to rich country per capita income

country's GDP will reduce the time needed to converge from 13.9 years to 13.3 years – a reduction of only 4%.

Opening the economy to foreign competition can also affect the production function – a possibility not examined in the paper. It forces producers to sell at world market prices and to adopt more efficient production techniques. For example, one of the premises of the EC's single market programme is that increased foreign competition will induce greater efficiency in Member States' economies. Closing economies to foreign competition and foreign techniques isolates them from technological progress and stunts growth. The Communist regimes of Eastern and Central Europe are clear examples.

Small increases in potential growth rates can significantly reduce the time needed for convergence. (In terms of Figure 5A.1, an increase in the growth rate shifts the growth path upward. For an unchanged R_0, the time to convergence is reduced from t_0 to t_2.) For example, if R is initially 0.5, and the growth differential increases from 2% to 2.5%, the time needed for convergence declines from 35 years to 28 years, a decline of 20%. Such increases in growth rates are certainly possible, as an economy opens itself up to foreign competition. A recent case in point is Southern China.

In sum, openness to foreign competition is likely to be more important than openness to foreign capital. Large inflows of foreign capital with an unchanged production function will not significantly accelerate convergence. That was essentially the case in Latin America in the 1970s, and the paper's empirical results bear this out. However, opening the economy to foreign competition can improve the production function. This will accelerate convergence, even if the actual inflow of foreign capital is relatively small. That is prospectively the case in Central and Eastern Europe.

Part IIA
Case studies – financial markets and economic development

6 The role of finance in economic development in South Korea and Taiwan

YUNG CHUL PARK

1 Introduction

The economic performance of South Korea (Korea henceforth) and Taiwan over the last three decades has been exceptional by any international standard. Building on overpopulated and agriculture-dominated economies belonging to the poorest group of countries in the 1950s, both Korea and Taiwan have succeeded in sustaining rapid growth and industrialization to join the ranks of newly industrialized countries over a period of three decades.

The two countries share a similar Confucian cultural background, in which education is highly valued and obedience to the authorities and frugality are emphasized. They are also poorly endowed in terms of natural resources, making it necessary to trade with other economies. In fact, both Korea and Taiwan stand out as the two most successful cases of economic development and industrialization through the promotion of exports of manufactures.

Because of their colonial heritage and economic dependence on Japan, Korea and Taiwan have developed a financial system that is quite similar to that of Japan in its structure and role, which is bank-oriented, highly regulated, and which was until recently insulated from world financial markets. Joining the worldwide trend of financial liberalization and internationalization in the 1970s, Japan has managed a substantial deregulation and opening up of its financial markets and industries, and Korea and Taiwan have embarked on a similar course of financial adaptation since the early 1980s.

The exceptional economic performance of Korea and Taiwan, characterized by rapid growth, stable prices (in Korea not until the 1980s), and strong balance of payments have attracted a great deal of research interest in and has subsequently spawned a voluminous literature on development strategies and industrial transformation of the two

121

economies. However, relatively little is known about the working and evolution of the financial system and, as a result, very little about the contribution of finance to economic development in the two countries during the post-war period.

Over the three decades of following an export-oriented development strategy, both Korea and Taiwan have developed a very large trade sector and a relatively liberal trade regime. In sharp contrast, however, their financial systems are still subject to a myriad of regulations and remain relatively closed, even after almost a decade of financial liberalization and market opening.

In fact many free market advocates claim that the financial systems of the two countries are 'backward', underdeveloped, or inefficient, although the set of criteria by which such a characterization is made is seldom articulated. These critics go one step further by arguing that financial underdevelopment is primarily caused by financial repression[1] or government intervention in finance and that it could become a major bottleneck to economic development. According to these free market believers, financial liberalization is the most effective and perhaps the only solution to the problem of financial underdevelopment (Shaw, 1973; McKinnon, 1991).

However, the financial experiences of the two countries do not necessarily support this view; at least at the macroeconomic level, financial repression and closedness do not appear to have interfered with either financial expansion measured by various ratios of financial assets to GNP (or wealth) or GNP growth and industrialization, certainly not as much as the free market approach could make us believe. Does this observation suggest that the high degree of financial control has been dictated by and effective in mitigating the adverse consequences of financial market failures in the two countries? Could we infer from the experience of the two economies that finance does not matter in promoting economic development as much as is claimed, at least under certain circumstances? Does the mounting evidence on financial instability and institutional failures associated with financial deregulation in both developed and developing countries justify the restrictive financial policies of Korea and Taiwan?

This paper attempts to answer some of these questions by analysing the role of finance in economic development in Korea and Taiwan for the past three decades. Section 2 discusses the growth and structural changes of the financial systems of Korea and Taiwan. Section 3 examines the effectiveness in mobilizing saving and the efficiency of credit allocation of the financial system. Section 4 analyses some of the apparent cases of financial market failures that may have justified government intervention in finance in the two economies. Section 5 discusses the allocative consequences of financial restrictions in a trade-dependent economy. Concluding remarks are found in a final section.

2   Growth and structural changes in the financial system

At the end of World War II, Korea and Taiwan inherited a financial system that had been introduced and managed by the Japanese during their colonial periods. Since then both countries have developed a relatively elaborate financial system with a variety of modern and specialized institutions. Although the two systems are still dominated by banking institutions, since the early 1970s a host of non-bank financial intermediaries (NBFIs) have come into existence to complement and compete with commercial banks. The creation of money and capital markets and their rapid growth have transformed the two financial systems into highly diversified and modern ones in terms of financial products, markets, and institutions.

Financial services provided by various financial intermediaries range from those of fixed deposits at local credit cooperatives to cash management, investment banking and asset management for individual savers and institutional investors. Some institutions and markets have been established in response to the demand for new financial services whereas others have been created ahead of their demand and needs to develop a balanced and diversified financial system.

The financial authorities both in Korea and Taiwan have taken steps to relax their grip on finance, beginning in the early 1980s, as part of the overall liberalization of the economy. The financial deregulation has led to privatization of the existing nationwide commercial banks, creation of new banks and a host of non-bank financial intermediaries. It has also broken down to a considerable degree the artificial segmentation of financial institutions by product and service, even allowing commercial banks to underwrite and accept securities.

Although it has been partial and marked by relapses, the deregulation of interest rates has altered the behaviour of commercial banks and other financial institutions as well as the modus operandi of monetary policy. The *World Development Report* (World Bank, 1989) highlights Korea's experience as one of the successful cases in which financial reforms for liberalization led to rapid growth in the financial sector in the 1980s (p. 126).

For the past three decades, the financial sector has grown at a faster pace than the real sector of the economy in both countries. As a result, the size of the financial sector measured by the financial interrelation ratio (Table 6.1) almost doubled in Korea between 1975 and 1989. A similar

Table 6.1. *Macro and financial indicators, 1975–89*

		1975–79	1980–84	1985–89
GNP growth rate (%)	Korea	9.3	6.3	10.4
	Taiwan	10.2	7.0	9.0
Inflation (%)	Korea (1985 = 100)	16.7	12.6	4.2
(consumer prices)	Taiwan (1986 = 100)	6.1	7.9	1.3
Domestic saving/GNP	Korea	26.3	26.0	34.7
%	Taiwan	32.6	32.2	36.0
	Japan	32.4	31.1	34.4

		1975	1980	1985	1989
Per capital GNP	Korea	594	1,592	2,194	4,994
(US$)	Taiwan	956	2,311	3,304	7,478
M2-GNP	Korea	31.1	34.1	36.6	41.4
	Taiwan	56.8	65.4	106.1	145.8
	Japan	84.6	86.2	96.7	117.1
FIR[1]	Korea				
	Financial sector	0.81	1.04	1.67	1.98
	Non-financial sector	1.37	1.36	1.85	2.12
	Japan	1.79	2.07	2.55	3.22
		2.62	2.87	3.44	4.33
	Taiwan	0.98	1.14	1.36	1.76[2]
		1.84	2.26	2.52	2.85
	USA	1.51	1.57	1.83	2.12[2]
		2.65	2.86	2.98	3.08
	West Germany	1.36	1.55	186	1.94
		1.49	1.52	1.89	1.93
	United Kingdom	2.02	2.08	3.20	—
		2.12	2.00	2.55	—

Notes: (1) The Financial Interrelation Ratio is defined as total financial assets divided by nominal GNP. (2) Figures for 1988.
Sources: Major Statistics of Foreign Economy, various issues, National Bureau of Statistics, Economic Planning Board, Republic of Korea; *Economic Statistics Yearbook*, 1991, The Bank of Korea; *Taiwan Economic Statistics*, 1989, Overall Planning Department, CEPD.

development has taken place in Taiwan, where the FIR jumped to 4.61 in 1988 from less than 2.82 in 1975. During this period of rapid growth, the financial sector has evolved from a simple to a relatively sophisticated structure and in the process developed a number of structural characteristics that are relevant to our discussion. It should be noted, however, that rapid financial growth and modernization have been attended by restrictive financial policies of controlling the interest rates and asset management of financial institutions and protecting domestic money and capital markets from foreign competition.

One distinctive feature of finance in both Korea and Taiwan has been the predominance of indirect finance or the intermediated credit market. Although the business sector has increasingly relied on direct finance and as a result capital markets have grown in size and importance, direct holdings of stocks and bonds by household savers as a proportion of their total financial assets have not increased at the same pace. Instead, investment trust companies and many other non-bank financial institutions have added to their portfolios a growing share of new stock and bond issues. They have in fact become intermediaries between issuers and holders of stocks and bonds, thereby only partially shifting the risk of holding these assets to ultimate lenders. The problem of informational asymmetries between lenders and borrowers in capital markets appear to be the main reason for savers' preference for indirect securities and in part explains the dominance of intermediated credit.

A second characteristic is the repressive nature of the financial system. Even after a decade-long promotion of financial liberalization, to many liberalization advocates little has changed in the dominant role of the government in managing the financial system. The two governments have not given up the idea of controlling interest rates and can and in fact do interfere in the allocation of banks' loanable funds. The financial authorities not only regulate entry to financial industries but also determine the types of services and product banks, NBFIs and securities firms can offer. Financial industries are different from other manufacturing and service industries. Nevertheless, the free market advocates and even some interventionists would question whether the degree of financial control exercised by the Korean and Taiwanese financial authorities has been necessary or justifiable on efficiency grounds, although financial repression, despite its severity and protraction, does not appear to have interfered with economic growth and industrialization in Korea or Taiwan.

A third feature has been the closedness of the financial sector. For almost three decades of successful export promotion, Korea and Taiwan have developed large and very open trade sectors. Export earnings have accounted for almost 45 per cent of Korea's GNP in recent years. Yet, in both countries the monetary authorities and the public have been reluctant and resisted foreign pressure to open their money and capital markets to foreign investors. How should one explain this coexistence of an open trade regime with a closed financial sector?

A fourth feature has been a close correlation between the structure of finance and that of industrial organization. Korea's financial sector is dominated by a relatively small number of large financial institutions both in the banking and NBFI sectors. Korea's manufacturing sector is also dominated by about 30 large industrial conglomerates, which as a group account for almost 40 per cent of manufacturing value added. In contrast, a large number of small and medium-sized firms produce a large share of manufactured products in Taiwan. These smaller firms have a very limited access to institutional credit and obtain much of their credit needs through the informal financial system which consists of unregulated and atomistic financial markets where a large number of small borrowers and lenders are engaged in credit transactions (Biggs, 1988a and b; Shea, 1990). Does the structure of industrial organization shape the structure of finance? Or does the causality run the other way round?

Finally, one could also observe in Korea and Taiwan a large increase in financial layering and financial interpenetration as evidenced by the rapid growth of transactions among financial institutions including the central bank. The financial sector as a whole contributed almost 5.5 per cent of Korea's GDP and about 4 per cent in Taiwan in 1989, and its share has been rising. This level of GDP contribution is close to that of many OECD countries in recent years. Despite the rapid increase in the variety and number of financial institutions and proliferation of financial products, most financial institutions have been engaged in indirect finance through the issuance of deposits or deposit-like liabilities. Is this allocation of resources to the financial sector 'excessive'?

The process of financial growth and liberalization over the past three decades in Korea and Taiwan raises a number of important issues as to the role of finance in economic development. One issue is related to the question of whether liberal financial reform could contribute to financial growth and sophistication. Another is whether financial growth, irrespective of its sources including financial deregulation, could stimulate domestic saving and improve the allocative efficiency of the economy. A third issue would be whether one could identify a set of conditions under which repressive financial policies may not only not interfere with but rather support growth of both the financial and real sectors.

3   Financial factors in economic development

3.1   Financial liberalization and financial growth

In a recent book, McKinnon (1991) reaffirms the view he first advocated in his *Money and Capital* (1973) that financial liberalization in which real deposit rates are brought to a market-clearing level can and indeed does lead to rapid financial deepening measured by the M3 to GNP ratio and that financial growth can and does contribute to higher GNP growth (chapter 2). What are the channels through which financial liberalization promotes rapid financial growth, which in turn produces a major positive impact on rapid output growth?

Starting from a repressive financial regime, reforms for financial deregulation are likely to make the holdings of financial assets relatively more attractive than those of real assets, as they tend to increase the interest rates on and the variety of financial assets. As a result, household savers would shift out of real assets such as land, houses, buildings and capital goods and into bank deposits, bonds, and other financial assets. This is the portfolio substitution effect. This substitution effect will be reinforced by an income effect if financial growth or deepening provides strong stimuli for output growth. Citing a number of empirical studies, McKinnon (1991) claims that achieving financial liberalization has a real payoff in terms of rapid financial and real output growth (pp. 30). In this section it will be argued that as far as the experienced of Korea and Taiwan is concerned, there is no clear evidence suggesting that the causality between financial growth and real output growth runs from financial liberalization to financial deepening and then to higher output growth.

It is true that during the 1980s, when policies for financial deregulation were carried out, the stocks of M3 and total financial assets grew faster than nominal GNP, resulting in a large increase in the M3/GNP and FIR ratios in both Korea and Taiwan. However, neither ratio appears to be a relevant measure of financial deepening or the effect of substitution between financial and real assets. The presence of a strong substitution effect favouring the holding of financial assets associated with financial liberalization would, ceteris paribus, have moderated the increase in the nominal value of real assets. In both countries, the holdings of land, individual housing, and commercial buildings account for a major portion of total wealth. As shown in Table 6.2, the nominal values of these real assets increased at a rate higher than that of the nominal stocks of M3 or total financial assets in recent years. Measured by equity prices, the nominal value of capital goods such as plant and equipment had risen faster than the nominal stock of M3 or total financial assets before the collapse of the stock market in the two countries toward the latter part of the 1980s. Therefore, the proportion of total financial assets in total wealth including capital goods and real property did not appear to have increased as much as the M3-GNP or FIR ratios did.

As for the channels through which financial growth exerts a positive effect on output growth, McKinnon (1973 and 1991) and others (World Bank, 1989) put emphasis on the saving incentives and investment efficiency effect generated by financial deepening. In the following two

Table 6.2. *Land price and stock price indices in Korea and Taiwan 1980–90 (% changes)*

Year	Korea[1]			Taiwan[1]		
	Entire city land price	Seoul land price	Stock price index	Entire city land price[2]	Nominal housing price (Taipeh)[3]	Stock price index
1980	—	—	− 9.78	32.05	53.39	− 2.43
1981	7.10	3.00	16.08	34.52	3.00	0.35
1982	6.40	10.40	− 3.40	6.62	− 6.93	− 13.05
1983	16.10	47.60	4.67	3.83	− 0.15	37.11
1984	13.60	26.40	3.29	1.47	− 4.32	33.35
1985	11.30	10.30	5.31	0.39	− 0.31	− 14.54
1986	4.10	4.60	64.00	3.93	2.03	26.71
1987	9.60	4.00	83.32	—	79.94	125.99
1988	26.00	22.20	65.97	—	65.96	143.66
1989	33.90	35.80	32.53	—	—	65.62
1990	21.00	28.20	− 18.68	—	—	− 21.36

Notes: (1) All percentage changes are calculated by comparison with the same period of the previous year. (2) Lin Yuan-Hsin (1989); (3) Wu De-Hsien (1989).
Sources: Economic Statistics Yearbook, The Bank of Korea, 1991, *National Accounts*, The Bank of Korea, 1990, and *Financial Statistics Monthly*, various issues, Central Bank of China.

sub-sections we shall assume, for the sake of argument, that there has been a substantial financial deepening in both countries and then show that there is no evidence that the financial deepening measured by the M3-GNP or FIR ratio has increased private saving (as a proportion of GNP) or improved the allocative efficiency of the economy in Korea and Taiwan.

3.2　Financial deepening and domestic savings

The decade of the 1980s witnessed a dramatic increase of domestic saving (as a percentage of GNP) in Korean history, a performance that rivals the doubling of the average propensity to save between 1965 and 1969. The decade began with a saving rate of 23 per cent that was 6 percentage points lower than the rate two years earlier. Beginning in 1983, the saving-GNP ratio climbed rapidly, reaching an all-time high of 38.1 per cent in 1988. During the same period, the M3-GNP ratio more than doubled to 1.26 and the FIR moved up to 3.66 in 1989 from less than 3 in 1975. In Taiwan, the saving rate, starting from about 13 per cent in the early 1960s, had risen steadily to reach 32 per cent in 1972. Since then it has fluctuated between 30.4 in 1982 and 40 per cent in 1987. At the same time, the rise of the M2-GNP ratio has been phenomenal, and the FIR has almost doubled between 1975 and 1989 (see Table 6.1). Is there any causal linkage between the increase in domestic saving and financial deepening?

There are basically two arguments supporting positive effects of financial growth on the saving rate. The first argument stresses the saving incentives created by an increase in the variety of financial assets with high yields and low risks that are convenient instruments of saving and which could satisfy diverse portfolio preferences of different savers. A large menu of financial assets and a large network of financial institutions could induce households to save more out of their incomes because it is now more convenient and profitable to save than when financial instruments are limited (World Bank, 1989, p. 27). While this traditional view is intuitively appealing, it essentially argues that financial deepening raises, other things being equal, the interest rate on financial instruments adjusted for risk and liquidity and that the higher interest rate stimulates saving.

It is well known that the substitution effect and the income effect of an increased interest rate could cancel each other out, so that the net effect is in theory ambiguous. Financial decontrol may lead to an increase in the rate of return on financial assets adjusted for expected rate of inflation. It is also likely to increase the availability of credit for consumption expenditure. The net effect on saving of the increase in the real interest rate and household debts after financial deregulation will therefore be ambiguous even when the substitution effect is stronger than the income effect.[2]

The second argument focuses on complementarity between money that is broadly defined to include time and savings deposits and capital in developing economies (McKinnon, 1973). These two assets are claimed to be complementary, because savers, who are often investors themselves, must accumulate their savings in the form of deposits which is the only readily available asset, until the required investment balances for lumpy investment projects are reached. Therefore the higher rate of return on deposits, the more willing savers are to engage in the accumulation process. As Dornbusch and Reynoso (1989) point out, it is difficult to differentiate this view from one that posits the positive effect of a higher interest rate on saving.

A number of empirical studies using Korean data provide rather conflicting results on the effect of real interest on saving. Depending on the choice of sample period and independent variables, the interest rate effect on saving could be either positive or negative. Nam (1988) provides a new set of evidence showing that saving responds to higher real interest rates. According to his estimation, the ratio of household saving to disposable income is explained mostly by the level and the growth rate of per capita income during the 1964–84 sample period. The saving rate is also positively related to the curb market interest rate and negatively related to the ratio of financial assets to income. Shea (1990) also argues that the positive real interest in Taiwan since 1962 has contributed to a high rate of saving, although he does not provide any empirical results. We have estimated similar equations for both Korea and Taiwan with different real interest rates, but our results do not support either the positive or negative effect of changes in the real interest rates on saving.

In contrast, the correlation of financial deepening and the real interest rate appears to be tighter than that of saving and the real interest rate when a nominal deposit interest rate is used as the return variable (see Nam, 1988).[3] However, it is easy to see that an increase in the M3-GNP ratio or FIR does not imply a corresponding increase in the saving rate because the increase could be brought about by a portfolio shift out of real assets without any change in the saving rate. Furthermore, financial asset-GNP ratios could be regarded as proxy variables for the wealth-GNP ratio. An increase in the financial asset ratios could produce a negative effect on saving to the extent that the increase captures the wealth effect. This is basically what Nam (1988) finds in his estimation.

How should one then explain the simultaneous increase in the FIR, M2-GNP ratio and the saving rate in Korea and Taiwan? It is clear that the positive real interest rate throughout the period has no doubt been conducive to both saving and financial asset accumulation. However, the most powerful economic forces driving up the financial asset-GNP ratio and saving rate may have been the high rate of growth and price stability. We return to this argument in Section 5.

3.3   Financial deepening and allocative efficiency

Financial deepening caused by an increase in real interest rates may not necessarily contribute to a higher saving rate, but it could increase the proportion of savings that is channelled to investors through financial intermediaries and money and capital markets. Provided that financial intermediaries and markets are more efficient in selecting viable investment projects, greater intermediation and more developed money and capital markets will ensure that investment projects with high rates of return are financed and thereby increase the average productivity of investment and the rate of growth of output (World Bank, 1989, p. 31).[4]

By bringing together savers and investors, financial markets in a competitive setting can improve allocative efficiency of the economy as they allow deficit units to invest more than they save with borrowed funds. With scale economies in collecting and processing information and the ability to process risks, financial intermediaries can also alleviate financial market inefficiencies stemming from informational asymmetry between lenders and borrowers.

Financial intermediaries have more and better information about lenders and borrowers and the ability to finance lumpy investment projects by pooling small savings. Given these advantages, it is not difficult to see that financial intermediaries will be better at identifying viable projects than industrial savers. However, according to the free market approach, this will be true if financial intermediaries are left unregulated to operate in a competitive market environment. If instead government controls asset management and lending and borrowing rates of banks and other financial institutions and intervenes in financial markets, as most governments do in developing economies, free market advocates would argue that financial deepening may not necessarily improve resource allocation, if the deepening is artificially engineered.

For example, an increase in controlled deposit rates will most likely increase savers' demand for deposits and thereby expand the amount of savings allocated through financial intermediaries. If, however, the allocation of bank credit is not determined by banks operating in a competitive environment, but by the government to achieve its allocative objectives, greater intermediation will not necessarily raise the average rate of return to investment. As a result, the causality will run from financial development to economic growth if financial development is accompanied by financial market liberalization.

Disputing the free market view, Stiglitz (1991) and others argue[5] that in economies where markets are too few or information is imperfect unfettered competition in financial markets does not necessarily ensure Pareto-efficient resource allocation. For example, given informational asymmetries, banks are likely to ration their credit among the would-be borrowers in terms of non-price criteria. Therefore, some forms of government intervention such as taxes and subsidies could be Pareto-improving. One of the major implications of the market failure approach is that financial deregulation does not necessarily improve the allocative efficiency of the economy because it cannot remove the distortions related to equilibrium credit rationing and other non-competitive behaviour of financial institutions, although it could lessen the distortions caused by government intervention.

As noted earlier, Korea and Taiwan have followed a path of financial liberalization since the early 1980s, though the path has been marked by interruptions and backslidings. Have the liberal financial policies in the

1980s, such as the partial interest rate deregulation and the demolition of the walls separating banks from non-bank financial institutions, strengthened the linkage between economic growth and financial deepening through the productivity improvement channel? If they have, could these effects be measured empirically?

In order to test the productivity improvement hypothesis, I assume a Cobb-Douglas production function for the manufacturing sector as in Horiuchi and Otaki (1987):

$$Y = AK^a N^b$$

where Y denotes value added, K capital stock, N labour and A total factor productivity. Expressed in logs, we have

$$\log(Y/N) - a\log(K/N) = \log A + (a + b - 1)\log N$$

It is assumed that A is positively related to financial deepening measured by the ratio (F) of corporate bonds and long-term borrowings from financial institutions to total assets. Then, we have estimated the following equation;

$$\log(Y/N) - a\log(K/N) = a_0 + a_1\log F + a_2\log N$$

In this estimation I used cross-section – time-series data for eight manufacturing sub-sectors for the 1981–89 period obtained from the bank of Korea's *Financial Statements Analysis*. a is the income share of capital. I have estimated this equation for the entire manufacturing sector and also for large and small and medium-sized firms. The results which are reported in Table 6.3 do not show any positive effect of financial deepening on the allocative efficiency of the economy.

Because of data limitations and specification problems, I do not have much confidence in the estimation results in Table 6.3. Are there any other ways of measuring the investment efficiency effect? In the short run financial liberalization will reduce the number of concessional interest rates and other financial subsidies in the form of availability, collateral requirements, and the terms of loans and as a consequence could lower the differences in the lending rates of financial intermediaries to different sectors and industries.

Cho (1988) argues that financial liberalization leads to similar costs of borrowing for different borrowers except for risk premium or transactions costs. Using the data from *Financial Statements Analysis* published by the Bank of Korea, he shows that the variance of borrowing costs for 68 manufacturing industries declined significantly from 43.14 in 1972 to less than 6 in 1984. I have run a similar test for a longer period from 1971 to 1988 for 28 (3-digit classification) and 68 (4-digit classification) manufacturing industries.[6,7] In general the results reported in Table 6.4

Table 6.3. *Productivity improvement and financial deepening*

	Constant	F	N	R^2	D.W.
Total[1]	− 5.241	− 1.379	0.018	0.175	1.598
	(− 2.124)	(− 1.027)	(0.151)		
Large firms	− 5.391	0.016	0.022	0.001	1.578
	(− 2.639)	(0.086)	(0.176)		
Small firms	− 2.237	− 0.023	0.033	0.003	2.403
	(− 3.168)	(− 0.016)	(0.436)		

Note: (1) The eight manufacturing subsectors are: (1) Food, beverages and tobacco; (2) Textile, wearing apparel & leather industries; (3) Wood & wood products including furniture; (4) Paper & paper products, printing & publishing; (5) Chemicals, petroleum, coal, rubber & plastic products; (6) Non-metallic mineral products; (7) Basic metal industries; (8) Fabricated metal products.
Sources: Monthly Bulletin, various issues, The Bank of Korea and *Financial Statements Analysis,* various issues, The Bank of Korea.

Table 6.4. *Variance of return to and cost of capital*

	3-digit		4-digit	
Year	Rate of return to capital	Cost of borrowing	Rate of return to capital	Cost of borrowing
1979	146.35	45.55	240.52	58.42
1972	109.78	17.05	199.48	43.57
1973	85.47	13.58	113.33	21.18
1974	134.66	8.63	189.80	21.55
1975	130.56	9.47	331.69	20.99
1976	121.40	19.32	214.59	20.71
1977	226.60	12.00	186.19	355.42
1978	239.97	24.31	172.12	17.64
1979	121.02	9.89	565.69	12.89
1980	267.94	245.68	133.30	23.05
1981	149.65	13.84	83.71	16.16
1982	116.11	7.92	58.95	10.02
1983	73.23	7.60	71.71	11.10
1984	90.70	59.04	73.63	20.14
1985	62.43	6.02	104.85	6.26
1986	67.29	3.27	88.98	15.55
1987	73.57	4.83	90.58	8.44
1988	71.70	5.11	68.07	6.95

Source: Financial Statements Analysis, various issues, The Bank of Korea.

confirm Cho's findings, but do they imply an improvement in the allocative efficiency of the economy?

Even in a liberal financial regime, I have suggested that financial intermediaries differentiate their borrowers in terms of their credit worthiness, ration credits among them, and charge different interest rates to different borrowers. If indeed financial intermediaries ration credit in terms of non-price criteria including the expected rate of return on investment projects of different borrowers, the reduction in the differences in borrowing costs is not an adequate measure of the allocative efficiency improvement associated with financial liberalization. This measure should be complemented by an estimation of the rates of return on investment in different sectors and industries, with the assumption that competitive financial markets will tend to reduce the differences in sectoral rates of return to capital in the long run.

Reliable data for such estimation are not readily available. As a proxy variable, I have used the sectoral ratios of gross value added to capital from *Financial Statements Analysis* compiled by the Bank of Korea as proxies for sectoral rates of return to capital in manufacturing industries classified by 2, 3, and 4-digit codes. Except for the case of the 2-digit classification, the variances of the rates of return on capital for 28 3-digit and 68 4-digit industries have declined in the 1980s in Korea. However, one should be cautious about taking these results at their face value because it is not clear how closely the rate of return data approximate actual rates of return to capital.

An improvement in the allocative efficiency of the financial system could be measured by the degree of integration of segmented financial markets along the path of financial liberalization. As a first approximation, the deregulation of interest rates at financial institutions and the relaxation of market segmentation by product and service will tend to lower the differences between the interest rates prevailing in the unregulated money markets and those in the regulated markets as they facilitate financial market integration. That is, through the interest rate decontrol, financial transactions in the unregulated money market will be in part absorbed or integrated in the organized financial system. An expansion of the intermediation capacity of the organized financial sector following financial deregulation is likely to result in smaller interest rate differentials between the regulated (or organized) and unregulated financial sectors. The financial integration will also stabilize the rate differentials between the two sectors.

I have examined these hypotheses using the Korean data from 1971 to 1988. The differences between the interest rate in the unregulated money market and the bank lending rates (or the yields on corporate debentures) are highly correlated with changes in the M3-GNP ratio or the FIR during the 1971–88 sample period except for 1983. I have also used the estimates of the return to capital in manufacturing instead of the bank lending rates in our estimation. The result is the same; the rate differentials have moved closely with changes in the M3-GNP ratio and the FIR. In Taiwan, however, I could not obtain similar results, simply because the rate differentials between the regulated (organized) and unregulated (informal) financial markets have varied very little since the mid-1970s.

In order to show the stability of the rate differentials between the regulated and unregulated financial sectors, I have calculated the standard deviation of the ratio of the unregulated money market and bank lending rates from 1971 to 1989. The differences between the two rates were large and moved around a great deal between 1973 and 1984. Since then the differences have become smaller and stable. Once again, in my view this result does not necessarily support the efficiency improvement hypothesis of financial liberalization, because the substantial fall in the expected rate of inflation in recent years has been largely responsible for the decline in the differentials between the two rates in Korea.

A decrease in the expected rate of inflation may tend to lower both informal and official lending rates, but much more the former. The reason is the following. In the unregulated money market, changes in the expected rate of inflation would, other things being equal, lead to changes in market rates of interest as they affect the demand for and supply of informal loans. However, in the organized financial system, the monetary authorities may not adjust the controlled lending rates when the expected rate of inflation falls, if the controlled rates were initially set below a market equilibrium level, so that the decrease in the expected rate of inflation could bring up the real official lending rate closer to the level of the real unregulated rate.

Using Taiwan data, Shea (1990) estimated a number of credit allocation equations. He specifies the ratio of the amount of credit supplied by financial institutions to total borrowings of ith industry as the dependent variable which is related to a variable representing financial market conditions, collateral requirements, capital productivity (measured by gross capital income divided by total assets of firms), the previous relationships with financial institutions (measured by the lagged dependent variable), and industrial dummies measuring sectoral preferences of financial institutions. The estimated equations covering five industries that include manufacturing, construction, and other service industries for the 1965–88 period show that capital productivity is the least important variable for the credit allocation of financial institutions. All other variables are significant.

Shea's analysis, while lacking in rigour, implies that financial liberalization has not altered to any significant degree the lending behaviour of financial intermediaries in Taiwan. In a competitive environment, it is likely that the viability of investment projects would be one of the most important considerations for making loan decisions, but Shea's results do not support this view.

In summary, what can be said about the effects of financial liberalization on the allocative efficiency of the economy in terms of the pieces of evidence we have been able to put together? Largely because of data and specification problems and lack of confidence in my estimation results, I am not at this stage prepared to make any judgement. Free market advocates could argue that the results simply reflect that the progress of financial liberalization in both countries has been much less than it is claimed to be. On the other hand, those who believe in the seriousness of financial market failures may not be surprised by my results.

4   Imperfections in the financial markets and government intervention

As noted in Section 2, the governments of Korea and Taiwan have maintained highly interventionist financial policies in which the management of assets and liabilities of financial institutions and market interest rates have been controlled in a rigid manner. A natural and important question arises as to what characteristics and roles of the financial markets and institutions make them so unique and different from other markets and institutions that they have been under government control for so long and so much.

One of the major reasons for the regulation of the financial sector rests on the argument that both the payments system and public confidence in financial institutions and instruments bears the qualities of a public good. The financial system must be built on the public's confidence in the integrity of both financial instruments and institutions, and trust that financial contracts will be honoured and that a legal framework exists for their enforcement. The confidence needed to resolve information asymmetries between lenders and borrowers is a public good, and the role of financial regulation is to provide that public good (Friedman, 1985).

Since free market competition by itself cannot achieve and protect the social benefits of a stable payments system, the government should supply the store-of-value characteristics of a monetary unit of account such as currency, and should allow the banking industry to supply inside money (deposits) as a convenient substitute for currency. If unfettered competition among intermediaries is likely to increase the probability of bank failure and hence the risks of default and breakdown of the payments system, banks, it then follows, should be regulated.[8]

Another justification for financial regulation often refers to the characteristics of the financial system in which financial institutions do not behave competitively and in financial markets a competitive equilibrium may not exist because of the information imperfections and scale economies in financial intermediation.

Deregulation of financial firms which will free them to pay whatever interest is required to obtain funds and to charge whatever interest is bearable to borrowers, may not result in an efficient allocation of resources. In the bank loan market, information imperfection leads banks to screen loan applicants in terms of non-price criteria. Adverse selection and moral hazard may severely reduce the market-clearing role of the interest rate.[9]

Banking in many countries including Japan, Korea, and Taiwan has been shown to display considerable economies of scale in every aspect of banking operation. There exists considerable disagreement on the relevant concept of bank output and operating costs for the estimates of scale economies. Using bank revenues or total earnings as bank output, however, a number of studies have demonstrated that banks in Korea and Taiwan enjoy considerable scale economies (Yang, 1990; Park and Kim, 1990). The existence of economies of scale may result in a highly concentrated banking industry dominated by a few large banks in the absence of any entry restrictions.[10] The major sources of scale economies appear to be indivisibilities in bank assets and innovation in financial technologies.

There are two other features of banking unique to East Asian countries that may explain non-competitive banking behaviour. One feature, which is most apparent in Japan, Korea, and Taiwan, is that banks do not necessarily maximize profits, but scale or market share measured by the volume of deposits. It is well known that in all three countries bank branch managers and senior executives are always rewarded in terms of promotion and bonus on the basis of their ability to attract deposits, not to earn profits.

Several hypotheses have been advanced to account for the market share maximizing bank behaviour in East Asia. In a regulated financial regime, where deposit rates are controlled below bank lending rates, banks' profits will increase as their deposits increase with the assumption that the cost function in terms of real resources for deposit mobilization exhibits scale economies. Another argument is that scale maximization in the short run is consistent with profit maximization in the long run. A third argument, which is relevant to our discussion, suggests that a scale maximization behaviour is built into the internal organizational structure of banks (Kitagawa and Kurosawa, 1990).

Banks may be geared to increase their scale of operations to exploit economies of scale and to reduce default risks of their loan portfolios. In all three countries, bank executives and managers tend to believe that their social status varies with the size of their banks. The larger scale also generates more jobs for the management, in particular more future opportunities for middle managers. Finally, it may be also true that the public believe that the larger a bank, the safer it is. Banks may also generate network externalities to their depositors and borrowers. These externalities are likely to increase with the increase in the scale of bank operations.

Another unique feature of banking in East Asian countries (also in Germany) is that financial intermediation is a device for establishing a long-term relationship between borrowers and lenders (Mayer, 1988, and Hellwig, 1990). Suppose long-term relationships between borrowers and lenders are valuable; there are reasons to believe this is true. In a competitive financial environment, however, such relationships may not develop because of the problem of time-inconsistency. *Ex ante*, a long-term relationship is desirable, but *ex post*, the borrower or the lender has the incentive to renege. Since both the lender and borrower are aware of this incentive problem, such a relationship never develops in the first place. Why can commitment to a long-term relationship be established through contractual arrangements? How does the bank overcome the incentive problem and help develop such long-term relationships? Mayer (1988) and Hellwig (1990) emphasize the difficulty of writing a complete and binding contract covering all future actions and outcomes for a longer period of time. Given this limitation, financial intermediaries could mitigate the time-inconsistency incentive problem as they have the advantage of having more information about their clients than outside financiers. This information advantage suggests that exclusive financing of a firm by one financier could reduce possible conflicts between financiers.

Following this line of reasoning, it is possible to argue that competition in financial markets may undermine the ability of the firm to commit itself to the bank and the bank to the firm (Mayer, 1988). Why do we need the bank as an exclusive financier in Mayer's framework? It is because when outside capital is diffuse, exclusive financing is possible and efficient through intermediation.

Why are the financial systems in Korea and Taiwan heavily repressed? Some of the failures of financial markets explain the need for the control – or prudent regulation – in part. Governments in Korea and Taiwan have also intervened extensively in the allocation of credit, in the apparent belief that without such intervention credit allocation would not reflect social and economic priorities often set by the governments themselves. In general, when a government assumes the role of the leading sector in economic development, it is only natural that it represses the financial system by controlling interest rates and the management of financial intermediaries so as to dictate the allocation of financial resources in the desired direction. Therefore, the overriding reason for government intervention in finance in Korea and Taiwan has been the pursuit of an industrial policy in which exports of manufactures have been promoted. Financial markets and institutions have been used as instruments to support such a policy.

Efficiency and equity are not the only considerations that lead to government intervention in credit allocation in Korea and Taiwan. Markets for labour, foreign exchange and commodities are also subject to a variety of imperfections and are often as heavily regulated as financial markets. The imperfection in, and control of, other markets often mandate alternative allocations of resources and consequently invite government intervention in credit allocation.

5   Consequences of a repressive financial regime

Financial liberalization since the turn of the 1980s in Korea and Taiwan has been uneven, intermittent and piecemeal. In the case of Korea, it has often relapsed into reregulation. Nevertheless, there is no denying that since the early 1980s the financial environment has become relatively freer, with less government control over financial markets and institutions than in the past. Have financial reforms indeed led to rapid financial growth in the two economies as the 1989 World Bank survey of finance claims? Our empirical work, though limited in scope shows no evidence that high real interest rates are positively correlated with high propensities to save. The expansion of the financial sector has increased the proportion of investment resources allocated through financial markets and institutions. Once again, there is no convincing evidence that this increased allocation capacity has led to any increase in the average productivity of investment.

Our conclusion is that the rapid financial growth Korea and Taiwan have experienced in the 1980s should be explained by high rates of growth of the economy, the rising propensity to save, and stable prices. The causality has run from changes in the real to the financial sector, not the other way around. To substantiate this point, we will first argue in terms of the experiences of Taiwan and Korea that differences in the structure of industrial organization primarily explain the differences in financial structure, not vice versa, at least in these two economies. We will then argue that efficiency of export-led development strategy has been responsible for minimizing allocative inefficiencies of the financial system. This may have been true regardless of whether financial inefficiencies originated in government or financial market failure.

5.1   Industrial organization and financial structure

According to a recent study by Biggs (1988b), Taiwan had almost 115,000 firms in 1986, 98 per cent of which had fewer than 300 employees and 48 per cent of which fewer than 5 workers. This small enterprise dominance has been the same since the early 1960s. Not surprisingly, these small and medium-sized firms have produced almost 50 per cent of manufacturing value added. Most of these small and medium-sized firms are family-owned and independent enterprises. In sharp contrast, in Korea the 30 largest industrial groups, the majority of which are also controlled by families, have produced almost 40 per cent of manufacturing value added in recent years.[11]

Although Taiwanese small and medium-sized firms produced a large share of manufacturing value added in the 1960s and 1970s, they were getting a disproportionately small share of bank loans, only about 20–25 per cent on average. Since then the Taiwanese banks have become much more accommodating than before the credit needs of small and medium-sized enterprises with the massive increase in their liquidity. Yet, even in 1987, more than 90 per cent of firms interviewed indicated that they could not get bank credit to enter business (Biggs, 1988b).

The large commercial and specialized banks in Taiwan directed their loans to large public and private enterprises, which in turn became de facto intermediaries, on-lending to smaller firms – many subcontractors and suppliers. Because of high transactions and information costs of processing a large number of small-sized and information-intensive loans, these large banks have no advantage in making small loans and have traditionally discriminated against small- and medium-sized firms. The Taiwan government could have created a host of institutions designed to serve the credit needs of small borrowers. Instead, it has left most of these borrowers to be served by a variety of unregulated financial institutions and markets that include financial instalment companies, leasing firms, financial investment companies and credit unions. Realizing the valuable services of the informal financial system, the Taiwan authorities have allowed the unfettered development of an active curb market to complement the role of regulated financial institutions (Shea, 1990, and Biggs, 1988).

The Taiwanese experience with financial development demonstrates that in an economy characterized by the predominance of small and medium-sized enterprises, the majority of borrowers would require financial resources for relatively short-term periods distributed in small blocks. In a competitive unregulated environment, this would be conducive to the development of atomistic money and capital markets, consisting of many small-sized and specialized financial institutions.

In Korea the financial sector is dominated by a relatively small number of large financial institutions both in the banking and NBFI sector. Despite the doubling of the number of nationwide commercial banks in the 1980s, the five large nationwide commercial banks still control an oligopolistic market structure. Among NBFIs, ten large investment finance companies, three large investment trust companies, and six large insurance companies exercise the controlling influence on non-banking financial intermediation. Korea's large industrial groups are also majority shareholders of NBFIs and securities firms and could easily control the management of the five largest nationwide commercial banks if the equity ownership restriction were removed. The structure of banking and non-banking financial intermediation together with the pattern of ownership of financial institutions corresponds very closely to the pattern of distribution of economic power, that is, the concentration of industrial power in the large industrial conglomerates.

Although the industrial groups are barred or restricted from exercising their voting rights, they have not been above abusing their influence. Not surprisingly, these groups are the largest borrowers at commercial banks and NBFIs. Although it is difficult to document any evidence, a large number of Korea's small and medium-sized firms belonging to the subcontracting network developed by or affiliated to the large groups appear to obtain finance from or through these groups.

As in Taiwan, there exists an informal financial sector in Korea. This sector accounted for a very large share of total finance until the early years of the 1970s. Since then, the Korean financial authorities, unlike their counterparts in Taiwan, have taken an active policy of integrating the informal with the formal and organized financial system with considerable success. In our view such a policy has been successful largely because underlying industrial structure – a high degree of industrial concentration – is conducive to financial concentration even in an unregulated environment.

In the early 1960s when the export-led development strategy was launched, efficiency of export industries in many cases required adoption of increasing returns technologies. This constraint conflicted with Korea's limited availability of domestic and foreign resources and forced support of one or at most two large producers in the industries promoted for exports. Since there was no market mechanism of choosing and concentrating resources in these potential monopolies and duopolies, it was perhaps natural for the government to assume the task. The banking system was used to channel domestic and foreign savings to these large firms and as a de facto partner, the government was drawn to participate in their business decisions. During the 1960s these large firms became successful exporters and with the growth of the economy also developed into industrial groups, dominating the manufacturing sector.

The concentration of economic power in the hands of a few industrial conglomerates has been the most important constraint on financial liberalization in Korea. Despite the continuing efforts to bring about a more balanced dispersion of economic power, these large groups have been able to maintain their relative share in total value added of the economy. What types of financial structure would be most efficient in meeting the financial needs of these conglomerates? It would not be a system which consists of atomistic money and capital markets, but one that is dominated by a small number of large financial institutions, as in Korea. Korea's industrial policy has been largely responsible for its industrial concentration, and the financial sector has adjusted itself to the structure of industrial organization and its changes.

5.2   *Export promotion and financial efficiency*

Given the propensity of financial markets to failure, it is not correct to argue that a liberal financial regime is likely to be more efficient in resource allocation than a repressive and closed system. However, it would also be presumptuous to argue that the Korean and Taiwanese governments have been so efficient and effective that they have been able to correct financial market failures through intervention while not committing government failures.

What have then been the consequences of a repressive financial regime in Korea and Taiwan? It will be argued that financial systems of the two economies have been able to avoid much of the inefficiency cost associated with government intervention and in this limited sense have been efficient or neutral in their effects on resource allocation, as they have been directed to support an export-led development strategy, which proved to be superior to an import substitution strategy. It will also be argued that government intervention in finance may have neutralized some of the adverse effects of financial market failures in Korea and Taiwan.

Exporters in the two countries have always been most favoured borrowers at financial institutions. At an early stage of export promotion, they were accorded an automatic short-term credit facility at a subsidized interest rate which tied the amount of short-term credit extended directly to export earnings and did not require any collateral and domestic value-added content. Successful exporters have had easier access to other types of bank credits as well and to many small and medium-sized firms, engaging in export and export-related activities has been the easiest way of gaining access to bank credits. There is little doubt that the financial systems in Korea and Taiwan have been geared to support the governments' export-promotion policies and allocated the bulk of resources to export-oriented industries (Park, 1990, and Shea, 1990).[12]

Export-producing firms must compete against foreign producers in the international market place. This necessity makes the firms more efficient than otherwise. In a credit-rationed economy, firms' success and survival critically depends on their access to bank credits. Korean and Taiwanese exporters were no exceptions to this reality and had to generate export earnings as soon as possible when they began production, and hence had to be cost efficient. Under the export-promotion strategy of Korea and Taiwan, foreign competition has functioned as a constraint on economic behaviour of both firms and policy-makers and provided feedback to them as to the success or failure of policies in terms of their objective.[13] Therefore, largely because of the relative efficiency of the export-led development strategy in resource allocation, the repressive financial system, which has been passive and oriented to support the export-oriented industries, many have been able to minimize the adverse effects of government intervention in finance.

Does Korean and Taiwanese experience provide any credible evidence that government intervention in finance has contributed to correcting financial market failures that could have presented serious obstacles to the promotion of export-led development? To respond to this question, it would be convenient to ask whether a market-oriented financial system could have supported export-promotion policy as well as a repressive system in Korea and Taiwan. It may not have for a number of reasons.[14]

Some of the reasons are well known and do not require any further discussion. In order to remain competitive and to cultivate new foreign markets, exporters often bear large costs of gathering and processing information, product advertisement, and other marketing activities. Learning and acquiring foreign technology and developing indigenous technology are vital to the very survival of many exporters. Investment in these activities generates signifciant externalities and is subject to economies of scale and scope in that it could reduce costs for new entrants in export-oriented industries. Since the returns to these types of investment are largely inappropriable, free market financing arrangements may not result in an optimum level of investment in these activities.[15]

It is shown that a coordinated investment programme across sectors could lead to the expansion of markets in all sectors and hence can be self-sustaining, whereas investing alone no firm can make profits because of the presence of profit spillovers across sectors (Murphy *et al.*, 1989). This big-push argument suggests that developing economies could achieve industrialization of each sector by implementing a coordinated investment programme at a lower cost in terms of tariffs and subsidies than when undertaking piecemeal industrialization.[16] Since the rates of return to investment are likely to differ from sector to sector at an early stage of industrialization, it is highly unlikely that a deregulated financial system could support such a coordinated investment programme without government intervention.

There are two characteristics of financial markets that are likely to frustrate the effective implementation of an export-led development strategy in the absence of government control of finance. One characteristic is that the speed of adjustment in financial markets is much faster than that in the product or labour markets. Another is that financial asset prices fluctuate much more than what is warranted by changes in fundamentals as they respond to changes in investor sentiment and to news.[17] The combination of these two characteristics makes returns on assets riskier and hence raises the cost of financing. These features also make it difficult to predict with any degree of accuracy the cost and availability of finance in the future.

New information and developments which may have little relevance to fundamentals could move prices of certain stocks and change credit ratings and availability for individual producers in an indiscriminate and unpredictable manner. This volatility problem could be more serious to those producers specializing in export production. In addition to domestic news and events, exporters will have to bear the costs of financial market volatility the causes of which are developments and new events in foreign markets that are harder for domestic financial markets to assess accurately than those of domestic origins. The high speed of adjustment and price volatility could then discourage physical investment, shorten expectation horizons of firms, and bias the choice of investment projects against long-term ones, in particular those for developing new products and technology.

Investment in export-oriented industries may be subject to a higher degree of risk than in domestic market-oriented sectors largely because of the lack of information about the foreign demand for export products. Unable to assess accurately, and responding instantaneously in an irrational manner to foreign news and information, domestic financial markets could amplify the risks involved in exportation. Volatile movements in stock prices and their effects on bond markets in Korea and Taiwan in recent years demonstrate how serious the bubble problem could be when a system with many narrow and shallow financial markets is deregulated (Shea, 1990, and Park, 1990).

In transiting from a repressive to a liberal financial regime, one often encounters the virtual disappearance of long-term finance, as shown by the Southern Cone experience (Diaz-Alejandro, 1985). This problem appears to be more acute in an unstable environment with a high rate of inflation. When market-determined interest rates are high and volatile, commercial banks – the traditional asset transformers – tend to match the maturities of their assets and liabilities and become more like information brokers.

Household savers become more sensitive to change in interest rates and more receptive to new financial assets that are liquid and yield higher rates of return than existing ones when prices are expected to rise continuously. Commercial banks lend at the short end of the market as long as they borrow at that end and often securitize their credit obligations to minimize the interest-rate risk. One advantage of the repressive financial system in Korea, and to a lesser degree in Taiwan, may have been its ability to supply long-term finance. This advantage was more critical at the early stage of export promotion.

Commercial banks can and do in fact transform assets and maintain mismatched balance sheets. However, the informational asymmetries, political and social unrest, and more and higher risks Korean and Taiwanese firms were exposed to as exporters during the earlier periods of export promotion would have made the risks of extending long-term loans unbearably high to banks and NBFIs. Without government intervention, profit-oriented behaviour of the commercial banks and NBFIs would have resulted in a dearth of long-term finance.

Due largely to information problems, the rate of return on investment in export-oriented industries, ceteris paribus, could be lower than that on a similar investment oriented to the domestic market. How efficiently would financial markets and institutions in a laissez-faire financial environment assess the risks in selling to foreign markets and shift them efficiently to ultimate lenders? Other things being equal, would not they favour domestic market-oriented producers and their investment? In Korea, the heavily regulated financial system has been utilized to absorb these export-related risks by providing subsidized credits and foreign loan guarantees and then to disperse them as widely as possible throughout the economy.

This risk-absorption and dispersion by financial institutions raised the effective rate of return on investment in export-oriented industries.

Together with the availability of long-term finance, this feature of the financial system provided strong incentives to exporters. The costs of absorbing the risks were extremely high in some cases, as demonstrated by the costs of industrial restructuring in the 1980s in Korea. In other cases the costs have been manageable and been paid for by seigniorage, and by withholding dividend payments to bank stockholders. The Korean government could have chosen a different system for risk-absorption and dispersion, but the use of the banking system has been least objectionable to the public and hence politically expedient.

6   Concluding remarks

In Korea and Taiwan, financial deregulation in the 1980s, though somewhat limited in scope, has contributed to strengthening competitive forces in financial markets. New financial and communications technology has greatly reduced the costs of collecting and processing information. Despite these developments, it has been difficult to identify any significant changes in the behaviour of financial institutions and markets that may indicate their attempts to adjust to changing financial environment. There has been no discernible change in the relationships between the government and financial institutions.

There is no evidence that financial growth, whether its source is financial reforms or output growth, has exerted any positive effects on saving or been associated with a higher average productivity of investment. Rapid growth in the financial sector has been the result of the high rate of growth of the economy, the rising propensity to save and stable prices. The discussion in Section 5 also suggests rather that finance has adjusted in a passive manner to changes in the real sector in Korea and Taiwan. Does this mean that finance does not matter? It does not; in market-oriented economies, the financial system plays a vital role. What our analysis suggests is that investment in building the financial infrastructure beyond a certain level may not be as productive as it is often claimed to be.

Some may also argue that it is too early to detect any effects of financial liberalization in the two economies. Others may claim that financial reforms in the two economics have been so uneven and protracted that our conclusions are hardly surprising. While these views are not disputed, our discussion also casts serious doubts as to whether further deregulation could make any significant contribution to sustaining rapid growth and stability in either Korea or Taiwan.

NOTES

The author is grateful to Susan Collins, Alberto Giovannini and Helmut Reisen for their helpful comments on an earlier draft.

1 An economy is said to be financially repressed if governments tax or otherwise distort their domestic capital markets by imposing usury restrictions on interest rates, heavy reserve requirements on bank deposits, and compulsory credit allocations (McKinnon, 1991, pp. 11).

2 A recent OECD study (1990) shows that with reduced liquidity constraints, private consumption has become less sensitive to changes in transitory income in the US, Canada and Japan. The same study also observes an inverse correlation between household borrowing and saving ratios, among OECD countries from early to mid-1980s.

3 According to Nam's specification, the desired household consumption to disposable income, (C/Y) has the following functional form:

$$C/Y = C\{(Y, Y^2), FA/Y, r, DEM/SSI\},$$

where FA is financial asset holdings, and DEM/SSI refers to demographic factors, social security and insurance programmes.

4 Gelb (1989) shows that higher real deposit rates of interest contribute to GNP growth through increased investment efficiency measured by the incremental output-capital ratio rather than through an increased saving (investment)-GNP ratio in his cross-section study of 34 countries.

5 See Stiglitz (1991) for references.

6 The cost of borrowing is approximated by total interest and other costs divided by total borrowings. The data are from the Bank of Korea's *Financial Statements Analysis*.

7 Because of the unavailability of data, we could not conduct a similar test for Taiwan.

8 As Friedman and Schwartz (1986) point out, however, it is an open question whether a complete deregulation of banking is desirable, or feasible, without government restrictions on banking activities.

9 For the literature on information imperfection and financial market failures, see Stiglitz (1991).

10 Since the early 1970s, the Japanese monetary authorities have encouraged mergers among smaller financial intermediaries such as credit cooperatives to take advantage of scale economies. A similar policy of creating a banking industry with a small number of large banks has been suggested in both Korea and Taiwan.

11 See Park (1990) for the cause of different industrial organizational structures in the two economies.

12 The export financing system was unique in that export credit incentives did not discriminate between activities and exporters and were determined contingent on export performance, which resulted in greater conformity in incentives, and also provided a test in foreign markets for potential recipients of subsidized credit. The market test feature also made more apparent to the policy-makers the cost of credit allocation to different industries and activities and allowed them to reallocate resources whenever the costs became excessive.

13 See Krueger (1980, 1981, 1985) for the relative efficiency of an export promoting regime to that of an import substitution regime.

148 Yung Chul Park

14 Citing the development experience of Hong Kong and Singapore, one may
   argue that a free market system could promote exports as efficiently as the
   interventionist regimes of Korea and Taiwan. We do not address this issue.
   Instead, we are examining whether a particular type of industrial policy –
   export promotion in our discussion – can be consistent with market-oriented
   finance.
15 Westphal (1990) argues that the state intervention through credit rationing
   and import quotas may not be the appropriate means to ensure the realization
   of the latent externalities unless it is combined with state actions to compel
   warranted investment in these activities.
16 Murphy *et al.* (1989) cite the Korean experience as a successful example of
   such a strategy.
17 As Shiller (1981, 1990), Stiglitz (1990) and Shleifer and Summers (1990) have
   shown, the variability of interest rates and stock prices could be excessive,
   given the flow of underlying information which markets are deemed to consider relevant. If asset prices do not reflect fundamentals, then one could make
   a persuasive case that the market determination of financial asset prices does
   not necessarily increase the allocative efficiency of the economy. Although this
   does not mean that the government can replace the price mechanism, nevertheless the excessive volatility of asset prices that has often little to do with
   changes in the real sector of the economy may make the monetary authorities
   less receptive to the idea of complete interest deregulation.

REFERENCES

Biggs, Tyler S. (1988a) 'Financing the Emergence of Small and Medium Enter-
    prise in Taiwan: Financial Mobilization and the Flow of Domestic Credit to
    the Private Sector, Efficiency Intermediation', EEPA Discussion Paper No. 15.
    (1988b) 'Financing the Emergence of Small and Medium Enterprise in Taiwan:
    Heterogeneous Firm Size and Efficiency Intermediation', EEPA Discussion
    Paper No. 16.
Cho, Yoon Je (1988) 'The Effect of Financial Liberalization on the Efficiency of
    Credit Allocation: Some Evidence from Korea', *Journal of Development
    Economics* **29**, 101–10.
Diaz-Alejandro, C.F. (1985) 'Good-bye Financial Repression, Hello Financial
    Crash', *Journal of Development Economics* **19**, 1–24.
Dornbusch, R. and A. Reynoso (1989) 'Financial Factors in Economic Develop-
    ment', *American Economic Review, Papers and Proceedings* **79**, 204–09.
Friedman, B.M. (1985) 'Monetary and Regulatory Policies for Developing Finan-
    cial Systems', in *Monetary Policy in a Changing Financial Environment*, The
    Bank of Korea.
Friedman, M. and A.J. Schwartz (1986) 'Has Government Any Role in Money',
    Journal of Monetary Economics **17**, 37–62.
Gelb, Alan H. (1989) 'Financial Policies, Growth and Efficiency', World Bank
    Working Paper, Country Economics Department, No. WP5202, Washington,
    D.C.
Hellwig, Martin F. (1990) 'Banking, Financial Intermediation and Corporate
    Finance', in A. Giovannini and C. Mayer (eds.), *Financial Integration*, Cam-
    bridge: Cambridge University Press.

Horiuchi, M. and A. Otaki (1987) 'Kinyu – Seifu Kinyu to Ginko Kashidashi no Juyosei (Finance, Government Lending and the Importance of Bank Loans)', in K. Hamada, M. Kuroda and A. Horiuchi (eds.), *Nihonkeisai no Macro Bunseki*, Tokyo, Todai-Shuppamkai.

Kitagawa, H. and Kurosawa, Y. (1990) 'The Behavior and Efficiency of Financial Institutions in Japan', presented to conference on 'Financial Development in Japan, Korea and Taiwan', Taipeh, ROC.

Krueger, Anne O. (1980) 'Trade Policy as an Input to Development', *American Economic Review, Papers and Proceedings* **70**, 288–92.

—— (1981) 'Export-Led Industrial Growth Reconsidered', in L. Krause and W.T. Hong (eds.), *Trade and Growth of the Advanced Developing Countries in the Pacific Basin*, Korea Development Institute, Seoul, Korea.

—— (1985) 'The Experience and Lessons of Asia's Super Exporters', in Vittorio Corbo, Anne O. Krueger and Frenando Ossa (eds.), *Export-Oriented Development Strategies*, Boulder and London: Westview Press.

Lin Yuan-Hsin (1989) 'On Methods of Compiling Price Indices for Real Estate', *Journal of National Chengchi University* (in Chinese).

Mayer, Colin (1988) 'New Issues in Corporate Finance', *European Economic Review* **32**, 1167–89.

McKinnon, R. (1973) *Money and Capital in Economic Development*, Washington: Brookings Institution.

—— (1991) *The Order of Economic Liberalization, Financial Control in the Transition to a Market Economy*, Baltimore and London: The Johns Hopkins University Press.

Murphy, K.M., A. Shleifer and R.W. Vishny (1989) 'Industrialization and the Big Push', *Journal of Political Economy* **97**, 1003–26.

Nam, S.W. (1988) 'The Determinants of National Saving in Korea – A Sectoral Accounting Approach', Korea Development Institute Working Paper No. 8821.

OECD (1990) *Macroeconomic Consequences of Financial Liberalization*, Paris.

Park, Yung Chul (1990a) 'Growth, Liberalization, and Internationalization of Korea's Financial Sector', presented to conference on 'Financial Development in Japan, Korea and Taiwan', Taipeh, ROC.

—— (1990b) 'Development Lessons from Asia: The Role of Government in South Korea and Taiwan', *American Economic Review, Papers and Proceedings* **80**, 118–21.

Park, Yung Chul and Dong Won Kim (1990) 'The Behavior and Efficiency of Commercial Banks in Korea', presented to conference on 'Financial Development in Japan, Korea and Taiwan', Taipeh, ROC.

Shleifer, A. and L.H. Summers (1990) 'The Noise Trader Approach to Finance', *Journal of Economic Perspectives* **4**, 19–33.

Shaw, E.S. (1973) *Financial Deepening in Economic Development*, New York: Oxford University Press.

Shea, Jia-Dong (1990) 'Financial Development in Taiwan: A Macro Analysis' presented to conference on 'Financial Development in Japan, Korea and Taiwan', Taipeh, ROC.

Shiller, R.J. (1981) 'Do Stock Price Move Too Much to be Justified by Subsequent Changes in Dividends'?, *American Economic Review* **71**, 421–36.

—— (1990) 'Speculative Prices and Popular Models', *Journal of Economic Perspectives* **4**, 55–65.

Stiglitz, J.E. (1990) 'Symposium on Bubbles', *Journal of Economic Perspectives* 4, 13–18.
   (1991) 'Government, Financial Markets, and Economic Development', NBER Working Paper No. 3669.
Westphal, L. (1990) 'Industrial Policy in an Export-Propelled Economy: Lessons from South Korea's Experience', *Journal of Economic Perspectives* 4, 41–59.
World Bank (1989) *World Development Report 1989*, Oxford University Press.
Wu De-Hsien (1989) 'A Study of Business Cycles in the Construction Industry and the Environment of Housing Supply', Ph.D. Dissertation.
Yang, Ya-Hwei (1990) 'A Micro Analysis of the Financial System in Taiwan', presented to conference on 'Financial Development in Japan, Korea and Taiwan', Taipeh, ROC.

Discussion

SUSAN M. COLLINS

Both (South) Korea and Taiwan present something of a puzzle to analyses of the financial markets and economic development. Despite relatively closed financial markets and pervasive government intervention in financial institutions, both countries are examples of successful economic development. They have achieved high and persistent rates of growth and domestic saving, international competitiveness and increasing industrial diversification.

Yung Chul Park's paper tackles many of the issues involved in reconciling this combination. It provides a useful and interesting summary of some of the key features of the financial systems in the two countries. (The discussion of attitudes towards banking and finance in Korea gives an especially stimulating perspective on developments in that country.) Much of the paper focuses on links between government intervention, financial systems, saving, credit allocation and export orientation. These pieces help to shed light on the question of why the government intervention was not inconsistent with successful performance. Overall, the paper is interesting, provocative and goes a long way toward explaining the 'puzzle'.

The paper covers a lot of ground. The rest of my comments will focus on four of the many points it contains. It is helpful to begin by summarizing them – not necessarily in the order they are made in the paper and in some cases with my own emphasis:

(1) The Korean and Taiwanese governments viewed their countries' financial systems primarily as a tool for helping to achieve their export-led growth strategies. This led to active intervention, including direct allocation of credit for approved projects.

(2) The export focus of government activities minimized the distortions caused by pervasive government intervention.

(3) Both countries have high saving rates and high rates of return to fixed capital formation. It is unclear whether financial market deregulation or growth of financial markets has contributed substantially to either of these two outcomes.

(4) In fact, government intervention is likely to be preferable to free markets – because of inherent market failures – for two reasons. The government encouraged (a) long-term relationships between borrowers and lenders and long-term loans and (b) loans to exporters; both of which free markets were likely to discourage.

I agree quite strongly with the first two points but have mixed reactions to the next two points. These reactions are discussed below.

The first point is made implicitly in the paper. In my view, it warrants much stronger emphasis. For example it is interesting to contrast these governments perceptions of financial markets with typical perceptions elsewhere. Unlike many other developing (and developed) countries, banks were *not* seen as the central means to finance budget deficits (and negative government saving). Similarly, there has been little push to develop private bond markets. The implication of this view is that financial flows were to be channelled to the private sector. There is also an interesting contrast with Hong Kong and Singapore, where internationally competitive financial institutions were seen as a source of economic growth and employment. Opening up to international competition has only recently become an issue in Korea and Taiwan.

There is a second reason to emphasize the view that financial markets were a tool to achieve export led growth: the implications for the government's role as lender of last resort. In both Korea and Taiwan this has meant that loans were typically extended under Ministry of Finance direction, making it difficult to hold banks responsible when loans went bad.

I also agree with Park's argument that the government's emphasis on export performance helped to minimize the distortions from government intervention. This is a major part of the explanation to the puzzle about why intervention went hand in hand with economic growth. In an environment with extensive domestic government interference, international competitiveness can act as a relatively efficient screen for the allocation of credit. (Note that it will not provide equal access to activities that are nontraded, such as the provision of certain types of services.)

However, I believe that the export focus is only part of the resolution to the puzzle. It would have been interesting for the paper to discuss other characteristics of the government interventions in Korean and Taiwanese financial markets that may help to resolve the puzzle. For example, these countries' experiences suggest that direct credit allocations – at low interest rates – to high expected return activities is preferable to simply setting a low interest rate ceiling. In the latter, banks may choose between the many potential lenders through bribes or nepotism. There is no presumption that the allocation mechanism will foster growth.

The third point is about the relationship between financial market development on the one hand and saving and investment performance on the other. On the saving side, I think we reach the same conclusion. There is at best weak evidence that financial market deregulation – in particular, raising domestic interest rates – contributed to the strong domestic saving. (Some studies find no role for interest rates; others find a small but positive role.) In fact, despite Korea's widely acclaimed interest rate reform in the mid-1960s, real deposit rates were negative during part of the 1970s. As Park states, the most important factor in explaining the rise in saving appears to be the rapid growth in real household incomes. Some of my own work points to relatively sluggish response of consumption behaviour to rising current (and expected permanent) incomes.

On the investment side, Park asks whether financial 'liberalization' in the 1980s raised growth by improving the allocative efficiency of financial markets. I found this discussion provocative, but unsatisfying, and would be very interested in the results of further analysis. 'Liberalization' is measured by a proxy for financial deepening (F): corporate bonds and long-term borrowing as a share of total assets. (Given the lack of liberalization during 1980–88, the question should be rephrased in terms of access to external financing for firms in different sectors of the economy.) As part of the discussion, it would have been helpful and interesting to know how this indicator has behaved. Has F risen and converged for most sectors during the 1980s? Or has financial deepening been concentrated within a few sub-sectors of manufacturing? In addition, if the null hypothesis is that an improved *allocation* of credit has raised growth, simply including a measure of the *amount* of financing is not enough. Instead, F could be entered interactively with some indicator of improved allocation, such as the variance of borrowing costs across sectors. Further analyses of the relationships between the availability and allocation of financing for investment and economic growth may provide very interesting lessons.

There is another puzzle about saving and investment that Park does not address. Unlike the Korean experience, in which both saving and investment rose to more than 30 per cent of GDP, and remained strong in the last half of the 1980s, investment in Taiwan fell sharply, from more than 30 per cent of GDP to just 16–17 per cent in the mid-1980s. It would be interesting to explore whether financial sector repression has played any role in this development.

The final point that I will discuss from the paper is that market failures in a laissez faire regime can mean that financial markets perform more poorly without government intervention than they do with government intervention. I certainly agree with the overall point. It is difficult to see how, with diferent financial institutions, either country could have had better overall economic performance, or faster export growth. I would add another argument for why government intervention in the early stages of Korean and Taiwanese development might have facilitated export growth relative to free financial markets that might view exports as especially risky. The government had additional information about, and control over, export viability because it could adjust the exchange rate. However, it becomes increasingly difficult to see why government intervention was needed to support exporters during the 1970s and the 1980s. More generally, one omission in Park's discussion is that it does not adequately distinguish between the role for government intervention during the early stages of development, and its role more recently. In my view, many of the very persuasive arguments for government intervention used historically have become less and less convincing as these countries have developed. Korea in particular promises to continue to provide interesting lessons about the role for government intervention at various stages of development.

HELMUT REISEN

What can be learned from Korea and Taiwan's approach to finance and development? While Yung Chul Park's thoughtful and provocative paper does not directly answer that question, he equips us with several elements to do so.

Both Korea and Taiwan have achieved extraordinarily high GNP growth, and promotion of industry and exports has been the key to growth. In both countries the financial system has been based on indirect finance and thus on banks, and their financial system has been (and still is) quite remarkably repressed and insulated. In particular, the government has actively intervened in credit allocation, and credit policies have been a major instrument of industrial policy. The combination of successful economic performance and active government credit allocation is a provocation, likewise for McKinnon and Shaw as for the *Financial Times*. According to McKinnon and Shaw, financial repression (defined as distortion of financial prices) reduces both the size of the financial system relative to non-financial magnitudes and the real rate of growth. According to the *Financial Times*, Korea and Taiwan's financial system is simply backward, and that should from now on at least retard further growth, if it did not do so already in the past. According to Yung Chul Park now, financial repression and closedness in Korea and Taiwan have at least not interfered with growth and industrialization, and building the financial infrastructure beyond a certain level may not be as productive as it is often claimed to be. What can Eastern Europe learn from all this?

When judging the contribution of a financial system to overall growth performance, it is helpful to distinguish three concepts of efficiency: operational efficiency, allocative efficiency, and macroeconomic efficiency.

- When the *Financial Times* is talking about the backwardness of Korea's financial system, it is probably talking about operational inefficiency. Real resource costs of providing financial services and the interest or fee margin between savers and investors are excessive if a financial system is operationally inefficient. Let us take that for granted in the case of Korea and Taiwan.
- What about allocative efficiency? Let us define this as the degree to which resources flow, through the financing process, to the most productive investments. And, giving the concept an intertemporal dimension, let us define allocative efficiency as the degree to which the financial system mobilises savings today for consumption tomorrow.
- Finally, macroeconomic efficiency. For our purposes, let me define this as the degree to which the financial system helps to transmit monetary policy to the real economy, to target monetary aggregates and the real exchange rate simultaneously, and to avoid macroeconomic instability.

Reisen and Yèches (1991) have recently produced a time-varying parameter estimation of the Edwards-Khan model of interest determination in semi-open economies. Their findings indicate a low degree of capital mobility for both Korea and Taiwan, and no trend over the 1980s towards more financial openness (except recently in Taiwan's interbank market). Therefore, capital controls and domestic regulations seem until now to have equipped the authorities in both Korea and Taiwan with considerable scope for an independent short-term monetary policy.

As for allocative efficiency, Eastern Europe can perhaps learn more from Korea's experience during the period mid-1960s to end-1970s than from the 1980s, which Park emphasizes in this paper. The 1960s have been qualified as a great success, the 1970s as a failure. In all subperiods, as Park emphasizes, the overriding reason for government intervention in finance has been the pursuit of industrial policy and export promotion.

In the early 1950s and early 1960s, the financial system was quite heavily repressed, with low deposit rates in the nationalized banking system, and an active curb market. When the government raised bank interest rates substantially in 1965, the banking system expanded rapidly. Interest reform therefore shifted assets from the unregulated curb market to areas under government control. The switch from severe to mild repression thus equipped the government with plenty of domestic resources to run an effective credit policy. By authorising every foreign loan (which interest reform had made cheaper than domestic borrowing), the government also commanded influence on the allocation of foreign resources.

During the same period, problems of adverse selection, moral hazard and rent-seeking, that have bedeviled the credit policies of many other countries, were largely avoided in Korea. I collect several explanations for this (especially in Cho, 1989, and in Vittas and Wang, 1991). First, Korean credit policy was not industry-specific, but was oriented towards exports and industrial development. Second, the government exercised discipline over credit subsidy recipients by imposing strict performance standards (output and export performance in exchange for subsidies); firms that failed to meet performance standards were denied further credit. Third, industrial policy encouraged entrants with minimum equity stakes and stimulated competition by allowing them access to credit; this left firms highly leveraged and thus vulnerable to the reduction of government credit.

It seems to me then that government intervention at that time was successful in overcoming financial market imperfections originating from poor information flows and inadequately developed institutions and markets:

– Banks were forced to assume the downside risk of investment in industry. This raised the expected return of industrial firms. In Korea, credit to industry as a fraction of GNP was higher than elsewhere, while finance for consumption and services was restricted.

– In the absence of direct securities markets at that time, government interference provided risk-sharing which banks would have been unlikely to provide. Banks are averse to lend to risky ventures and they emphasize current profitability, rather than output and export performance as the government did.

It is difficult to conceive, therefore, that at the early stage of Korea's development, a market-based financial system would have done better.

As countries move up in the hierarchy of the international product cycle, it becomes more difficult for the government to pick winners. For Korea, the 1970s mirror these difficulties, when the HCI drive led the country into HIC status (HCI stands for heavy and chemical industries, HIC for highly indebted country). Investment in heavy and chemical industries carried long gestation periods and uncertain returns, hence Korean business was reluctant to invest in HCI unless the government provided strong incentives. Government credit policy turned industry-specific, and triggering the risk of bankruptcies, it also turned size-specific. Since large corporate borrowers were not allowed to go bust, distress borrowing and moral hazard prevailed in the 1970s. There was also adverse selection now as the unsupported sector was forced to borrow at very high rates on the informal market: the dual structure of the credit system created an imbalanced industrial structure. The banking system was saddled with nonperforming loans, requiring depressed deposit rates for banks' survival, which in turn lowered domestic savings and stimulated foreign borrowing.

The synthesis of these observations is that government interference in the financial system to support industrial policy can be successful under certain conditions. These conditions are:

– keep government finance strong enough to obviate the need for severe financial repression;
– build well-functioning bureaucracies and information systems for effective monitoring;
– keep credit and industrial policy in line with world prices and aim for international competitiveness in not too distant a future;
– keep credit and industrial policy general and access to finance contestable enough to avoid moral hazard and adverse selection, but give incentives for industry and exports to avoid diversion of subsidised credit into speculative assets.

Note that some of these conditions – macro stability, good information systems, effective monitoring – are quite the same for the smooth operation of market-based financial systems. This coincidence obviates to a certain extent Park's nagging question whether observed inefficiencies in the Korea of the 1980s are due to government interference or due to failures of a liberalized financial system.

REFERENCES

Cho, Yoon Je (1989) 'Finance and Development: The Korean Approach', *Oxford Review of Economic Policy* **5**, 88–102.

Reisen, Helmut and Hélène Yèches (1991) 'Time-Varying Estimates on the Openness of the Capital Account in Korea and Taiwan', OECD Development Centre Technical Papers No. 42, forthcoming in *Journal of Development Economics*.

Vittas, Dmitri and Bo Wang (1991) 'Credit Policy in Japan and Korea: a Review of the Literature', World Bank Working Paper Series No. 747.

7 Finance and development: the case of Southern Italy

RICCARDO FAINI, GIAMPAOLO GALLI
and CURZIO GIANNINI

1 Introduction

In his pioneering work on the development of the Mezzogiorno, Hollis Chenery (1962) highlighted the fact that despite massive capital inflows the accomplishments of the Southern Italian economy had been in many respects disappointing and, at any rate, had not matched the performance of the North. Thirty years later, Chenery's judgment is not really open to dispute. Almost half a century of development policy, fostering large-scale transfer of income and capital to Southern Italy, has failed to narrow in any significant manner the output gap between North and South (Table 7.1).

To be sure, today's South is no longer poor: in per capita GDP, it fares no worse than the North in 1970 or Spain today; it is considerably better off than Ireland, Portugal and Greece (Table 7.2). In forty years it has undergone significant change, as witnessed by the fall in the share of agricultural employment from 49 to 16 per cent; local manufacturing has unambiguously taken off along the Adriatic coast and around Naples.

However, the fact remains that convergence has not been achieved, nor is it anywhere in sight. Investment has been high, but productivity in both the public and the private sectors has lagged behind. As a result, 36 per cent of the Italian population lives in a region that has become heavily dependent on public subsidies. This condition has become the source of increasing political strain, since socially painful central government budget cuts have become necessary to redress the public finances. A view broadly held by public opinion, and endorsed by reputable scholars,[1] is that the money spent in the South has been a source of waste, has fed corruption and has nourished rather than curbed organized crime; it has perpetuated and aggravated a long history of dependency on external aid, rather than promoting economic growth. Surely, government intervention

Table 7.1. *The South and the Centre-North: main indicators (per cent)*

	1951–60	1961–70	1971–80	1981–90	1990
Share of South in Italian:					
– population	37.2	36.0	35.1	36.1	36.6
– GDP	24.4	24.1	24.1	24.7	24.7
– consumption	28.1	28.2	27.9	29.9	30.3
– fixed investment	26.1	29.0	31.2	29.0	26.9
South/Centre-North					
– GDP per capita	54.5	56.6	58.6	58.2	56.7
– consumption per capita	66.2	70.0	71.4	75.4	75.1
Investment/output					
South					
– whole economy	22.4	25.6	26.0	24.5	22.0
– industry	14.7	20.6	24.5	22.8	22.0
Centre-North					
– whole economy	20.3	20.0	18.2	19.7	19.6
– industry	21.3	16.9	13.8	17.4	18.6
Net imports/GDP					
– South	15.4	17.9	20.0	20.8	20.3
– Centre-North	– 2.8	– 4.8	– 3.9	– 5.2	– 6.0
– Italy	1.6	1.8	1.8	1.2	0.5
Unemployment rate					
– South	9.1	6.4	9.6	16.3	19.7
– Centre-North	6.8	4.5	5.2	7.6	6.5
Employment shares					
South					
– agriculture	49.1	35.9	27.3	18.1	15.6
– industry	23.1	29.1	29.3	23.4	21.8
– private services	18.4	22.3	26.7	38.2	41.5
– public sector services	9.4	12.7	16.7	20.3	21.0
Centre-North					
– agriculture	31.1	18.6	10.4	8.4	6.9
– industry	34.5	40.9	41.3	34.6	33.1
– private services	24.4	28.8	33.1	40.3	43.1
– public sector services	9.5	11.7	15.2	16.7	16.9

Sources: Istat and Svimez (various years).
Note: In 1987, Italian national accounts underwent a substantial revision. Columns 1–3 of the table refer to the old accounts, columns 4–5 to the revised accounts. The main change concerns investment, which has been revised upward, especially in the Centre-North; employment statistics (but not the unemployment rate) now refer to standard labour units rather than number of employees.

Table 7.2. *GDP per capita in Europe*[1] *(EUR 12 = 100)*

Italian Regions			European Countries		
1	Lombardia	137.3	1	Luxembourg	125.4
2	Valle d'Aosta	132.9	2	Denmark	113.7
3	Emilia Romagna	127.7	3	Germany	113.5
4	Trentino A.A.	121.6	4	France	109.2
5	Piemonte	120.7	5	United Kingdom	105.3
6	Liguria	120.4	6	Netherlands	104.5
7	Lazio	120.2	7	Italy	104.4
8	Veneto	119.0	8	Belgium	100.7
9	Toscana	116.4	9	Spain	74.0
10	Friuli V.G.	115.0	10	Ireland	64.2
11		110.0	11	Greece	54.3
12	Umbria	95.0	12	Portugal	53.7
	CENTRE-NORTH	123.7		EUR 12	100.0
13	Abruzzo	87.6			
14	Sardegna	77.1			
15	Molise	75.3			
16	Puglia	73.6			
17	Sicilia	70.1			
18	Campania	68.7			
19	Basilicata	61.5			
20	Calabria	58.7			
	MEZZOGIORNO	70.7			

Source: Guglielmetti and Padovani (1989).
Note: 1 Purchasing power parities (1987).

in the South no longer commands the widespread intellectual support it enjoyed in the 1950s and 1960s, and is losing its political appeal.[2]

It is against this rather bleak background that the current debate on finance and development is taking place in Italy.

In this area, the government has done much of what good economic theory used to suggest. The literature cited lack of long-term capital as a main constraint on growth in less developed areas (Gerschenkron, 1962; Goldsmith, 1969; Rybczynski, 1974); insufficient local savings and retained earnings, widespread uncertainty and risk-aversion were deemed to hamper the agglomeration and channeling of long-term funds from savers to investors. In this perspective, it was necessary to promote the creation of a local financial structure and, above all, of Special Credit Institutions (SCIs); these were not very different from the Development Finance Institutions created in many developing countries with the support of the World Bank. The mandate of such institutions, created after the war, was soon substantially broadened to include the selection of projects eligible for public subsidies; a regulation was introduced fixing the interest rate that SCIs could charge on subsidized loans.

Our analysis starts from the consideration that external aid has been massive and capital scarcity is not (or, at least, is no longer) the key problem (Section 2). We must thus confront the 'productivity puzzle', which is at the centre of much current literature on development, not only in Italy (see, among others, Lucas, 1990, and Greenwald and Stiglitz, 1991). Total factor productivity is unambiguously lower in the South, even in private manufacturing. This brings up a long list of problems, ranging from still deficient infrastructure and the inefficiency of government services to issues of market structures, increasing returns, localized learning etc.; it also suggests the possibility of policy-induced distortions. The questions that we ask focus on the role of finance. Can inefficiencies of the financial sector be legitimately added to the list? And, if so, to what extent can they be attributed to inadequate policies?

In order to assess these issues, we document the unhappy state of finance in today's Mezzogiorno, stressing the role of a large body of regulation, in tune with good old theories, that until recently has been a major factor in segmenting the banking markets, hampering competition and efficiency (section 3). We then analyse the functioning of the system, building on a number of contributions that have gone well beyond the traditional 'channeling' approach. Influential works by McKinnon (1973) and Shaw (1973) have argued that a system of directed credits and low interest rates discourages lending for riskier and longer maturity projects, impedes competition within the financial sector and plays a role in credit rationing, with no guarantee that credit will be granted to the more productive projects.[3] More recently, the traditional approach has been criticized by a number of scholars (see, for instance, Stiglitz, 1989, and Hellwig, 1991), on the grounds that it does not deal with informational problems and misses the crucial function of financial institutions, i.e. the allocation of capital to the most productive uses. If informational and other market imperfections are substantial, as is often the case in less developed regions, then the simple availability of capital at the macro level may not be sufficient to promote development. What matters is that capital be channeled to firms and projects with high social rates of return. In this spirit, we perform a number of tests to assess the allocative efficiency of Southern financial markets (section 4).

In section 5, we bring the evidence together and offer our view on what ought to be done to enhance the contribution of the financial system to the development process.

2   The 'dependent region' model

The economic condition of the South can be described in terms of what has often been called the 'dependent region' model. Its key features are large government transfers, high wages and consumption, low productivity and persistent external deficits. A few numbers suffice to give an idea of the size and persistence of these phenomena.[4]

2.1   Regional development policy and transfers

The engine of the model is government transfers. The fact is that the overall primary deficit of the Italian public sector is the resultant of a much larger deficit in the South and a surplus in the Centre-North.

As is shown in Table 7.3, in 1988 the excess of non-interest spending over total public sector revenues was 31 per cent of regional GDP in the South and minus 8 per cent in the Centre-North. In fact, for at least three decades the primary public sector deficit in the South has been no less than 20 per cent of the region's gross product (Banca d'Italia, 1989). Since interest spending is of course a consequence of primary deficits, this accounting implies that the formation of the entire Italian public debt, now 104 per cent of GDP, can be imputed to the excess of primary spending over revenues in the South.

Transfers are largely the result of the automatic functioning of the tax and social security systems coupled with the lack of financial autonomy for local authorities. But other factors, more directly linked to regional development policy are also important, notably labour and capital subsidies, exemptions from corporate taxes and special public works programmes.

A glance at the main items of the government budget, displayed in Table 7.3, highlights these points. Four facts stand out. The share of personnel spending in the South is 44 per cent of the national total, outstripping the regional share of both GDP (25 per cent) and population (36 per cent). Expenditure on social benefits is three times as great as social security contributions, while in the rest of the country the two items are roughly in balance; this is in part the result of labour subsidies (in the form of reduced social security contributions) that now amount to some 20 per cent of labour costs in manufacturing (see Bodo and Sestito, 1991).[5] The South's share in direct taxation (20 per cent) is smaller than its share of GDP because of progressivity and, more importantly, regional exemptions from corporate taxes on new investment. The ratio of capital spending to GDP in the South is twice as high as in the Centre-North, as a result of efforts in two areas of regional policy: public works infrastructure

Table 7.3. *Main aggregates of public sector finances by region, 1988*

	South			Centre-North			Italy		
	(a)	(b)	(c)	(a)	(b)	(c)	(a)	(b)	(c)
Total expenditure	9.2	73	34	10.4	46	66	10.0	53	100
Current expenditure	8.2	65	33	9.4	42	67	9.0	48	100
personnel	3.2	25	44	2.3	10	56	2.6	14	100
welfare	3.0	24	34	3.4	15	66	3.2	17	100
contrib. to prod. activities	0.3	3	40	0.3	1	60	0.3	2	100
interest payments	0.5	4	11	2.2	10	89	1.6	8	100
Capital expenditure	1.0	8	39	0.9	4	61	1.0	5	100
public investment	0.8	6	35	0.8	4	65	0.8	4	100
investment subsidies	0.3	2	53	0.1	1	47	0.2	1	100
Total revenues	4.8	38	22	9.7	43	78	7.9	42	100
direct taxation	1.4	11	20	3.2	14	80	2.6	14	100
indirect taxation	1.5	12	29	2.1	10	71	1.9	10	100
social security contributions	1.1	9	16	3.5	15	84	2.6	14	100
Total balance	−4.4	−35	78	−0.7	−3	22	−2.1	−11	100
Primary balance (1)	−4.0	−31	296	1.5	8	−196	−0.5	−3	100
Current balance	−3.5	−27	110	0.2	1	−10	−1.1	−6	100

Sources: Micossi and Tullio (1991) and Scandizzo (1991).
Notes: (a) Current values (million lire) per capita; (b) % ratios to GDP; (c) % shares in national totals. (1) Total balance, net of interest payments.

– a key objective of regional policy since the inception, in 1951, of the 'Cassa per il Mezzogiorno' – and financial subsidies to investment; the latter, introduced in the 1960s, now reduce the cost of long-term capital in Southern manufacturing by about 40 per cent.

The macroeconomic consequences of government transfers have been high local consumption and a persistent regional trade deficit (Table 7.1). Total per capita consumption is 75 per cent of that of the Centre-North, much higher than the comparable figure for GDP (57 per cent).

Investment has also been high, but its poor productivity has curbed the growth of potential output. The trade balance has therefore been in the red since the 1950s; the deficit expanded significantly in the 1960s and has since oscillated around 20 per cent of the area's GDP (Table 7.1). As of 1990, Italy's national deficit (6 trillion lire, 0.5 per cent of GDP, by the ESA definition) was resultant of a deficit of 65 trillion lire in the South and a surplus of 59 trillion lire in the Centre-North.

In principle, a trade deficit may be considered natural in a less developed area, if imported saving is put to productive use. What is striking about the Mezzogiorno, however, is that the external deficit has persisted for decades, and nothing suggests any impending reversal. It is quite clear that the external deficit reflects the permanent weakness of the productive structure and continuous dependence on external aid.

2.2   The productivity puzzle

A large body of research has demonstrated that the North-South productivity gap cannot be accounted for by the different composition of output, either by sector of activity or by size and property structure of firms (see, among others, Svimez, 1991, and Banca d'Italia, 1990). Some of the key numbers are reported in Table 7.4; labour productivity in private manufacturing is about 20 per cent lower than in the rest of the country. The capital productivity gap is wider, value added per unit of productive capital being only about half as much in the South as in the Centre-North. The high capital/output ratio measured from firms' balance sheets is no surprise in view of the national accounts data, which show that the ratio of gross investment to output has always been much higher in the South, both in the industrial sector and in the whole economy (see Table 7.1). The contribution of direct investment flows from outside the area has been essential: about 60 per cent of total manufacturing employment is with firms whose main operations are not in the South.[6] Cumulating net additions to the capital stock Galli and Onado (1990) have computed a theoretical North-South output gap assuming equal efficiency of investment and equal factor proportions in the two areas. In this exercise, per capita GDP in the South should be between 75 and 80 per cent of that of the rest of the country, depending on assumptions concerning depreciation rates and the initial distribution of the capital stock in 1951. The difference between this figure and the actual ratio of 57 per cent is accounted for by lower total factor productivity and higher capital intensity of Southern production. The capital/labour ratio in Southern manufacturing (as is implied by the first two rows of Table 7.4) is 1.6 times higher than in the Centre-North. Differences of this order of magnitude are found in almost all sectors of activity and size categories of private firms. They can be attributed to the system of subsidies, which strongly favours capital-intensiveness (see Siracusano and Tresoldi, 1990; Galli and Onado, 1990; Dini, 1989).[7]

Various other indicators confirm the low productivity of the Southern private sector. For instance the turnover of inventories is much lower, indicating less efficient storage and production methods (see Siracusano and Tresoldi, 1990). More important, corporate profits (including subsidies) in the South appear to be lower for local firms and only slightly higher for large multiregional firms.

What are the reasons? Why has productivity failed to catch up in spite of large-scale investment? A recurrent explanation in the Italian literature is lack of economic infrastructure (transportation, water, electricity, telecommunications, etc.). Yet while this argument certainly contains more than a grain of truth (see Biehl, 1986), it is not entirely convincing. Public investment in infrastructure has been substantial, at least since the 1950s, and although programmes have resulted in much waste, the South does now offer several sites where firms could settle with little disadvantage as the gap with the rest of the country is not very large. The recent trade performance of the Asian NICs has shown that the importance of transportation costs can easily be overstated.

Rigidities in the labour market provide a more convincing explanation. Labour subsidies and income transfers have made it politically feasible for the trade unions to impose, since the early 1970s, equal pay scales throughout the economy. Wages have thus been made unresponsive to local labour market conditions and to productivity differentials between regions and between firms; the lower cost of labour per employee in the South is entirely due to social security contribution relief for employers. At the same time, the expansion of employment in the public sector and increasing transfers to households have impaired labour mobility, another key ingredient in a properly functioning market economy (see Attanasio and Padoa-Schioppa, 1991; Micossi and Tullio, 1991); rent controls, introduced on a large scale in the late 1970s, have also impaired mobility by virtually drying up the rental market for housing. Finally,

Table 7.4. The productivity gap in the private sector (percentages)

	South		Centre-North		South/C.N.	
	Non-financial firms	Manufacturing	Non-financial firms	Manufacturing	Non-financial firms	Manufacturing
A.						
value added per employee (1)	47.9	44.3	57.7	53.9	83.0	82.2
value added/net plant and equipment	83.0	92.4	151.0	185.0	55.0	49.9
labour costs per employee (1)	28.7	28.0	33.8	33.0	84.9	84.8
labour costs/value added	59.9	63.2	58.6	61.2	102.2	103.3
debt servicing/financial debt	13.3	13.2	14.2	14.9	93.7	88.6
B.						
long-term debt with intermediaries/value added	120.8	88.9	66.0	55.7	183.0	159.6
short-term debt with intermediaries/value added	70.1	52.6	44.0	36.0	159.3	146.1
equity/value added	123.1	131.5	86.1	85.7	143.0	153.4
debt/equity	118.2	80.5	102.2	85.6	115.6	94.0
bonds/total liabilities	0.7	0.5	1.5	1.5	46.6	33.3

Sources: Galli and Onado (1990), based on 1987 data of Company Accounts Data Service.
Note: (1) Millions of lire.

political constraints on hirings and lay-offs are much more stringent in the South than elsewhere, not only for public enterprises but also in the private sector.

The inefficiency of the public administration places a large burden on existing firms. A disproportionate share of managers' time and energy is devoted to dealing with public officials; acts that should be immediate and practically automatic (from issuing a licence to the repair of a telephone line) often take years; bribes and parallel markets are widespread; lawyers and accountants flourish.

The main inefficiency is probably related to the administration of justice, not only in connection with the fight against organized crime (which itself is an enormous burden and risk for firms in some areas of the South); much more generally property rights are less well established and guaranteed than elsewhere in the country: it may take a decade and huge costs for a creditor to see his claim recognized in court.

Another factor may be returns to agglomeration. There are several reasons why proximity to an area with an established and diversified network of industries may enhnance productivity. The main one is that information (about technologies, markets, prospective entrants into the industry, etc.) circulates much more easily. Acquiring it is thus much less costly and time-consuming than elsewhere. For this reason (not just because of transport costs) it may be easier to diversify suppliers and clients and adopt more efficient models of specialization. In fact, Southern firms are often highly dependent on a single supplier or a single customer; also, they are typically more vertically integrated than Northern firms, which may again be related to geographical isolation.

Apart from these generally recognized causes of the failure of Southern private-sector productivity to catch up, the rest of this paper addresses possible explanations specifically inherent in the field of finance.

3   The state of finance in the Mezzogiorno

The fundamental fact to emerge from a large body of research is that the financial industry of the South differs considerably from that of the rest of Italy (see, in particular, Banca d'Italia, 1989 and 1990; Messori and Silipo, 1991). In spite of rapid change in the 1980s, it is still not clear that the relative backwardness of the South is less marked in the financial sphere than in the rest of the economy. Apparently the South's being an integral part of a wider monetary area subject to common fiscal and financial regulations and the gradual liberalization of markets in the last decade have not been sufficient to bring about the expected convergence in financial conditions.

In the present section we document the most obvious regional disparities in the financial behaviour of households, firms and banks; we also provide a brief account of the regulatory framework. This exposition is a useful background to the more complex matter of the reasons for the differences and their effects on the economy.

3.1   Households and firms

Table 7.5 shows the composition of households' financial wealth. In the South, almost three-fourths of the total consists of bank and postal deposits, as against less than half in the North. The chief financial innovation of the 1980s (the development of a huge securities market to fund Italy's rapidly growing public debt) has had relatively little impact on the investment habits of Southern households, in spite of enormous interest rate differentials (up to 600 basis points) between T-bills and deposits of the same maturity. As a consequence, the ratio of bank deposits to GDP has remained quite stable in the South while falling by more than 13 percentage points in the North.

As regards firms, the main interregional differences stem from the productivity gap. Ratios of financial stocks (debts, equity, liquid assets etc.) to real economic flows (value added, sales, profits etc.) are much higher in the South because it takes twice as much physical capital to produce a unit of value added (see Table 7.4, Panel B).

Debt/equity ratios are not far from unity in both areas, but the sources of equity finance differ, with government grants playing an important role in the South and the stock market playing no role at all. Partly because of their smaller size, Southern firms are virtually absent from the stock market and account for less than 3 per cent of the Milan Stock Exchange. Bonds are a minor source of finance in the North and a negligible one in the South. Because financial subsidies apply only to long-term debt, this item is more important in Southern balance sheets, at the expense of short-term bank loans.

Overall, the bond and the stock markets are not very important in either area of the country and are virtually irrelevant in the South; the main sources of finance are retained profits and loans from financial intermediaries.

3.2   The efficiency gap in the financial industry

Five distinctive features have characterized the system of financial intermediaries in Italy, essentially since the banking reform of 1936; some of them have had different implications for the functioning of the system, depending on region.

Table 7.5. *The financial assets of households (per cent)*

	South		Centre-North	
	1980	1987	1980	1987
Bank deposits	64.1	47.1	65.5	39.6
Postal deposits	30.7	24.6	8.3	5.3
Securities	5.2	23.1	26.2	48.0
Investment funds	—	5.2	—	7.1
Total	100	100	100	100

Source: Banca d'Italia (1989).

(1) Separation between banking and commerce. Banks are generally not allowed to purchase the shares of commercial firms or to have any direct stake in their management. The reverse relation (firms holding bank shares) is subject to strict limits.

(2) Distinction between short and long-term banking. Commercial banks (CBs) are generally not allowed to operate on maturities beyond 18 months, on either the liability or the asset side; only in the bond market are they allowed (and at times have been obliged) to hold assets with longer maturities. Special Credit Institutions (SCIs) operate in the long end of the market: they have traditionally been viewed as the key intermediaries for investment finance.

(3) A large body of regulations to ensure the stability of the system, through barriers to entry. The rules have included a virtual ban (until 1985) on establishing new banks, regulations on branch openings and transfers (subject to authorization until 1990) and restrictions on lending by small and medium-sized banks outside the geographical area in which their branches are located. Lending ceilings, used intermittently in the 1970s and part of the 1980s as a tool of monetary policy, have also tended to limit competition (see Cottarelli *et al.*, 1986).

(4) Public ownership of banks. Directly or indirectly, the public sector controls most Italian banks, including the largest ones, and their directors are designated by political authorities.

(5) Fragmentation, especially in short-term banking. Italy has more than a thousand banks; very few are large by European standard; most are very small, often with just one or two branches.

The rationale behind the first two types of regulation was to avoid the entanglement of credit institutions with the corporate sector and maturity mismatching, which were viewed as key causes of the banking crises of the interwar period. Likewise, the third type of restriction was aimed at bolstering stability during post-war reconstruction (see Banca d'Italia, 1947) by preventing the proliferation of banks and branches that occurred after the first world war and eventually resulted in a huge number of failures (3,000 banks, two-thirds of the total, disappeared between 1927 and 1947). For many years, this philosophy was not questioned even by market-oriented economists: the system had indeed proved quite stable and, above all, capable of financing the rapid growth achieved by the economy during the 'Italian miracle'.

The fourth feature, i.e. public ownership, is largely the legacy of the wave of failures of private banks in the interwar period, perpetuated by the prohibition on opening new banks.

Except for the first one, the above restrictions have become less rigid over time. In line with the Second EC Banking Directive, the financial industry has gradually been liberalized. Proposals to attenuate the distinction between short and long-term banking have reached the political agenda, as German universal banks will be allowed to operate in the domestic market starting in January 1993. Steps towards privatization have been taken, although a recent law enshrines the principle that the government should generally maintain 51 per cent of the shares of the banks that it currently owns. The fragmentation of the system, also largely a historical heritage, has been perpetuated by fiscal problems and a number of legal provisions, now being phased out, that made mergers and acquisitions virtually impossible.

The regulatory environment for special credit institutions differs somewhat by geographical region and their structure and operating features have been affected by the Southern development programme. In fact, three main SCIs operating in the South (accounting for 17 per cent of the national market) were created in the 1950s as part of the programme, and the Cassa per il Mezzogiorno still holds a majority stake in them. Investment subsidies are a major area of overlap between regional policy and financial intermediation. A firm investing in the South acquires entitlement to the subsidies when it is granted a loan on an eligible project by an authorized SCI. The interest rate on subsidized loans is fixed by the government.

Research conducted at the Bank of Italy (Galli and Onado, 1990, and Sabbatini, 1990) has shown that the regulatory environment, the interference of regional policy objectives and the property structure of Southern SCIs have impaired efficiency and made the institutions more like bureaucratic apparatuses than banks. Their operating costs are much higher (several fold!) than those of Northern SCIs, mostly because of the larger share of staff classified as 'managers'; productivity is lower (for instance, the number of borrowers per employee is 65, against 76 in the rest of Italy); and net income is lower (0.47 per cent of total resources, against 0.69 in the rest of Italy, on average from 1980 to 1988). Additional problems were a higher share of bad loans and a lower level of equity, a direct consequence of low profits.

As regards commercial banks, the regulatory environment is uniform nationwide. There is no significant North-South disparity in the availability of banking structures (number of banks and bank branches); the degree of concentration, as measured by the Herfindahl index is only slightly higher in the South (see Table 7.6). However, many of the rules cited earlier have impeded competition and fostered the geographical segmentation of the market: this has permitted the development of substantial interregional differences in banks' operating features.

The key differences, emerging again in studies conducted at the Bank of Italy (Ciampi, 1984, Marullo Reedtz, 1990; Banca d'Italia, 1990), can be summarized as follows:

– The main Southern banks operate in clearly defined, distinct territories; medium-sized banks, which have proved to be the most dynamic in the North, are virtually absent; most banks are very small, many one-branch operations, owing in part to the past policy of authorizing the opening of only tiny local banks (rural and artisans' banks).

– Operating costs as a share of total resources, of the banks with headquarters in the South (about 300, accounting for 68 per cent of total bank lending in the South) are about 20 per cent higher than those of the banks located elsewhere in the country. The gap is accounted for mainly by differences in physical productivity.

– Average loan quality is considerably worse for Southern banks. Bad loans make up about 14 per cent of the total, compared to 8 per cent in the rest of the country (see Table 7.7).

– A number of relatively new activities that have proved lucrative for Northern banks (foreign currency lending, securities dealing, consumer credit, etc.) have developed quite slowly in the South.

– The lending rates charged by Southern banks are higher than the national average by about 2 percentage points (see Section 4 below), while deposit rates are roughly the same.

– Net profits, and hence equity, are considerably lower than in the Centre-North.

The last decade has witnessed a number of significant changes. Efficiency has increased, thanks to deregulation, the increased presence of Northern banks and the growing competitive pressure exerted by the burgeoning market for Treasury securities. Two developments in particular warrant mention. The first is that the share of Southern branches belonging to

Table 7.6. *The availability of banking structures, 1988*

	South	Centre-North
Number of special credit institutions	22	69
Number of commercial banks	317	784
Number of bank branches	3,652	11,795
Ratio to bank branches of:		
population	5,742	3,092
GDP	64.3	63.4
bank deposits	35.3	41.4
Concentration index (1)	0.17	0.15

Source: D'Onofrio and Pepe (1990).
Note: (1) Herfindahl index computed on the basis of bank loans in each of the 95 provinces of Italy; the index ranges between 0 and 1, with the latter value indicating a situation of monopoly.

Table 7.7. *Bad loans/total loans, 1988 (percentages)*

	Location of borrower		
Location of bank	South	Centre-North	Total
South	16.0	8.2	14.0
Centre-North	12.0	7.8	8.2
Total	14.3	7.9	8.9

Source: Onado *et al.* (1990).

Northern banks, which for 30 years was stable at around 14 per cent, has now risen to over 21 per cent (see Table 7.8). The second is that the gap in terms of unit costs (though still a substantial 20 per cent, as noted) has actually been halved, from the 40 per cent differential registered at the end of the 1970s (see Figure 7.1).

Overall, despite recent progress, Southern banks are still considerably less efficient and more fragile financially. Perhaps surprisingly, it cannot really be said that the banking sector is more 'advanced' than the rest of the Southern economy: in particular, the productivity gap is of the same order of magnitude as in manufacturing. It would rather appear that given the partial segmentation in industry, banks have closely mirrored the problems of their local environment.

Table 7.8. *Distribution of bank branches by area (percentages)*

	South			Centre-North		
	1951	1978	1988	1951	1978	1988
Southern banks	85.5	85.8	78.7	1.4	1.7	1.7
Other banks	14.5	14.2	21.3	98.6	98.3	98.3
Total	100	100	100	100	100	100

Source: D'Onofrio and Pepe (1990).

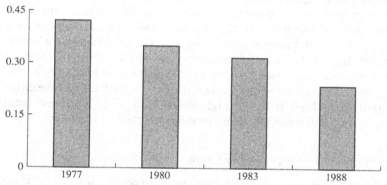

Figure 7.1 Banks' operating expenses/total resources (South/Centre-North).
Source: Galli and Onado (1990).

4　Informational imperfections in financial markets: are they greater in less developed regions?

The relative inefficiency of the financial system in the Mezzogiorno would not be of major concern if intermediaries did not have a crucial role in allocating saving and resources or if, nothwithstanding their low productivity, Southern banks performed this role no differently from other banks. This is what we try to assess here, building on the literature that stresses the informational aspects of financial intermediation. According to this literature (see Hellwig, 1991, for a recent survey), given widespread informational asymmetries, intermediaries are most useful either because they can monitor borrowers more efficiently (Diamond, 1984) or because, by establishing long-term relations with their customers, they can enlarge the information set available to the market, thereby helping to overcome imperfections. However, customer relations cut both ways: while enlarging the information set available to the lender, they also expose the borrower to the risk of being 'informationally captured' by its bank (Sharpe, 1990); the latter may exploit the monopoly power implicit in the informational advantage it has acquired over its competitors. This outcome is more likely the wider the bank's information advantage (i.e. the greater the extent of informational imperfections), the slower the reaction speed of 'exploited' borrowers (i.e. the lower their 'mobility'), and the heavier the weight the bank attaches to current as opposed to future profits. Customer relations, then, cannot be taken unambiguously as the sign of efficient resource allocation. Especially in the context of underdevelopment, they may signal inefficiencies and may be coupled with widespread credit rationing.

Our inquiry into these issues starts with an analysis of why lending rates are higher in the South. Higher risk, while an important factor, turns out to be only part of the story. In the South: (i) information problems are particularly heavy and customer mobility low; (ii) local banks are 'informationally' sheltered: outside banks, less informed, have to resort to rationing practices in various forms; (iii) the allocative efficiency of the banking system is lower: in particular, it appears that innovative firms (those that carry high risk and high yield) tend to be excluded from external finance and must rely more heavily on retained earnings.

4.1   Why are lending rates so much higher in the South?

Figure 7.2 plots the average rate on bank loans in each of the 95 provinces of Italy against per capita GDP. The two variables are quite clearly correlated. The interest rate differentials between the richest and the poorest provinces can be as large as 400 basis points. The average North-South differential of 200 basis points is hence the result of a much more pervasive phenomenon. As is shown in Figure 7.3, the differential has persisted over a long period of time. And, surprisingly, no regulation has ever kept individuals or firms from borrowing outside their local areas: a large number of banks have always been allowed to lend throughout the national territory. Moreover, Northern banks hold a 32 per cent share of the Southern loan market; as is shown in Table 7.9, the average rate they charge in the South (14.96 per cent) is considerably lower than that charged by local banks (15.84 per cent).

On the basis of a cross-section of bank lending rates referring to 1988 (Figure 7.2), D'Amico et al. (1990) have found that the average North-South differential is explained mainly by GDP per capita (accounting for 53 per cent of the differential) and by a variable that controls for the composition of lending in terms of size and economic sector of borrowers.[8] Small borrowers, which are more risky nation-wide, have a

Table 7.9. *Lending rates[1] (geographical distribution of banks and of operations) (%)*

Area of bank	Area of operations		
	South	North	Total
South	15.84	13.56	15.13
North	14.96	13.31	13.46
Total	15.36	13.32	13.62

Source: Central Credit Register, September 1988.
Note: (1) Interest rate on short-term lending in lire to resident customers. Geographical distribution of operations is based on the location of the bank's branch issuing the loan. Geographical distribution of banks is based on the location of the banks' headquarters.

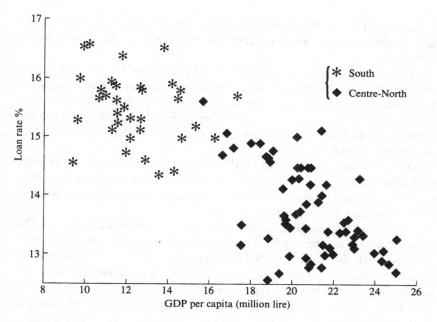

Figure 7.2   Loan rates and GDP per capita in the 95 provinces of Italy
Note: Interest rates on banks' loans in lire to domestic borrowers. Geographical distribution of operations is based on the location of the banks' branch issuing the loan.
Source: Central Credit Register.

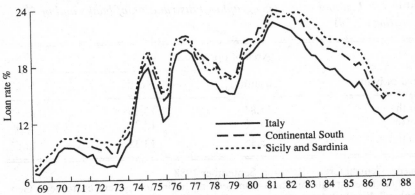

Figure 7.3   Loan rates in the two Southern sub-regions and the national average
Note: Interest rates on banks' loans in lire and in foreign currency to domestic customers. Geographical distribution of operations is based on the location of the banks' branch issuing the loan.
Source: D'Amico *et al.* (1990).

larger weight in the South: mainly for this reason the composition variable explains a significant portion (34 per cent) of the North-South differential.[9]

Bad loans, an imperfect measure of risk, explains 11 per cent of the differential. The Herfindahl concentration index is barely significant and explains no more than 2 per cent; a simple version of a 'structure-performance' model does not account for regional disparities, essentially because, as we have already noted, the degree of concentration is comparatively uniform.

This regression confirms that GDP per capita is an important variable, even after controlling for the sector and size of borrowers: thus a textile manufacturer of a given size is likely to be charged a higher rate if most of his borrowing is done in a poor province.

To gain further insight, we consider data on individual loans. The data-set comprises observations on 35,711 contracts (amount and interest rate) between 76 banks and 9,127 firms in a single year (1988). Each bank-firm relation appears only once, implying that on average each firm had dealings with 4 banks; a few firms having relations with a single bank have been eliminated (see Appendix A for further details on the data and the methodology).

Table 7.10 reports results based on a simple analysis of variance, corresponding to the following regression

$$r_{ij} = a + \sum_i \beta_i b_i + \sum_j \gamma_j f_j \qquad (1)$$

Table 7.10. *Analysis of banks' and firms' fixed effects*
(Dependent variable: bank rates on overdraft loans)
Differences between the average coefficients of South or Centre and those of the North

A. Entire sample

	Banks (β_i coefficient)	Firms (γ_j coefficient)
Centre-North	0.44	0.54
South-North	1.26	1.05

	Entire sample	Manufact.	Engin.	Text.
B. Small firms (less than 20 employees)				
Centre-North	0.54	0.62	2.10	0.18
South-North	1.03	0.91	0.86	3.20
C. Intermediate firms (20 to 200 employees)				
Centre-North	0.49	0.48	0.02*	0.48
South-North	0.95	0.96	0.96	1.40
D. Large firms (above 200 employees)				
Centre-North	0.38	0.36	0.11	0.44
South-North	0.50	0.31	0.33	0.37*

Notes: $R^2 = 0.639$; Standard Error = 1.54; Mean of dependent variable = 13.83; Number of observations = 35,711; Number of firms = 9,127; Number of banks = 76. Both the banks' (β_i) and the firms' (γ_j) coefficients are significant at the 1 per cent level, according to an F test. All t tests for differences with the North are significant at the 1 per cent level, except those marked with *.

where: r_{ij} = interest rate on an individual overdraft credit from bank i to firm j;
     b_i = dummy variable for bank i;
     f_j = dummy variable for firm j;
     a, β, γ are parameters.

We therefore regress the price of individual loans on a constant and on 75 dummy variables for banks and 9,126 dummy variables for firms. This analysis allows us to attribute the variation in observed interest rates to two separate effects: those resulting from differences between banks and those resulting from differences between firms. The β_i coefficients are non-zero if different banks (because, say, of different costs or monopoly power) charge different interest rates to identical firms; the γ_j coefficients inform us about the characteristics of the firms, holding constant those of the banks.

The regression has a fairly low R^2, (0.639), which means that a large part of the variance is not explained either by the characteristics of the banks or by those of the firms. Other important factors, which we address in the next section, affect the specific relation that develops between each bank and its customers.

The basic result is that the differential is due, more or less in equal proportion, to different characteristics of both banks and firms. The first column in panel A of Table 7.10 shows the difference between the average coefficients of banks located in the Northern regions of the country (roughly, north of Florence) and those of banks located respectively in the Central and Southern regions: rates charged by Southern banks are 1.26 percentage points higher than those charged by Northern banks to identical firms. For comparison, note that the differential between the Centre and the North, although statistically significant (there are more than 26,000 degrees of freedom), is only 0.44 percentage points.

Quite clearly this reflects higher costs and, possibly, greater market power of Southern banks.

To assess the role of operating costs, we have run another regression, replacing the banks' dummies with a number of numerical variables capturing banks' characteristics: in addition to costs, we have introduced various balance-sheet ratios (see Appendix A). The basic result is that operating costs *alone* explain almost the entire within-banks variation: with only this variable included (instead of 75 banks' dummies) the uncorrected R^2 and the standard error are virtually the same as those of the previous regression (see regressions 1 and 2 in Table 7A.1).

Concerning firms, our results show that those located in the South are charged higher rates, regardless of the location of the bank from which they borrow. The second column in panel A of Table 7.10 shows that the average South-North difference is 1.05 percentage points. Quite clearly banks view Southern firms as riskier. The higher riskiness is only partly accounted for by differences in size and sector. Panels B, C and D replicate the analysis of panel A focusing on different sizes and sectors of activity.[10] The North-South differences are larger for small firms, as one would expect given the greater market power that banks wield in their regard. But sizable differences also show up with respect to medium-sized and large firms and, within those, individual sectors of activity (of which only a few are displayed in the table). These results confirm those of previous research based on firms' accounts (Siracusano and Tresoldi, 1988; D'Amico *et al.*, 1990). The variability of various measures of profitability (*ROI, ROE*, net income/sales etc.) has been shown to be unambiguously higher in the South for the different classes of firms and over time. To this evidence, we add that of Table 7.11 on rates of mortality,

Table 7.11. *Mortality rates of firms[1] (percentages)*

North-West	3.8
North-East	3.5
Centre excluding Lazio	4.3
Lazio	4.6
Continental South	4.8
Sicily and Sardinia	4.6

Note: (1) Ratio between the number of employees belonging to firms that fell out of social security files and the total initial number of employees in each year; average of 1984–89, per cent.

derived from the files of the social security system.[11] The figures of the table represent the number of employees belonging to firms that fell out of the file in a given year divided by total initial number of employees covered. The mortality rate, so computed, is 4.8 per cent in the continental South against 3.8 in the North-East and 3.5 in the North-West of Italy.

In conclusion, there is no doubt that Southern firms (even those of equal size and operating in the same sector) are generally riskier. Risk, however, accounts for only half the interest rate differential; the rest must be attributed to higher costs of banks and less competition.

4.2   Information and geography in financial markets

The previous section presents two interesting facts. The first is that different banks are able to charge the same borrower significantly different rates, mainly reflecting their operating costs. The second is that the residual variance of the regression in which banks' and firms' specific effects are fully taken into account is high.

Both these facts strongly suggest that informational problems are of great importance in the Italian banking market. This finding is of course neither new nor entirely specific to Italy. The extensive literature on customer relations builds on the notion that, even in an integrated monetary area, there are two layers in financial markets. In the upper layer, one finds the textbook case of perfectly mobile capital: securities issued by governments or other large borrowers, wholesale banking, etc. In the lower layer, there are bank loans, as well as deposits, which appear to be quite sticky. Here the particular relation that develops between the lender and the borrower is of paramount importance and may be heavily influenced by geographical considerations.

Greenwald and Stiglitz (1991) argue that information problems are likely to be magnified by the fragmented institutional and economic environment that typically characterizes underdeveloped regions. Indeed, as we have seen, Southern firms are generally younger, smaller and risker. In such circumstances it may take quite a lot of time and effort for a bank to gather enough information to determine the class of risk in which borrowers actually belong. In the absence of repeated interactions, banks will charge higher rates or resort to rationing practices of the kind exposed by Stiglitz and Weiss (1981). Most importantly, they may offer a lower quality credit facility, entailing the risk for the firm of not receiving finance when it is most needed or having to borrow very short-term.

Stable customer relationships (hence low mobility) are the natural result. To some extent they may be beneficial, in that they allow the bank to acquire more information about the firm. However, as Sharpe (1990) shows, the firm risks being 'informationally captured' by its bank, which may exploit the monopoly power conferred by its informational advantage over other banks.

The conjecture to test may thus be articulated as follows: (i) information problems are particularly heavy in the South, and stable customer relations tend to prevail; (ii) the informational advantage of local banks shelters them from outside competition: outside banks tend to practice rationing; (iii) because of low competitive pressure and low customer mobility, local banks can indulge in monopolistic behaviour and raise lending rates in line with operating costs.

In the end, the purpose is to assess the impact of information problems on the efficiency of intermediaries in performing their selection function.

That outside banks engage in credit rationing is already signaled by the size distribution of bank customers in the South. In our sample, firms that are very large by Italian standards (1,000 or more employees) account for about 50 per cent of outside banks' total lending in the South, against 17 per cent for Southern banks.[12]

To explore the matter further, we have performed two experiments.

From the same data set used for the regression in the previous section, we have taken a sample of firms on the basis of the following criteria: (i) location in Sicily; (ii) lines of credit with at least one Southern (in practice, Sicilian) and one outside bank (headquartered in the North or in the Centre of Italy); (iii) Southern bank credit lines accounting for at least 30 per cent of total borrowing. In short, we are examining firms that borrow both from local and from outside banks and for which local banks are not marginal. The latter proviso ensures that we are not considering small loans on which firms might more readily accept uncompetitive terms (in order, say, to maintain an open channel with a bank or the power group it may represent). The resulting sample is made up of 150 firms, for which we computed the unweighted average interest rate paid to local and to outside banks, the average utilization rate of lines of credit, the average incidence of each relation on the total amount of funds borrowed; we also break the sample down by firm size (see Table 7.12).

This test confirms that simultaneous borrowing from local and outside banks is done at different rates. The North-South differential in this sample is more than half a percentage point. Nevertheless, Southern firms get the bulk of their finance from local banks. Note that the share of borrowing from each outside bank is not negligible (on average about 20 per cent), which suggests that the rates charged by these banks are not dumping rates to facilitate the penetration of a new market.

Whether or not this is evidence of 'type 2' rationing behaviour by the outside banks is debatable. Utilization rates are certainly higher with these banks: 66 and 73 per cent, respectively, with banks located in the North and Centre as against 44 per cent with local banks. Yet while this is not a small difference, it remains unclear why firms do not borrow close to 100 per cent from outside banks and use lines of credit with local banks as buffers for short-term swings in their financing needs. To a certain extent, this may be due to the averaging out of individual positions. To obtain a more precise indicator of excess demand for credit, we have also computed for each category of firm the ratio between the total amount of unauthorized overdraft credit observed for that category and the total lines of credit outstanding: the higher the ratio, the greater the incidence of 'rationed' positions with respect to the category's total demand for credit. Values are considerably higher for Northern and Central banks (on average 5.3 and 8.9 per cent respectively) than for Southern banks (1.3 per cent); this is true for all classes of firms we considered (Table 7.12).[13]

The second experiment attempts to explain the bank-firm specific residual variance of the regression run in Section 4.1. Rates charged on individual loans are regressed on two sets of dummy variables (firms' and banks' specific effects) and a number of additional regressors to capture the variation that does not depend on the characteristics of either bank or firm *per se* but is specific to a particular bank-firm relationship.

The additional regressors include the past duration of a contract, credit line utilization rates, measures of geographical proximity, and measures of the importance of the bank for the firm and of the firm for the bank (see Appendix A and Table 7A.1).

An interesting finding concerns one particular measure of geographical proximity: a dummy variable set at 1 when the province of the borrower coincides with that of the bank's headquarters and zero otherwise. The coefficient of this variable is close to 1 and statistically highly significant in the South. Elsewhere it is very low and not significant.

Taken literally, this result suggests that geographical proximity matters

Table 7.12. Credit market indicators for Sicilian firms

Category of firms	Northern Banks				Central Banks				Southern Banks			
	Average interest rate	Relative size of the loan (1)	Utiliz. rate (2)	Unauthor. overdraft (3)	Average interest rate	Relative size of the loan (1)	Utiliz. rate (2)	Unauthor. overdraft (3)	Average interest rate	Relative size of the loan (1)	Utiliz. rate (2)	Unauthor. overdraft (3)
Small firms	15.9	0.24	74.8	6.1	16.1	0.26	70.7	6.0	16.5	0.49	60.4	5.3
Medium firms	15.1	0.20	64.1	3.8	15.0	0.16	78.1	6.1	15.8	0.42	61.4	1.2
Large firms	13.9	0.11	39.3	9.5	14.3	0.21	51.4	13.3	14.2	0.38	41.3	0.2
Total sample	15.3	0.21	65.5	5.3	15.2	0.19	73.3	8.9	15.9	0.44	59.5	1.3

Source: see Appendix A.
Notes:
(1) Weight of each loan in total borrowing of the firm; averages of individual firms.
(2) Percentage of credit actually utilized.
(3) Unauthorized overdraft as a percentage of total lines of credit.

much in the South but not elsewhere. When a Southern bank lends to a local firm, it charges almost 1 percentage point more than its average lending rate to firms of the same risk class (as measured, unambiguously, by the firm and bank dummy variables). This is consistent with the notion that Southern firms are 'informationally captured'; most likely it is in the interest of the firm, rather than the bank to maintain the relation; otherwise rates would be lower, not higher.

Another variable, the market share of the bank in the borrower's province (*WBP* in Table 7A.1), potentially measures geographical proximity; the fact that its coefficient is barely significant (and, if anything, has a negative sign) suggests that being a local bank is different from being an outside bank with local branches; only the former seem to enjoy additional market power. This may explain why penetration by outside banks has been so slow. In the last decade, the Bank of Italy has adopted efficiency standards in evaluating applications for new branches: as a result, the share of Southern branches pertaining to outside banks has risen from 14 to 21 per cent; however, their share of the lending market has increased by just 1.5 percentage points (from 30.7 to 32.2 per cent).

Further evidence of the relative stickiness of the Southern loan market is displayed in Table 7.13. The data of the Central Credit Register allow us to reconstruct the pattern of change in borrowers' relationships with their banks (as in Ciocca *et al.*, 1984). Five cases are considered, depending on whether the borrower has, in a given year: (i) established at least one business relation with a new bank, without breaking off any existing ones (increase without substitution); (ii) established more new relations than broken off old ones (increase with substitution); (iii) broken off at least one relation, without establishing a new one (decrease without substitution); (iv) broken off more relations than established new ones (decrease with substitution); (v) replaced old with new relations (substitution without increase or decrease).

The table shows that borrowers' mobility is significantly lower in the South than elsewhere, in all years considered and for all types of change. The lack of similar data for other countries makes it impossible to say whether the mobility of Italian borrowers is 'high' or 'low', but one point is worth underscoring: the two forms of mobility that presumably best reflect retaliatory behaviour on the part of borrowers (increase and decrease *with* substitution) are almost negligible (0.35 and 0.26 per cent respectively in the Southern area in 1988).

On the whole, the evidence suggests that informational problems are important, especially in the less developed regions. Southern banks have both the technical opportunity and the economic incentive to extract monopoly rents from their customers, because of their relative

Table 7.13. *Distribution of customers according to changes in business relationships with commercial banks*

| | Number of customers as a percentage of total customers (1) | | | | | | | | |
| | 1982 | | | 1985 | | | 1988 | | |
Type of variation	North	Centre	South	North	Centre	South	North	Centre	South
Increase without substitution	17.26	15.77*	15.16*	17.13	16.05	14.68*	13.17	12.73	11.81*
Increase with substitution	1.40	1.10	0.87	0.98	0.90	0.50*	1.01	0.63	0.35*
Decrease without substitution	7.31	6.82	6.34*	6.94	6.50	5.88*	7.38	6.80	5.95*
Decrease with substitution	0.71	0.51	0.49*	0.53	0.50	0.33*	0.57	0.44	0.26*
Substit. without incr. or decr.	3.89	3.31	3.25	3.13	2.90	2.52	3.22	3.04	2.05*
Total variation	29.47	27.95	26.58*	28.21	27.29	23.85*	24.76	24.22	20.40*

Source: Central Credit Register data on about 350,000 individual borrowers based on loan account headings.
Notes: (1) An asterisk indicates values which are significantly different at the 1 per cent level from those of the North. To allow for different cell sizes, the comparison of means has been carried out on the basis of Tukey's studentized range test.

inefficiency, the extent of their informational advantage, and the relative immobility of their customers. Even in the absence of institutional barriers, informational problems limit the ability of external banks to compete in Southern credit markets. Most likely, when entering a local market in the South, outside banks have to resort to various forms of rationing to avoid getting the worst borrowers.

4.3 Screening and resource allocation

Ultimately, the most important question concerns the ability of financial markets to perform their screening function, in light of the regulatory framework.

The evidence set forth in Section 4.2 on the stability of customer relationships and the low mobility of borrowers suggests that informational problems are heavier in less developed regions. On this basis alone, it may be argued that screening is less efficiently performed. The linkage between information and screening has been clarified by the theoretical literature initiated by Stiglitz and Weiss (1981). While that article focused on credit rationing, subsequent work (De Meza and Webb, 1988; Hillier and Ibrahimo, 1991) has stressed the consequences of informational asymmetries on the allocation of resources.

As we view it, the bottom line is that when banks are not 'well' informed, credit may be misallocated, in both possible senses: some bad projects are financed and some good ones are not. Two simple inequalities capture the essential aspects of the problem:

$$x \geq \frac{(1 + \rho)}{p} \tag{2}$$

$$x \geq a \frac{(1 + \rho)}{p} + (1 - a)(1 + r) \tag{3}$$

where x is the unit return on a project (if the project is successful), ρ is the risk-free rate of interest, p is the probability of success of the project, r is the bank lending rate and a the share of equity financing (and $1 - a$ the amount borrowed from the bank). The project is assumed to have a binomial distribution: the return is x with probability p or zero with probability $1 - p$.

Inequality (2) is the condition for social optimality. The project should be undertaken if its expected return, $x \cdot p$, is greater than the risk-free interest factor $(1 + \rho)$.

The second inequality gives the condition under which the firm will be willing to apply for the loan at interest rate r: the expected rate of return on the project net of interest costs, $[x - (1 - a)(1 + r)] \cdot p$, must be sufficient to cover the cost of own funds, evaluated at the risk-free rate.[14]

The two inequalities would coincide and no inefficiency would arise if the bank rate on each project were fixed according to the following criterion:

$$(1 + r) = \frac{(1 + \rho)}{p} \tag{4}$$

The inefficiency stems from the assumption that the bank does not know the probability of success, p (at least for some borrowers or groups of borrower) and hence cannot fix the lending rate according to the optimal criterion.

Exactly how the lending rate is determined depends on the definition of a full equilibrium model of the credit market. Even without defining such model, a number of interesting propositions follow from the observation that r is some fixed number, greater than the risk-free rate and independent of the specific risk characteristics of the project. In Figure 7.4 the SE (socially efficient) line represents equation (2) (taken with the equal sign); all projects above this line are socially efficient and should be financed. Likewise the SS (self-selection) line represents equation (3); all firms with projects lying above this line will apply for a loan.

The shaded areas identify the two types of inefficiency. The lower right corresponds to the underinvestment case analysed by Stiglitz and Weiss (1981): i.e. projects with low return in case of success and low risk (high p). The reason why firms contemplating such projects do not apply for loans is essentially that, given their low risk, the interest rate charged by the bank is too high. The upper-left identifies cases of overinvestment (De Meza and Webb, 1988). Firms in this area seek financing even though the expected return, $x \cdot p$, is lower than the risk-free interest factor. They do so because they can transfer part of the risk to the bank: for these high-risk, high-return projects, the lending rate is too low. Firms proposing these projects are 'liars': they know their high risk but do not tell the bank. This is not true of the Stiglitz-Weiss firms, which may honestly try to persuade the bank of their low riskiness but fail to allay the bank's suspicions.

Note that adjusting the lending rate does not solve the problem as long as the bank fails to differentiate among individual projects: for instance, a higher rate merely shifts SS upward and increases the number of deserving projects that are excluded.

The share of debt financing (the parameter $1 - a$) is important: self-evidently, when borrowing is small (a is large), the inefficiency stemming from asymmetric information between the borrower and the lender is reduced. In the limiting case in which a is one (one hundred per cent equity) there is no inefficiency.[15]

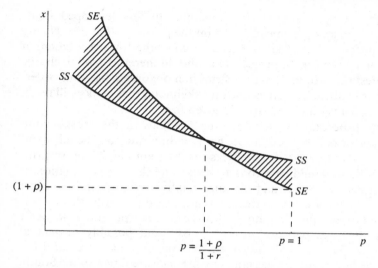

Figure 7.4   The efficiency of bank screening under asymmetric information

While our description has focused on self-selection, the model also accounts for moral hazard. Suppose, for instance, that a firm can choose between a low-risk project falling in the lower shaded area and a high-risk one in the upper area: it will obviously choose the latter, at the expense of the bank and of social efficiency.

The general conclusion is that lack of information may result in too much money being invested in high risk projects and too little in safe projects. Empirically, this argument is rather appealing, helping to reconcile the widespread complaint that Southern firms are denied access to credit (because it is too costly or rationed) with the high ratio of bad loans by Southern banks. But this is certainly only part of the story. Information problems may manifest themselves in many other ways. One is simple misjudgment by the bank: bad projects are deemed deserving or vice versa. Nor is asymmetry the only source of informational inefficiency: it may be that both the bank and the borrower equally misjudge the merits of the project. Even shying away (as we do) from a Schumpeterian view of the bank, we have no doubt that the intermediary has an important role in elucidating the borrower as to his project's likelihood of success. Charlatans, of which – we agree with Stiglitz (1991) – there is an infinite supply, are yet another problem. The charlatan may be in good faith and truly believe that his project is a surefire success. The efficient bank certainly cannot content itself with what the loan applicant believes: it must assess what he can actually do.

These, of course, are universal problems; the question is whether their consequences are more disruptive in economically less developed areas. We have thus run an experiment, based on the postulate that if screening is efficient different banks should tend to converge toward a common evaluation of a given firm or project. They should therefore tend to charge similar interest rates, or at least rank firms in more or less the same order. If screening is inefficient, there is a strong likelihood that banks will reach differing judgments on the merits of a given firm.

Our testing procedure is based on the residuals of the cross-section regression performed in Section 4.1, with lending rates on the left-hand side and firms' and banks' fixed effects on the right-hand side. In principle, the residuals would be zero if all banks had the same evaluation of individual firms, i.e. if they had the same relative ordering and the exact numerical position of firms on the risk scale. In other words, the lending rates charged to *the same firm* should be the same, except for a scale factor reflecting differences between banks in costs and possibly in general market power. We have already seen that the residuals are far from negligible: we now want to ascertain whether they are larger in the South.

Table 7.14 (Panel A) gives the average of the absolute values of the residuals for different locations of firms and banks. Considering the marginal means for banks (the last column), we see that the residuals (given, like interest rates, in percentage points) are considerably larger in the South (1.22 against 0.85 in the North). The reported t-statistic (17.4) testing for the difference between these two means is significant at the 1 per cent level. This confirms the presumption that screening is impaired by informational problems in the South. The surprising new feature of this table is that the residuals do not differ greatly between *firms* of different areas. The means are 0.97 for firms located in the South, 0.98 for those of the Centre and 0.88 for those of the North. Moreover, correcting for size class of bank, residuals of Southern firms are no larger than those of other firms. Rather, in each column, i.e. for each type of firm, residuals increase as we move from Northern and Central to Southern banks. Taken literally, this indicates that Southern firms are no harder to screen than others; it is Southern banks that perform the screening less efficiently. We are inclined to take this result with some caution in the light of possible problems in extrapolating from our sample to the entire population (see Appendix A). Indeed, the results about firms change somewhat when we consider homogeneous subsections. Panels B and C of Table 7.14 reflect the same tests as in panel A, but taking the residuals pertaining to a specific size category of firms (20–200 employees) and, within it, two specific industries (engineering and textiles). Again, we find that the residuals are significantly larger for Southern banks: for instance, in the textile sector (panel B), they come to 1.75 percentage points against 0.84

for Northern banks, with a t of 6.7. Looking at differences across firms (i.e. along the rows), we find that the residuals are generally somewhat larger for Southern firms, but at a much lower level of significance than for banks: in the textile sector, the marginal mean for firms (the last row of Panel B) is 1.38 in the South and 0.89 in the North, with a t of 2.9. The difference is significant only at the 5 per cent level and results exclusively from the behaviour of Southern banks; in fact, in the first two rows of the table (relating to banks of the North and of the Centre) differences between firms are small, not statistically significant, and in one case of the wrong sign.

On the whole, these tests suggest that screening might be more difficult in the South; for sure, they indicate that the difficulties are aggravated by certain specific features of the financial system.

Table 7.14. *Absolute value of the residuals of regression 1 of section 4.1; means by area of banks and firms*[1]

(A) Entire sample

Banks	Firms North	Centre	South	Total
North	0.84 21,505	0.90 1,568 (2.7)	0.90 744 (1.7*)	0.85 23,817
Centre	0.99 4,818 (10.4)	0.98 4,274 (2.6)(0.7*)	0.93 648 (0.7*)(1.2*)	0.98 9,740 (12.2)
South	1.27 956 (13.9)	1.32 453 (7.8)(0.7*)	1.08 745 (3.8)(3.2)	1.22 2,154 (17.4)
Total	0.88 27,279	0.98 6,295 (7.6)	0.97 2,137 (4.2)	0.90 35,711

(B) Intermediate firms[2]; textile sector

Banks	Firms North	Centre	South	Total
North	0.84 1,225	0.83 125 (0.1*)	0.93 32 (0.3*)	0.84 1,382
Centre	1.10 230 (3.7)	1.03 291 (1.7*)(0.7*)	1.06 10 (0.5*)(0.1*)	1.06 531 (4.3)
South	1.24 28 (2.2)	2.2 17 (5.1)(2.0)	2.5 51 (2.3)(2.4)	1.75 96 (6.7)
Total	0.89 1,489	1.02 433 (2.3)	1.38 93 (2.9)	0.92 2,009

Table 7.14. (*cont.*)

(C) Intermediate firms[2]; Engineering sector

Banks	Firms							
	North		Centre		South		Total	
North	0.92	1,704	0.96	59	0.92	16	0.92	1,779
			(0.4*)		(0.1*)			
Centre	1.13	454	1.02	184	1.16	19	1.10	657
	(3.8)		(0.3*)	(1.2*)	(0.5*)	(0.2*)		(3.8)
South	1.19	80	1.74	29	1.23	33	1.32	142
	(2.4)		(3.0)	(2.0)	(1.8*)	(0.1*)		(4.3)
Total	0.97	2,238	1.08	272	1.11	68	0.98	2,578
			(1.7)		(1.0)			

Source: see Appendix A.
Notes: (1).
– In the upper left corner of each cell, cell means are reported;
– in the upper right corner of each cell, the number of observations in the cell is reported;
– t statistics for comparison with the North are in parenthesis; comparisons along the columns are reported on the left of each cell; comparisons along the rows are reported on the right of each cell. An asterisk indicates that the test is *not* significant at the 5 per cent level.
(2) 20 to 200 employees.

4.4   Evidence from corporate behaviour

Providing a direct quantitative assessment of the real consequences of the numerous inefficiencies which, as we have documented so far, plague the financial sector in the South is a most challenging task. In what follows, we take a simple but indirect route. We look first at the determinants of corporate borrowing and ask whether there are significant differences in the pattern of financial choices between Southern and Northern firms. We focus in particular on the impact of the system of subsidized credit applying to long-term loans issued by Special Credit Institutions in the South. The so called 'financial repression' hypothesis holds that a system of directed credits and administrative interest rates may discourage lending for riskier and longer maturity loans and contribute to widespread credit rationing and misallocation of resources (McKinnon, 1973; Shaw, 1973).

We rely on an econometric analysis based on a sample of balance-sheet data for 2,132 small firms located in both Northern and Southern Italy over the period 1982–87. Sample characteristics and methodology are described in Appendix B and, in greater detail, in Bonato *et al.* (1991). Here it is enough to say that we rely throughout on market rather than book values of both long-term debt and physical capital stock. The intent is to identify significant differences in the pattern of corporate borrowing and investment between firms located in the North and those in the South, focusing in particular on the role of financial constraints and risk.

Initially, we consider long-term debt and follow the literature in assuming a simple partial adjustment mechanism. The equilibrium debt/sales ratio for firm i at the time $t(B^*_{i,t})$ is a linear function of its determinants. The latter include risk factors (measured by the volatility of earnings), tax considerations (proxied both by the effective tax rate for the firm and the ratio of taxable earnings to fiscal depreciation, with the latter measuring the importance of non-debt tax shields), liquidity (i.e. cash-flow), the share of fixed assets (to capture Myers' effect) and the ratio of the aggregate stock market index to the CPI. Whenever appropriate, the variables are normalized by the level of sales. We expect greater earnings volatility to reduce corporate borrowing on two accounts, namely the larger probability of financial distress and the more limited value of debt as a tax shield.[16] A greater share of fixed assets should be associated with more debt to the extent that it indicates lower discretionary investment possibilities (Myers, 1977). Similarly, profitable firms (i.e. those with large *ex-post* tax liabilities) with limited non-debt tax shields should rely to a greater extent on borrowing. The impact of cash-flow, by contrast, is ambiguous: greater cash-flow may reduce the need for external finance, but may also signal greater long-run profitability and be used as collateral for further borrowing. Finally, the stock market index, though not directly relevant for most Southern firms, is included, as it is typically found to exert a negative and significant effect in many empirical debt studies (MacKie-Mason, 1988; Taggart, 1977). In estimation, we distinguish between time-varying and time-invariant determinants of debt. We also control for dynamic panel data biases (see the Appendix for details).

Column 1 in Table 7.15 presents the estimates from the first-stage regression on the time-varying determinants of debt. The ratio of physical capital to sales has a significant impact on long-term debt, whereas no significant cash-flow effect is found. Presumably, the various conflicting effects of larger cash-flow on debt offset one another. The results of the second-stage regression on time-invariant factors are presented in the first column of Table 7.16. All variables have the expected sign, including our indicators of the tax position of the firms.

The only variable for which a significant difference between Northern and Southern firms could be detected is our measure of risk (*STDE* in Table 7.16). As expected, this varies inversely with corporate borrowing;

Table 7.15. *The determinants of corporate borrowing: time-variable determinants, small firms*
Dependent variable: B/Y

	Long-term debt	Short-term debt
Constant	− 0.005	0.003
	(2.93)	(1.51)
$(B/Y)_{t-1}$	0.574	0.569
	(13.1)	(38.9)
$(CF/Y)_t$	− 0.083	− 4.46
	(0.17)	(1.98)
$(K/Y)_t$	0.276	11.1
	(3.06)	(1.76)
SMI_t	0.0007	−
	(1.99)	
Wald χ^2	328.8 (4)	1,559.9 (3)
Sargan χ^2	5.45 (6)	13.3 (9)
AR2	− 0.843	− 1.54

Legend:
B: financial debt (long-term or short-term)
Y: sales
CF: cash-flow
K: capital stock
SMI: stock market index
Note: t-statistics are shown in parentheses. The AR2 test is distributed as a standard normal variable. Numbers in parentheses after χ^2 tests are degrees of freedom. See Appendix B for further detail. The regression on long-term debt is reproduced from Bonato *et al.* (1991).

its effect is significantly stronger in the South than in the North. Even a locational dummy (taking a value of one for firms located in Southern Italy) turned out not to be significant and was therefore dropped from the equation.

The strong negative impact of risk on outstanding debt in the South apparently supports the claim that interest rate regulation on long-term borrowing crowded out riskier projects. This test of the financial repression hypothesis is considerably more direct than tests found in the literature, which focus on the relationship between investment (or growth) and time deposit interest rates (Fry, 1988) or on differences in borrowing patterns as a function of firm size (Tybout, 1984). Yet the larger role of risk in the South could be predicated on other factors. We accordingly look further at borrowing decisions, and now focus on short-term debt. The

Table 7.16. *The determinants of corporate borrowing: time-invariant determinants, small firms*
Dependent variable: individual firms' effects from Table 7.15

	Long-term debt	Short-term debt
Constant	− 0.943	− 2.40
	(4.54)	(8.38)
τ	0.63	2.81
	(1.30)	(4.37)
E/DEPR	0.209	0.370
	(8.54)	(10.07)
Y'	1.58	2.24
	(2.94)	(3.10)
STDE	− 7.581	− 3.85
	(2.98)	(1.12)
STDE/(E/DEPR)	− 1.745	− 2.944
	(1.49)	(1.61)
STDES	− 13.27	− 28.99
	(1.96)	(2.54)
Φ	62.6	67.4

Legend:
τ: effective tax rate (corporate taxes/taxable earnings)
E: earnings
DEPR: depreciation allowances
Y':   growth rate of sales
STDE: standard deviation of earnings normalized by sales
STDES: STDE * DUMSUD
DUMSUD: dummy variables for firms located in the South
Φ: percentage of correct predictions
Note: t-statistics are shown in parentheses. See Appendix B for further detail. The regression on long-term debt is reproduced from Bonato et al. (1991).

results of the first stage regression are presented in Table 7.15 (column 2). The most noticeable result is that cash-flow now has a significant, negative impact on short-term debt. The greater availability of internal finance is reflected in lower demand for short-term rather than long-term debt. Turning to the second stage regression, we find again that tax and risk considerations play a significant role (column 2, Table 7.16). More important, risk, as measured by the standard deviation of earnings, is once again the only variable with a significantly different coefficient between Northern and Southern firms; and it has a larger impact in the South. This result concerning short-term debt shows at the very least that interest rate regulation is not the only factor at work.

Searching for other factors, one might posit that bankers in the South are more risk-averse. However, this explanation does not fully square with the fact that default rates are much higher in the South (see Table 7.7), an indication that banks in the South have indeed taken considerable risks (Fazio, 1985; Galli and Onado, 1990). Another possibility is that risk has a larger effect in the South because Southern entrepreneurs lack collateral to back their demand for finance. The firm's assets are not deemed to be sufficient collateral by banks because of capital losses and liquidation costs in the event of default. Weak law enforcement in particular may significantly raise liquidation costs. In principle, collateral (for which we are not able to control in our estimates) should affect both the level of debt and the impact of risk on borrowing.[17] The first effect did not show up in our estimates, since the locational dummy proved to be insignificant: differences in the availability of collateral between Northern and Southern Italy might be present, but they certainly do not play a decisive role.[18] Finally, it could be claimed that the availability of subsidized loans and investment grants in the South exacerbated risk-taking behaviour by local entrepreneurs and may therefore account for an overly prudent attitude by local bankers.[19]

None of the previous approaches provides a totally satisfactory explanation of why risk has a more marked effect on corporate debt in the South. We are therefore left with the initial argument, namely that risk just matters more in a relatively backward economy. This simple statement of course leaves unanswered whether this state of affairs subsists because banks in the South perform their screening tasks less efficiently or, alternatively, because information about borrowers and their projects is simply more difficult to evaluate in a developing area.[20] We believe that our previous results allow us to cast some light on this issue. In Section 4.3 we found indications that Southern borrowers are not significantly more difficult to screen than those of other regions and concluded that bank inefficiencies, i.e. less well developed screening capabilities, were important. The results of this section show that these factors have a substantial impact on corporate balance sheets and compound the difficulties of small, relatively risky firms in getting their projects financed.

The bias against riskier projects would not be a matter of concern if this type of project also yielded low social return. Suppose, however, that banks can distinguish, on the basis of observable characteristics, between say n groups of potential borrowers. Within each group, borrowers are observationally indistinguishable. If the observed average characteristic of any group lead the bank to believe that it is relatively risky, then this group may be rationed or redlined. The argument of both Stiglitz and Weiss (1981) and Cho (1986) is that such groups *may* be the most

Table 7.17. *Cash flow and investment (149 small firms in the South)*
Dependent variable: $(I/Y)_t$

	Coefficients	*t*-statistics
$(I/Y)_{t-1}$	0.487	2.47
ccap	− 0.174	− 1.34
Y'	0.233	3.37
$(B/Y)_{t-1}$	− 0.007	− 1.79
$(K/Y)_{t-1}$	− 0.334	− 4.27
$(CF/Y)_{t-1}$	0.503	1.77
Wald χ^2	30.82 (6)	
Sargan χ^2	11.1 (11)	

Legend:
I: investment
B: financial debt
Y(Y'): sales (growth rate)
CF: cash flow * *DUMR*
ccap: cost of capital
DUMR: dummy variable for high-risk firms
K: capital stock
Note: Numbers in parentheses after χ^2 tests are degrees of freedom.

productive ones, i.e. those with highest average returns. In what follows, we take a closer look at this possibility. Our approach is very simple; we estimate an unrestricted investment function where the decision to invest is assumed to depend on output growth, the real cost of capital, the availability of cash flow and lagged debt. We interpret a significant value of the coefficient of cash flow to imply that firms are willing to undertake investment projects, but can only do so if internal finance is available.[21] Such projects are likely to be characterized by relatively high expected returns; otherwise the firm would not be willing to finance them internally. We then ask whether cash-flow effects on investment are more significant for riskier firms. We find that this is indeed the case (Table 7.17). We interpret this as indicating that high-risk firms in the Mezzogiorno are endowed with profitable investment projects, which sometimes cannot be undertaken because of a lack of internal funds. This finding is consistent with the previous result that high-risk firms are at a disadvantage in the markets for long-term and for short-term credit alike. In the estimation, the Arellano-Bond procedure was used to allow for the dynamic structure of our specification. We also experimented with both gross and net investment to avoid any spurious correlation that may arise from the fact that our definition of cash-flow availability includes additions to depreciation funds and may therefore be correlated with gross investment. Our results proved quite robust with respect to this modification. Overall, therefore, we feel justified in concluding that the financial system in the South shows a bias against high-risk, high-yield projects.

5   The implications for financial policy

The evidence set forth points to some rather clear conclusions about the nature of the South's relative backwardness and the role of finance. First of all, it is hard to deny that the experience of the Italian Mezzogiorno includes countless examples of government failure; it should be a potent antidote to the belief that wholesale infusions of capital are a panacea for the ills of underdevelopment. Efforts to sustain the South have been massive. Transfers have ranged between 20 and 30 per cent of the area's GDP for decades. Almost every conceivable measure has been attempted to promote growth, ranging from infrastructure and public works to industrial subsidies, tax exemptions, special projects for enterprise creation and training; the objectives of regional policy have shaped the strategies of large government-owned enterprises and affected financial markets and intermediaries in some of their key structural features. Investment has taken place at very high rates, attracted by subsidies rather than by market conditions; moreover, a large share of investment (more than half) has been undertaken by outside firms.

As much of modern development theory suggests, the crux of the matter is the efficiency of investment. Our evidence clearly indicates that the poor performance of the Southern economy is to be imputed to low total factor productivity. As we have argued, this observation calls into question a long list of possible explanations, from agglomeration economies and increasing returns to the inefficiency of government services (including law enforcement). It strongly suggests the possibility of policy-induced structural distortions, especially in the labour and financial markets. There is little doubt that labour subsidies and other income transfers bear a large responsibility for the rigidities in the labour market. Labour mobility, which was massive until the 1960s, has virtually ceased. Wages have been made almost completely unresponsive to local labour market conditions and to productivity differentials between regions or firms. Political constraints on hiring and dismissal have been considerably more stringent in the South than elsewhere in Italy, also for private firms.

Concerning finance, this paper has provided ample evidence of the operating and allocative inefficiencies that have developed in the South, under the regulatory regime that has prevailed until very recently. To be sure, the old regime had solid motivations in both economic theory and experience. The protection of local banks, the promotion of specialized regional institutions, interest subsidies and interest rate ceilings were essential ingredients in a global development strategy aimed at overcoming the lack of saving and of long-term capital, which were perceived as the key obstacles to growth. On another ground, barriers to entry and slack competition have helped prevent any repetition of the disruptive bank crises that had marked the interwar period; and they did not keep Italy from achieving among the highest economic growth rates in the Western world for many years.

These motivations now appear outdated. For one thing, low productivity, not lack of capital, is the key impediment to growth in today's Mezzogiorno. And for another, experience has shown that stability and efficiency are not necessarily conflicting goals; with appropriate prudential regulation, they may reinforce each other if efficiency leads to lower costs and better quality of assets.

We have shown that financial intermediaries' operating costs are higher in the South, while productivity, profits and own capital are lower. The gaps are wider for special credit institutions, which have been more heavily affected by the regional development programmes; interest rate regulation on subsidized loans is only one of the several factors that have impaired competition in the Southern market for long-term credit.

The environment in which Southern banks operate is unquestionably more difficult. Our analysis of the lending rates of commercial banks and the evidence on firms' profits and balance sheets demonstrate that risk is certainly greater in the South. Yet we have also shown that risk can explain no more than half the observed rate differential. The rest must be attributed to less competition and higher bank costs.

There are persuasive indications that informational problems are heavier, leading to more intense rationing, captive relations between banks and firms, and poorer screening. Some of this evidence is worth recalling. First, Southern firms that borrow simultaneously from local and outside banks do so at different rates; the cost of credit from outside banks is systematically and significantly lower. Certain data (concerning the size distribution of customers and rates of utilization of lines of credit) suggest that outside banks resort more to rationing practices. Building on the asymmetric information literature, we attribute this to the presumption that they are less well informed about local firms. The latter may hence be 'informationally captured' (viz. Sharpe, 1990) by their local banks. This presumption is reinforced by our analysis of customer mobility: direct evidence on individual loan contracts show that Southern firms are less likely to break off a business relation with a bank or to open a new one.

Relevant indications also emerge from a cross-section regression explaining interest rates charged on individual loans as a function of firms' and banks' specific effects. In an ideal efficient market, the variance of lending rates should be fully explained by differences in risk between firms; instead we find that banks' effects are significant (mainly capturing differences in operating costs) and, more importantly, that the bank and firm effects combined explain little more than half of the observed variance. The residual variance may depend essentially on two factors: differences in banks' assessments of individual firm risk (coupled with the limited mobility of borrowers) and specific bank-firm interactions leading to stable customer relations. These factors operate nationwide. In the South, however, the residual variance is larger, especially when the comparison is between banks rather than firms. We take this as indirect yet rather strong evidence of lower screening efficiency on the part of Southern banks.

Moreover, in an attempt to capture bank-firm interactions (using such variables as past duration of loan contracts, measures of geographical proximity and of the importance of the bank to the firm and vice versa), we have found that one special gauge of geographical proximity (coincidence of the borrower's province with that of the headquarters of the bank) has a significant positive coefficient only in the South: Southern banks tend to charge such local borrowers much higher rates than those they charge on average to other firms with identical risk characteristics. Quite interestingly, another potential indicator of geographical proximity (share of a bank's branches in the province of the borrower) is not significant: we interpret this evidence as suggesting that being a local bank is different from being an outside bank with local branches; only the first case seems to give rise to additional market power. This fact may explain why penetration by more efficient outside banks has been extremely slow in the last decade, despite a substantial increase in the number of their branches located in the South.

The final piece of evidence derives from econometric analysis of corporate behaviour, suggesting that high-risk high-return firms are more likely to suffer credit rationing in the South than elsewhere. In an investment equation, cash-flow constraints are considerably more stringent for risky firms. In short and long-term debt equations, risk has more significant negative effects in the South.

Overall, there is good cause to complain about the state of finance in the Mezzogiorno. Banks have certainly not performed the Schumpeterian role of promoting large-scale development projects. And the same goes for special credit institutions, even though these were created specifically to perform this function on behalf of the public sector. Intermediaries have also displayed shortcomings in such less ambitious but nonetheless important tasks as screening and monitoring. At best, they have played the role of followers, providing finance when it was demanded in the private and especially in the public sector.

What can be done to redress this situation? Which specific feature of the regulatory system should be changed?

In our view, one feature of overriding importance concerns competition. Slack competitive pressure affects not only costs and prices but also the 'quality' of the banking product. In this regard, financial liberalization (which started slowly in the early 1980s and has recently accelerated) will prove to be of major benefit to the efficiency of entire Southern economy, not just the financial system; more will come with the full implementation of the Second Banking Directive, which will allow Community banks to operate everywhere in Europe on the basis of home country regulation. Our analysis of customers' relations and of the role of outside banks does suggest, however, that structural change will be a very lengthy affair unless measures are taken to make the ownership of banks more easily contestable. As we have seen, geographical proximity to the borrowers is of paramount importance: since it is hard to envisage a massive increase in the number of bank branches in the South (which would imply very high adjustment costs for both outside and local banks), the only practicable way for outside banks to exert additional competitive pressure is by purchasing branches and local banks.[22] This requires appropriate fiscal rules as well as political decisions concerning the property structure of public banks; in particular, we favour the elimination of any provision that reserves to the government 51 per cent of the shares of the banks that it currently owns.

Similar decisions are also needed to enhance bank size. Theory clearly points to the importance of size and economies of scale in screening and monitoring (Diamond, 1984). There is little doubt that tiny banks with just a branch or two are in a poor position to evaluate customers. They have contact with very few firms, are not aware of the alternatives, cannot set up the technical structure for efficient screening and monitoring and cannot diversify to an appropriate extent. In addition, the fragmented structure of the Italian banking system, especially in the South, leaves ample room for reducing costs through economies of sale (Conigliani *et al.*, 1991; Grillo, 1987). And since most banks are public, policy decisions are needed to remedy the situation.

Another questionable feature of the current system is the separation between commercial banks and special credit institutions, which may impair financial intermediaries' ability to perform a key aspect of loan selection: matching firms and projects. The commercial banker knows the firm, which is typically also a depositor and has a continuing business relationship, while the special credit banker knows the investment projects that are submitted to him intermittently, i.e. when a new investment is undertaken. Thus, neither is in the best position to evaluate the suitability of a given project for a given firm. This problem has been more pervasive in the South: elsewhere, the connections between short and long-term banking have been closer, because of special agreements or direct property ties. Furthermore, it can be argued that economies of scope between the two types of institutions are more relevant in less developed regions, where a global view of market opportunities is at once more urgently required and less readily obtainable.

The final feature on which we focus is the system of financial subsidies, which greatly impairs the efficiency of the special credit institutions. On the one hand, it burdens them with functions and responsibilities, including legal ones, that are typical of government (judging whether a project is eligible for subsidies); on the other it tends to relieve them of the main responsibility of the banker: evaluating the economic merits of a project. Administered interest rates on subsidized loans, besides impairing competition among intermediaries, also downgrade the screening function of the institutions. When the interest rate is fixed exogenously by a government agency, the banker will only be concerned with the lower tail of the distribution of returns: he has to make sure that bad outcomes have a low probability and that the risk is covered by collateral. As we have seen, risky projects tend to be rejected, regardless of expected returns. As a consequence, what is sometimes called 'development finance' (relating to projects with high return and high risk) is virtually nonexistent: new product and technology ideas, growth-oriented firms, etc. have little or no access to long-term capital. This is a most unfortunate situation. Development needs development finance, for at least two reasons. First, in an area that is totally open to external trade, local firms cannot grow simply by copying what is done in mature areas. They must generate new ideas, in terms of technology, organization, products etc.: in a word, they must take risks. Second, in the Mezzogiorno, and presumably in the less developed areas of other industrial countries, firms are either very large (typically outside or public corporations) or very small (typically, the local firms). While efficiency does not always grow in direct proportion to size, it is clear that very small firms may not be able to develop the technical structures, marketing organization and so on that are required to survive and, *a fortiori*, to prosper. Moreover, expanding a firm's size usually requires a discontinuous jump with the financing of new projects that are large compared to the existing concern. Once again, risk-taking emerges an important feature of development.

While other financial institutions, such as merchant banks and venture capital companies, may be better suited for this task and should certainly be encouraged, the most important changes nevertheless concern the traditional intermediaries, which still account for the lion's share of finance.

In conclusion, our view is that government intervention in the South should be revised and, in many areas, reduced. The financial system also requires thoroughgoing transformation, for which liberalization and increased competition are necessary but not sufficient conditions.

Appendix A: Interest rate regressions

1.1   Structure of the sample

The data used in sections 4.1, 4.2 and 4.3 derive from three different sources: the Centrale dei Bilanci (Company Accounts Data Service), the Centrale dei Rischi (Central Credit Register) and the Financial Statistics of the Bank of Italy.[23] The first source publishes standardized figures on the balance sheets of about 30,000 Italian firms. The second, which is a section of the Bank of Italy's Statistical Department, collects data on individual transactions undertaken by banks. The data cover the amount of individual loans larger than 80 million lire and the interest rate charged. While loan sizes are reported by all Italian banks, interest rate data are provided, on a voluntary basis, by 79 banks only, which account for about 70 per cent of total bank lending. Since the explanation of interest rate differentials was our main objective, we decided to concentrate on this smaller data-set. The third source contains data on the balance sheets of financial institutions and on their branch networks.

We have collated the three sources by bank and by firm, proceeding as follows. We first extracted from the Company Accounts Data Service a balanced sample (over the period 1982–88) of about 15,000 firms. We then eliminated firms whose data were incomplete, missing or unavailable for our purposes of interest rate studies. More precisely, we excluded firms if: (a) the wage bill was lower than 100 million lire; (b) net interest expenses, ordinary depreciation allowances, liquid assets, financial debt or net capital were non-positive.

The resulting sample of about 10,000 firms was then collated with the other two sources. We then concentrated on overdraft lending. We eliminated observations pertaining to very small loans, excluding: (a) lines of credit smaller than 5 million lire; (b) actual utilized credit (yearly average of daily figures) of less than 500,000 lire. The reason for these cuts was to control for 'spurious' interest rates resulting, in particular, from the practice of including among interest expenses – from which the figures on interest rates are worked out – commissions and fees payable by customers even if they are not borrowing or are borrowing very small amounts.

To further control for noise (which would bias especially our variance experiments), we also eliminated observations for which the interest rate was either higher than 25 per cent or 3 points lower than the rate on 3-month Treasury-bills. Finally, in order to make the ANOVA experiments meaningful, we eliminated a few firms with only one bank relation.

The resulting sample consists of 35,711 'contracts', which summarize the dealings between 9,127 firms and 76 banks; each bank-firm interaction appears only once, meaning that on average firms have relations with 3.9 banks. For *each firm*, we know the interest rate and the actual amount borrowed for each outstanding overdraft loan, plus detailed information on the company's balance sheet. For each bank, we also have information on overall deposits, loans, bad loans, compulsory reserves, branches (by province) and market shares (also by province).

Almost all firms (98 per cent) are in the private sector. By sector, the bulk of the sample consists of manufacturing firms (60 per cent), followed by enterprises in the distributive trades and services (20 per cent), in transport and communications (7 per cent), and in mining (4 per cent).

The average interest rates by area of banks and firms are the same as those of the entire Credit Register sample, except for the cell corresponding to the lending of Southern banks to Northern firms for which there are (in the real world and, *a fortiori*, in our sample) very few observations: here our sample exceeds the population interest rate by 1.6 percentage points.

1.2   Econometric estimates

The results are shown in Table 7A.1. Regression 1 is the ANOVA experiment commented on at length in Section 4.1.

In regression 2 the *BANK* dummy has been replaced with the ratio of operating costs to deposits. As can be seen, operating costs alone account for almost all the variance explained by the *BANK* dummy: the R^2 in this case is 0.606 and standard error is 1.61. We then added balance-sheet ratios (regression 3). All variables are significant and carry the correct sign: an increase in compulsory reserves, in bad loans, or in total lending (each divided by deposits) has the effect of increasing the interest rate charged to the borrower. The deposits variable (capturing the effects of bank size), although significant, contributes very little to the explanatory power of the equation. The lending-to-deposits ratio allows

Table 7A.1. Interest-rate regression[1]
(dependent variable: interest rate on bank advances)   Number of observations: 35,711

Variables	Regression 1 $R^2 = 0.639$ SE = 1.54	Regression 2 $R^2 = 0.606$ SE = 1.61	Regression 3 $R^2 = 0.618$ SE = 1.58	Regression 4 $R^2 = 0.653$ SE = 1.51	Regression 5 $R^2 = 0.632$ SE = 1.55
1. Banks' dummies (BANK)	— (42.13)			— (35.03)	—
2. Operating costs/deposits (OP)		19.32 (26.67)	11.88 (11.51)		9.77 (9.58)
3. Lending/deposits (L)			19.43 (17.32)		19.18 (17.22)
4. (Lending/deposits)² (LSQ)			−16.10 (−17.87)		−15.76 (−17.66)
5. Bad Loans/deposits (BD)			4.08 (18.21)		4.15 (18.88)
6. Compulsory reserves/dep (ROB)			10.93 (15.02)		10.12 (14.03)
7. Deposits (DEP)			0.007 (5.80)		0.005 (3.85)
8. Weight of the firm for the bank (WFB)					
North				2.40 (1.34)	
Centre				−6.84 (−1.96)	
South				2.57 (0.56)	
9. Weight of the bank for the firm (WBF)					
North				−1.76 (−21.5)	−1.62 (−23.68)
Centre				−1.56 (−9.69)	
South				−2.07 (−8.87)	
10. Weight of the bank in the province of the borrower (WBP)					
North				−0.002 (−1.06)	
Centre				−0.005 (−2.07)	
South				−0.007 (−1.05)	

Table 7A.1. (cont.)

Variables	Regression 1	Regression 2	Regression 3	Regression 4	Regression 5
11. Weight of the borrower's province for the bank (WPB)					
North				−0.001 (−0.01)	
Centre				0.075 (0.41)	
South				−1.090 (−1.01)	
12. Duration of relation (DUR)					
North				−0.02 (−0.93)	
Centre				−0.08 (−1.77)	
South				0.06 (0.12)	
13. Volatility of utilized credit (VOLAT)				1.22 (11.48)	1.42 (13.09)
14 Utilization rate (UTR)				−0.19 (−14.22)	−0.21 (−15.58)
15. Relative size of the firm and the bank (SIZEFB)					
North				−0.006 (−0.06)	
Centre				0.089 (0.60)	
South				0.367 (0.87)	
16. Dummy 'local-to-local' (LT)				0.023 (0.63)	
17. Dummy 'local-to-local in the South' (LS)				0.81 (3.26)	1.15 (8.06)
18. Dummy 'Northern bank-Southern firm' (DNS)				0.024 (1.82)	

Note: (1) All regressions include dummy variables (*FIRM*) capturing firm-specific effects; in all cases these dummies proved jointly significant at the 1 per cent level. *T*-statistics (or *F*-statistics where appropriate) are shown in parentheses.

List of variables used

Name	Description

Numerical variables

OP	Ratio of bank operating costs to deposits.
L	Lending-to-deposits ratio.
LSQ	Lending-to-deposits ratio squared.
BD	Ratio of bad loans to deposits.
ROB	Compulsory reserves as a percentage of total deposits.
DEP	Total deposits.
WFB	Ratio of a firm's loan to total loans of the bank.
WBF	Ratio of a firm's loan to total borrowing of the firm.
WBP	Ratio of the number of the bank's branches in the province to total branches in that province.
DUR	Number of years for which the particular bank–firm relationship is observed without interruption in the sample.
VOLAT	Volatility of utilized credit, as proxied by the ratio between average and end-of-period loan.
UTR	Ratio of utilized credit to the total line of credit.
SIZEFB	Ratio of the bank's total deposits to the firm's value added.

Dummy variables

BANK	Dummy for bank-specific effects.
FIRM	Dummy for firm-specific effects.
LT	Local-to-local dummy: it takes a value 1 if the headquarters (not the branches) of the bank are located in the same province in which the borrower resides.
LS	Same as *LT*, but refers only to Southern provinces.
DNS	It takes a value of 1 when a bank located in the North or in the Centre lends to a borrower located in the South.

for the fact that banks with below-average lending have an incentive to lower interest rates in order to increase the proportion of loans in the overall portfolio: in this case we also included a quadratic term, which turned out to be negative. Overall, however, balance-sheet ratios add little to the effect of operating costs: the R^2 increases only from 0.606 to 0.618.

In regression 4 the rates charged on individual loan contracts are regressed on the two sets of dummy variables (firms' and banks' specific effects) that appear in regression 1 and, in addition, a number of regressors designed to capture the variation that does not depend on the characteristics of either the bank or the firm but is specific to a particular bank-firm relationship.

Although several of these variables are statistically very significant, the unexplained variance is reduced only marginally relative to the regression on the bank and firm individual dummy variables alone (regression 1). The uncorrected R^2 increases from 63.9 per cent to 65.3; the standard error is reduced from 1.54 to 1.51. This standard error (measured in percentage points) strikes us as being still very large, suggesting that, aside from possible noise in data collection, we are still far from having a satisfactory empirical explanation of specific bank-firm relations. It should be noted in this regard that collateral, possibly an important variable in this regression, is missing for lack of data: different rates may be charged to the same firm because of different choices by both the firm and the bank with respect to collateral. Note, however, that the specific effect of firms or banks (such as total assets of the firm, personal wealth of the entrepreneur, and average degree of collateralization of a bank's loans) cannot be used in the regression, as they are already captured by the relative dummies.

Four variables turn out to be statistically significant. The first, and most interesting, is the LS variable (local to local in the South), which has a coefficient of 0.81 and is significant at the 1 per cent level.

As noted in the text, the LT variable has instead a very low coefficient (0.023) and is not statistically significant.[24] The WBP variable (weight of the bank in the borrower's province) is barely significant and has, if anything, a negative sign, suggesting that being a local bank is different from being an outside bank with local branches.[25]

The WBF variable (weight of the bank for the firm) is also a possible gauge of customer relationships. Prima facie, its negative sign might be interpreted as the result of banks' more careful screening and monitoring of the firms that are highly dependent on them, hence a greater willingness to charge them lower rates. But this is hardly convincing, as the WFB variable (weight of the firm for the bank) is not significant and has a positive sign in two of the three areas of the country; if anything, one would expect banks to be particularly careful when monitoring firms to whom they extend a loan which is large in relation to the size of the bank, not the firm. We are hence inclined to interpret the negative sign of the *WBF* variable simply in terms of the demand function for credit (firms borrowing more where the cost is lower, other things being equal).

Another variable potentially measuring the importance of customer relations (the *DUR* variable) is not significant. Of the remaining significant variables in this regression, *VOLAT* has a simple interpretation: its positive sign may stem from banks charging higher rates when the utilization of lines of credit is volatile, complicating their short-run liquidity management. However, the negative sign of *UTR* (the utilization rate) is puzzling, as one would expect rates to be higher when firms draw larger shares of their lines of credit. It might be that the size of the facilities is seldom revised by banks, so that utilization turns out to depend essentially on the behaviour of demand, yielding a negative correlation with interest rates.

Column 5 offers a highly concise summary of the previous results concerning operating costs, balance-sheet ratios and bank-firm specific interactions. There is little variation in the coefficient values: the banks' coefficients (variables 2–7) are very close to those of regression 3, while those relating to bank-firm interactions (variables 8–17) are close to those of regression 4.

Appendix B: Corporate borrowing and investment regressions

The empirical analysis of Section 4.4 is based on a sample of 2,132 firms' balance-sheet data from the Company Accounts Data Service. We only consider small manufacturing firms, i.e. those with sales of 1–10 billion lire in 1982. We also exclude firms whose data are incomplete, missing or unreliable; specifically, if: (a) the capital and the depreciation accounts do not square; (b) sales grow on average at a rate higher than 100 per cent or decrease on average by more than 50 per cent; (c) assets and liabilities do not square; (d) the firm has been involved in a merger and/or acquisition operation; (e) we find non-positive values for the capital stock, the number of employees, or the level of financial debt. We compute the capital stock at replacement cost. We use 1982 as a benchmark year (in 1982 Italian firms were allowed to update the capital stock value in their balance sheet) and the perpetual inventory method subsequently. We rely on market rather than book value of long-term financial debt. In computing the market value, we use the Brainard *et al.* (1980) procedure, allowing for some specific features of debt issues in Italy, in particular for the fact that debt is reimbursed progressively until maturity.

In the estimation of equation (1), with $B_{i,t}^*$ replaced by a linear function of its determinants, we allow for the fact that because of the short time-span covered by our sample, fixed-effect estimation would result in biased and inconsistent coefficients (Nickell, 1981). We follow Arellano and Bond (1991) and take the first differential of the original equation to remove the firm's fixed effect. We then use a generalized method of moments approach[26] with the dependent variable lagged twice as an instrument. This leaves just four observations for each firm. Under these circumstances, it is difficult to believe that factors such as the tax position of the firm or its riskiness will vary significantly over our sample period. We therefore follow a two-step estimation strategy. First, we regress the debt-sales ratio on its time-variable determinants. Then, using the estimated coefficients, we compute the individual firm effects. In the second step, we regress the individual firm effect on the time-invariant determinants of borrowing. At this stage we use both a standard OLS procedure and a logit specification where the probability for a given firm that its fixed effect is larger than the sample median is taken to be a logistic function of the time-invariant determinants of borrowing. The two approaches yield very similar results. The tables report only the results of the second procedure. To capture the effect of other time-varying factors we use both a trend (i.e. a constant in the first-difference specification) and a set of time dummies. The latter, however, are found to have little explanatory power.

NOTES

The views expressed are those of the authors and do not involve the responsibility of either the CEPR or the Banca d'Italia. We would like to thank R. Camporeale, A.P. Caprari, S. De Mitri, F. Farabullini and A. Mendolia for editorial and data handling assistance. We are also very grateful to L. Bonato, L. Cannari, C. Cottarelli, G. Parigi, M. Ratti and the participants in seminars at IGIER, the University of Modena and the London School of Economics for very helpful discussions and comments.

1 See Meldolesi (1990).
2 The abolition of the Ministry for the Mezzogiorno, with much of its apparatus of transfers and subsidies, is proposed in a referendum, promoted by members of a broad spectrum of political parties. In addition, Northern resentment, even separatism, latent for many years, is now a concrete political problem; it threatens, if not the integrity of the Italian state, the electoral base of the main political parties.
3 McKinnon (1973) also argues that financial repression discourages saving and investment; we do not pursue this approach here since, as we shall see, capital scarcity is not at issue in the Italian case.
4 For a broader overview of the structure and performance of the economy of

the Mezzogiorno see Banca d'Italia (1990), D'Antonio (1988), Graziani (1984), Marzano and Murolo (1985) and Sylos-Labini (1985).

5 Other factors are the higher incidence of irregular and unemployed workers and more generous welfare policies (see F. Padoa-Schioppa, 1990).

6 See Giannola (1986).

7 As we have noted, subsidies cut the cost of capital by about 40 per cent and the cost of labour by 20 per cent.

8 D'Amico et al. (1990) have disaggregated the data into 264 cells according to the size and sector of activity of the borrowers. The average national rate in each cell has then been weighted with the share of lending pertaining to that cell in each province.

9. Their preferred regression is the following:

$$LR = 15.2 + 0.9 \, COMP - 0.11 \, GDP + 0.03 \, BL + 0.01 \, HERF - 1.8 \, DUAG$$
$$\quad (25.7) \ (7.6) \qquad (6.6) \qquad (2.6) \qquad (1.8) \qquad (1.8)$$

$\bar{R}^2 = 0.845$; standard error = 0.43; number of observations = 95

where: LR = average lira lending rate charged by bank branches located in the province;

$COMP$ = composition effect, computed on the basis of economic sector and size of borrowers;

GDP = GDP per capital in each province;

BL = ratio of bad loans to total loans reported by local branches;

$HERF$ = Herfindahl index for each province computed on the basis of bank loans reported by local branches;

$DUAG$ = dummy variable for the province of Agrigento (Sicily).

10 The regression is the same as for panel A, but the tests refer to subsets of the firms' coefficients. Note that, because of composition effects, the value of the average differential is not the average of the differentials displayed in the individual subsets of the sample; in general, average differentials turn out to be larger than those of any subsample.

11 We thank A. Gavosto of the Banca d'Italia for collecting these data and making them available to us.

12 In the terminology of Keeton (1979), this may be interpreted as evidence of 'type 1' rationing.

13 A greater intensity of rationing in the South has been pointed out also by Pittaluga (1991), who however does not discriminate between Northern and Southern banks.

14 It is assumed that the loan is indispensable, as the own resources of the firm are insufficient to cover the cost of the (fixed size) project.

15 At least on the implicit assumption that equity finance is not affected by agency problems. This is not a bad assumption when describing local firms in which owner coincides with manager and the alternative to bank financing is retained earnings, not external equity.

16 To distinguish between the risk and the tax effects of greater earnings volatility, we include in the list of regressors the ratio of earnings volatility ($STDE$) to a measure of non-debt tax shields, i.e. earnings divided by depreciation allowances ($E/DEPR$). In this way, we should capture the fiscal effect of $STDE$ (larger volatility makes debt less palatable as a tax shield; this effect will be more pronounced if the firm can rely on alternative tax shields).

17 Consider the simple case in which projects are successful with probability p and returns x or unsuccessful with probability $1 - p$ and returns equal to zero. All projects yield by assumption the same average return. Lower values of p therefore signal riskier projects. The true value of p is known both to the entrepreneur and to the bank. In a competitive equilibrium we have:

$$1 + r = (1 + \rho)/p - (1 - p)/p(C/B)$$

where r and ρ indicate respectively lending and deposit rates and B and C denote the loan and the collateral. A large amount of collateral is associated with a lower r and, as a result, greater borrowing. Similarly a lower value of p, i.e. a riskier project, would call for a higher interest rate. The extent of the effect on r of a decline in p varies inversely with the availability of collateral.

18 Notice also that the impact of collateral is not unambiguous. As shown by Stiglitz and Weiss (1981) entrepreneurs with more collateral may also be less risk-averse. On this issue, however, see also Bester (1985).

19 In a Stiglitz-Weiss set-up, however, investment subsidies lead to an improvement in the pool of applicants and feebler adverse selection effects. This is because in this model the marginal project is the best, i.e. the least risky, project. An investment grant therefore draws into the applicant pool new, less risky entrepreneurs. This by itself should improve the average return to the banks' portfolio and force the interest rate down. Less credit demand from each individual entrepreneur (who can rely at least partly on government financial help) would work in the same direction. At the same time, though, the number of applicants would go up, putting upward pressure on the lending and the deposit rates.

20 Slightly more formally, let us suppose that banks observe the volatility of firms' earnings, i.e. they know $STDE$. The latter, however, is only a noisy measure of the true risk (σ_i) for firm i, i.e. $\sigma_i = STDE_i + \epsilon_i$ where ϵ_i is a stochastic term. It could then be argued that the variance of ϵ_i is larger in the South. This would explain why $STDE$ exerts a larger effect on debt in the South, but would still leave unanswered the question of why the variance of ϵ_i is larger.

21 Larger cash flows may indicate an improvement in the firm's future profitability and therefore lead to higher investment. A positive coefficient for the cash-flow variable does not therefore necessarily capture the existence of a financial constraint on investment (Fazzari et al., 1988), despite the fact that we try to control for other possible determinants of investment. Our results, however, do not merely indicate that cash-flow matters, but suggest that it matters more for riskier firms. Therefore, even if the cash-flow coefficient is a biased indicator of the importance of financial constraints, it could still be argued, on the assumption of a constant bias, that such constraints are more important for riskier firms.

22 On this point, see Vives (1991).

23 Data collected by the Bank of Italy on individual banks and customers are subject to a legal provision forbidding their publication; for this paper, they have been handled only at the central bank by authorized persons.

24 Given the parametrization of this regression, the coefficient of LT measures the effect of the local-to-local variable in the Centre-North. The effect in the South is given by the sum of the coefficients of LT and LS.

25 The WBP variable is significant (at the 4 per cent level) only in the Centre; its

negative sign might be explained in terms of the demand function for loans (lower rates leading to higher market shares).
26 The estimation package for dynamic panel data (DPD) was developed by Arellano and Bond (1988).

REFERENCES

Arellano, M. and S. Bond (1988) 'Dynamic Panel Data Estimation Using DPD – A Guide for Users', Institute for Fiscal Studies Working Paper No. 15.
    (1991) 'Some Tests of Specification for Panel Data: Monte Carlo Evidence and an Application to Employment Equations', *Review of Economic Studies* **58**, 277–97.
Attanasio, O. and F. Padoa-Schioppa (1991) 'Regional Inequalities, Migration and Mismatch in Italy', in F. Padoa Schioppa (ed.), *Mismatch and Labour Mobility*, Cambridge: Cambridge University Press.
Banca d'Italia (1947) *Assemblea annuale dei partecipanti. Relazione del Governatore sull'esercizio 1946. Considerazioni finali*, Roma.
    (1989) *Assemblea annuale dei partecipanti. Relazione del Governatore sull'esercizio 1988*, Roma.
    (1990) 'Il sistema finanziario nel Mezzogiorno', edited by G. Galli, special issue of the *Contributi all'analisi economica*, Roma.
Barro, R.J. and X. Sala-i-Martín (1991) 'Convergence across States and Regions', *Brookings Papers on Economic Activity*, (1), 107–82.
Bester, H. (1985) 'Screening vs. Rationing in Credit Markets with Imperfect Information', *American Economic Review* **57**, 850–55.
Biehl, D. (1986) *The Contribution of Infrastructure to Regional Development. Final Report*, Luxembourg, Office for Official Publications of the European Communities.
Bodo, G. and P. Sestito (1991) *Le vie dello sviluppo. Dall'analisi del dualismo territoriale una proposta per il Mezzogiorno*, Bologna, Il Mulino.
Bonato, L., R. Faini and M. Ratti (1991) 'Le scelte di indebitamento delle imprese in Italia', in V. Conti and R. Hamaui (eds.), *Operatori e mercati nel processo di liberalizzazione – I. Le famiglie e le imprese*, Bologna, Il Mulino.
Brainard, W.C., J.B. Shoven and L. Weiss (1980) 'The Financial Valuation of the Return of Capital', *Brookings Papers on Economic Activity*, (2), 453–502.
Chenery, H. (1962) *Politiche di sviluppo per l'Italia meridionale*, Roma, Svimez-Giuffrè.
Cho, Y.J. (1986) 'Inefficiencies from Financial Liberalization in the Absence of Well-Functioning Equity Markets', *Journal of Money Credit and Banking* **2**, 191–99.
Ciampi, C.A. (1984) 'Intervento' to the Conference 'Banche e imprese per lo sviluppo delle economie locali del Mezzogiorno', Bari, 22 June 1984, Banca d'Italia, *Documenti*, 129, June.
Ciocca, P., A.M. Giannoni and C. Nanni (1984) 'An Analysis of Customer "Mobility" in the Bank credit Market 1979–1980', in Banca d'Italia (ed.), *Italian Credit Structures: Efficiency, Competition and Controls*, London, Euromoney Publications.
Conigliani, C., R. De Bonis, G. Motta and G. Parigi (1991) 'Economie di scala e

di diversificazione nel sistema bancario italiano', Banca d'Italia, *Temi di discussione*, 150, Feb.

Cottarelli, C., G. Galli, P. Marullo Reedtz and G. Pittaluga (1986) 'Monetary Policy Through Ceilings on Bank Lending', *Economic Policy* 1, (3), 673–94.

D'Amico, N., G. Parigi and M. Trifilidis (1990) 'I tassi d'interesse e la rischiosità degli impieghi bancari', in Banca d'Italia, 'Il sistema finanziario nel Mezzogiorno', special issue of the *Contributi all'analisi economica*, Roma, 305–47.

D'Antonio, M. (1988) 'Sviluppo economico e redistribuzione: il caso Mezzogiorno', *Economia & Lavoro* 1, 3–24.

De Meza, D. and D.C. Webb (1988) 'Credit Market Efficiency and Tax Policy in the Presence of Screening Costs', *Journal of Public Economics* 36, 1–22.

Diamond, D.W. (1984) 'Financial Intermediation and Delegated Monitoring', *Review of Economic Studies* 51, 393–414.

Dini, L. (1989) 'Relazione introduttiva' to the Isveimer Workshop *Il fattore Finanza per la competitività dell'Azienda Mezzogiorno*, Capri, 11–12 November, Banca d'Italia, *Documenti*, 267.

D'Onofrio, P. and R. Pepe (1990) 'Le strutture creditizie', in Banca d'Italia, 'Il sistema finanziario nel Mezzogiorno', special issue of the *Contributi all'analisi economica*, Roma, 207–50.

Fazio, A. (1985) 'Credito e attività produttiva nel Mezzogiorno', Banca d'Italia, *Bollettino Economico*, No. 5, October, 27*–42*.

Fazzari, S.M., B.C. Petersen and R.G. Hubbard (1988) 'Financing Constraints and Corporate Investment', *Brookings Papers on Economic Activity*, (1), 141–206.

Fry, M. (1988) *Money, Interest and Banking in Economic Development*, Baltimore, J. Hopkins University.

Galli, G. and M. Onado (1990) 'Dualismo territoriale e sistema finanziario', in Banca d'Italia, 'Il sistema finanziario nel Mezzogiorno', special issue of the *Contributi all'analisi economica*, Roma, 1–63.

Gerschenkron, A. (1962) *Economic Backwardness in Historical Perspective*, Cambridge (Mass.), Harvard University Press.

Giannola, A. (1986) 'Problemi e prospettive di sviluppo nel Mezzogiorno', in Ente per gli Studi Monetari, Bancari e Finanziari L. Einaudi (ed.), *Oltre la crisi. Prospettive di sviluppo dell'economia italiana e il contributo del sistema finanziario*, Bologna, Il Mulino, 209–44.

Goldsmith, R.W. (1969) *Financial Structure and Development*, New Haven, Yale University Press.

Graziani, A. (1984) 'Produttività insufficiente. Scoprire le cause profonde', *Delta* 12, 5–6.

Greenwald, B.C. and J.E. Stiglitz (1991) 'Information, Finance, and Markets: the Architecture of Allocative Mechanisms', NBER Working Paper No. 3652, March.

Grillo, M. (1987) 'Concorrenza, monopolio, regolamentazione', in D. Cossuta and M. Grillo (eds.), *Concorrenza, monopolio e regolamentazione*, Bologna, Il Mulino.

Guglielmetti, P. and R. Padovani (1989) 'L'economia della Sardegna a fine '88: tendenze recenti e prospettive di sviluppo', mimeo.

Hellwig, M. (1991) 'Banking, Financial Intermediation and Corporate Finance', in A. Giovannini and C. Mayer (eds.), *European Financial Integration*, Cambridge (UK), Cambridge University Press.

Hillier, B. and M.V. Ibrahimo (1991) 'A Partial Equilibrium Model of the Credit Market with Asymmetric Information about Project Means and Variances', paper prepared for the Second International Macroeconomics Programme Meeting, Madrid, 7–8 June.

Keeton, W.R. (1979) *Equilibrium Credit Rationing*, New York, Garland Publishing Inc.

Lucas, R.J. (1990) 'Why doesn't Capital Flow from Rich to Poor Countries?', *American Economic Review* **80**, 92–96.

MacKie-Mason, J.K. (1988) 'Do Taxes Affect Corporate Financing Decisions?', NBER Working Paper No. 2632.

McKinnon, R.I. (1973) *Money and Capital in Economic Development*, Washington (DC), The Brookings Institution.

Marullo Reedtz, P. (1990) 'La redditività delle aziende di credito', in Banca d'Italia, 'Il sistema finanziario nel Mezzogiorno', special issue of the *Contributi all'analisi economica*, Roma, 251–76.

Marzano, F. and A. Murolo (1985) 'Il ruolo del sistema creditizio nello sviluppo del Mezzogiorno: alcune considerazioni critiche', *Mezzogiorno d'Europa* **1**, 45–61.

Mayer, C. (1990) 'Financial Systems, Corporate Finance, and Economic Development', in R.G. Hubbard (ed.), *Asymmetric Information, Corporate Finance, and Investment*, Chicago: The University of Chicago Press, 307–32.

Meldolesi, L. (1990) 'Mezzogiorno con gioia', Università di Napoli, mimeo.

Messori, M. and D. Silipo (1991) 'Un'analisi empirica delle differenze territoriali del sistema bancario italiano', CESPE Paper, 6, 90.

Micossi, S. and G. Tullio (1991) 'Fiscal Imbalances, Economic Distortions, and the Long Run Performance of the Italian Economy', paper prepared for the International Workshop on 'Global Macroeconomic Perspectives', Roma, May 29–30, 1991.

Myers, S.C. (1977) 'Determinants of Corporate Borrowing', *Journal of Financial Economics* **2**, 147–75.

Nickell, S.J. (1981) 'Biases in Dynamic Models with Fixed Effects', *Econometrica* **49**, 1417–26.

Onado, M., G. Salvo and M. Villani (1990) 'Flussi finanziari e allocazione del risparmio', in 'Il sistema finanziario nel Mezzogiorno', Banca d'Italia, special issue of the *Contributi all'analisi economica*, Roma, 65–102.

Padoa-Schioppa, F. (1990) *L'economia sotto tutela. Problemi strutturali dell'intervento pubblico in Italia*, Bologna, Il Mulino.

Pittaluga, G.B. (1991) 'Economie regionali e squilibri nel mercato del credito', in *Il razionamento del credito: aspetti teorici e verifiche empiriche*, Milano, Franco Angeli, 117–54.

Rybczynski, T.M. (1974) 'Business Finance in the EEC, USA and Japan', *Three Banks Review* **103**, 58–72.

Sabbatini, P. (1990) 'I conti economici degli istituti di credito speciale', in Banca d'Italia, 'Il sistema finanziario nel Mezzogiorno', special issue of the *Contributi all'analisi economica*, Roma, 277–304.

Scandizzo, P. (1991) 'I trasferimenti pubblici e la loro distribuzione sul territorio' in ISPE, *I trasferimenti pubblici e la loro distribuzione sul territorio in Italia*, Roma.

Sharpe, S.A. (1990) 'Asymmetric Information, Bank Lending, and Implicit

Contracts: A Stylized Model of Customer Relationships', *The Journal of Finance* **45**, 1069–87.

Shaw, E.S. (1973) *Financial Deepening in Economic Development*, New York, Oxford University Press.

Siracusano, F. and C. Tresoldi (1988) 'Evoluzione e livelli dei margini di profitto dell'industria in Italia e nei principali paesi industriali', in Banca d'Italia, 'Atti del seminario: Ristrutturazione economica e finanziaria delle imprese', Roma, 27–28 June, special issue of the *Contributi all'analisi economica*, Roma, 269–333.

——— (1990) 'Le piccole imprese manifatturiere: diseconomie esterne, incentivi, equilibri gestionali e finanziari', in 'Il sistema finanziario nel Mezzogiorno', Banca d'Italia, special issue of the *Contributi all'analisi economica*, Roma, 103–67.

Stiglitz, J.E. (1989) 'Markets, Market Failures, and Development', *American Economic Review, Papers and Proceedings* **79**, 197–203.

——— (1991) 'Government, Financial Markets, and Economic Development', NBER Working Paper No. 3669, April.

Stiglitz, J.E. and A. Weiss (1981) 'Credit Rationing in Markets with Imperfect Information', *American Economic Review* **71**, 393–410.

SVIMEZ, *Rapporti sull'economia del Mezzogiorno*, various years.

——— (1991) *I differenziali di produttività Nord-Sud nel settore manifatturiero. Un'analisi microeconomica*, edited by L. Prosperetti and F. Varetto, Bologna, Il Mulino.

Sylos-Labini, P. (1985) 'L'evoluzione economica del Mezzogiorno negli ultimi trent'anni', Banca d'Italia, Temi di discussione No. 46.

Taggart, R.A. (1977) 'A Model of Corporate Financing Decisions', *The Journal of Finance* **5**, 1467–84.

Tybout, J. (1984) 'Interest Controls and Credit Allocation in Developing Countries', *Journal of Money, Credit and Banking* **4**, 474–78.

Vives, X. (1991) 'Banking Competition and European Integration', in A. Giovannini and C. Mayer (eds.), *European Financial Integration*, Cambridge, Cambridge University Press.

Discussion

PATRICK HONOHAN

This is a fascinating paper whose importance is not limited to the light it casts on Southern Italy, but which has potentially much wider implications for the question of informational barriers to entry in European banking.

With the deregulation of cross-border banking in Europe an important question is: to what extent will informational barriers limit the potential consumer gains? A high proportion of the prospective welfare gains for the whole Single Market as presented by the Cecchini report of the European Commission was to be accounted for by the elimination of differentials in intermediation margins. These estimates have been criticized for making no allowance for information and contract problems such as are addressed in this paper (Grilli, 1992).

Because of the high intermediation margins that have prevailed, it is usually thought that Italy, along with Greece, Portugal, Spain and Ireland, will have the most adjustment to make. But if local banks have powerful informational advantages, then comparatively little might change.

Conventional wisdom about the elimination of regulatory entry barriers in Australia and Canada would have it that the entry, or threat of entry, of foreign banks reduced gross bank margins considerably, but that residual inherent entry barriers were sufficient to prevent the newcomers from prospering; none captured a big market share.

The paper presents evidence not for a whole country, but for a region (Southern Italy) apparently displaying significant contrasts with the rest of the country, not only in financial structure and average interest rates, but also in a wide range of other economic indicators.

The authors' main purpose is to tell us if financial intermediation is in fact different in the South. They conclude that it is, and that a model based on informational barriers is the relevant one for explaining this difference. This is a serious piece of data analysis, and stands up well to scrutiny. I think that their conclusions drawn are, on the whole, plausible. But I would like to provide a caution regarding the magnitude of the effects we are looking at and the conclusiveness of the evidence.

There are several distinct substantial parts to the data analysis in the fairly complex structure of this paper. I would like to concentrate on what is to me the most important, the discussion of why Southern firms pay higher interest rates. The raw average here is 210 basis points, and the exercise carried out by the authors is to try to see how much of this is explained by observable characteristics. We immediately discover that about one-half of the 210 points is explainable by firm characteristics (using firm dummies). Thus the average Southern firm pays 100 basis points more to its Southern bankers than it does to its Northern bankers.

Note that there is no analogous effect in the North. The average Northern firm does not pay its Northern bankers more than its Southern bankers. This suggests that the conclusion that Southern Italian banks have special information advantages which allow them to extract monopoly rents from local firms may not generalize to other peripheral countries in Europe. We cannot say, *ex ante*, whether Spain is more like Northern or Southern Italy in this regard.

Why do Southern firms pay a higher interest rate to their Southern bankers? The answer given by the authors is that the Southern banks have captured a monopoly rent from their local knowledge or informational advantage. This interpretation is supported by the supplementary information that a firm pays (roughly) a further 100 basis points more to a bank whose head office is in the same province as the firm.

Now there could be a bit of a problem with the interpretation here since we also know that the Southern banks have lower profits than the Northern ones. Within the authors' interpretation we have to assume that a second level of rent capture is occurring, with the staff of the bank taking some or all of the rent obtained from informational advantage.

Some alternative interpretations to the rent capture theory are possible. For instance, it may be that the Southern banks specialize in information gathering and monitoring of local borrowers. From this perspective one might suppose that such behaviour allows them to screen more effectively, but it is costly and thus results in higher interest rates to cover higher operating costs even in a competitive environment. An attraction of this alternative theory is that it could explain both the high interest rates and the high operating costs of the Southern banks. However it would provide serious competition for the authors' preferred theory only if the higher operating costs of Southern banks could be shown to be correlated with better loan appraisal – and indeed the authors argue the contrary.

Another possibility is that some kind of side payments are prevalent in the relationship between Southern firms and their local bankers. For instance if the banking relationship is not strictly armslength, there might be some reasons (e.g. taxation) to effect additional payments from firm to bank by means of surcharges on the economic rate of interest. Or a firm might be paying higher interest on its short-term loans in order to secure subsidized, and hence rationed, long-term loans from a financial institution that is not wholly independent from the bank. In this case the bank would be exploiting monopoly power, but that power would not be based on information advantage.

Finally there is the question, largely unresolved in the paper, of the nature of the loan. The risk and cost of lending by a bank differs considerably depending on the degree and quality of collateral and on the flexibility of repayment schedules. These characteristics could differ systematically as between Northern and Southern banks lending to Southern firms. Indeed it is plausible that Northern banks, lacking information, would tend to confine themselves to self-liquidating documentary credits and the like. In that case the Northern banks would be offering essentially a different product to the Southern banks. If so, the lower interest rate they were charging might only reflect objective risk differentials, and not the exercise of monopoly power by Southern banks.

Thus, even though the information story is plausible, there may be other factors which tend to reduce what is already a rather small effect. There is a presumption that by conditioning on such further factors, were data on them available, the 100 basis points would shrink. It is noteworthy that the, presumably more homogeneous, sub-sample of Sicilian firms results in a differential of only 50 basis points.

Standing back to interpret these findings, let us recall from the first part of the paper that we know that the South of Italy is a very different economy from the North – with, for example, an overall 30 per cent productivity differential. Furthermore there have until recently been restrictions on bank branching, so the picture is not one of a completely open regulatory environment for a lengthy period. Against this background I have to say that even a 1 percentage point interest differential seems to me remarkably low.

The other main results in the paper are perhaps less persuasive than that on average interest rates, not so much because of methodological issues but because the magnitude of the effects is rather small. The authors make much of statistical significance in reporting their results, but with thousands of data points, even tiny effects can be statistically significant. The quantitative importance of the effects is small. Thus, for example we are told that Southern firms are less likely than Northern ones to change their bankers; but this is based on the observation that 24 per cent of Northern firms changed their bankers in a certain period compared with 21 per cent of Southern firms – hardly an enormous difference, and much smaller than many other North-South contrasts. Likewise, I am not convinced that Southern banks are much less efficient in evaluating risk on the basis that the mean absolute error in the relevant interest rate equation is 120 basis points instead of 90.

REFERENCE

Grilli, V. (1989) 'Europe 1992: Issues and Prospects for the Financial Markets', *Economic Policy* 4 (9), 387–421.

ANTONIO S. MELLO

The paper by Faini, Galli and Giannini is a very interesting piece of a scarcely explored field of economic research. It tries to investigate whether the inefficiencies in the workings of the financial sector can explain the gap between the Northern and the Southern regions of the same country (Italy). This hypothesis is verified when two conditions can be met: (1) Finance in the South is different from that in the North (by finance one must mean not just the intermediation process, but how property rights are established and exercised, bankruptcy procedures differ, as well as the structure of corporate governance and control); and (2) the reported differences in finance do not result from differences in the economic fabric, the state of economic development, industry specialization and corporate structure, but instead contribute to these differences. Assuming that the hypothesis holds, one must then explain what perpetuates the survival of financial intermediates that operate with costly and inefficient methods.

The authors start the analysis by looking at different measures of sources of capital. From the information provided one can see that the debt to equity ratios are roughly the same in both the North and the South; the proportion of long-term to short-term debt is also not different; also neither the North nor the South seems to rely on bonds for long-term financing, though the percentage in the North seems slightly higher. What seems to differ is that firms in the South are more heavily capitalized. Moreover, equity financing in the South is achieved mainly by retaining earnings and long-term debt in this region is often available through a state development agency – the SCI. These two important findings, involving the quantity and the cost of capital may be interrelated, but the authors leave unshown whether this is, in fact, the case.

What is the effect of a lower participation by southern firms in the capital markets? This is potentially significant, because when firms do not contract in the capital markets, there is no objective benchmark for the opportunity cost of capital to guide investment decisions. But why are firms in the South not in the stock market? Here, again, the authors do not provide an answer, although they talk about smaller size. But if size is what matters (and no statistical evidence of a size effect is given) then one must ask what makes southern firms smaller when presumably easier access to capital should, instead, make them larger? I think control is part of the story: maybe most companies in the South are smaller, because owners simply do not want to give up control; without a market for corporate control, inefficiencies tend to arise. Moreover, if growth implies giving up control in family-owned businesses, then failure to exploit available economies of scale may occur, with the corresponding inefficiencies.

So much for demanders of capital. What about financial intermediation? Institutional restrictions seem to be similar both in the North and in the South: prohibition of establishing new banks, requirement of authorization to open new branches, credit ceilings and limitations on the ability of small banks to lend outside the area in which branches are located. What then could explain the finding that banks in the South charge higher fees to southern firms than do northern banks operating in the South? I suspect size and segmentation: southern banks are smaller, maybe because companies in the South are smaller: recall the restriction that banks cannot lend outside the area of location of their main branches: so if customers do not expand geographically, banks may not expand either. Also, smaller size could be the simple result of the existence of a state development agency provider of a substantial part of the credit. I do not find in the study any evidence that banks in the South are indeed smaller, but I am able to conclude that the financial system is more fragmented in the South: (small) private banks concentrate on short-term financing, whilst government agencies provide long-term funds.

If southern banks are smaller and there are economies of scale beyond their size, then their average costs are higher and profits are lower. Higher costs could also occur because of greater investment in information (although the authors seem to imply that southern banks are less efficient in screening borrowers, of which, from the statistics presented, I am not at all convinced), higher deadweight costs of bankruptcy and a less diversified portfolio of loans.

The question that the authors then ask is what explains the apparent survival of southern banks alongside their northern counterparts when the former charge higher rates. They say monopoly rents in an informationally captured economy. This is plausible, but by no means tells the whole story, and does not necessarily imply the existence of rents. Southern banks could charge more to local companies than their northern competitors if they provided additional services to local companies: for example, means to finance the consumption needs of owners, as well as other services; this is the case, especially when in small businesses, family and company assets are not clearly separate. One must also remember that this represents a potential form of tax evasion. The higher rates could result, as well, from the fact that in bad times southern banks would not stop extending credit as early as northern banks, especially when these have better opportunities elsewhere (greater regional diversification) or are less informed about idiosyncratic risks. This is somewhat equivalent to establishing an effective priority of claims – which also ties in with the observation that companies do not seem to exhaust the credit lines of cheaper banks – some kind of implicit collateral. Moreover, it is related to some sort of specialization in the information collection process: while northern banks are better in economy/market wide information, southern banks would collect regional and local company-specific information, presumably more difficult to get. In such a separating competitive equilibrium, both types of banks would survive with southern banks charging higher rates.

My final remark is about the way the authors treat risk. They report that risk seems to account for one-half of the spreads in loan rates charged by southern banks. The rest should be explained by monopoly power. However, it is very hard to make statements of this sort without a proper model to measure risk. If I had to do it myself, I would start by assuming that markets were segmented: the price of risk would then differ as different models would be applicable. In fact, segmentation is one of the most clear contributions of this fine paper: the authors have provided evidence that segmentation (induced by regulatory actions) can occur within the same country and is not just a subject relevant to international capital markets.

Finally, this paper also teaches us that scarcity of capital may not be a sufficient reason for less economic development. Indeed, the less developed and poor South has greater capital-intensity than the rich and developed North. What matters is how capital is allocated and utilised in the economy.

Part IIB:
Case studies – government policies

8 Macroeconomic control in liberalizing socialist economies: Asian and European parallels

RONALD I. McKINNON

This paper explains why price inflation and a general loss of macroeconomic control are almost endemic in a liberalizing socialist economy – whether in Asia or in Eastern Europe. In their rush to decentralize decision-making, privatize, and dismantle the apparatus of central planning, reformers inadvertently upset the pre-existing system for sustaining macroeconomic equilibrium. The ability of the reform government to collect taxes and control the supply of money and credit is unwittingly undermined by the liberalization itself. Thus, the first part of the paper seeks to understand how the preexisting system of financial control under Stalinist central planning actually worked, and why it tends to break down once liberalization begins.

The Stalinist system of financial control was remarkably similar across all the socialist economies – whether in, say, the Soviet Union before 1985 or in China before 1979. In Eastern Europe, however, the liberalization process itself is being confounded by the simultaneous breakup of whole countries – as in the former Soviet Union and Yugoslavia. Similarly, the precipitate decline of the old CMEA trading regime in 1990–91 has severely disrupted even those Eastern European economies which are managing to hold together politically.

In contrast, the Asian socialist economies – China, Vietnam, Laos, Mongolia and Myanmar – are culturally and politically more homogeneous. Their economic liberalizations are not being confounded by simultaneous attempts to redraw national political boundaries. For China, Laos, and Myanmar, the importance of CMEA trade was more marginal and its break up of little significance. Although both Mongolia and Vietnam are severely impacted by the decline of CMEA trade and by the cessation of terms-of-trade subsidies from the Soviet Union, both are more agrarian; neither has an extensive capital stock in heavy industry so dependent on the old CMEA trading system as do the smaller Eastern European economies.

Thus, compared to their Eastern European counterparts, our five Asian economies have the option of choosing a more deliberate liberalization strategy – though Mongolia is opting for a 'big bang'. Because of the absence of calamitous civil disorders or unmanageable external shocks, the Asian socialist economies may well be more instructive examples for studying the 'optimum' order of economic liberalization. Even with their more gradualist approaches to liberalization, however, China, Vietnam, Laos and even Myanmar have experienced problems qualitatively similar to those in Eastern Europe in raising tax revenue, balancing the government budget, and controlling the system of money and credit. Actual or incipient inflation has been a serious problem.

In the second part of the paper, therefore, more effective monetary and fiscal measures for containing inflation in a socialist economy in transition are spelled out. Rather than a 'big bang' abolishing all planning controls simultaneously, moves to dismantle the apparatus of central planning, decontrol prices, privatize property, free foreign trade, and so on need to be supported by a proper sequence of fiscal, monetary, and foreign exchange measures. Building on the more comprehensive treatment in McKinnon (1991) and drawing on both Asian and European experience, this paper sketches a more appropriate financial order for maintaining macroeconomic stability as liberalization proceeds.

1   Financial control under classical socialism

The centrally planned Soviet economy, before the advent of perestroika and the current financial breakdown, is our model of classical socialism. Although not addressed at all in this paper, the hierarchical system of command and control and its institutional structure in the traditional Soviet economy is extremely complex – as nicely summarized by Richard Ericson (1991). Here I focus on the main elements of the financial system, which were also adopted to a greater or lesser extent by the smaller countries of Eastern Europe and our five socialist economies in Asia – even in Myanmar, which, under 'the Burmese way to socialism', never adopted rigorous central planning.

In the classical socialist economy, the financial system has two essential features that differentiate it from its capitalist counterpart. First, the system of taxation is largely *implicit* and uncodified. Second, the system of money and credit for enterprises is entirely *passive*. In the absence of central planning, the monetary system itself does not restrain the ability of enterprises to bid for scarce resources.

Consider the fiscal system first. Because the government owns all the industrial and agricultural property, surpluses are extracted from enterprises (and indirectly from households) with relatively little codification in formal tax law. In addition, the controlled price system is rigged to extract a relatively large economic surplus from agriculture. Rather than the government appropriating this surplus directly from agricultural procurement agencies, the surplus is first gathered as 'monopoly' profits in industrial enterprises which the government itself owns. Only at this point of one remove is the surplus expropriated by some combination of taxes and profit remittances.

'The pre-reform fiscal system in China . . . shares in common with other Soviet-type fiscal systems an overwhelming dependence on industry, and a reliance on profits of state-owned enterprises, along with taxes for government revenue. Using administrative prices that systematically discriminate against agricultural and raw materials producers in favor of industry, artificially high profits are created in the industrial sector. These are then captured for government coffers through a combination of turnover taxes and expropriation of profits.' (Wong, ADB Study, 1991, p. 10.)

If industrial enterprises are used as tax-collecting vehicles, no system of consumer excises (sales taxes) need be formally codified if the preexisting system of price controls keep the retail cost of consumer 'luxuries' – liquor, tobacco, automobiles, and so on – arbitrarily high. Then enterprises producing these goods would run with large cash surpluses (government revenue) which reverted to the state. Of course, the government can also lose revenue if prices of some goods, say basic foods, are set below their costs of production. The implicit consumer excise tax rate on these goods is then negative.

Similarly, no law establishing a personal income tax is necessary if all enterprises essentially withhold household income at its source. As long as the state owns the capital stock, it must set or limit the wages of workers and managers to ensure that enterprises, on average, do generate cash surpluses. Otherwise, if managers or workers' councils can determine their own wages with an indirect claim on the firm's physical capital, they will pay themselves 'excessive' wages that tend to decapitalize the enterprise (Hinds, 1990). With the necessary industrial wage controls already in place, maintaining a parallel system of personal income taxation is an unnecessary expense. Moreover wages can be more easily kept down relative to the prices of industrial goods if agricultural procurement prices for foodstuffs are kept low – which also 'automatically' keeps the incomes of farmers low.

Correspondingly, any organized system for collecting taxes on real property is redundant. Keeping agricultural procurement prices low – however distorting that may be – obviates the need for a separate land tax.

And all profits, really economic 'surplus', generated in the protected industrial monopolies is already controlled by the socialist government – thus obviating the need for a separate tax on industrial property.

Under classical socialism, having enterprise 'profits' – really residual cash surpluses which do not allow for depreciation of fixed capital or the drawing down of inventories – simply revert to the state is not an inefficient method of taxation. (The state must then provide financing for authorized new investments by recycling funds back to enterprises.) It can provide great revenue buoyancy to the government when industry is growing rapidly relative to agriculture. Christine Wong (1991) shows that Chinese government revenue rose by about 8 percentage points of GNP during the Maoist period from 1952 to 1978.

What about adverse incentive effects to enterprise managers from appropriating enterprise surpluses? In the presence of centralized price controls, output targets, and input allocations, which enterprises generate surpluses and which generate deficits is largely arbitrary, anyway. Thus, appropriating cash surpluses is the only feasible method for the government to tax enterprises. As long as all decisions for allocating resources are actually made by the central planning agency, seizing enterprise profits *ex post facto* need not be particularly damaging to managerial incentives.

In contrast, generalized business taxes that work well in a liberalized market context, say a value-added tax, might not even be collectable in the classical socialist economy when price controls prevent the tax from being shifted forward to the final user. Similarly, levying a formal gross turnover tax directly on enterprises (as socialist governments do) may simply reduce residual profits, which would otherwise revert to the state. As long as the final prices of goods sold are controlled by the government, whether revenue is formally collected from a turnover tax or from residual profit remittances to the state is a distinction without a difference. (However, the distinction is important once prices begin to be liberalized.)

Even under centralized price and output controls, however, enterprise surpluses remain somewhat uncertain. Variability in the technology, uncertainty in the availability of inputs, unknowns in inventory accumulation, and so on make enterprise cash surpluses difficult to predict *ex ante*. Hence, enforcing revenue collection in the absence of formally codified tax law requires that these surpluses remain 'blocked' as they are generated *ex post*. Under classical socialism, therefore, enterprise deposits with the state bank cannot even be spent on domestic goods and services without permission, nor are enterprises allowed to hold 'cash' – coin and currency that could be spent without being traced. This internal or 'commodity inconvertibility' of enterprise money in socialist economies is much more restrictive than mere inconvertibility into foreign exchange (McKinnon, 1979, Ch. 3),[1] which of course is a more common phenomenon in nonsocialist economies as well.

Within a classical socialist economy like, say, the Soviet Union's before 1985 or China's prior to 1979, therefore, we have two monetary circuits: the (blocked) deposits of enterprises held with the state bank – sometimes in several designated accounts – and households' coin and currency. Households can spend their cash freely for goods and services without getting permission from the government (if they can find them in the shops) or deposit it into personal savings accounts that can be later withdrawn without restraint.[2] To prevent an overhang (at fixed retail prices) of domestically convertible household money which leads to more than the normal 'tautness' in aggregate demand in the socialist economy, the amount of the blocked enterprise money which is converted through wage or other payments for personal services must be strictly limited. Indeed, having the state bank carefully monitor the conversion from enterprise to household money complements the system of wage controls.

By itself, the Stalinist system of enterprise money and credit is essentially passive on both the loan and deposit sides of the state bank's balance sheet. On the loan side, enterprises are restricted neither by interest rates (which are kept trivially low) nor by fixed credit lines. If any enterprise had insufficient funds on hand to purchase supplies as allowed under the plan, it could borrow without restraint from the state bank. On the deposit side, the demand for 'money' by enterprise is indeterminate. Blocked deposit accounts simply build up with the State Bank until they are expropriated or the government gives the enterprise permission to buy something. But with all spending mandated by the central planning agency, whether or not the enterprise has 'cash' on hand does not affect what it can or cannot do.

Even before its liberalization policy of 'doi moi' in 1986, planning in Vietnam was less detailed and comprehensive than in the Soviet Union. Nevertheless, monetary policy remained essentially passive.

'(Vietnam's) monetary policies consisted of little more than rules and practices adopted to implement the public sector's credit and cash plans, both of which were part of annual economic plans. The credit plan set forth the amount of credit to be granted to different sectors of the economy, while the cash plan specified the banking sector's receipts and payments. The banking system was thus accommodating, and both the government and state enterprise managers paid comparatively little attention to monetary issues'. (Fforde and de Vylder, ADB Study, Aug. 1991, p. 49).

In summary, the financial system does not constrain enterprises from bidding for scarce resources under classical socialism. However, as long as the central planning mechanism imposes a rough balance between supply and demand for each product, this absence of financial restraint on enterprises need not debilitate the macroeconomy. If the old method of implicit tax collection – based largely on the expropriation of enterprise surpluses – generates enough revenue, the government can prevent inflation by limiting the buildup of liquid (unblocked) cash balances owned by households.

2   The breakdown of financial control in the transition

Once liberalization begins, the formal apparatus of central planning is weakened, as decision-making and effective property rights devolve more to the (state-owned) enterprises themselves, and perhaps to a newly enfranchised private or cooperative sector. Price controls may or may not be removed in this transitional period. However, by giving up control over state property, the government in effect gives away its tax base! Because of the implicit nature of the old system of taxation, no formal internal revenue service exists for clawing back revenue from entities that are no longer controlled by the government. Enterprises can no longer so easily be used as revenue (cash) cows, or as vehicles for indirectly taxing households.

However, this decline in revenue involves more than just the transfer of some property away from direct government control. Indeed, with the exception of Mongolia's big bang in 1991, the pattern in China, Vietnam, and Myanmar has been for central or local governments to hang on to as many of the traditional industrial enterprises as they can after liberalization begins. Nevertheless, each government's revenue position is still severely impacted once markets for commodities and services are given freer rein. First, the price system can no longer be rigged to keep agricultural procurement prices – and thus real product wages – artificially low so as to transfer an easily captured surplus to industry. Second, industrial enterprises – owned by the central or diverse local governments that had generated monopoly profits – may now face substantial competition from each other (as among township industries in China), from newly enfranchised private or cooperative enterprises, and (possibly) from freer imports. The upshot is that the industrial profit base itself will tend to decline as the monopoly positions of the old state-owned industrial enterprises are undermined.

In a liberalizing socialist economy, 'profits' taxes in any form can no longer remain the major source of government revenue once the economy becomes highly marketized. Indeed, in mature market economies, we see that total profits as share of GNP are modest, and profits taxes as a share of government revenue are tiny. In the United States in 1990, for example, before-tax corporate profits (the main profit flow in the economy) amounted to about $297 billion dollars and was only 5.4 per cent of American GNP. On this base, total corporate profits taxes collected by the US federal and state governments in 1990 amounted to $134 billion, which is only 2.3% of American GNP and 7.5 per cent of the consolidated revenues of the US federal and state governments (*Economic Report of the President*, February 1991).

Compare this to the consolidated revenue of the central and local governments in China under classical socialism. In 1978, Table 8.1 shows that revenue from enterprises in the form of profits taxes and remittances amounted to 20.6 per cent of Chinese GNP and almost two-thirds of total government revenue. But this revenue position is simply not sustainable as marketization begins and the (monopoly) profit position of socialist industry begins to erode – and enterprise profits as a share of GNP begin to fall toward levels observed in the United States and other mature market economies. With the failure to develop a personal income tax or expand the base of commodity taxation, China, the Soviet Union and the smaller socialist economies of Asia and Europe naturally experience a sharp decline in the revenue share of the consolidated government as liberalization proceeds. Starting from classical socialism before 1978, China provides the longest continuous revenue series on a decentralizing socialist economy: through the massive agrarian reforms in 1979–84 where land was leased back to households to the development of township industries and those in 'free' economic zones in the late 1980s. Table 8.1 shows that consolidated revenue of the central, provincial, and local governments fell from over 34 per cent of GNP in 1978 to only 19 per cent in 1989. Table 8.1 also shows that virtually all of this decline can be explained by a fall in 'profit remittances' from enterprises, and that revenue from business product taxes – turnover and value added taxes – held up rather better (Blejer *et al.*, 1991).

This overall revenue decline forced the central and local governments to curb growth in expenditures – so that measured fiscal deficits were only 2 to 3 per cent of Chinese GNP. But this understates the 'true' fiscal deficit. Because government-financed investment expenditures fell so sharply as a share of GNP, local governments in particular pressured the banks to lend to the enterprises they owned or controlled to finance infrastructure investments in their localities. Besides fostering unhealthy fiscal competition among governments for control over enterprises and thus revenue (Wong, 1990), this 'forced' extension of excessive bank credit to

Table 8.1. *China: government revenue, 1978–89*
(In percent of GNP)

	1978	1979–81	1982–84	1985–87	1988	1989[1]
Total revenue[2]	34.4	30.0	27.0	24.8	20.4	19.0
Revenue from enterprises	20.6	17.1	12.5	8.3	5.6	4.0
Of which:						
Profit remittances	(19.1)	(16.1)	(11.4)	(0.4)	(0.3)	(0.3)
Profit tax	(1.5)	(1.0)	(1.1)	(7.9)	(5.3)	(3.7)
Taxes on:						
Income and profits[3]	21.5	17.8	13.3	7.9	5.3	3.7
Goods and services[4]	11.3	10.6	10.1	10.6	9.1	8.6
International trade	0.8	0.9	1.1	1.8	1.1	1.1
Other taxes	—	—	1.5	3.2	3.0	3.0
Nontax revenue[5]	0.8	0.8	1.0	1.3	1.7	2.4

Source: Blejer, Mario, David Burton, Steven Dunaway and Gyorgy Szapary, *China: Economic Reform and Macroeconomic Management*, International Monetary Fund, Occasional Paper 76, Washington, D.C., January, 1991, p. 23.
Notes:
1 Budget.
2 Total revenue includes nontax revenue.
3 Includes profit remittances.
4 Includes product, value added, and business taxes.
5 Excluding profit remittances.

enterprises throughout the Chinese economy undermined monetary control from the mid-1980s into the 1990s.

Similarly in Vietnam, we observe a sharp decline in transfers from state enterprises since the liberalization programme known as 'doi moi' (national renovation) began in 1986. Although the data are still very preliminary, transfers from state enterprises to the government budget appear to have fallen from 17.2 per cent of GNP in 1986 to 7.1 per cent in 1990 (Fforde and Vylder, August 1991, p. 44).

In the same year 1986, the Lao People's Democratic Republic in November introduced their new economic mechanism (NEM) with a major decontrol of agricultural and industrial prices in 1987, the decollectivization of agriculture in 1988, and the growth of private ownership in industry through disinvestment from the state sector in 1989–90 (Vokes and Fabella, ADB Report, August 1991). Although successful in many other economic dimensions, the fiscal consequences were highly adverse. Current transfers to the government from public enterprises declined from 9.5 per cent of GNP in 1986 to 1.7 per cent in 1989 (World Bank, 1990).

In the early 1990s, all five Asian economies are suffering from declining or inadequate public sector revenues as the traditional fiscal system based on the generation of high profits in the state-owned industrial sector is undermined by the liberalization itself – without being replaced by new institutions and mechanisms for collecting revenue from farms, enterprises, or households.

In the former Soviet Union, the period for observing the fiscal effects of liberalization was shorter – but the (less reliable) Soviet fiscal data tell a similar story. From 1985 when Mikhail Gorbachev took office through 1989, Table 8.2 shows government revenue falling over six percentage points of GNP. About half this fall is attributable to declining remittances from state enterprises; special factors, such as diminished sales of alcohol at home and petroleum abroad, account for the remainder. Because the Soviet government did not reduce its expenditures as revenue declined, by 1988–89 'formal' Soviet fiscal deficits had already reached 9 to 11 per cent of GNP. In 1990–91, the fiscal decline in the Soviet Union became more precipitate from burgeoning deficits on which we have little reliable information. Because of the struggle between the central government and the republics for control over revenue-generating enterprises, the republican governments refused to hand over revenue to the Soviets – an important factor in the debasement of the ruble and the collapse of the power of the Soviet central government in the summer of 1991. Now, in Russia itself, enterprise surpluses continue to erode as prices are decontrolled and competition increases.

Because interest rates are pegged below market-clearing levels, fiscal deficits cannot be financed by the direct issue of government bonds to the non-bank public. Liberalizing socialist governments typically cover their revenue shortfalls by borrowing from the (state) banking system which funds itself by issuing modest-yield saving deposits and liquid cash balances to households, and partly by allowing the blocked deposit money owned by enterprises to increase. Because of this monetary overhang, incipient price increases are large should price controls be removed. Thus even reformist governments become reluctant to eliminate price controls over a wide range of goods and services, and normal market development is severely impeded.

Monetized government deficits are not the only culprit in the inflation process, nor is inflation *per se* the only reason why markets fail to work as the apparatus of central planning is dismantled. The passive system of money and credit makes the budget constraints on enterprises unduly soft. Loss-making enterprises – those which are very inefficient or have their output prices pegged too low – continue to borrow from the state bank in order to prevent unemployment in their workforces; and this

Table 8.2. *USSR: fiscal development, 1985–89*
(In percent of GNP)

	1985	1986	1987	1988	1989 (estimate)
State budget revenue	47.3	45.8	43.6	41.7	41.0
of which:					
From state enterprises	14.9	15.8	15.0	13.2	11.9
Turnover taxes	12.6	11.5	11.4	11.5	11.8
State budget expenditure	49.7	52.0	52.0	51.0	49.5
of which:					
Investment in the economy	8.2	8.3	8.7	8.7	10.6
Subsidies	8.9	9.4	9.3	10.1	10.6
Overall balance	− 2.4	− 6.2	− 8.4	− 9.2	− 8.5
Adjusted balance[1]	—	—	− 8.8	− 11.0	− 9.5

Source: The Economy of the U.S.S.R.: Summary and Recommendations, International Monetary Fund, Dec. 19, 1990.
Note: 1 Includes cost of extrabudgetary agricultural price support, but excludes balance of centralized fund operations.

perverse flow of bank credit contributes to the loss of control over the money supply. In addition, once planning controls are removed, profitable enterprises will be anxious to spend their previously blocked cash balances lest they be seized or refrozen – thus exacerbating the inflationary pressure.

But this is not the end of the inflation story for the economy in transition. The productivity of physical capital – both fixed assets and inventories of inputs and goods in process – could fall. Absent of attractive monetary assets, whether liquid cash, or time deposits bearing a positive real rate of interest, newly liberalized enterprises will overbid for storable material inputs, foreign exchange, capital goods and so forth. In effect, decentralized enterprises will carry 'excess' inventories of all kinds as *substitute monetary stores of value* (McKinnon, 1991). The abysmally low productivity of physical capital in socialist economies could worsen during liberalization, thus adding to the net inflationary pressure as the supply of goods for sale falls relative to the aggregate demand for them.

Finally, once central planning is dismantled but the uncodified tax system based on the seizure of accumulated enterprise surpluses remains in place, it can hardly fail to undermine managerial incentives. The syndrome of the 'soft budget constraint' (Kornai, 1986) is aggravated: firms making incipient losses get compensated by subsidies (including cheap credit), and 'successful' firms have their surpluses removed. In addition, the desperate need for revenue induces the government to continually reintervene in enterprises in order to extract surpluses; and these unpredictable reinterventions are made easier when the highly visible deposits of enterprises with the state bank are easily (re)frozen or seized.

Such reinterventions make it virtually impossible for a liberalizing socialist government to commit to lasting tax or monetary agreements, or for enterprises to make long-term contracts with each other. Whatever tax, property, or credit arrangements are promulgated, they are continually overturned as economic events unfold. This chronic instability in the 'rules of the game' may well be characteristic of any socialist regime where political and economic power is monopolized by one party as in the former Soviet Union (Litwack, 1991). However, it is greatly aggravated if a government is fiscally straitened and must grab economic surpluses whenever they become visible.

3   Creating an internal revenue service

Suppose a socialist government begins liberalizing. It frees wholesale and retail markets from price and output controls so that agricultural procurement and other raw materials prices (including energy) increase to market-clearing levels. The operation of state-owned enterprises and collective farms is decentralized, and cooperative or private firms begin to operate more freely. How then can financial equilibrium be better maintained? What domestic fiscal and monetary reforms would be necessary and sufficient to balance the public finances on the one hand, and to constrain enterprises and households from overbidding for the economy's scarce resources on the other?

On the fiscal side, let us focus just on the central government by itself – although fiscal relationships among central, provincial, and local governments can be tangled (Wong, 1990). At the outset of the liberalization, an organized internal revenue service (IRS), a major central-government bureaucracy for collecting taxes from households and liberalized enterprises, should be in place. Operating under stable tax laws, the IRS can collect revenue directly from households and from enterprises in the rapidly growing liberalized sector. Then, as the relative size of surpluses in traditional state-owned enterprises inevitably declines, the government's fiscal position need not deteriorate.

Institutionally, the new IRS must break away from the socialist tradition of associating the power to tax with the actual formal ownership of property. In China since 1978, we know from Table 8.1 that profit remittances (or taxes) have declined sharply – although indirect taxes on goods and services from the industrial sector have been rather better maintained. In 1990, over two-thirds of tax revenues was still being (narrowly) collected as taxes or other remittances from industrial enterprises – reflecting the relative failure to collect much revenue from the personal income tax, from agriculture *per se*, or from international trade (Wong, 1991). In the absence of a generalized IRS, this unduly narrow focus of revenue sources in Chinese industry reflects the fact that the central and local governments continue to own most significant-scale industrial enterprises – and these are convenient administrative vehicles for collecting both commodity taxes and profit remittances.

The revenue position of the Chinese central government has been particularly weakened. Because of the huge expansion of township and other locally owned and controlled industries, the traditional tax base of the central government, i.e., the enterprises it owns, has declined relatively. Of the 83,000 or so industrial enterprises in China in 1990, less than 2,000 (albeit some of the bigger ones) are now owned by the central government. This has resulted in various forms of contracting by which the central government designates local governments to be its tax collecting agents for sharing revenues from local industry – a form of 'fiscal federalism' which has worked badly. In inflationary circumstances, revenue buoyancy to the central government has decreased because intergovernment transfers have been specified in nominal terms. In addition, by diverting local-industry revenues from budgetary to extrabudgetary channels, local governments can understate the volume of tax revenues actually being collected (Wong, 1991). Contracting has proven so unsatisfactory that old rules are continually being scrapped, and the whole system is in a state of flux as governments try to (re)negotiate new contracts.

Fforde and de Vylder (ADB Report, August 1991) report the same impasses in negotiations between the central and local government authorities in Vietnam when the former attempts to force the latter to remit 'surplus' revenues. They quote (pps 91–92) a Vietnamese official Tran Vinh who accuses local officials of

'. . . hiding of revenues, expenditures outside the system, fraudulent over-reporting, for example of the number of pupils in schools, nurseries, kindergartens, primary schools and training establishments. When accompanied with extra staff recruitment, this confused situation leads to highly contradictory reports and to fierce arguments'.

The effect has been a sharp fall in central government revenue in Vietnam from about two-thirds of total revenue in the early 1980s to about a planned 25 per cent in 1991 (p. 87).

Associating tax revenues with the ownership of industry also encourages an unhealthy form of intergovernmental mercantilistic rivalry. In China (as in Vietnam), local governments vie with each other for new (taxable) industries, and strive to protect old ones from 'foreign' competition – imports from enterprises in adjacent local jurisdictions.

'Most problematic was the apportionment of revenues between the central and provincial governments on the basis of enterprise ownership, which linked local revenues with income of local enterprises . . . Faced with intense budgetary pressures, local governments had little choice but to engage in industrial expansion. Not only has vigorous local expansion been a major source of overheating and macroeconomic imbalance through the 1980s, the distorted price and tax signals ensured that much of the investment was wasted in duplicative and irrational projects. Moreover, the dependence of local budgets on the financial health of local industry in turn induced officials to intervene to protect the welfare of their enterprises whenever possible, perpetuating bureaucratic management and exacerbating the tendency toward regional protectionism.' (Wong, ADB Study, August 1991, p. 49.)

Clearly, institutional change to divorce tax collection by different levels of government from their ownership of industrial property is of first-order importance for the liberalizing socialist economy. For the central government, this can be accomplished by the formation of a broadly based internal revenue service for collecting taxes *directly* from all enterprises in industry and agriculture – whether they be owned privately, by cooperatives, by local governments or by the central government itself. Presuming that such an institutional change can be effected, what forms of taxation would be particularly appropriate?

4   Procurement prices and the taxation of agricultural land

Consider agriculture first. Compared to their European counterparts, our five liberalizing Asian socialist economies are much more agrarian, with between 60 and 70 per cent of the population still in agriculture – despite ongoing population shifts toward urban areas. However, with collectivization of agricultural land under 'classical' socialism, and with the reduction of agricultural procurement prices as method of extracting an economic surplus from agriculture that were captured by generating 'monopoly' profits within industrial enterprises, direct tax revenues from agricultural land have fallen dramatically. In China, Christine Wong (1991, p. 39) estimates that the share of agricultural revenues fell from 40 per cent in 1950 to less than 5 per cent of total government revenue by 1960. In part because of ongoing price inflation, for which land assessment could not be updated, the formal taxation of agriculture accounts for less than 2 per cent of total government revenue in 1990.

Although Myanmar's economy remains overwhelmingly agrarian today, with about two-thirds of the population employed directly in agriculture, the fall in government revenue – both direct taxes and indirect extractions – from agriculture has been going on for a long time.

'Before World War II, the main method of taxing agriculture was the land revenue system based on periodic settlements for the assessment of the land tax. . . . . In the early days of British rule, the land tax yielded as much as half of total revenues. But with the expansion of other sources, especially customs duties, excise duties, and taxes on income, the contribution of land revenues declined in importance; in 1939/40 they yielded 22.6% of total revenues.

In the early postwar years, a government owned State Agricultural Marketing board was established which was given the monopoly of exporting rice and rice products. Domestic purchase prices were fixed below international prices in order to give huge profits to the government. . . . In 1961/62, implicit taxes on the marketing of rice amounted to 15% of total revenues . . . while land revenues amounted to another 3.4% of total revenues. . . .

The liberalization of agricultural prices and abolition of government monopoly of the rice trade in 1987–88 have eliminated implicit taxes on agriculture; . . . As a result, taxation of the agricultural sector is now essentially about 1% of tax revenues and 0.5% of total revenues.' (U Tun Wai, ADB Report, August 1991, pp. 66–68.)

This remarkable fall in the government's 'take' from agriculture in China and Myanmar (as well as in Laos and Vietnam) is, in part, a (welcome) consequence of liberalization where procurement prices seen by domestic farmers have risen to market-clearing levels. In an optimum order of liberalization, however, as the position of farmers improved through price reforms, agricultural land taxes should have been phased in to replace some of the lost revenue. In none of our five Asian economies has there been sufficient effort to systematically tax agricultural property once the commodity prices received by farmers increased.

True, in developing countries more generally, relatively few countries have followed the almost universal advice of economists to raise money by suitably constructed land taxes in agriculture.

'Very few countries collect as much as 10 percent of total government tax receipts from direct taxes on agricultural land. There are no countries in which land taxes account for more than 20 percent of revenues. In most, all kinds of taxes on property bring less than 5 percent of central government revenues.' (John Strasma et al., 1990, p. 439.)

Even by this weak standard, the effort to collect land taxes in our five liberalizing socialist Asian economies has been inadequate – given their strongly agrarian status and market-oriented commitment to improve agriculture's terms of trade. To mobilize popular support for land taxation, such revenues could be earmarked as the primary source of funding for (badly needed) infrastructure improvements in agriculture – to be mainly undertaken by local governments under the threat that bank credit for such investments is to be phased out and 'monopoly' profits in locally owned industry will continue to dissipate.

However, assessing the value of real property – particularly agricultural land – can only be carefully and fairly done with substantial lags. This year's tax liability in cash typically depends on the assessment of the land's potential productivity made a year or more ago. Thus the real proceeds from a cash-based property tax can be greatly diminished by ongoing inflation. Given the failure of all five of our Asian economies to bring inflation under control, governments may have to consider doing the assessments and imposing land taxes in kind by using some common regional crop as the numeraire – although actual payments would still be made in money terms on the day the tax becomes due.

5   Personal income taxation and VAT

In a liberalizing socialist economy, the traditional tax base – the huge 'protected' flow of monopoly profits in state-owned industrial enterprises – will largely disappear as the economy becomes more competitive. In addition to land taxation by local governments, what new revenue sources can be tapped?

In the longer run, a 'global' personal income tax, i.e., one that consoliates all forms of household income into the same taxable schedule, should eventually become the principal tax base in the economy. In the United States, consolidated government revenue from the personal income tax was almost 13 per cent of American GNP in 1990 – and was 41 per cent of the revenue collected by all levels of the American government. However, personal income taxes are more difficult to collect when per capita incomes are still low. Although the most advanced of our five countries in developing a personal income tax, China still collects less than 1 per cent of GNP in this format. In a largely agrarian developing country, institutions for tracing and collecting personal income taxes in a nondistortionary fashion will take some years to put in place. But it is important to start immediately in levying a *moderate* rate personal income tax – say 25 to 30 per cent after a basic exemption for the poor – as soon as possible.

But what about the immediate fiscal crisis and fall in government revenues in each of our five countries? Our hypothetical fledgling IRS will still need enterprises as administrative vehicles for collecting taxes. However, the old format based on 'profits' appropriation needs to be dramatically changed toward uniform taxation of commodities and services. Once prices are decontrolled, shifting to a *uniform* value-added tax on industrial enterprises is both feasible and necessary. With a determined effort over one or two years, large amounts of revenue can be raised rather quickly in a nondistortionary fashion – as shown by the experience of Chile in the late 1970s (Edwards and Edwards, 1987).

'No public finance development of the last half century can rival the emergence and spread of the value-added tax. It is difficult for contemporary economists to believe that, barely fifty years ago, there was no such thing as a value-added tax. The French were the first to institute such a tax, in the 1950s. What is astounding is the degree to which the idea thus planted has in subsequent decades proliferated around the world – in both developed and developing countries.' (A.C. Harberger, 1990, p. 27.).

In the industrial sector, the way the new IRS works vis-a-vis liberalized enterprises – as distinct from enterprises remaining under government ministerial control – must be spelled out. The debilitating practice of seizing the cash surpluses of profitable enterprises while subsidizing loss-makers must end. But the recent history of the reform socialist governments of the Soviet Union after 1985, China in 1989–90, and the smaller economies of Eastern Europe and Asia, is one continual reintervention to seize high profits and to subsidize losses. This moral hazard in public policy is now so pronounced that major institutional changes in both the fiscal and monetary systems are necessary if government reintervention is to be credibly foreclosed. On the fiscal side, I suggest that *reforming socialist governments replace the taxation of profits generated within domestically owned enterprises in the liberalized sector with a broadly based and uniform value-added tax.*[3] (Profits paid out to individuals – whether in the form of interest, dividends or capital gains – would be subject to withholding against the personal income tax.)

Once output prices are decontrolled and production decisions are made freely – but not until then – a full-scale value-added tax (VAT) can be effectively imposed. Thus, new enterprises, or existing enterprises just entering the liberalized sector, would immediately register to pay their VAT as a condition for getting an operating license and legal protection from the state. For example, imposing a flat 20 per cent VAT rate on all liberalized enterprises whether profitable or not is straightforward. Whatever their corporate form – cooperative, private, or owned by the central or local governments – their VAT liabilities would be unambiguous.

Provided that the fledgling IRS also imposed a full-scale personal income tax, supplemented by consumer exercises, taxing the profits of *liberalized* enterprises should be unnecessary for securing sufficient revenue.[4]

Traditional enterprises whose output and input prices remain under direct state control, as described below, would remain subject to the old-style full taxation of residual profits. For accounting purposes, however, a 'shadow' VAT might also be imposed on them. Although this shadow VAT reduced residual profits one-for-one much like the old socialist turnover tax used to do, the government would then have a better accounting measure of 'true' profits and losses in traditional enterprises.

Unlike the old-line industrial ministries, or local governments sponsoring specific industries, the new IRS would deal with households and liberalized enterprises throughout the economy. A VAT is levied at a flat rate on enterprises' gross sales less the tax embedded in purchased supplies. If profit taxation is officially abandoned, no accounting measure of enterprise profits is necessary for collecting the VAT, which would help shelter the IRS from pressure to seize 'inordinate' enterprise profits. (Operating under our moderate-rate personal income tax, the IRS would still want to catch dividends and capital gains paid out to individuals.) Moreover, because the incidence of the VAT is eventually passed forward to retail buyers, pressure to exempt liberalized loss-making enterprises, those which the state is no longer sponsoring, from paying this well-defined tax would be minimal.

Although China has a VAT as one of several commodity taxes, it is neither uniform nor widespread. Instead, the government tries to hit liberalized enterprises with highly progressive profits taxes.

'Since 1950, the industrial and commercial tax has been levied on the profits of collective enterprises on an 8-grade progressive scale that begins at 10% with annual profits of 1,000 yuan or less, reaching 55% with profits over 200,000 yuan. In practice many enterprises are exempted.

In response to their growing numbers during the process of reform, the government introduced a new tax in 1986 to cover all privately owned businesses in industry, commerce, construction, and service trades. This tax has a 10-grade progressive scale, with rates that rise from 7 to 60%. In addition, a surtax of 10–40% is levied on annual profits over 50,000 yuan.' (Wong, ADB Report, August 1991, pp. 37–38.)

This Chinese approach of taxing collective or private enterprises 'progressively' confuses the role of a uniform business tax necessary for raising revenue efficiently with the desire of the authorities to have a progressive tax on personal incomes. It comes uncomfortably close to the old discredited idea of the government seizing 'excess' profits. Personal income taxation and business taxation should be separated. The most natural approach is to impose a uniform VAT of say 20 per cent on *all* private, collective, or otherwise liberalized enterprises. Besides being well-defined *ex ante*, the VAT format provides institutional protection against the government seizing 'inordinate' profits of collective or private enterprises *ex post facto*. Then, income actually paid out to individuals could be subject to a progressive personal income tax – against which all enterprises would be liable for withholding at the source to help the government collect the tax.

6 Gradualism or a big bang?

Even with a fledgling IRS in place for dealing with households and liberalized enterprises, the fiscal position of the reforming socialist government is likely too precarious, and its ability to collect tax revenue from the private sector too weak, to afford any massive giveaway of claims on earning assets. For fiscal reasons alone, an early attempt at a 'big bang' privatization by giving common shares in large state-owned enterprises or in natural resource industries to households on a widespread basis could be seriously misplaced. However, this argument does not preclude a one-time restructuring of formal ownership rights in state enterprises to better recognize the implicit claims of existing stakeholders – workers, banks, pension funds, and the public treasury – by the distribution of explicit equity shares that validate these claims (Lipton and Sachs, 1990). Nor does it preclude rapid effective privatization in agriculture – as the Chinese demonstrated with the break up of the communes and the advent of their 'family responsibility system' after 1978.

However, breaking up large industrial concerns in the context of a 'big bang' is a more dubious proposition (Murrell, 1990) – although one can move quickly to liberalize small-scale industry and agriculture. Indeed, capitalism is best grown from modest beginnings in small-scale enterprises that provide a sorting mechanism for successful and unsuccessful entrepreneurs (Kornai, 1990). Many years might have to pass before domestic entrepreneurs with proven managerial expertise accumulate sufficient capital to buy state-owned industrial assets on a large scale. Correspondingly, massive sales of domestic assets to foreigners at the outset of the liberalization could even delay the development of domestic entrepreneurship – although joint ventures, in which domestic partners retain the principal ownership claims, can sometimes be useful vehicles for absorbing foreign technologies.

All five of our Asian economies moved sharply towards the effective privatization and marketization of agricultural activities. However,

China, Vietnam and Myanmar have moved rather slowly in changing the ownership and control structure of the traditional state-owned industrial enterprises (SOEs). In China, in particular, small-scale private and collective enterprises have simply grown in and around 'the commanding heights' of the socialist economy – which remain state-owned and controlled. Only in special economic zones such as Guangdong, have fully liberalized – largely private – enterprises become the dominant mode of economic activity.

In contrast, Laos has opted more for a 'mini bang' in allowing highly autonomous and decentralized operations of its SOEs since 1988, but without first putting proper financial controls – including wage controls – in place. The result has been a wage explosion and significant decapitalization in traditional industries.

'The freeing up of wages and the ability of managers and workers to vote themselves bonuses, led to a pay explosion. From a situation of rough parity with the levels of pay in the civil service in late 1987 and early 1988, pay levels within state enterprises are now reported to be as much as five times those in the government. . . .

Given the diversion of a major part of after-tax profits to bonus payments, the ability of SOEs to fund investment from their own resources is severely limited. At the same time, enterprise managers have a strong incentive to invest. By borrowing funds to raise the capital intensity of the production process, the consequent increase in labor productivity will be available for higher real compensations, in the form of wages and bonuses, while government held equity goes unremunerated.' (Vokes and Farbella, ADB Report on Laos, August 1991, pp. 35–36.)

Going much further than the Laotians, Mongolia is opting for a 'big bang'. Starting from a situation where its government owned and controlled virtually all property in an extreme version of the old Stalinist model, the legal and institutional structures in Mongolian society are to be changed in 1991–92 so as to radically transform the economy into a market system based on private property.

A radical form of privatization is to begin in July 1991. Privatization of (formerly) state-owned property is to take place in two stages over a 14-month period. Between July and October 1991, all small units and assets (shops, livestock, farm equipment, trucks etc.) are to be auctioned off; and in the subsequent 12-month period, ownership in the remaining large enterprises is to be transfered (through) vouchers, which are to be distributed to every citizen on an egalitarian basis.' (Y.C. Kim, ADB Report on Mongolia, August 1991, p. 35.)

But it appears as if the financial controls necessary to allow such an economic programme to succeed are not yet in place. Neither the fiscal system nor the banking system has been reconstructed to compensate for this massive loss of resources by the State.

'A new law on customs duties has gone into effect in March 1991, and the new Tax Law in January 1991. The Tax Law introduced income taxes for individuals, enterprises and cooperatives – replacing then-existing profit transfers. Yet, it is said that little income taxes are being collected because (a) no system of tax collection has yet been set up; and (b) because of very bad economic conditions, enterprises have no "taxable" income. . . .

Timing in implementing the privatization program is said to have been moved up in order to minimize the hemorrage in the fiscal budget resulting from ever-increasing government subsidies to enterprises. At the same time, it is universally acknowledged that virtually no newly privatized enterprises would become financially viable under the country's present and near future economic conditions. Simply to pass the bankruptcy law (June 1991) will not address the wholesale insolvency of the country's enterprises even after privatization.' (Y.C. Kim, ADB Report on Mongolia, August 1991, pp. 36–38.)

Instead of a big bang, I will simply presume for the remainder of the paper that our model economy adopts a more gradualist approach in which appropriate financial controls are put in place as liberalization proceeds from 'the bottom up', i.e., starting with small-scale farming, manufacturing and services. Although in agriculture, the transformation to small-scale 'virtually' private farming best takes place very quickly – as in China in 1979–81 – presuming that a suitable system of land taxation can be put in place as agricultural procurement prices increase.

7   Enterprise financial constraints in the transition: a tripartite classification

Before the transition to a full-fledged market economy is effected, therefore, both traditional enterprises with soft budget constraints and liberalized enterprises with hard budget constraints would likely coexist for some years – but under somewhat different monetary and tax regimes in order to better maintain financial control. Focussing on the industrial sector, I have tried in Table 8.3 to summarize what financial arrangements would be consistent with the degree of liberalization or mode of operation of each class of enterprise. Three relatively gross classifications are distinguished.

First, *traditional enterprises* remaining under state ownership would remain subject to some price controls on their outputs, and perhaps to state materials allocations for some inputs (including credits from the

Table 8.3. *Alternative financial arrangements for enterprises in transition*

	Traditional enterprises[1]	Liberalized enterprises	
		State-owned[2]	Private
Taxation	Expropriation of surpluses[3]	Uniform value-added tax	Uniform value-added tax
Deposit money: domestic commodity convertibility[4]	Restricted	Unrestricted interest-bearing	Unrestricted interest-bearing
Credit eligibility	State Bank	Non-bank capital market	Non-bank capital market
Wages	Government determined	Government determined	Market determined
Residual profits	Accrue to government	Dividends to government – retained earnings for investment	Dividends to owners[5] – retained earnings for investment or lending to other private enterprises
Foreign exchange	Restricted	Current account only	Current account only

Notes:

1 Traditional enterprises are those whose output and pricing decisions are still determined by a central government authority or planning bureau with centrally allocated inputs and credits from the state bank to cover (possible) negative cash flows.

2 'State owned' can refer to any level of government. Nevertheless, the VAT and restrictions on bank credit would apply equally to liberalized enterprises owned or controlled in different jurisdictions.

3 Although residual profits revert to the state, they could include a 'shadow' VAT levy in order to better understand the 'true' profitability of traditional enterprises.

4 'Commodity convertibility' here means the freedom to spend for domestic goods and services or to buy and hold domestic coin and currency – but need not imply convertibility into foreign exchange.

5 Dividends would be subject to the personal income tax when paid out to private owners, but retained earnings would not be taxed.

state banking system). They could include both natural public goods such as utilities, energy-producing resource-intensive industries, and infrastructure activities like roads and irrigation facilities. In addition, industrial basket cases – those running with negative cash flows even when prices are fully liberalized, but which the government could not immediately close down for social reasons – would also fall into this 'traditional' category.

This distinction between liberalized enterprises with hard budget constraints and traditional enterprises need not preclude substantial rationalization of relative prices in the latter. Indeed, although I am eschewing a 'big bang' (a massive transfer of ownership claims to industrial property at the outset of liberalization), widespread *marketization* of economic transactions where government-controlled prices are set closer to market-clearing levels is both feasible and highly desirable. For example, in the energy sector, which one would expect to remain under state ownership and control much like a public utility, a sharp decrease in the economy-wide price of energy to approximate world levels should be charged to all enterprises at the outset of the transition process. Otherwise, liberalized enterprises will begin using, or continue to use, energy wastefully. Even though traditional enterprises may not economize on energy use very rapidly, the reduction in their accounting profits as the price of energy is increased would be a better signal to the government of their true profitability. Higher energy prices would allow the government to better tax the economic rents (surplus) associated with the exploitation of this natural resource.

Second, in *state-owned liberalized enterprises*, output and input decisions would be freely determined by the enterprise management – who could also bargain freely over commodity prices in pursuit of higher profits after paying the value-added tax. State-owned manufacturing concerns could fit into this liberalized category as long as the government exerted its ownership claim over capital to maximize profits. Although managers of liberalized state-owned enterprises would operate freely in commodity markets, the government would continue to set wages and salaries for managers by direct participation in wage bargaining. The government would also determine the division of profits between dividends reverting to the state and earnings retained by these enterprises themselves.

Third, *private liberalized enterprises* would have no direct government restraints on their making output, price, wage and dividend decisions in the pursuit of higher profits. Along with their liberalized state-owned counterparts, these private or cooperative enterprises would be liable for the value-added tax but not for any separate profits tax. However, the IRS would also enlist their cooperation in withholding personal income taxes on any wages, interest, dividends, or capital gains paid out to individuals.

For each of these three enterprise classifications, the columns in Table 8.3 list consistent tax, monetary, credit, wage and profit arrangements. Down column 1, for example, traditional enterprises continue to be taxed by the expropriation of their surpluses (although this would include a 'shadow' VAT calculation); their deposits in the state bank remain blocked, and could be considered simply an extension of the government's treasury accounts. Being thus incapacitated in terms of their own financial resources, traditional enterprises would still be eligible for loans from the state bank at positive real interest rates to finance new investments or to cover ongoing losses. As under classical socialism, their freedom of financial action remains highly circumscribed. In contrast, columns 2 and 3 of Table 8.3 show that liberalized enterprises – whether private or state-owned – are subject to a uniform VAT but not to a profits tax.

8   Hardening the system of money and credit: banks and liberalized enterprises

What system of money and credit for the newly liberalized sector would be consistent with this different tax regime? The answer depends partly on the initial conditions that the transitional economy faces. Suppose it faces a near 'worst-case' scenario in two important respects.

First, a fiscal deficit forces the government (and traditional enterprises) to continue borrowing heavily from the banking system despite the best efforts of the newly created IRS. As of 1991, all five Asian economies had this problem of falling tax revenues and inflationary pressure from excess government direct or indirect borrowing.

Second, the state banking system itself, with an enormous bad loan portfolio from past lending to loss-making enterprises at the government's behest, has yet to be restructured to avoid similar moral hazard in future lending. The need for a complete recapitalization of existing divisions or branches of the state banking system, before normal lending on commercial terms can begin, has been stressed by Brainard (1990). The current state of bank lending in China is also indicative of bank portfolios in Vietnam, Laos, Myanmar and Mongolia.

'"Bad" loans is a concept that has no specific definition in Chinese banks. ... One reason for not distinguishing between irrecoverable "bad" loans and overdue loans is the lack of clear guidelines for identifying and treating defaults on loan payments ... At present, many bankers report that loans are automatically rolled over if a request is made 7 days prior to maturity. At the same time there is little follow up on the rolled over loans to distinguish between those caused by the unrealistically short repayment terms, and those encountering real financial problems. Another reason for the low percentage of "bad" loans is that a high percentage of industrial loans are guaranteed by the supervisory bureaus or corporations, so that outright defaults are rare.

In the view of many economists in China, the issue of bad loans in the banks is currently impossible to solve, since many of the bad loans were either inherited (such as when the Industrial Commercial Bank inherited the portfolio of the People's Bank of China when the latter devolved its commercial operations) or they had been under administrative orders in the first place. . . . The situation deteriorated in 1989–90, when the government ordered banks to make loans that were clearly problematic – to allow enterprises to meet payroll and build inventories of unsold goods.' (Christine Wong, ADB Report on China, August 1991, pp. 58–59.)

At the macroeconomic level, the ongoing fiscal deficit implies that no room exists for noninflationary bank lending to the liberalized sector. At the microeconomic level, moral hazard in existing monetary intermediaries, whose deposits must be insured to protect the payments system, implies that they cannot be trusted to lend safely on commercial terms anyway.

Nor could traditional enterprises with 'soft' budget constraints be trusted to lend to, or borrow from, other enterprises – particularly those in the liberalized sector – on any substantial scale. The recent financial history of partial 'liberalizations' in the 1970s and 1980s in many Eastern European countries is that loss-making traditional enterprises overborrow from their suppliers by simply not making payments on their trade credits – thus throwing suppliers into financial difficulty. To prevent general industrial collapse the State Bank is often forced to intervene to provide (inflationary) credit to all concerned.

In our model, free trade on commodity account would prevail between the traditional and liberalized sectors, but they would be insulated financially. In order to maintain control over the aggregate supply of internally convertible ('household') money, the government would have to carefully monitor and limit the cash deficits of the traditional (and general government) sector with households and liberalized enterprises – as shown in Table 8.3. But this insulation and monitoring becomes more difficult as marketization proceeds.

'As in other Soviet-type economies, there are separate circuits for enterprise and household money. In the prereform period, all enterprises were required to have an account with PBC, and all transactions of value greater than Y50 were required to go through bank transfers. Cash holdings of enterprises were restricted to three days currency requirements in location with a bank branch, and to two weeks elsewhere. Payments to households and to rural collectives were made in cash supervised by the PBC. Control over currency outstanding was relatively simple, though manipulating wage policies and the supply of consumer goods.

With monetization of the economy in the reform period, the control of the currency has been complicated by the much greater transactions demands for currency among farm households and among non-state and private traders. The development of extra-plan trade and the growth of nonstate enterprises have increased the use of cash in enterprise transactions, weakening the separation between the two monetary circuits. After 1985, when enterprises were allowed to open accounts with more than one bank, the accounting and monitoring functions of the banking system were further eroded. While enterprise transactions are still required to take the form of checks, monitoring has become more difficult. The unpopularity of checks in the service trade in Beijing indicates that cash payments are still preferred (perhaps to facilitate tax avoidance). In an effort to control spending by state organizations, some accounts were frozen by the banks, and transactions were blocked.' (Wong *op. cit.* pp. 56–57)

Traditional state-owned enterprises in China are inevitably now more bound up with the cash economy because of the general liberalization. However, the government can still maintain a tight line on extensions of new credits beyond those needed to refinance old debts, on giving or receiving more than 'normal' trade credit, and on new funding for investment. Other than investment in important infrastructure activities, a deliberate decision could be made to scale back (bank-financed) investments in traditional manufacturing (including township industries) while continuing to restrict the ability of traditional enterprises to spend from their own accumulated deposit money or cash – as indicated in Table 8.3 above. The relative size of this traditional sector would then shrink as the economy grew.

However, new or financially reorganized state-owned enterprises with clean balance sheets could be put wholly onto the 'cash' economy. Old debts and deposits would be cancelled on the presumption that these now-liberalized enterprises could be financially autonomous in the future. Other than auditing against fraud, what they did with their owned cash balances – including deposit money – for new investments or the purchase of supplies would be unrestrictied. Checking accounts would still be held with the state bank to ensure the integrity of the payments mechanism.

Along with households, liberalized enterprises could still hold interest-bearing savings accounts that were unrestricted for deposit or withdrawal. The important caveat, however, is that these *financially liberalized state-owned industries could no longer borrow from the state banking system* – or from any monetary intermediary. Like private or independent cooperative enterprises, they would have to seek funding from the non-bank capital market, and from building up their own cash positions, i.e. from self-finance.

Given the macroeconomic need to restrain inflation and the current incapacity of the banks to be 'responsible' lenders, how might domestic banking arrangements best evolve with respect to the liberalized sector? Imagine two successive stages in the transition.

> Stage One: Liberalized enterprises are confined to self-finance and to borrowing from the nonbank capital market not involving traditional enterprises. Bank lending to liberalized enterprises is prohibited.
> Stage Two: Commercial banks begin limited and fully collateralized short-term lending to liberalized enterprises according to the 'Real Bills Doctrine'. That is, they lend only to finance the build up of 'productive' short-term assets, such as inventories or accounts receivable, that can be easily realized if assumed.

At the outset of Stage One, which is portrayed in Table 8.3, all urban and rural liberalized enterprises, whether state-owned, cooperative, or private, become ineligible for credit from banks (that is, from deposit-taking monetary intermediaries). Nor can they borrow from traditional enterprises who continue to have access to bank credit. But borrowing and lending in the nonbank capital market among liberalized firms and individuals could take place freely. Apart from 'normal' trade credit, however, non-bank sources of finance are likely to be quite small for some years. Instead, liberalized enterprises would depend mainly on their owners' equity and subsequent untaxed retained earnings for investment finance. These earnings could now accumulate in currency and demand deposits, or in interest-bearing time deposits, that were now fully convertible for domestic spending. Banking institutions would be rearranged so that the government could no longer conveniently monitor, appropriate, or freeze the financial asset positions of the liberalized enterprises. When a state-owned enterprise was declared to be 'liberalized', it would lose the privilege of borrowing from the state bank, but be compensated with the right to accumulate internally convertible domestic money and other financial assets.

A primary goal of Stage One is to encourage firms to use monetary assets as a store of value, rather than physical assets. As households and liberalized enterprises build up their liquid asset positions, excess inventories and other forms of low-yield capital would be voluntarily disgorged and replaced with more attractive monetary assets. Thus could the average productivity of physical capital increase from the outset of the liberalization – despite industrial restructuring.

Decreasing the demand for physical assets as a store of value will also help disinflate the economy. If monetary assets are to be attractive, however, the efficiency of the payments mechanism becomes critically important to all liberalized enterprises, whether private or state-owned. To facilitate free convertibility of enterprise deposits into domestic goods or currency, rapid check clearing and money transfers are essential. In effect, the monetary circuit of liberalized enterprises would be unified with that of households as both could hold coin and currency as well as domestically convertible deposits. (However, the monetary deposits of traditional enterprises would remain blocked – their funds could not be spent or converted into cash without permission).

In addition, the government would set substantially positive real interest rates on time deposits in the mode of successfully disinflating developing economies – such as Taiwan in the late 1950s and Korea in the mid-1960s. What the socialist government can afford to pay on deposits, however, is limited by its own fiscal position and its success in increasing the yields on the government-owned assets that dominate the loan side of the state bank's balance sheet. In order to achieve high real financial growth in households and liberalized enterprises, setting real deposit rates in this 3 to 6 per cent range is consistent with the experience of other countries (McKinnon, 1991) – provided that these deposits are not subject to being blocked.

Such reliance on self-finance is the simplest technique for imposing financial restraint on liberalized enterprises while simultaneously increasing the productivity of physical capital. Bankruptcy would be virtually automatic if the internal cash flow of a liberalized enterprise became negative for any significant length of time. The effective wages paid to workers and the (implicit) yield to all owners of the firm's equity would vary directly with the firm's success in the open market. Self-finance avoids the issue of moral hazard in lending by government-owned or insured banks. It also has the great advantage of bypassing the difficult problem of how to establish a more elaborate corporate structure, with different forms of accountability to outside lenders.

However, self-finance works for liberalized enterprises if and only if output prices have been decontrolled fully and firms can negotiate freely over input prices and wages. As long as no liberalized enterprise can borrow from the state bank, nor from traditional enterprises which still have access to credit from the state bank, then all liberalized enterprises will be in the same competitive position. In competitive equilibrium, therefore, profit margins should be sufficiently wide for liberalized enterprises, on average, to finance their own ongoing investments.

Are there historical examples of this widening of profit margins in a regime of self-finance? The successful liberalization of Chinese agriculture from 1979 to about 1985 relied almost exclusively on Chinese farm households building up their own cash positions in order to finance on-farm investments.[5] For enterprises to build up sufficient cash, however, depends on the absence of any significant tax on current profits, and on having broad money bring a positive real deposit rate – that is, not be significantly taxed by inflation. In the early years (1979–84) of China's agricultural liberalization, the price level was quite stable – although inflation later became a serious problem – and Chinese farmers built up their cash positions remarkably rapidly (Wong, 1991).

True, self-finance has its limitations. Large scale infrastructure investments for roads, pipelines, major irrigation facilities and so forth would have to remain in the government (traditional) sector, although with a better set of commodity prices and positive real interest rates to guide decision-making. Unless they could attract additional equity finance, even successful liberalized enterprises with excellent investment opportunities would have to wait a bit longer (compared to borrowing externally) to generate internal funds sufficient to overcome indivisibilities in purchasing capital goods. Nevertheless, by building up or drawing down bank deposits at positive real interest rates, liberalized enterprises and households would be engaging in a limited form of intertemporal arbitrage. Without access to external credits, liberalized enterprises would aim for rather larger average stocks of liquid assets (including deposits) to cover unexpected contingencies – like shifts in their terms of trade – that might suddenly reduce current cash flows.

As the non-bank private capital markets develop – say, unsubsidized rural credit cooperatives or urban markets in short-term commercial bills – the severe credit constraints on liberalized enterprises would relax naturally, but these private lenders would also face bankruptcy if they made bad loans or charged interest rates below market levels. Compared to lending by the state-owned or state-insured banks, moral hazard in lending would be dramatically reduced. The government role would be to serve as ultimate enforcer of all debt contracts through the judicial system; and to give the liberalized sector a stable unit of deferred payment by securing the price level.

Suppose such monetary control is established and fiscal deficits are reduced to the point that the government plus traditional enterprises no longer fully absorbed the lending resources of the state banking system. The price level has stabilized. Moreover, enforcement of debt contracts in the liberalized sector is secured, and open markets in some debt instruments, like commercial bills, have begun to develop in the non-bank capital markets. Then, and only then, is Stage Two feasible: to begin fully collateralized bank lending to the liberalized sector on strictly commercial terms. The prior existence of a commercial bill market could provide a natural vehicle for providing that collateral; in fact, established bill brokers might be the most technically qualified applicants with sufficient capital to be granted private commercial bank licenses. Checkable and interest bearing deposits could be offered to the general public provided that these authorized banks invested in a diversified portfolio of commercial bills with well-defined secondary markets, and with more or less the same term to maturity as their deposits.

Alternatively, appropriately recapitalized divisions of the state bank could be designated as 'commercial'; these would mobilize additional saving by offering higher yield time deposits, and then use the fund to begin 'for profit' lending to the liberalized sector. However, tight regulations on collateral for securing their loans – perhaps inventory bills of lading or accounts receivable – would have to be in place to prevent moral hazard through the nonrepayment of loans from developing all over again.

In the optimum order of liberalization, therefore, the development of ordinary commercial banking may well have to be deferred for some years after liberalization begins, and to wait until overall monetary and fiscal control is secured. Putting the matter more negatively, premature efforts to break up the monolithic state bank (associated with classical socialism) into a central bank and more loosely regulated commercial banks (associated with mature capitalist economies) could lead to a disastrous loss of overall monetary control and a worsening of moral hazard in bank lending in transitional economies. This pattern occurred in Poland in 1988–89 with the partitioning of the state bank aggravating the underlying inflationary pressure[6] and is happening in the former Soviet Union in 1990–91 with the formation of hundreds of wildcat 'commercial' banks controlled by the old state enterprises (McKinnon, 1991).

In Vietnam, the experience with new 'private' unregulated banking institutions – which the Vietnamese prefer to call credit cooperatives – has not been successful.

'Today in Vietnam, there are some 7,500 rural credit cooperatives with total assets of about 90 billion dong. However, the portion of uncollectable loans is very large, estimated at some 50 percent.

Urban credit cooperatives are a more recent phenomenon. The cooperatives have been providing funding for private enterprises that have not been able to get funding from the state banks, but some state enterprises have been involved both as depositors and borrowers. In the beginning of 1990, around 300 urban credit cooperatives of various sizes were reportedly in operation, controlling deposits of around 400 billion dong, or almost $US100 million.

Until the credit crashes of 1990, most urban credit cooperatives operated like pyramid schemes, attracting deposits by offering interest rates of up to 15 percent per month. But beginning in Ho Chi Minh City in March 1990, a number of credit cooperatives – largely unregulated and poorly supervised, and with no system of reserve assets or deposit insurance – started to go bankrupt. Some of the worst cases of pyramid schemes – involving grossly fraudulent behavior on the part of owners – were closed down by the authorities, and several well-known managers were arrested. The scandals panicked depositors, who rushed to withdraw their money, forcing many cooperatives out of business. The bankruptcies also caused the collapse of more than 2,000 small private enterprises.' (Fforde and de Vylder, ADB Report on Vietnam, August 1991, pp. 51–52.)

Vietnam's problems with the premature sanctioning of private bank-like institutions has both obvious and not-so-obvious dimensions.

As in any more mature market economy, regulating against fraud – usually in the form of some kind of Ponzi game or pyramid scheme – is a problem but an obvious one. Small savers are particularly vulnerable if deposits in the past had been government guaranteed – and they feel an implicit guarantee still exists.

In socialist economies, however, it can be particularly inappropriate for state-owned enterprises to begin sponsoring their own commercial bank – or to make deposits in, and to receive loans from, 'private' commercial banks (credit cooperatives) which they indirectly own or control. The classical socialist method for the government to collect (implicit) taxes from traditional state-owned enterprises is simply to impound their cash surpluses in the state bank. However, the SOE may well avoid paying this implicit tax if it can deposit funds in its own commercial bank – or one that it indirectly controls. Then the SOE can convert otherwise blocked balances into expendable funds – possibly by directing loans from this 'commercial bank' to whom it designates.

The result is a further fall in government revenue in the transitional socialist economy. Before the final collapse of the Soviet Union itself in late summer of 1991, the revenue position of the central government had been completely undermined by a number of factors – one of which was the rapid spread of 'cooperative' commercial banks which were mainly fronts for SOEs. From virtually none in 1989, about 1,700 of these new banking institutions had sprung into existence by May of 1991 – leading the authorities to lose control over the rate at which 'inconvertible' enterprise deposit money was transformed into cash. The result was a wild inflation.

Clearly, keeping liberalized enterprises confined to self-finance and to the non-bank capital market (Stage One above), while also keeping tight control over (state) bank credit to traditional enterprises, is a straight-forward – albeit very draconian method – of securing financial control. If at the same time the public finances are also improved through expenditure reduction and the broadening of the tax base, price inflation could be rather quickly eliminated. Then, the economy would be ready for Stage Two: a deliberate, but very careful, broadening of the base of bank lending to include the liberalized enterprises. With the price level firmly under control with positive real interest rates on time and savings accounts, the stage would be set to allow liberalized enterprises to grow very rapidly compared to the shrinking relative size of the still-credit-constrained traditional sector.

9   Foreign trade and foreign exchange: a concluding note

This paper has focused on domestic financial policy: how to reconstruct the public finances and the system of money and credit in a step-by-step transition from classical socialism toward a market economy. In foreign trade, however, the optimum order for liberalizing quotas, tariffs, and exchange controls in parallel with the freeing of domestic trade is as complex as it is important. Commercial policy governing foreign trade, and financial arrangements governing the foreign exchanges, should parallel and complement these domestic tax and monetary arrangements.

For example, traditional enterprises whose deposits remain blocked for domestic transactions could hardly be allowed to exercise convertibility of this money into foreign exchange. In contrast, the money of liberalized enterprises could be freely convertible for current-account transactions, for importing or exporting, provided that the country's foreign commercial (tariff) policy was simultaneously well-defined under a unified exchange rate. These distinctions appear in the last row of Table 8.3.

However, the severe domestic credit constraints imposed on the liberalized enterprises as a matter of policy would be undermined if such enterprises could freely borrow (or deposit) abroad. Until the domestic capital market matured with borrowing and lending at market interest rates, foreign exchange convertibility on capital account would be inappropriate, even for liberalized firms.

What about tariffs, quotas, and commercial policy affecting the current account of the balance of payments? Again the pace of liberalization would depend heavily on the socialist economy's initial conditions: the production distortions arising out of the preexisting system of protection and the extent to which the government remained dependent on the surpluses of state-owned industrial enterprises for revenue.

In a traditional centrally planned Stalinist economy, protection for domestic manufacturing is almost entirely implicit. From exchange controls and the apparatus of state trading, disguised subsidies to users of energy and other material inputs are coupled with virtually absolute protection from competing foreign manufactures. Although no formal tariffs appear in any legal codes, the implicit structure of tariff equivalents 'cascades' downward from very high levels for domestic production of finished consumer goods through manufactured intermediate products through industrial raw materials and energy, which are negatively protected because of implicit export taxes (or import subsidies). This implicit structure of protection in foreign trade parallels and supports the Stalinist system of internal price controls where industrial raw materials and primary food products are underpriced relative to finished industrial goods.

This highly cascaded structure of implicit tariffs in socialist economies raises effective protection in finished goods to the point where most manufacturing may well exhibit negative (or very low) value added at world market prices. In such circumstances, a precipitate move to free trade could provoke the collapse of most domestic manufacturing industries – no matter how the exchange rate is set, and no matter that some of this industry might eventually be viable at world market prices (McKinnon, 1991).

Moreover, a sudden move to world relative prices would accentuate the decline in the surpluses of the state-owned industrial enterprises – thus further undermining the government's revenue position. In the absence of an effective internal revenue service, the government will need the revenue from profit remittances from state-owned industry for some years into the transition. Thus, reforms to make commercial policy more explicit *and* preserve the revenue position of the government should accompany efforts to make the currency convertible on current account.

Consider the outset of the liberalization as the domestic economy moves to a market-based system with suitable credit constraints in place and a unified foreign exchange rate. Then, I suggest (McKinnon, 1991) the 'tariffication' of quantitative restrictions on competing imports of manufactures and industrial goods coupled with the elimination of implicit export taxes (or import subsidies) on energy and material inputs. As the domestic prices of energy and raw materials rise relative to wages, (temporary) offsetting tariff protection for domestic manufacturing industry is necessary to prevent a collapse in industrial output and in net government revenue. A cascaded tariff, with manufactured consumer goods receiving the highest protective rates, simply recognizes the pre-existing production distortions – from which the economy must be given time to adjust. Tariffication is, itself, a substantial market-oriented liberalization in comparison with the old system of quantitative import and export restrictions. Moreover, the government would receive the tariff revenue directly while the profit remittances from the state-owned industrial sector would be better maintained.

Once made explicit, the highest tariffs in the cascade can then be phased down step-by-step to zero (or a low uniform level) over a preannounced five-to-ten-year time horizon. The optimum speed with which the newly marketized economy should then converge to free foreign trade would then depend on (1) its success in setting up an *internal* revenue service to replace tariff revenue and profit remittances from state-owned enter-prises, and (2) some estimate as to how fast the industrial sector can reequip itself to eliminate undue dependence on energy and other raw materials – keeping in mind that any massive borrowing from the domestic banking system would be inconsistent with the all-important objective of maintaining macroeconomic stability.

NOTES

1 John Williamson (1991) further clarifies various concepts of internal and external currency convertibility.
2 This normal monetary guideline of classical socialism was violated by the Soviet monetary 'reform' of January 23, 1991, when large-denomination ruble notes were cancelled and withdrawals from personal savings accounts were restricted.
3 There remains a strong case for moderate domestic taxation of domestic profits repatriated in some form to foreigners. Not only does the socialist government need the revenue, but the foreign-owned firm can typically claim equivalent tax credits against its own corporate income tax liabilty in its home country.
4 The pros and cons of different forms of taxation under classical socialism in comparison to a more liberalized economy are reviewed in McKinnon (1991).
5 This and other examples are discussed further in McKinnon (1991).
6 I am indebted to Professor Arnold Harberger for pointing out this ill-advised feature of financial reform in Poland prior to the more successful price-level stabilization of 1990.

REFERENCES

Blejer, Mario, David Burton, Steven Dunaway and Gyorgy Szapary (1991) *China: Economic Reform and Macroeconomic Management*, International Monetary Fund, Occasional Paper 76, Washington, D.C., January.

Brainard, Lawrence J. (1990) 'Reform in Eastern Europe: Creating a Capital Market', *The AMEX Bank Review: Special Papers*, No. 18, November, 1–22.

Edwards, Sebastian and Alejandra Cox Edwards (1987) *Monetarism and Liberalization: The Chilean Experiment*, Cambridge, MA: Ballinger.

Ericson, Richard E. (1991) 'The Classical Soviet-Type Economy: Nature of the System and Implications for Reform', *Journal of Economic Perspectives* 5, 11–27.

Fforde, Adam and Stefan de Vylder (1991) *The Socialist Republic of Vietnam*, Report to the Asian Development Bank, Manila, August.

Harberger, Arnold C. (1990) 'Principles of Taxation Applied to Developing Countries: What Have We Learned?', in M. Boskin and Charles McLure (eds.), *World Tax Reform: Case Studies of Developed and Developing Countries*, San Francisco: ICS Press.

Hinds, Manuel (1990) 'Issues in the Introduction of Market Forces in East European Socialist Economies', The World Bank, Internal Discussion Paper, IDP-0057, April.

International Monetary Fund (1990) *The Economy of the USSR: Summary and Recommendations*, December.

Kim, Young C. (1991) *Economic Liberalization in Mongolia*, Report to the Asian Development Bank, Manila, August.

Kornai, Janos (1986) *Contradictions and Dilemmas: Studies on the Socialist Economy and Society*, Cambridge, MA: MIT Press.

(1990) *The Road to a Free Economy*, New York: W.W. Norton.

Lipton, David and Jeffrey Sachs (1990) 'Privatization in Eastern Europe: The Case of Poland', *Brookings Papers on Economic Activity* (2), 293–341.

Litwack, John (1991) 'Legality and Market Reform in Soviet-type Economies', *Journal of Economic Perspectives* 5, 77–89.

McKinnon, Ronald I. (1979) *Money in International Exchange: The Convertible Currency System*, New York: Oxford University Press.

(1991) *The Order of Economic Liberalization: Financial Control in the Transition to Market Economy*, Baltimore and London: Johns Hopkins University Press.

Murrell, Peter (1990) 'Big Bank Versus Evolution: Eastern European Reforms in the Light of Recent Economic History', *PlanEcon Report*, June 29.

Strasma, John et al. (1990) 'Agricultural Taxation in Theory and Practice', in R.M. Bird and O. Oldman (eds.), *Taxation in Developing Countries*, 4th edition, Baltimore and London: Johns Hopkins University Press.

Vokes, Richard and Armand Fabella (1991) *Economic Reform in the Lao People's Democratic Republic*, Asian Development Bank, Manila, August.

Wai, U. Tun (1991) *Economic Reform in Myanmar*, Report to the Asian Development Bank, Manila, August.

Williamson, John (1991) *The Opening of Eastern Europe*, Institute for International Economics, Policy Analysis 31, May.

Wong, Christine (1990) 'Central-Local Relations in an Era of Fiscal Decline: The Paradox of Fiscal Decentralization in Post-Mao China', Working Paper No. 210, University of California, Santa Cruz, September.

(1991) *Economic Reform in China*, Asian Development Bank, Manila, August.

World Bank (1990) *Lao PDR: Issues in Public Economics, 1990*, Washington, DC.

Discussion

RICHARD PORTES

This is in some respects an easy paper to discuss: it distils some of the lessons of Ron McKinnon's 1991 book and adds comparative material, with a more explicit prescriptive scheme for economic reform; it covers a very wide range; and it is often controversial. But I agree with a number of the controversial points, and I am familiar only with China among the Asian countries used for comparison with Central and Eastern Europe. Nor is there a formal model on which to focus. So I shall offer a number of disparate remarks.

The main points in the paper for me are the following: (1) The fiscal revenue base will erode as a consequence of economic decentralization; this will lead to inflation; a value added tax (VAT) is an urgent priority. (2) The preferred reform strategy should be gradualism with an explicit sequencing, rather than 'big bang', in the sense of trying to do as much as possible as fast as possible, with little concern for sequencing. (3) There should be an explicit distinction between 'liberalized' and 'unliberalized' or 'traditional' firms; they should operate under quite different rules, which would change as the sequence went from stage to stage. (4) In the first stage, there should be no bank lending whatsoever to firms of either kind; investment should be financed by a combination of retained earnings and a form of 'primitive capital accumulation'. (5) During the extended period of adjustment required to move to a free market economy, there should be significant tariff protection, more for 'senile' than for 'infant' industries.

I fully endorse the emphasis on the disastrous macroeconomic consequences of partial decentralization without effective fiscal and monetary controls. McKinnon describes the monetary system of the 'classical socialist' (centrally planned) economy. In that system the key element of monetary control is bank control over wage expenditures (Portes, 1983). The 'soft budget constraint', which was not in fact particularly important in the 'hard' command economy, does become dangerous when planning relaxes and banks let 'passive money' finance wages. This was the key factor in the Soviet macroeconomic disintegration from 1985 onwards (Portes, 1991), though it was exacerbated by weak oil prices, the anti-alcohol campaign, and Gorbachev's effort to 'accelerate' growth from 1987 onwards (Roland, 1992).

I do have some quibbles with the analysis and a major difficulty with the solution. The turnover tax was not collected from industrial firms, but rather at the wholesale distribution level, and almost all of it fell on consumer goods, not intermediates. A misunderstanding here leads McKinnon to misinterpret the relation between consumer prices and the profits of industrial firms. That said, turnover tax and 'deductions from profits' were indeed substitutable under the old system, and there was a trend shift from the former to the latter, which McKinnon ignores. If turnover tax had remained the source of two-thirds of tax revenues, as it was in the 1950s, the erosion of industrial enterprise profits consequent upon decentralization would not have been quite so disastrous fiscally. It is also important to note that the erosion in the tax base corresponded to some extent to reductions in central (budget-financed) expenditures, in particular, with the shift towards the enterprises of decision-making authority and financial responsibility for investment.

McKinnon is right to stress that the key to solving the fiscal problem is VAT, which he characterizes as feasible, necessary, and straightforward. Indeed – but even he says it will take a year or two to introduce, and in practice this seems to be an underestimate. Nor is it easy to enforce the complementary personal income tax that he recommends, in economies which hitherto used such a tax mainly to try to catch the dubious (to the authorities) earnings of private artisans and suppliers of minor services.

The gradualist approach McKinnon recommends would proceed from the 'bottom up'. He specifies clearly the different arrangements for different types of firms. It is clear, too, that price liberalization would come early; that there would be little or no centrally implemented demonopolization; and that both privatization and the development of a two-tier banking system would be delayed. Current account convertibility would come immediately for 'liberalized' firms.

McKinnon does not consider how corporate governance and incentives are to be improved without privatization or at least the prospect of it (Carlin and Mayer, 1992); how well a 'mixed' price system will work; and the likelihood that 'traditional' firms could arrange transactions with 'liberalized' firms in order to get access to foreign exchange. More seriously, he does not suggest how the restructuring of industry is to proceed (Hughes and Hare, 1992): when the 'traditional' firms are to be 'liberalized' (or closed); how, meanwhile, the central planning of their inputs and outputs and fixing of their prices can be consistent with a free market environment for 'liberalized' firms that sell to or buy from the traditional firms. What about the fiscal consequences of the continuing 'soft budget constraint' for 'traditional' firms – and why keep it anyway? (Begg and I, 1992, suggest cash-limited subsidies for specified periods for the state enterprises that have not yet been privatized.) Is the system robust to the (ultimate) failure of the traditional firms that do not adjust?

I believe McKinnon's proposals to delay modernizing the banking system and to prohibit bank lending to firms in the first stage are unnecessarily extreme responses to the problems posed by the overhang of enterprise bad debt and the correspondingly weak capital base of the banking system. These problems must be attacked directly and urgently – there are feasible solutions (see Begg and Portes, 1992), and they should be at the top of the sequence. A financial cleanout that deals with bank-enterprise relationships will also eliminate the problem of 'excessive' or 'unjustified' trade credit, because such a cleanout will make it possible to enforce bankruptcy. The proposal that the second stage shold limit lending to that which can be justified under an appropriate version of the real bills doctrine is questionable, since that was precisely the rule of crediting applied under the classical CPE system (Portes, 1983), and bad habits will doubtless persist.

My final remark is simply to endorse McKinnon's advocacy of temporary protection through tariffs, as a second- or third-best policy (see also Flemming, 1992). It is not clear that East Germany, where the real wage quickly rose to grossly unjustified levels that made most industrial production unprofitable, is a good argument for this policy; but Poland most certainly is. Despite the arguments for immediate and complete opening to imports (e.g. Berg and Sachs, 1992), I believe the case for gradual adjustment is gaining ground.

REFERENCES

Begg, D. and R. Portes (1992) 'Enterprise debt and economic transformation: financial restructuring of the state sector in Central and Eastern Europe', paper for CEPR-Fundacion BBV conference, San Sebastian, forthcoming in C. Mayer and X. Vives (eds.), *Financial Intermediation in the Construction of Europe*.

Berg, A. and J. Sachs (1992) 'Structural adjustment and international trade in Eastern Europe: the case of Poland', *Economic Policy* 7, (14), 117–73.

Carlin, W. and C. Mayer (1992) 'Restructuring enterprises in Eastern Europe', *Economic Policy* 7, (15), 311–52.

Flemming, J. (1992) 'Relative price shocks and unemployment: arguments for temporarily reduced payroll taxes or protection', paper for TAPES Conference, Munich, June.

Hughes, G. and P. Hare (1992) 'Industrial policy and restructuring in Eastern Europe', CEPR Discussion Paper No. 653.

Portes, R. (1983) 'Central planning and monetarism: fellow travellers?', in P. Desai (ed.), *Marxism, Central Planning and the Soviet Economy*, Cambridge, MA: MIT Press.

(1991) 'The transition to convertibility for Eastern Europe and the Soviet Union', in A. Atkinson and R. Brunetta (eds.), *Economics for a New Europe*, London: Macmillan.

Roland, G. (1992) 'The political economy of transition in the Soviet Union', CEPR Discussion Paper No. 628.

9 Regional imbalances and government compensatory financial flows: the case of Spain

JUAN RAMÓN CUADRADO, GUILLERMO
de la DEHESA and ANDRÉS PRECEDO

1 Introduction

Different levels of economic growth among regions is a fact common to most countries, although with a wide variety of degree and character.

Regional economics has tried to find scientific explanations for those differences, borrowing from general theories of growth, development, capital and international trade but, at the same time, applying specialized theories about space and location in economics.

Starting from different approaches, hypotheses and assumptions, Neoclassical models (Meade, 1963); Cumulative causation models (Myrdal, 1957; Kaldor, 1957, 1970); Export base models (Bolton, 1966); Agglomeration models (Lösch, 1954; Giersch, 1949; von Böventer, 1970); Location theory models (Isard, 1956; Beckman, 1968); Urban monocentric models (Alonso, 1964); and Innovation models (Grossman and Helpman, 1991) among others, have tried to explain why growth rates differ among countries and regions.

If there is a common ground to most of their findings, this is that production and consumption tend to concentrate spatially due to economies of scale, economies of transport and external economies, and therefore tend to produce divergence among different areas or regions in a country, or among different countries. There are, nevertheless, two extreme positions. In Neoclassical models growth rates tend, in the long run, to be more balanced due to decreasing returns to capital and countries and regions tend to converge and, at the other extreme, cumulative causation models show that there is a permanent tendency for countries and regions growth rates to diverge. The rest of the models fall in the middle between these extremes.

In the last four years, regional issues have been getting more attention due to two developments. On the one side, the appearance of endogenous

261

growth and factor accumulation models (Lucas, 1988; Romer, 1986, 1988; Barro, 1989) showing that long-term growth can be generated without relying on diminishing returns to capital and exogenous changes in technology or population, as in neoclassical models, but by constant or increasing returns in the factors that can be accumulated. These models are establishing new grounds for explaining increasing regional divergence and for supporting regional government intervention. On the other side, the regional effects of European integration are coming to the centre of the regional debate. The renewed fashion of the pioneering works by Giersch (1949) showing the perverse regional impact of economic and monetary unions, and by Mundell (1961) showing the importance of factor mobility in determining optimal currency areas, is the basis for a new and vigorous debate about the 'Two speed EMU' (Dornbusch, 1990) and about the importance of a compensatory transfer system (Cohesion) to avoid larger regional divergences.

In this regard, the comparative studies between a long-time consolidated economic and monetary union (USA) and another being born (Europe) are extremely useful. The works by Krugman (1991a, 1991b, and 1992) Blanchard and Katz (1992), Eichengreen (1990), Sala-i-Martín and Sachs (1991) and Bertola (1991), among others, try to show that an economic and monetary union may produce a lack of convergence by, on the one side, eliminating or reducing the use of the traditional policy instruments of adjustment and compensation to regional shocks (monetary, fiscal and exchange rates policies) and, on the other side, concentrating economic activity through economies of scale and externalities.

The first issue is goods and services mobility, due to a single market. It seems that opening markets and reducing transaction costs increases the importance of economies of scale and concentrates production in the central areas (Krugman, 1990; Faini, 1983; Krugman and Venables, 1990).

The second issue in the debate is whether factor mobility, due to economic and monetary integration, reinforces the tendency of economic activity to concentrate or not. Some analyses (Klaassen and Molle, 1982; Vanhove and Klaassen, 1987) show that both migration and capital mobility have tended to reinforce greater concentration. Labour has tended to migrate to the centres of economic activity and banks have channel savings from 'peripheral' regions to 'centre' regions where the demand for capital is higher. Greater capital mobility should help borrowers from local segmented markets who today pay higher rates (Branson, 1990), provided marginal borrowers are not crowded out by tighter financial and credit discipline. Nevertheless, in the last few years there has been exceptions to these trends. Spain and Portugal have received large flows of foreign direct investment and labour has not migrated (De la Dehesa, 1989).

In any case, the market mechanism seems to reinforce concentration of economic activity through goods, services and factor mobility and the accumulation of those factors can induce greater economic divergence among regions. The actual results depend, naturally, on the initial situation of each region and its capacity to react.

As the evidence of these theories is still inconclusive, the first objective of this paper is to try to collect and analyse data to show regional growth trends both in Europe and in Spain, and try to see if they fit with those concentrating and diverging tendencies. This is what we do in section 2, and we reach the conclusion that regional convergence, both in Europe and Spain has stopped in the last few years and does not show any clear tendency to improve but, if anything, is diminishing.

The second issue to discuss, here, is government intervention. The majority of the regional analyses of European economic and monetary union (Krugman, 1992; Bertola, 1991; Molle, 1989; Neven, 1990; Sala-i-Martín and Sachs, 1991) integration call for government intervention to avoid market failures and perverse effects of excessive concentration. The EC Commission has also realized that some measures of regional policy are necessary to compensate the countries and regions more negatively affected by integration, to avoid the future of the community being in jeopardy (Padoa-Schioppa, 1987). The whole 'Cohesion' effort is trying to achieve just that (Braga de Macedo, 1991).

There are three basic arguments that are mainly used in Europe to justify government intervention through regional policy (Molle, 1991). The social, political or 'equity' argument is the one more widely used to support intervention both at national and Community level. It is based on the idea that an integrated EC should be based not only on the market mechanism of free movements of goods, services and factors, but also on the principle of solidarity of prosperous with less prosperous nations and regions. This is the same kind of argument that is used by governments for the redistribution of personal income. The economic or 'efficiency argument' is based on the idea that an inefficient distribution of productive factors, public goods and economic activity may prevent the EC from achieving its potential growth (Baldwin, 1989) because production may be bigger with a more even and less concentrated productive structure, since private mobility decisions lead to excessive concentration of production (Bertola, 1991).

The third argument could be called the 'integration success argument'. A European common currency will bring about inter-regional shocks that will generate unemployment in some regions and inflation in others, threatening the very survival of the economic, monetary and even political union: therefore, redistributive fiscal federalism is necessary. (Sala-i-Martín and Sachs, 1991).

If we agree that governments should intervene, many questions need to be answered. Which government; the regional, the national, or the Community one?

Up to now, most regional policies have been carried out by regional and national governments, EC regional policy being a small percentage, in volume of financial resources. The problem with regional government intervention is that running a deficit today to compensate for a present regional shock may induce more taxes tomorrow, and, if the shock tends to be more permanent, the policy will be ineffective and expensive to the region (Krugman, 1992; Sala-i-Martín and Sachs, 1991).

Therefore, regional compensatory policy should be either national or at the EC level. The problem here is that the budget of the EC is too small in relation to the national ones and it is 'crowded out' by agricultural policy.

The second question is: which kind of regional policy? In section 3 we try to argue that there are two kinds of regional policies: explicit and implicit ones. The first are those traditionally classified as regional. The second are also very important but are never regarded as 'regional' since they are mainly 'sectoral' or 'personal', but, in fact, they have very important regional effects; sometimes, as in the case of Spain, they are even more important than the explicit ones.

The third question is with what instruments and measures is it most efficient to intervene? Public investment, transfers to regional governments, personal transfers, lower taxes, education, infrastructure, or R & D? We try also in section 3 to look at this issue. Our view is that, as policies have been more frequently based on political ideas about compensation and redistribution than on the search for economic efficiency in the backward regions, the instruments (compensatory transfers) have not been appropriate to enhance economic development and the results of regional policies are very poor. The examples of Italy (Faini, 1990) and Spain are paradigmatic.

2   Recent evolution of regional disparities in Europe and Spain

The economic development disparities among regions can be analysed in different ways. The one that we follow here is only one of them, the one we think is the most suitable for achieving our ultimate objective, that is, to present the fundamental outline of the evolution of the disparities, at a regional level, in the context of the European Community, and, more particularly, in the Spanish case.

Before commenting on the results obtained in our descriptive analysis it may be useful to examine some methodological aspects.

2.1 Data base, selected indicators and methodology

The Netherlands Economic Institute has recently prepared an adjusted regional data base which covers the period 1968–88 and which includes the 171 regions (NUTS II) of the present members of the European Community, taking into consideration that some of the twelve member countries were incorporated in the EC at intermediate or very recent dates.[1] To analyse the Spanish case, apart from this source, which allowed us to make comparisons between member countries, we have also used the series which the Banco de Bilbao has produced for some years, since their temporal coverage is very superior to the one published, since 1980, by the Instituto Nacional de Estadística.

The indicator which is here taken as a reference to measure the disparities between regions is GDP per inhabitant, which we feel reflects, better than others, the evolution of the level of development of the countries and regions, although certain insufficiencies arise, such as the exclusion of self-production, and, as we will see later, the problem of subsidization.

The relationships between GDP and the standard of living, output and the level of development, in general, pose several relevant questions which we will not deal with here. However, comparison between the countries and regions of the EC makes it necessary to choose values that avoid distortions due to exchange rates and purchasing power differentials. For this reason GDP values have previously been translated to terms of purchasing power parity standards (PPS) and, as a second alternative, to ECU.

On the other hand, it would be useful to remember that the NUTS II regions of the EC have a very unequal dimension and weight, and that the way economic data are accounted for leads sometimes to an undervaluation or an overvaluation of the importance of some regions. The cases of Hamburg and Groningen are two good extreme examples of this. Hamburg has a heavy productive concentration in a reduced territory and many persons who work there live in other adjacent regions, with a corresponding incidence in its GDP per inhabitant. In Groningen the value of the natural gas extracted in its administrative territory is included in its output, which substantially increases its GDP, in spite of the fact that it has very limited effects on employment and income in the region.

The techniques used here for analysing the evolution of the disparities are simple, In the case of the EC as a whole, the standard deviation coefficients, weighted by the importance of each region, offer clear and illustrative results. In the Spanish case, we have also used Theil indexes since they permit us to differentiate the influence which productivity, level of employment and total population have, or have had, on the historic evolution of the disparities between Spanish regions. Note 2 contains a condensed exposition of both techniques.[2]

2.2   Evolution of regional disparities in the EC

The magnitude and evolution of regional disparities can be viewed both at the Community level and within each different country.

The differences between regions at the EC level are, as it is well known, very important. They represent, substantially, more than twice those registered in the USA (although the regions subjected to comparison are quite different). Taking the average GDP per inhabitant corresponding to the period 1986–1987–1988, the richest European region – Groningen – is over 4.6 times the level of the poorest – Voreio Aigaio – in Greece. The ten richest European regions had a GDP per inhabitant in 1988 equivalent to more than three times that of the ten poorest of the Community ranking. In total, 104 of the 171 Community regions have a per capita GDP, in PPS values, below the average and of those, 43 regions are below 80 per cent of the average (Commission of the European Communities, 1991).

The recent historic evolution of these inter-regional differences are of special interest and, for this reason, we have analysed their variation using standard deviations. Figure 9.1 shows standard deviations of GDP per inhabitant both in PPS and in ECU, and shows that regional disparities tend to decrease until 1975–77, when the impact of the first energy shock introduces a temporary increase. However, from the beginning of the eighties the convergence has remained stable, but with a slight tendency to decrease, becoming even clearer when calculations are made in PPS values.

The historic inter-regional convergence which has been noted until the middle of the seventies seems then to have halted. The energy and industrial crisis, the decline of traditional industries, the emergence of new technologies, the concentration of production in some central areas of Europe reinforcing the, so called, European 'Hot Banana', that covers an area 1,500 km long by 250 km wide going from London to Milano, the recent extension of that centre toward the South of Europe through the 'Mediterranean Arch' (Figure 9.2) and the anticipation of the competitive effects of the 'single market' contribute in different degrees to explain this

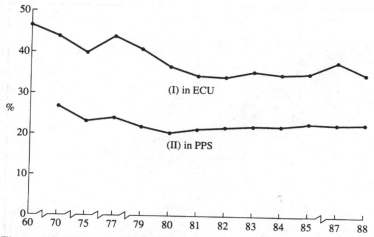

Figure 9.1   Regional imbalances in the EC (weighted standard deviation as a percentage of the average)

non-convergence. The lack of mobility of the population, observed in the EC during the last few years, in contrast to what happened in the sixties and at the beginning of the seventies – a remarkable fact taking into account the differences of GDP per inhabitant – has also largely contributed to explain such a lack of convergence. We will come back to this issue later.

If we look more closely at the changes in the relative position of the regions in the European ranking, we can see that, as a general rule, regions located in the more peripheral countries of the EC (Greece, Portugal, Spain, Ireland and even Italy) tend, apparently, to worsen their relative position, while regions which are situated in the countries that form the European 'core' (United Kingdom, The Netherlands, Belgium, Denmark and Germany), as well as in the new emergent zones of Southern Europe (the Mediterranean Arch) tend to improve their position. On the other hand, most of the 'objective 1' regions of the EC (that is to say, those which are eligible for ERDF funds because of their relative underdevelopment) have grown less than the European average. There are notable exceptions, however, such as part of Ireland, Abruzzi and Molise (Italy); Macedonia (Greece); Centro (Portugal), and part of Spain (Andalucía, Canarias, Comunidad Valenciana, Extremadura, Galicia and Murcia), all of which have, somewhat, slowly improved their relative position in the European ranking. Such different behaviour shows that EC regional compensatory policies do not appear to offset spatial growth dynamics.

Existing regional disparities within each country also give us some

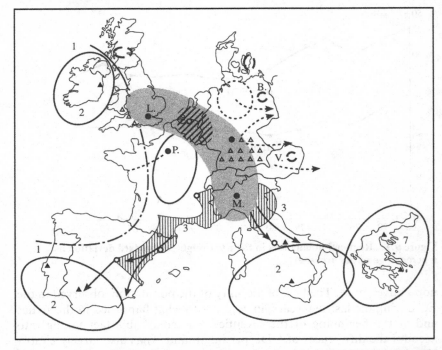

Figure 9.2   The European 'hot banana'. *Source:* adapted from GIP–RECLUS, 1989

points of interest. Figure 9.3 shows that regional divergences have always been smaller in two rich countries: Germany and Great Britain, and two lower income level countries, Spain (against what is very often maintained) and Greece.

On the contrary, regional differences are appreciably higher in Portugal, Italy and France. In the last two countries regional divergence – always in terms of GDP per inhabitant – has increased even in recent years, from 1983 to 1988.

The European panorama shows, then, complex situations and different behaviour, when each of the member states is studied. But, what seems clear to us is that from the first third of the eighties, a new regional growth dynamics has begun to appear which affects as much the situation of each of the regions in the European hierarchy, as the increase, stability, or decrease of inter-regional differences within the different countries. In any case, what is undeniable is that, first, at Community level, regional convergence has ceased during the eighties and even worsened slightly following an apparent 'core-periphery' pattern, with some important exceptions. And second, that this tendency could continue during the next

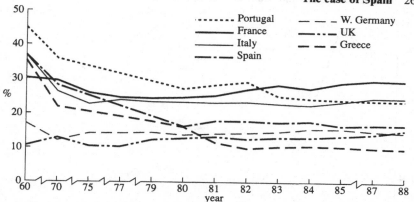

Figure 9.3   **Evolution of income disparities within member states in PPS (weighted standard deviation as a percentage of the average)**

few years, helped by the probable centripetal effects of the free factor mobility imposed by the 'single market'.

2.3   The Spanish case

The convergence results obtained by using a Theil index for the 1960–87 period in Spain are those shown in Figure 9.4. Leaving aside the 1960–64 stage, two very clear stages appear. In the first, from 1964 to 1979, there is an outstanding inter-regional convergence in GDP per inhabitant terms. Nevertheless, when total values are analysed, both for production and population, it can be clearly seen, in this phase, that an important concentration was produced in the more industrialized areas (Cataluña, País Vasco and Madrid). In the second phase (1979–87) the aforementioned convergence process is suddenly halted, worsening in 1983 and remaining almost stable afterwards.

The splitting of the Theil index allows us to be more precise. In the first stage, the tendency towards a greater equality of output per worker by region (Theil 1) is reinforced by the population/inactive and unemployed population ratio (Theil 2). The important inter-regional migratory movements which occurred during this period (from the poorest to the richest and most dynamic areas) underlie both facts and particularly the second.

However, from 1977, (although from 1976 the deviation is already clear) output per worker has continued its tendency toward a regional approximation, while the inactive and unemployed population component (with higher levels in some regions than in others) is the factor that seems to contribute most of the persistence of inter-regional differences in GDP

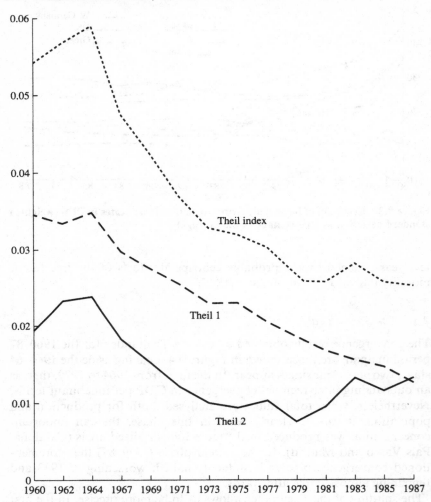

Figure 9.4   Regional disparities in Spain: Theil index for 1960–87

per inhabitant, contrary to what happened in the past, when considerable mobility of the population and the work force existed.

Such an evolution of the inter-regional differences in Spain needs some additional insights which will allow for a better understanding of its underlying facts. In concrete, we refer to three of them: the distance between rich and poor provinces; the link between national and regional growth; and the recent evolution towards a new economic-regional map of Spain, as a consequence of the unequal regional development of the last decade.

With regard to the first, it should be pointed out that an analysis of the disparities at a provincial, less aggregated, level, shows that the process of inter-regional convergence, that we have previously observed, has been due much more to a reduction of the distances between the rich provinces and the national average, than to an advance of the poor ones towards the national average. For instance, the province which in 1973 occupied the lowest position (Lugo in Galicia) had a GDP/inhabitant equivalent to 57 per cent of the Spanish average; in 1985, Granada (Andalucía), occupied this position with a GDP/inhabitant equivalent to the 57.5 per cent and, in 1989, Jaén (Andalucia), the poorest Spanish province had 58.6 per cent. In contrast, the relative retrogressive tendency toward the average by the richer provinces has been – in general – more notable, some historically rich provinces (Vizcaya, Cantabria, Guipuzcoa and even Barcelona) have been especially affected by the impact of the crisis and decline of traditional industries that caused important losses in their previous positions, and, at the same time, a rise of various intermediate provinces (Gerona, Zaragoza, Valencia, La Rioja and, of course, Baleares) (Preedo, 1989).

The second fact worth noting is that, in the same way as the Spanish GDP growth and that of the EC show an increasing correlation, the growth of most Spanish regions is more and more closely related to the growth of the national GDP and, thus, to that of the EC. Table 9.1 shows the correlation coefficients obtained between the growth of GDP of the different autonomous regions (Raymond, 1991) and the growth of the Spanish and EC GDP for the period 1962–90. Only in the cases of Extremadura (still primarily agricultural), La Rioja (a very small region, also dedicated to agriculture and the wine industry) and the Canary Islands (a distant region specializing in the tourist trade and some specialized home agrarian production) did the correlation coefficient reach lower values in relation to the evolution of the Spanish GDP.

Therefore, the Spanish economy functions increasingly more in step with that of the EC and the majority of the regions follow the fluctuations of the Spanish economy. This synchronization has always been accompanied by a tendency towards equalizing the productive structure of the regions. The average index of inequality of regional structures in relation to the national economy shows, for each year, the degree of structural disparity between regions.[3] If, as a whole, the regions are increasingly more similar, this average index should tend to decrease with time, as has actually happened. Figure 9.4 shows the tendency of the average index between 1962 and 1990, from which it is clear that the regions are ever more similar regarding the structure of their output, although in terms of employment this approximation still shows notable differences.

This convergence in the productive structure is reflected, logically, in a certain convergence of GDP growth rates, given that the behaviour of the

Table 9.1. *Correlation between regional and national and EC growth*

Correlation coefficients between GDP growth of autonomous communities and GDP growth of

	Spain	EC
Andalucía	0.88	0.69
Aragón	0.85	0.68
Asturias	0.90	0.71
Baleares	0.72	0.84
Canarias	0.61	0.86
Cantabria	0.72	0.66
Castilla – La Mancha	0.90	0.74
Castilla – León	0.82	0.57
Cataluña	0.98	0.74
Extremadura*	0.38	0.36
Galicia	0.91	0.77
Madrid	0.89	0.61
Murcia	0.80	0.75
Navarra	0.88	0.67
País Vasco	0.88	0.57
La Rioja*	0.64	0.64
Valencia	0.72	0.72

Source: Raymond (1991).
Note: * indicates not significant at 1 per cent level.

productive sectors at a national level is usually relatively homogeneous.[4] The disparity index based on GDP growth for the period 1962–90 shows a significant negative tendency (*t*-statistic of 3.6) which indicates that the regions have tended to converge in their GDP growth rates, although maintaining relatively moderate standard deviations (see Figure 9.5).

Precisely, the third fact that we wish to emphasize here is that this greater homogeneity of the behaviour of the Spanish regions during the last few years has not prevented some regions, as in the past, from growing faster than others, due to a better adjustment and/or response of their industry and services to the evolution of markets, as well as a greater dynamism in productive investments, both domestic and foreign.

Since the end of the seventies the different rates of growth of the Spanish regions has shown (Cuadrado, 1988, 1990 and 1991; Alcaide, 1988 and 1991; Alcaide *et al.*, 1990), that as a general rule, the regions with faster growth have been those geographically closer to the 'European core' and/or integrated in the emergent 'Mediterranean axis or arch'.

Figure 9.6 shows that the higher growth regions, since EC integration, are located in the 'Mediterranean axis' (Cataluña, Valencia, Alicante,

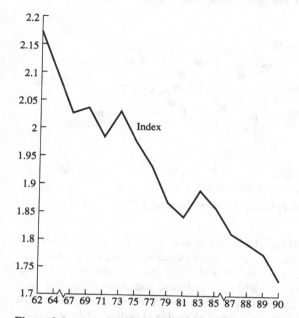

Figure 9.5 Regional inequality index. *Source:* Raymond (1991)

Murcia and Almería, plus Baleares), and its derivative the 'Ebro axis' (Navarra, La Rioja and the centre of Aragón). The exceptions to this general rule are: the País Vasco and Cantabria, that have both suffered a strong restructuring of their declining traditional industrial sectors, Canarias, that has been going through a tourist boom and Andalucía, that has been the region receiving the highest volume of state transfers and investments in the last ten years.

3   Spanish regional policies

We consider in the Spanish case two kinds of regional policies: 'explicit' and 'implicit' ones. In most countries much attention has been given to 'explicit' regional policies and very little to 'implicit' ones. The first are those which are classified as such, using different figures (creation of 'development poles or cores', creation of infrastructure, localization of state-owned companies in backward areas, building of transport infrastructure, creation of economic promotion zones, etc.) and diverse instruments (financial and fiscal incentives, direct investments, etc.). 'Implicit' regional policies are a consequence of more personal or sectoral policies, that is to say, not specifically regional, but which can have a

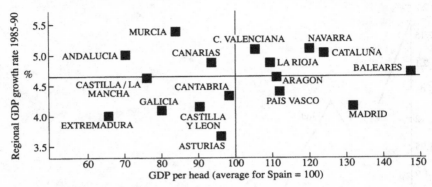

Figure 9.6　Regional growth in Spain, 1985–90. *Source:* FIES.

specific and differentiated effect at the regional level. All sectoral policies (agricultural, industrial, energy, etc.) have positive or negative effects on one or other region. The same occurs with investment decisions on public infrastructure and, of course, with tax policies, social security and personal transfers made by the State, etc. However, the regional incidence of some of these activities is not accounted as regional policy, although their actual importance may be greater than the explicit regional policies. This is why we try to include them in our analysis.

3.1　Explicit regional policy

Spain has a relatively long tradition of regional policies. The twenties saw, already, the birth of new plans for the regulation of large geographic areas, by the, so called, 'Confederaciones hidrográficas'. In the forties and fifties, apart from the work of reconstruction begun in various zones after the Civil war, policies of concentration and regulation of agrarian production were developed as well as of integral agrarian colonisation of new zones, (plans for Badajoz and Jaén), all of which with very unequal impact on regions.

Regional policy reached a much more prominent level during the stage of the strong boom of both the European and the Spanish economies (1964 to 1973–74).

The role played by regional policy during this stage is relatively well known and has been the object of diverse studies and evaluations.[5] The first three 'National Development Plans' clearly incorporated the intention to correct traditional regional differences that existed in the country. One of the tools used were the 'poles' of development (Lasuen, 1969), which by means of a concentration of actions, (infrastructure, fiscal and financial subsidies, low tariffs on imports, etc.) looked for the formation or the development of important new industrial centres, distributed among the last developed regions of the country. Another group of actions were directed, simultaneously, towards the development of tourist and agricultural zones of special interest, as well as the creation of industrial zones and areas to relieve congestion near the large cities. Andalucía, Extremadura, Galicia, both Castillas and Aragón were the principal regions to which these efforts were directed, which in some aspects followed a line comparable with other French and Italian experiences.

The results of these regional development policies have been the object of very different evaluations, sometimes of an excessively negative nature. The time which has elapsed permits, perhaps, to better qualify such judgments. In synthesis, it can be affirmed that the strategy of 'polarization' applied to the first two Development Plans (from 1964 to 1971) did not function as it was hoped. The relative success of the industrial areas of Zaragoza, Burgos and Huelva was not so much due to the incentives and subsidies granted to the enterprises which decided to establish themselves there, as to the strategic location of those centres and to the actual industrial decentralization process which occurred in Spain, similar to what happened in other countries. The industrial areas also show some unequal results. Better results were obtained in the urban centres which already had a certain dynamism, mainly those which were near Madrid and Barcelona, or which had some advantages of location regarding transport facilities. The best results were obtained in the development of an important tourist infrastructure in the Mediterranean coastline that helped to accommodate the increasing number of foreign tourists, but, unfortunately, it was built with very little planning and deteriorated the urban environment of the whole Mediterranean coast.

It is worth pointing out, on the other hand, that the regional policy of this period was always subordinated to the sectoral policies included in the Development Plans. Nevertheless, for the first time, an effort was made to systematize the measures which should be applied, in order to try to correct regional imbalances. A notable advance in the plans of regional policy was associated with trying adequate articulation/regulation of the whole territory and not only in the industrialization of underdeveloped zones. This was particularly clear in the III Development Plan (1972–75), although it was not implemented, because of both the general evolution of the economy and the transition towards democracy.

The 1975–85 period was one of an almost total regional policy vacuum in Spain. Some of the instruments and measures inherited from the past still existed, but explicit regional policies practically disappeared from the priorities of the Government. There were various reasons for this which are explained elsewhere (Cuadrado, 1987). First, because the industrial and economic crisis, in general, moved the priority to macroeconomic and sectoral restructuring. Second, because the available resources for regional actions were of residual character and very limited. And finally, because the political change toward greater autonomy for the regions required redesign of the jurisdictions of the central and regional governments.

In this context, 'explicit' regional policy remained practically in hibernation, with the sole exception of actions of a compensatory character urgently implemented in declining industries which gave birth to the 'Urgent Reindustrialisation Zones' (ZUR). The balance of costs and results of these is yet to be made, but the available data show some uneven results: rather successful in the areas located in the most dynamic zones (Barcelona and Sagunto) and failures in the rest (Cádiz and to a lesser degree, the whole of the North).

From 1985 it is necessary to talk again about an 'explicit' regional policy in Spain, although with three main differences from previous stages. The first one, and the most important, is that the protagonism of this policy is no longer of a single agent (the central government) but of three: the EC Commission, the central government and the newly autonomous regional governments. This is so not only because the latter now have the capacity and power to implement policies in their own region, but also, because the three agents mentioned have been obliged to cooperate on some concrete regional actions, especially in those financed by the EC structural funds (ERDF, EAGGF and ESF).

The second characteristic of the new regional policy is that Spain has had to be subject, in this as in other fields, to the directives and limitations approved by the EC. This has involved the elaboration, for example, of Regional Development Programmes of a triennial (and moveable) character to revise and regulate 'regional investment incentives'[6] – one of the new key instruments – and to select the priorities for public investments linked to regional policy. Spain, as opposed to other countries, has given almost absolute priority to the construction of infrastructure (development of a motorway plan, roads, new 'high speed' trains, improvement of the railways, airports and harbours). Table 9.2 shows the amount of ERDF transfers to the regional autonomies.

Finally, the third new aspect is the creation, by constitutional mandate, of an 'Interterritorial Compensation Fund' (FCI), oriented to the redistribution of part of the new public investment in favour of the less advanced regions of the country. At the beginning such a fund suffered clear

Table 9.2. *ERDF transfers to Spanish regions (million pesetas)*

	1987	1988	1989	1990	1991	Total
Andalucía	1,778.1	8,102.6	12,589.3	10,507.9	10,604.1	43,582.0
Aragón	157.0	393.5	601.4	254.1	555.9	1,961.9
Asturias	969.2	1,271.2	1,540.8	410.6	7,875.5	12,067.3
Canarias	1,534.1	2,131.7	300.8	3,153.6	7,646.8	14,767.0
Cantabria			126.0	225.8	1,129.6	1,481.4
Castilla – León	1,443.6	1,457.5	2,980.0	2,168.9	8,776.8	16,826.8
Castilla – La Mancha		1,401.8	2,656.4	4,186.8	2,639.0	10,884.0
Comunidad Valenciana			3,286.3	561.1	8,183.4	12,030.8
Cataluña		1,728.4	1,406.5	6,983.7	3,509.3	12,727.9
Extremadura*	855.6	1,764.9	3,882.0	978.2	7,171.5	14,652.2
Galicia	1,751.6	3,748.7	4,256.0	6,443.7	3,242.5	19,442.5
Madrid			1,136.2	7.2	986.1	2,129.5
Murcia	101.9	455.1	866.7	972.7	2,921.1	5,317.5
Navarra			174.6	271.3	365.6	811.5
País Vasco			1,570.3	2,988.2	1,035.1	5,593.6
La Rioja*					517.1	517.1
Total	8,591.1	22,455.4	37,373.3	40,113.8	67,159.3	174,493.0

deviations with respect to its main objective since it also benefited some of the most developed regions. The modifications introduced most recently have brought the FCI somewhat closer to its constitutional meaning, but its redistributionary character continues to be rather questionable. Table 9.3 shows the evolution of the participation of the different autonomous communities in the FCI from 1983 to 1989. In this last year the resources of the Fund amounted to 214,814 million pesetas (around 2 billion dollars). It is interesting to point out that Spanish regional funds are much more important than those received from the EC. Five years of ERDF funds add, in all, to less than one year of FCI funds, showing once more that 'fiscal federalism' in Europe is still very small. For the period 1989–93 the structural funds to be received by Spain will represent only 1.2 per cent of total regional GDP, while in the case of Ireland, Greece and Portugal they will be 2.9 per cent, 2.3 per cent and 3.5 per cent respectively.

3.2   Implicit regional policy: two examples

What we have previously justified as implicit regional policy has a very wide content. It includes, in reality, any act of economic policy by the authorities which has different effects on different regions, as all such actions have to a greater or lesser extent.

Here we concentrate on two concrete and important examples which result in a differential treatment of the Spanish regions. The first one is through taxes and public sector expenditure, that is to say, via personal redistribution; the second, is through the distribution of government investment by region.

A good way of approaching 'implicit' regional policies is by using not only regional GDP as an indicator, but also disposable family income (RFD) by region. This indicator incorporates wages, salaries and incomes received directly by families, transfers from the public sector (pensions and other social security transfers, health subsidies, unemployment subsidies, subsidies to agricultural day labourers, complementary pensions and other transfers from Public Administrations), deducting, at the same time, social security contributions paid by workers and taxes paid by families. This means, in a few words, that the disposable family income indicators per inhabitant of each region or province are the result of the redistributive action by the public sector, collecting revenue from some regions or provinces and transferring incomes to others.

So, the comparative data of regional GDP and RFD per inhabitant during the period 1967–87 shown in Table 9.4 allows us to confirm, that, even if some oscillations are observed, whose explanation requires a more

Table 9.3. *Regional participation in the 'Fondo de Compensacion Interterritorial' (FCI)*

	1983	1984	1985	1986	1987	1988	1989
Andalucía	26.84	27.74	27.73	26.90	25.36	24.43	23.21
Aragón	2.25	2.50	2.46	2.35	2.17	1.92	1.99
Asturias	2.29	2.17	2.16	2.13	2.45	2.31	2.22
Baleares	1.06	1.07	0.85	0.80	0.83	0.68	0.72
Canarias	6.74	5.34	4.68	4.60	5.09	5.79	5.47
Castilla – León	8.85	9.19	9.33	9.45	9.02	7.60	7.50
Castilla – La Mancha	6.58	6.78	7.60	7.57	7.51	7.15	7.00
Cataluña	7.85	8.34	8.60	7.47	7.13	9.77	11.12
Extremadura	7.64	7.67	7.17	8.51	8.01	6.20	5.93
Galicia	10.67	10.19	10.61	10.65	10.91	10.78	10.66
Murcia	2.04	2.12	2.17	2.01	1.92	2.17	2.36
Navarra	0.64	0.66	0.67	0.71	0.71	0.65	0.68
Valencia	5.87	5.98	5.27	5.95	6.21	6.28	6.28
País Vasco	3.36	3.20	3.54	3.66	5.27	6.98	7.44
Madrid	5.73	5.44	5.34	5.38	5.52	5.72	5.81
La Rioja	0.34	0.33	0.34	0.35	0.33	0.30	0.30
Cantabria	0.77	0.82	0.88	0.93	0.94	0.80	0.82
Ceuta	0.24	0.23	0.31	0.32	0.34	0.26	0.27
Melilla	0.24	0.23	0.29	0.26	0.28	0.21	0.22
Total	100.0	100.0	100.0	100.0	100.0	100.0	100.0

Sources: Ministry of Economy and Finance.

detailed study, there are a series of backward regions which show clearly a net increase in their disposable income through transfers from the rest of the country, via central and regional governments. That is the case of Extremadura, Andalucía, Galicia, Murcia and Castilla-La Mancha, while others see their RFD reduced, correspondingly, such as País Vasco, Madrid, Baleares, Navarra, Aragón and Cataluña, and a last group of regions moves between a net receiver or a net giver of income, according to the year taken into consideration.

In this way, Government carries out a policy which tends toward a greater regional equality which does not exactly respond to the regional development policy schemes but to actions of redistribution of personal income (via taxes and expenditure) and to other policies that imply transfer of income.

Social Security is also a very significant example of the latter. Table 9.5 collects the results of the analysis of the contributions paid to Social Security by each region and the amounts received from it. As can be observed, several regions classified as most backward, Extremadura,

Table 9.4(a). *Transfers from the general government received by families resident in the region (% of total income)*

	1967	1969	1971	1973	1975	1977	1979	1981	1983	1985	1987
Extremadura	11.5	14.5	9.5	13.4	16.2	14.3	14.6	16.0	16.3	16.5	18.4
Andalucía	6.9	9.3	7.3	6.8	6.0	7.0	9.9	10.9	11.7	13.2	16.2
Galicia	6.1	5.5	10.3	12.2	13.2	13.4	15.3	9.1	7.1	7.6	8.9
Murcia	0.6	1.7	1.2	0.3	-2.7	1.3	3.7	-0.2	5.2	7.2	6.8
Castilla – La Mancha	0.7	1.3	0.3	2.1	3.2	4.8	7.6	1.8	7.0	4.8	7.9

Source: Serie BBV.

Table 9.4(b). *Withdrawal of regional family income due to transfers by general government to other regions (% of total income)*

	1967	1969	1971	1973	1975	1977	1979	1981	1983	1985	1987
País Vasco	1.7	2.9	3.2	5.3	7.2	11.7	11.8	5.8	7.1	10.4	10.0
Madrid	0.2	1.3	-1.4	-5.2	3.3	5.9	9.5	7.0	7.1	8.0	12.3
Baleares	3.2	3.1	5.7	13.8	4.6	-0.1	1.2	1.0	1.2	8.2	13.0
Navarra	2.4	-0.4	0.8	1.2	2.2	3.1	4.2	5.7	4.7	5.8	7.2
Aragón	1.8	2.6	3.7	3.8	1.7	1.3	-0.8	2.5	7.5	4.1	3.3
Cataluña	5.1	5.6	5.6	5.4	4.4	4.4	3.9	3.3	2.5	3.6	2.8

Source: Serie BBV.

Table 9.4(c). *Addition or withdrawal of income related to transfers from or to general government (% of total income)*

	1967	1969	1971	1973	1975	1977	1979	1981	1983	1985	1987
Asturias	−4.0	−7.3	−10.1	−12.7	−5.4	−0.9	−0.3	5.3	−1.9	−0.2	0.7
Cantabria	−4.6	−2.9	−4.6	−5.7	−0.3	−2.2	−3.8	2.7	0.5	0.8	2.3
Castilla – León	1.9	3.6	0.5	1.6	5.9	5.0	1.3	1.2	−0.3	1.8	3.6
La Rioja	1.3	2.1	0.4	0.0	0.4	4.2	1.1	−2.8	−1.8	1.5	6.0
C. Valenciana	0.1	1.6	−0.1	−0.8	0.5	3.7	3.9	0.4	2.9	3.7	3.3
Canarias	−3.9	−7.9	−8.8	−5.5	2.8	2.2	0.0	−4.2	−0.8	−4.3	−7.1

Source: Serie BBV.

Table 9.5. *Comparison between social benefits received and contributions paid to social security, 1967–87 (%)*

	1967	1969	1971	1973	1975	1977	1979	1981	1983	1985	1987
Extremadura	125.05	141.59	146.12	178.24	138.54	133.99	170.19	218.35	188.02	190.32	223.54
Andalucía	101.77	122.77	129.30	134.03	122.47	106.15	124.74	192.70	166.17	161.81	185.26
Castilla – La Mancha	110.53	114.72	131.40	141.91	111.57	103.96	124.70	176.61	151.07	148.82	171.13
Galicia	80.58	97.37	118.56	110.86	106.25	100.71	126.28	162.20	146.01	149.25	161.17
Murcia	100.86	122.05	136.82	131.40	110.01	95.47	107.34	184.96	164.74	155.30	154.98
Asturias	86.62	84.02	97.02	94.27	87.59	76.15	83.06	160.21	104.62	113.47	145.14
Castilla – León	78.72	86.80	107.38	112.18	97.28	84.66	102.12	156.06	125.88	130.69	143.02
Comunidad Valenciana	72.60	86.10	97.66	93.34	81.40	69.92	81.81	134.66	120.47	129.64	135.61
Cantabria	72.36	104.78	94.80	84.12	77.78	60.42	79.67	143.09	120.74	122.60	132.75
La Rioja	62.40	64.81	82.45	83.13	70.64	59.03	73.11	123.60	109.74	115.74	129.72
Aragón	63.73	67.71	82.25	84.20	69.20	61.68	77.68	132.45	104.73	115.26	121.25
Canarias	72.68	96.96	99.50	88.22	92.21	78.88	82.05	123.56	108.02	118.84	113.05
Cataluña	56.89	65.00	79.34	69.84	60.00	50.58	61.02	106.87	103.18	106.24	111.88
Navarra	61.10	61.60	88.23	82.27	59.34	50.84	58.84	102.54	98.70	99.20	102.63
Baleares	58.95	62.27	82.51	77.55	76.42	76.26	85.92	123.57	98.95	111.47	100.78
País Vasco	64.28	65.06	78.41	67.08	52.19	43.67	57.61	99.38	92.06	92.20	99.10
Madrid	56.11	54.12	77.17	77.89	46.94	37.55	43.07	71.22	63.58	83.98	76.88
Ceuta and Melilla	0.00	0.00	0.00	0.00	0.00	0.00	0.00	0.00	115.14	126.01	125.59
Spain – total	70.61	78.68	94.82	90.95	74.41	63.99	75.63	123.10	109.04	116.86	122.31

Source: Serie BBV.

Andalucía, Castilla-La Mancha, Galicia and Murcia, appear among those that are clearly receptors, a position that has been reinforced when financing of most of the social security quotas has come to depend more on the Central Government budget.

Another interesting example of regional discrimination is, as was previously indicated, that of the distribution of government investment among regions. Its analysis poses, however, quite a few methodological difficulties and a clear lack of information. M.A. de Frutos (1990) has calculated the government capital stock by regions from the flows of government investment for autonomous regions, using different depreciation rates. Table 9.6 presents and compares, in per capita terms, GDP and state capital by regions.[7] Although the data should be interpreted with much caution due to deficiencies in the basic statistics, the correlation between GDP and capital stock is clearly negative and significant (correlation coefficient 0.71) which expresses that state investment policy is also oriented towards redistribution.

This performance can, undoubtedly, be applauded, but also gives room for discussion since, from a productive point of view, an efficient assignment of state capital should perhaps be allocated in a more balanced way, or even in favour of the regions in which the relation between state capital and GDP is lower, facilitating a greater growth of the regions with higher GDP and so achieving a higher growth for the country as a whole.

But, without forgetting that this is an area where there is plenty of room for different ideological and economic positions, a strict economic evaluation of those policies requires further analysis to see if the regions most helped in terms of RFD and of state investment are, or are not, those which are the most dynamic and where private investment reacts accordingly.

4   The growth response of regional economies to regional policies

As we have seen, a rigorous analysis of these issues is complex and, above all, presents almost insoluble technical problems, especially those of information. However, it appears possible to carry out a minimally acceptable approach.

As has already been indicated, the experience of the eighties shows that the growth of the Spanish regions, although quite homogeneous, shows fairly important differences. Table 9.7 shows the regional average annual growth figures for two periods. The first (1983–87) includes the last years of the economic crisis and the first of the strong recovery of the Spanish economy. The second (1985–90), includes only the recovery years, when,

Table 9.6. *Government capital distribution by region, 1988*

	GDP per capita (000)	State capital per capita (000)	State capital/ GDP per capita (%)
Andalucía	738.8	269.8	36.5
Aragón	1,163.3	321.6	27.6
Asturias	996.2	577.2	57.9
Baleares	1,547.7	198.3	12.8
Canarias	1,050.0	312.3	29.7
Cantabria	983.4	291.4	29.6
Castilla – La Mancha	806.6	316.3	39.2
Castilla – León	948.8	299.5	31.6
Cataluña	1,297.7	164.5	12.7
C. Valencina	1,127.0	162.2	14.4
Extremadura	674.7	345.9	51.3
Galicia	833.7	248.4	29.8
Madrid	1,325.0	262.2	19.8
Murcia	880.4	211.3	24.0
Navarra	1,168.2	179.8	15.4
País Vasco	1,156.5	162.9	14.1
La Rioja	1,124.0	227.5	20.2
Spain – total	1,044.6	246.2	23.6

Source: M.A. de Frutos (1990).

probably due to the EC integration impact, the regions of higher growth are located in the two axes: The Mediterranean and the Ebro, as well as the two archipelagos.

What is quite clear is that those regions which have grown most rapidly hardly coincide with those that receive more government transfers, except for Andalucía and, at a certain distance, Castilla-León. The relationship between growth and the indicator of large state capital stock/GDP per capita is not high, since it only occurs in the cases of Andalucía, Aragón and the Canarias. On the contrary, other regions that have also a high index of state capital stock/GDP do not achieve high growth figure (Cantabria, Castilla-La Mancha, Castilla-León, Extremadura and Galicia) while those which clearly grow more than the average have a state capital stock ratio inferior to the Spanish average (Baleares, Cataluña, Comunidad Valenciana, Navarra and La Rioja).

Another way to obtain an indicative reference about the relation between economic growth and government transfers and investment is through the analysis of the regional localization of private domestic industrial investment and of foreign investment.

Table 9.7. *Annual growth, 1983–87 and 1985–90 (% per annum)*

	1983–7	1985–90
Murcia	5.2	5.4
Comunidad Valenciana	4.1	5.1
Navarra	3.1	5.1
Andalucía	4.0	5.0
Cataluña	2.6	5.0
La Rioja	1.4	4.8
Canarias	6.2	4.8
Baleares	5.3	4.7
Aragón	3.1	4.6
Castilla – La Mancha	4.4	4.6
País Vasco	1.3	4.4
Cantabria	1.1	4.3
Madrid	2.7	4.2
Castilla – León	3.1	4.2
Galicia	3.2	4.1
Extremadura	6.9	3.9
Asturias	1.8	3.6
Spain – average	3.3	4.6

Source: Own calculations, based on Serie BBV and FIES.

The first indicator has been developed by Aurioles and Cuadrado (1989) taking into account the territorial localization of industrial private investment, both in new enterprises or plants and in expansions and reforms. The research covered the period 1980–87 and not only had an exhaustive analysis of the data about investment at a provincial level, but also an enquiry about the motives of enterprises when choosing a locality.

The results obtained can be summed up as follows (Table 9.8):

(1) The provinces where new investment reaches the highest levels are located in the Mediterranean and Ebro axis, as well as Madrid, Vizcaya, and to a much lesser extent Cádiz. There exists, then, in general terms, a very notable coincidence and correlation between the regions with greater new industrial investment and those which at the same time have grown most, and, on the contrary, a very low correlation with the ones that were helped by regional policies.

(2) The enquiry about the motives in the selection of a locality allows us to conclude that the most decisive factors were the following: personal relations in the zone; availability of a qualified work force; availability of input supply and subcontracting and, finally, market access via communications. The lowest ranked motives were the offer of subsidy and credit

Table 9.8. *Provinces with highest indicators of intensity of new investment, 1980–87*

	Indicator
Barcelona	4.664
Valencia	2.498
Madrid	2.177
Zaragoza	1.751
Tarragona	1.606
Alicante	1.475
Vizcaya	0.359
Castellón	0.307
Murcia	0.217
Navarra	0.205
Cádiz	0.118

Source: Own calculations, based on Aurioles and Cuadrado (1989).
Note: 1.0 = Spanish average industrial investment.

incentives, which, according to this study, only operate as an additional and complementary factor with respect to the rest.

The localization of foreign investment could also offer us an interesting indication of the preferred regions. The data on accumulated direct investment for the period 1986–89 are those contained in Table 9.9, which makes clear the preference of foreign investment for Madrid, Cataluña (particularly Barcelona) and Andalucía, followed, at a certain distance by the País Vasco, Aragón and the Comunidad Valenciana.

5   Main conclusions on the Spanish case

Spanish regional policies, both explicit and implicit, have had, mainly, a compensatory character and not a clear economic development objective, and this is, probably, the main reason for their lack of success in helping backward regions to converge with the Spanish and European GDP per capita averages. As we have seen in previous sections, government interventions have not been able to reduce the gap between poor and rich regions. Market dynamics and external shocks have been stronger elements in the growth behaviour of Spanish regions.

EC structural funds have not been able to increase convergence either, for three main reasons. One is that the total volume of funds is very small (1 per cent of GDP, before 1989 and 2 per cent after 1991). Another one is that agricultural funds (EAGGF) that are the biggest in volume do not have a redistributive role but the opposite. Finally, as most EC structural

Table 9.9. *Regional distribution of foreign direct investment, 1986–89 (%
of total)*

	Industry	Construction	Services	Other*	Total
Andalucía	10.3	10.0	8.0	9.9	9.0
Aragón	4.3	0.9	0.3	3.4	2.1
Asturias	0.2	0.1	0.1	1.0	0.1
Baleares	0.2	19.5	3.1	0.9	1.9
Canarias	0.4	4.7	1.8	1.6	1.2
Cantabria	0.3	0.0	0.6	0.1	0.5
Castilla – León	2.8	0.0	0.3	2.8	1.4
Castilla – La Mancha	0.7	0.0	0.1	3.2	0.5
Cataluña	37.7	20.6	18.2	38.5	27.0
Comunidad Valencina	3.2	2.6	1.5	2.7	2.3
Extremadura	0.2	0.0	0.0	1.5	0.1
Galicia	1.5	1.1	0.4	5.2	1.0
Madrid	18.9	32.3	57.1	23.4	39.8
Murcia	0.4	0.2	0.2	1.2	0.3
Navarra	1.0	2.2	0.7	0.8	0.9
País Vasco	4.8	0.0	1.4	2.8	2.8
La Rioja	1.9	0.0	0.3	0.8	1.0
Unidentified	11.2	6.0	5.9	0.1	7.9
Spain – total	100.0	100.0	100.0	100.0	100.0

Source: Own calculations, based on DGTE data.
Note: * Other includes agriculture and energy sectors.

funds have to be matched by domestic funds, they are imposing an
additional burden on the budgets of the poor regions.

Fiscal federalism in the US sense is almost absent in the case of the EC.
A clear example is that Spain is going to be a net contributor to the EC
budget in 1992 in spite of having an average GDP per capita that is 80 per
cent of the EC average.

Although the data on Madrid could include foreign investment which is
actually made in factories located in other regions, it seems clear that
there is a preference for the two great metropolitan areas of the country
where there is a higher population density, that is, access to markets,
(Madrid and Barcelona) and for the regions of the Mediterranean coast
(Valencia) and the Ebro (Aragón), that is, the two emerging axes, as well
as the tourist areas, (regarding construction and services). Andalucía,
which is also a tourist area and, to some extent, ties up with the Mediterranean axis, is the main exception, being a backward region.

From the indicators of industrial investment and of foreign investment we deduce, then, that, apart from a few exceptions, Andalucía in particular, both are concentrated in regions that are more dynamic in the eighties, which in turn, also with some exceptions, are not those that reach higher state capital stock-GDP ratios per inhabitant, and are not those that receive government transfers.

Except for the large government investment in infrastructure partly supported by ERDF and EIB funds and credits of the last few years, that is performing an important role by connecting regional cities and creating bigger local markets and by connecting regional markets and networks to those of the rest of the nation and the EC, most of the compensatory regional transfers have proved to be negative to growth either in the short run or in the long run, for the following reasons:

First of all, compensatory transfers have somehow protected the families and companies of backward regions from increasing competition, both domestic and foreign, and also from the macroeconomic discipline of a restrictive monetary policy and high interest rates derived from ERM membership. Therefore, they have just retarded adjustment without creating the productive conditions to overcome backwardness.

Second, high and long-lasting unemployment subsidies and large personal transfers have helped to avoid migration from backward to prosperous regions reducing labour mobility and avoiding necessary wage adjustment. Therefore, the backward regions have kept high wages and high unemployment, thus losing a clear comparative advantage that could attract labour-intensive investments and improve convergence in the medium run, in the first place, and creating, artificially, long-term unemployment with a corresponding increase in the Spanish NAIRU, in the second place.

Third, the central and regional governments have tried to avoid social conflicts in those regions by allowing large-scale social security fraud. There are today some backward regions that have registered a bigger number of workers as temporarily and permanently disabled than the active population! The same can be said about pensioners. Many families in those regions are still receiving the retirement pensions of long-dead relatives! As in the case of Italy (Galli, 1990) this permissive fraud is helping to create local 'mafias' or pressure groups that distribute personal transfers in exchange for political votes.

Fourth, strong family and personal subsidization is reducing not only the incentives of the unemployed to look for another job but also those of young potential entrepreneurs, who feel comfortable at home, relying on a few relatives' pensions, and lack the initiative either to get more educated or qualified or to start any kind of business. Large compensatory transfers, therefore, inhibit market incentives and create a class of 'indirect' government employees, who live off the budget but without any task to accomplish.

Fifth, the creation of state-owned industries in some of the backward regions has also proved counter-productive in the medium and long run. Given that wages in state-owned industries in Spain are much higher than in private industries, due to their higher trade-union presence, when they are localized in a backward region they tend to increase the average wage level of the region, inhibiting further private labour-intensive investment both national and foreign and creating an 'industrial desert' around it. The Asturias region is a paradigmatic case.

Finally, large personal transfers mean that the measure of convergence through GDP per capita may not be very explanatory of the real situation of those regions, since disposable income is higher than GDP per inhabitant. The unemployment level may be a better indicator, although unemployment rates are very high throughout Spain.

Therefore, the Spanish experience shows regional policies should rather try to concentrate on the creation of a favourable market environment, in order to attract productive investment, than to compensate directly the citizens' incomes. That means, to preserve wage moderation, to increase labour mobility, to increase education and qualification levels of the work-force and to create physical infrastructure.

NOTES

We thank David Begg, William Branson, Daniel Cohen, Susan Collins, Riccardo Faini, Giampaolo Galli, Alberto Giovannini, Paul Krugman, Stefano Micossi, Richard Portes, Luigi Spaventa, Joseph Stiglitz and Antonio Zabalza Marti for useful comments.

1 We thank the NEI for the use of its data base and for additional work done by J. Boeckhout.
2 The weighted standard deviation coefficient is the following:

$$S = \sqrt{\sum_i (X_i - X)^2 (W_i/W)}$$

where X is the average GDP per inhabitant (EC = 100%), X_i is average GDP per inhabitant of the region, W_i is total GDP of the region and W total EC GDP.

The Theil index for the regional GDP per inhabitant of a country's regions is

$$I = \sum_{i=1}^{n} \frac{Y_i}{Y} \log \frac{Y_i/P_i}{Y/P}$$

where Y_i is the GDP of region i and Y is the GDP of the country, P_i is the population of region i and P that of the country. This index can be separated, taking into account that if e_i is the example of region i,

$$Y_i/P_i = (Y_i/e_i)(e_i/P_i)$$

so that

$$I = \sum_i \frac{Y_i}{Y} \log \frac{Y_i/e_i}{Y/e} + \sum_i \frac{Y_i}{Y} \log \frac{e_i/P_i}{e/P}$$

The first part of this expression is simply the Theil index relating to GDP per occupied person in the regions of the country. The second part shows the influence of the rates of activity and unemployment, given that if a_i is the active population of the region:

$$e_i/P_i = (e_i/a_i)(a_i/P_i)$$

3 Raymond (1991) has proposed and calculated an index of inequality of each autonomous community with respect to the Spanish economy which is obtained through:

$$IDEP_i = [(I_i - I)^2 + (S_i - S)^2 + (C_i - C)^2 + (A_i - A)^2]/4$$

where I, S, C, A are the weights, respectively of industry, services, construction and agriculture in GDP, for region i with subscript i and for the nation as a whole without subscript. The average index of inequality for each year can be estimated by:

$$IDEP = \sum_{i=1}^{17} (IDEP_i)/17$$

4 There are nevertheless some exceptions, for instance in services, with high differences between services related to industrial production and those related to the financial and tourist sectors.
5 See Cuadrado (1981, 1987).
6 'Regional incentives' to investments were introduced to Spain by Law 50/85 following an EC directive. Its recent evolution can be seen in the report 'Politica Regional 1990', Ministerio Economia y Hacienda, 1991.
7 The depreciation rate, following Raymond, is 8%, derived from an average capital life of 14 years.

REFERENCES

Alcaide, J. (1988) 'Las cuatra Españas económicas y la solidadridad regional', *Papeles de Economía Española*, 62–81.
   (1991) 'La economía regional española en el quinquenio expansivo, 1985–1990', *Cuadernos de Información Económica*, FIES, No. 49, April.
Alcaide, J., J.R. Cuadrado and E. Fuentes (1990) 'El desarrollo económico español y la España desigual de las autonomías', *Papeles de Economía Española*, 2–61.
Alonso, William (1964) *Location and Land Use: Towards a General Theory of Land Rent*, Harvard University Press.
Aurioles, J. and J.R. Cuadrado (1989) 'La localización industrial en España. Factores y Tendencias', FIES, Madrid.
Baldwin, Richard (1989) 'The growth effects of 1992', *Economic Policy* 4, (9), 247–81.

Barro, Robert (1989) 'Economic growth in a cross section of countries', NBER Working Paper No. 3120.

Beckman, M.J. (1968) *Location Theory*, Random House: New York.

Bertola, Giuseppe (1991) 'Models of Economic integration and localized growth', Mimeo.

Blanchard, Olivier and L. Katz (1992) 'Regional evolution', *Brookings Papers*.

Bolton, R.E. (1966) *Defense Purchases and Regional Growth*, Brookings Institution, Washington D.C.

Braga de Macedo, Jorge (1991) 'Labour mobility, fiscal solidarity and the exchange rate regime: a parable of European Union and Cohesion', Economic Papers.

Branson, W. (1990) 'Financial market integration, macroeconomic policy and the EMS', in C. Bliss and J. Braga de Macedo (eds.), *Unity with Diversity within the European Economy: the Community's Southern Frontier*, Cambridge: Cambridge University Press.

Commission of the European Communities (1991) *The Regions in the 1990s (Fourth Periodic Report)*, Brussels. (Spanish version *Las regiones en la decada de los noventa*, Luxemburgo).

Cuadrado Roura, J.R. (1981) 'La política regional en los planes de desarrollo (1964–75)', in VV.AA. *La España de las Autonomías*, Espasa-Calpe, Madrid.

(1987) *Los desequilibrios regionales y el Estado de las Autonomías*; Orbis, Barcelona.

(1988) 'Tendencias económico-regionales antes y despus de la crisis en España', *Papeles de Economía Española* 17–62.

(1990) 'Una nota en torno a le evolución de las disparidades regionales en España', *Economistas*, 12–15.

(1991) 'Structural Changes in the Spanish Economy; their Regional effects', in L. Rodwin and H. Sazanami (eds.), *Industrial Change and Regional Economic Transformation. The Experience of W. Europe*, Harper Collins: London.

De la Dehesa, Guillermo (1989) 'North-South in the EEC', The Group of 30, mimeo.

Dornbusch, Rudiger (1990) 'Two track EMU, now!' in Karl Otto Pohl *et al.*, *Britain and EMU*, Centre for Economic Performance.

Eichengreen, B. (1990) 'One Money for Europe? Lessons from the US Currency Union', *Economic Policy* 5, (10), 117–87.

Faini, R. (1983) 'Cumulative Processes of De-industrialization in an Open Region: the case of Southern Italy, 1951–1973', *Journal of Development Economics* 12, 277–301.

(1990) 'Regional development and economic integration: the case of Southern Italy', paper presented at the conference 'Portugal and the internal market of the EC', Lisbon.

Frutos, M.A. de (1990) 'Una evaluación del stock de capital público en las comunidades autónomas', Working Paper No. 17, Instituto de Análisis Económico, Barcelona.

Galli, Giampaolo (1990) 'Il sistema finanzario del Mezzogiorno', Banca d'Italia, mimeo.

Giersch, Herbert (1949) 'Economic Union between Nations and the location of Industries', *Review of Economic studies* 17, 87–97.

Grossman, G. and E. Helpman (1991) *Innovation and growth in the global economy*, Cambridge, MA: MIT Pres.

Isard, N. (1956) *Location and Space-Economy*, New York: John Wiley and Sons.

Kaldor, Nicholas (1957) 'A model of Economic Growth', *The Economic Journal* **67**, 591–624.

(1970) 'The case for regional policies', *Scottish Journal of Political Economy* **17**, 337–48.

Klaassen, L.H. and W.T.M. Molle (1982) *Industrial migration and mobility in the EC*, Gower Press, Aldershot.

Krugman, Paul (1990) 'Increasing Returns and Economic Geography', NBER Working Paper No. 3275.

(1991a) 'Increasing returns and economic geography', *Journal of Political Economy* **99**, 483–99.

(1991b) *Geography and Trade*, MIT Press.

(1992) 'Integration, specialization and regional growth: notes on 1992, EMU and stabilization', Mimeo.

Krugman, Paul and Anthony Venables (1990) 'Integration and the Competitiveness of Peripheral Industry', in C. Bliss and J. Braga de Macedo (eds.), *Unity with Diversity in the European Economy: the Community's Southern Frontier*, Cambridge: Cambridge University Press.

Lasuen, J. Ramón (1969) 'On growth poles', *Urban Studies* **6**.

Lösch, A. (1954) *The Economics of Location*, New Haven: Yale University Press.

Lucas, Robert (1988) 'On the mechanics of economic development', *Journal of Monetary Economics* **22**, 3–42.

Mancha, T. (1987) 'Las desigualdades regionales en España', *Enciclopedia de Economía Española*, vol. 8, Barcelona: Orbis.

Meade, James E. (1963) *A Neoclassical Theory of Economy Growth*, London: George Allen and Unwin Ltd.

Molle, W. (1989) 'Will the completion of the internal market lead to regional divergence?', paper presented at the conference 'The completion of the internal market', Kiel, June 1989.

(1991) 'Regional policy', in Peter Coffey (ed.), *Main economic policy areas of the EEC toward 1992*, Kluwer.

Mundell, Robert (1961) 'A theory of optimum currency areas', *American Economic Review* **51**, 657–65.

Myrdal, G. (1957) *Economic Theory and Underdeveloped Regions*, London: Duckworth.

Neven, D. (1990) 'EEC integration towards 1992: some distributional aspects', *Economic Policy* **5**, (10), 13–62.

Padoa-Schioppa, T. (1987) *Efficiency, Stability and Equity*, Oxford: Oxford University Press.

Precedo Ledo, Andres (1989) 'Transformaciones espaciales y sectoriales de la industria en las regiones españolas', *Revista Geographicalia*.

Raymond, J.L. (1991) 'El crecimiento del PIB por Comunidades Autónomas: un análisis de la experiencia histórica, Cuadernos de Información Económica, FIES No. 49, April.

Romer, Paul (1986) 'Increasing returns and Long-Run Growth', *Journal of Political Economy* **94**, 1002–37.

(1988) 'Capital accumulation in the theory of Long Run Growth', in Robert Barro (ed.), *Modern Business Cycle Theory*, Harvard University Press.

Sala-i-Martín, X. and J. Sachs (1991) 'Fiscal Federalism and Optimum currency Areas. Evidence from Europe and the United States', NBER Working Paper No. 3855.

Vanhove, N. and L.H. Klaassen (1987) *Regional Policy: a European Approach*, Aldershot: Gower.

Von Böventer, E.G. (1970) 'Optimal spatial structure and Regional development', *Kyklos* **23**.

Discussion

STEFANO MICOSSI

This paper discusses trends in regional disparities in Spain (against the background of broad trends in the EC), the rationale and implementation of regional policies, and their results. The approach is descriptive, and a wealth of data are presented that highlight many important features in the Spanish experience; and the conclusions are quite sensible.

Section 2 discusses regional disparities in Spain, against the background of broad trends in Europe. It is shown, based on data on trends in per capita GDP,[1] that (i) Europe has higher divergences than, say, the US; (ii) convergence proceeded rapidly in the sixties and seventies, but seems to have worsened in the eighties in a number of countries (Italy, Greece and France), while stabilizing or continuing to improve in other countries (Spain, Portugal and Ireland).

The first fact can be seen as confirming that Europe will face growing pressure for increased specialization/concentration of the inter-industry type (Krugman, 1987; Emerson, 1988), and the importance of avoiding too rapid convergence in wage levels if less developed regions are to exploit their relative advantage (abundant and cheap labour; see Krugman and Venables, 1990).

The reasons for the second fact – halting convergence in some places, but not in others – are not well explained in the paper, although two candidates seem to be identified in decreased labour mobility and industrial restructuring processes. As for the latter factor, the paper itself acknowledges that in some instances in Spain restructuring processes have actually worked to reduce the gap between the more developed areas, of more ancient industrialization (since traditional industries were in some cases reducing their scale of operations and employment, being confronted with stronger external competition). On the whole, a fuller assessment of what was going on would require more detailed analysis of developments in sectoral value added (agriculture, industry, services) by region and for the total area.

Two other candidates in explaining halting convergence could be suggested. One is the shift, in the eighties, to a less inflationary environment, with high real interest rates and tight money: there is evidence that in some cases (e.g. Italy) the weaker, precarious economic fabric of less developed regions found it more difficult to adjust to this new environment. The second candidate, to an extent recognized in the paper, is the large increase in 'defensive' transfers, from the EC budget and from national governments, to shield both households and companies from the consequences of stronger macro (exchange rate) and micro (competitive pressure) discipline.[2] Both these aspects would certainly deserve further study.

Turning to Spain's experience with regional policies, two features should be emphasized. Regional development policies were not exclusively aimed at fostering industry, but tried to exploit specific geographic or cultural advantages, in particular by strongly promoting tourism, with considerable success. Moreover, to an increasing extent regional policies were concentrated on strengthening infrastructure and improving locational incentives, rather than on providing outright support to certain enterprises or sectors. On the other hand, Spain too experienced a very large increase in personal transfers and the virtual elimination of labour migration out of the poor regions.

On balance, it does not appear that efforts to foster development in less developed regions have been very successful, although they seem to have managed to stabilize GDP-per-head differentials.

A couple of other features in Spain's experience are perhaps not discussed as much as one would have liked. Spain experienced in the eighties a very large inflow of foreign capital; these investments led to high increases in total factor productivity, but little increase in labour productivity, so that they resulted in large increases in employment. It may be recalled that Spain is the place in Europe where Japanese companies have been concentrating their labour-intensive investments in Europe (Micossi and Viesti, 1991). Moderate nominal wage increases and a labour market reform that introduced considerable flexibility for new plants (Larre and Torres, 1991) were main factors in making these developments possible.

The regions where foreign investment concentrated were those that were growing more rapidly and not the regions where regional development policies tried to spur growth; the negative correlations reported in the paper between growth and public investment by region are therefore rightly interpreted by Cuadrado, de la Dehesa and Precedo as evidence of a 'compensatory' (redistributive) nature of public investment. This action was reinforced by substantial redistribution of income through the public budget; the data in the paper make it clear that the stabilization of GDP-per-head differentials has been requiring growing personal transfers, in absolute terms and as a ratio to GDP, in poor regions.

No wonder, therefore, that the paper ends with a sense of disillusion on the effectiveness of regional policies. The fact is that regional policies have not – in Spain, as in Italy and other places – been working to promote a market-friendly environment and a flexible labour market with moderate wages; rather, they have concentrated on slowing adjustment and compensating individuals for the inconvenience of living in a less developed region. The interesting aspect about Spain is that this country has at the same time been doing some of the 'wrong' and some of the 'right' things to foster development; but the right policies have in the main not benefited much the poorer regions, where market incentives were muted by massive transfers of a redistributive-compensatory nature.

A final point concerns the discussion in the paper of industrial policies (Section 3). The authors list in a rather loose way the traditional arguments for industrial policy interventions (increasing returns to scale, static and dynamic externalities, informational or market failures), with little critical discussion. In fact, the sense of disarray that one feels when reviewing industrial policy experiences in Europe, be it for regional, sectoral or other 'strategic' purposes, has a main cause in the difficulties involved in practice in identifying the cases when public intervention is warranted and in designing the appropriate intervention. In most known cases policies to directly promote specific industrial activities or technologies have not been a success, in many instances they have been outright failures (Grossman, 1989). It is important, in other words, to recognize that there is no such thing around as a ready-made 'right' industrial policy.

In sum, we remain with the following conclusions: (i) a key feature of good development policies is maintaining moderate wages, commensurate to productivity, and a flexible labour market; (ii) foreign investment can be at the same time the acid-test that the conditions are right for growth and a source of rapid and substantial productivity improvements; (iii) it is essential that what we do with the right hand, we do not undo with the left hand: regional policies can easily turn counterproductive if they work to weaken or eliminate incentives to adjust to increased competition in Europe's internal market.

NOTES

1 Calculated in PPS and in ECUs; the fact that the two measures lead to the same conclusion is encouraging on the significance of comparisons. It is not clear to me why regional data should be weighted.
2 The EC Commission (1991) and the OECD (Ford and Suyker, 1989) have extensively documented the prevalent defensive nature of industrial policies in the EC since the mid-seventies; the same feature was shared obviously by agricultural support policies (the infamous CAP) and by structural funds disbursements; and a considerable increase in personal transfers from the government has been observed in the eighties in Spain, Italy and Greece. It is possible that halting migration from poor to rich regions was a direct consequence of rising personal transfers.

REFERENCES

Commission of the European Communities (1991) 'Fair Competition in the Internal Market: Community State Aid Policy', *European Economy*, No. 48, September.

Emerson, M. (ed.) (1988) *The Economics of 1992 – The E.C. Commission's Assessment of the Economic Effects of Completing the Internal Market*, Oxford University Press.

Ford, R. and W. Suyker (1989) 'Industrial Subsidies in the OECD Economies', OECD Working Papers, December.

Grossman, G. (1989) 'Promoting New Industrial Activities: A Survey of Recent Arguments and Evidence', OECD, September.

Krugman, P.R. (1987) 'European Economic Integration: Some Conceptual Issues', in T. Padoa-Schioppa (ed.), *Efficiency, Stability and Equity: a Strategy for the Evolution of the Economic Systems of the European Community*, Oxford University Press.

Krugman, P.R. and A.J. Venables (1990) 'Integration and the Competitiveness of Peripheral Industry', CEPR Discussion Paper No. 363.

Larre, B. and R. Torres (1991) 'Real and Nominal Convergence in EMS: The case of Spain, Portugal and Greece', mimeo, OECD.

Micossi, S. and Viesti, G. (1991) 'Japanese Direct Manufacturing Investment in Europe', in L.A. Winters and A. Venables (eds.), *European Integration: Trade and Industry*, Cambridge: Cambridge University Press.

ANTONIO ZABALZA MARTI

Cuadrado, de la Dehesa and Precedo have undertaken a brave task, trying to make sense of the rationale behind Spanish regional policy. This is an effort that should be welcomed, both for its interest and for the difficulties it involves.

The interest lies in that it would be very informative to know, first, the objectives of regional policy, second, the criteria underlying the use of the different regional policy instruments now in existence and, third, the effect that these instruments have on the stated objectives. These are questions on which, whether as economic analysts or as ordinary citizens, we would all like to have an answer.

The difficulty, however, lies in the fact that many of the objectives of regional policy are not of an economic, but rather of a political nature and therefore economic analysis does not render itself very useful to accomplish this task.

This does not mean that economic analysis should be dismissed. On the contrary, it may help us to identify more clearly the patterns of behaviour that have some economic purpose in them, and therefore to isolate the residual elements that, not unlike the error term in regression analysis, have to be attributed to other, possibly, political motives.

I start with these considerations because I somehow miss in the paper a recognition of the inherent difficulties of an economic analysis of regional policy and of the limitations that economic tools may have in helping us to provide, in themselves, a sufficiently complete explanation of the problem.

My second and basic comment refers to what I identify as the main thesis of the paper: that in the regional dimension neither public investment nor public transfers are well correlated with economic development, from which it can be concluded that both public investment and public transfers are bad instruments for achieving a more equilibrated pattern of growth.

Concerning public investment, my first worry lies in the quality of the data. It is indeed very difficult to allocate public investment regionally, and I take it that official data tend to leave out a significant amount of investment whose location is not identified. I do not know to what extent these problems have been taken into account in deriving the figures for the stock of public capital, nor do I know whether this stock refers only to public infrastructures or also to investment in public firms. The very large figure for Asturias in Table 9.6 makes me suspect that maybe some public productive investment has been included, but if this is so it should have been included in a systematic fashion and this may be impossible given the difficulty of ascertaining the extent of the entrepreneurial public sector. Also, I would not recommend that line of analysis, as it is not clear that public productive investment is located on the basis of regional policy.

Another query I have concerns the measurement of the capital stock, which I take is done on the basis of investment flows. Do the available data provide long enough series of public investment to derive the stock figures?

My third point on this issue is that I have some difficulty in attaching a precise economic meaning to the correlation between public capital stock and GDP in a given region. Public capital stock, particularly if we refer to public infrastructures, acts like plant investment in a firm, the productivity of which will increase as production grows. With public infrastructures something similar happens. You need a given amount which may be quite unrelated to production, but without which you would never get anything produced. This is even more so when you consider the problem on a regional basis. A desert region located between two productive centres may have an infinite public capital stock–GDP ratio, and yet the motorway that crosses it be perfectly justified, even on economic grounds. So, even if the public capital stock figures were correct, we should not be surprised to see a lower average productivity of public capital in poor than in rich regions. To make a useful comparison here, I think you need public plus private capital.

Another related point is whether a more appropriate correlation would be between the capital stock (both public and private) and the rate of growth, rather than between capital and the level of GDP. I would rather think that the first is a more meaningful relationship. But even then, I suspect that if any relation exists, this is of a very long-term nature and a very structural one. I am not sure that this aspect is well captured by correlation indices between contemporaneous annual flows.

I point out these aspects because, although I have no empirical proof to offer, I am quite convinced that public infrastructures, particularly communication infrastructures and infrastructures related to human capital, are a necessary, although not sufficient, condition for economic development. And I think the Spanish experience tends to corroborate this assertion. All experts seem to agree, and the paper also shares this view, that the Mediterranean and the Ebro axis are economically the most dynamic Spanish areas. And it seems to me that a significant difference between these two areas and the rest of Spain is their much better developed road communications network. I am not saying that with a similar network other areas would also develop in a similar fashion; I am saying that without this network, the Mediterranean and Ebro axis would never have flourished.

This brings me to another question posed by this paper. What is the sequence of events? Do public infrastructures promote economic development, or is economic development, or at least the prospect of economic development, the reason that compels governments to locate public infrastructures? I think a bit of both. In some areas, and here economic and political factors both play important roles, public investment will come first whereas in others, public investment will follow.

The paper also attaches quite a lot of importance to the potential influence of personal transfers on economic growth. I think here the issues are very different. I would tend to separate the two problems and recognize from the outset the compensatory nature of personal transfers. I am not even sure that a regional approach is the most appropriate, as I think here we are dealing with a personal income distribution problem. Many of the patterns detected in the paper are more the consequence of our present tax and benefit system, which in itself has no explicit or intended territorial aims, than the result of a particular regional policy. The question then arises, why concentrate on the tax-benefit system and not include the other sectorial policies like R & D, industrial incentives, etc.? With respect to the public capital stock distribution given in the paper, these other policies would have an offsetting effect on the regional allocation of public resources, which may possibly be even positively correlated with regional output.

Also, and this is a minor related point, I am curious as to how the data concerning net transfers have been derived. I am referring specifically to the data in Table 9.4. These flows give rise to sensitive political issues, and it would be instructive if the paper were more explicit on the methodology used to derive them.

We are dealing here with an issue of personal income distribution. If one wants to insist on the territorial dimension of these flows, I think it is reasonable to assert that they are the result of economic development and should therefore be separated from other factors that, at least potentially, could be identified as causes of economic development.

I began my comment by saying that Cuadrado, de la Dehesa and Precedo have carried out an interesting and difficult task. I have concentrated on what I think are the difficult parts of the exercise, or at least the parts that have puzzled me most, but I would also like to point out that I have learned a lot from the paper. I think the authors identify the main issues in regional policy, pose the relevant questions and show that the answers are not always available. I think all those working on these issues will thank the authors for this effort, and I hope that this paper will generate more work, both by the authors and by other researchers on an issue which is very important both here and in the rest of Europe.

Part III:
Development finance

10 Financing and development in Eastern Europe and the former Soviet Union: issues and institutional support

PHILIPPE AGHION and ROBIN BURGESS

1 Introduction

As the citizens of Eastern Europe and the former Soviet Union (EESU) are rapidly discovering, transition involves a good deal more than adherence to the dogma of privatization and market forces: increases in personal freedom have not been accompanied by spectacular increases in the standard of living. Instead there is a recession in the region: demand has fallen, intra-EESU trade has collapsed, unemployment is rising, and fiscal deficits, debt and inflation have become problems. The challenge is to build on the new freedoms of economic agents to generate welfare improvements and growth in EESU countries.

The recent experience of Poland, Czechoslovakia (CSFR) and Hungary has shown that macro stabilization, price liberalization and a minimum degree of convertibility can be achieved rapidly. The more complex and fundamental issues of restructuring and privatization have yet to be properly addressed. These two processes in many ways define transition. The scope of the challenge is unprecedented in history and the costs of making these deep adjustments will be very large. Success in *maintaining* stability in the macro sphere and in pushing the overall reform process forward, however, depends on advances in these areas. Microeconomic reform now represents the central challenge of transition in EESU.

Our focus in this paper is on privatization, restructuring and foreign direct investment in EESU countries. These are likely to be slowed down by numerous market failures and imperfections, most notably the absence of sound banking and credit institutions; the inadequacy of physical infrastructures such as telecommunications, transport, and energy; the absence of a market for corporate control and management skills and the lack of access to international capital markets.

We shall argue that each of these market failures provides a rationale for intervention by multilateral institutions which can help the transition to

303

market economies, through involvement in privatization and restructuring, and through the creation and/or modernization of infrastructure and institutions necessary for private sector development.

In Section 2, we initiate the paper by setting out the financing constraints facing EESU countries and by showing how multilateral institutions can be effective at easing these constraints. The central contribution of the paper is contained in Sections 3 and 4, devoted, respectively, to privatization and restructuring. In each of these sections, we first try and carefully define the issues and problems associated with these two fundamental aspects of market transformation, and then we examine how international institutions can support these processes. The bulk of the examples are drawn from the experience of the European Bank for Reconstruction and Development (EBRD).[1] In Section 5 we offer some concluding remarks.

2   The financing gap

A natural way to approach the financing problem is to ask how much money is actually needed to rebuild EESU and to compare this to how much is available. Assuming that domestic variables remain constant, Collins and Rodrik (1991) note that about US$1.5 trillion a year in foreign capital will be needed to raise the amount of productive capital per worker in EESU to what would be required to achieve 7 per cent per annum growth which is compatible with reaching a Western capital-output ratio after a 10-year period.[2] If one compares these figures to actual and projected capital inflows, one realises that what can be expected is less by more than a whole order of magnitude. Collins and Rodrik (1991), for example, estimate likely capital inflows based on empirical data on current and future likely commitments of foreign (public and private) creditors and obtain a median figure of US$55 billion per annum for EESU. This figure is in the region of a Marshall Plan, that is one which would contribute a modest 2 per cent of recipient GNP per annum, corresponding to a flow of US$48 billion per annum (see Collins and Rodrik, 1991).

Recent empirical estimates of the *total* amount of credits pledged to EESU in 1991 are small (e.g. approx. US$37 billion, see ECE, 1991 and Handler *et al.*, 1991). A large part of these funds have not yet been disbursed. At this early stage of transition, roughly two-thirds of this total represents commitments by multinational institutions including the EBRD, IMF, World Bank and EC.

From the private side, capital inflows have (so far) been limited. While the level of interest among potential industrial investors is high, the actual flows are disappointingly low. As of October 1991, it is estimated that the aggregate foreign direct investment earmarked for EESU as recorded in registered joint venture and investment proposals had reached approximately US$13 billion, representing over 30 thousand investment projects.[3] The actual dollars disbursed and number of ventures which are operational are, however, at best 40 per cent of the recorded figures. A few small countries with favourable investment environments, however, have been relatively successful. Hungary, for example, attracted foreign direct investment in excess of $1 billion in 1991 alone. Increasingly, the CSFR is attracting investors.

Foreign direct investment could play a strategic role in Central and Eastern Europe and the former Soviet Union which goes beyond the flow of capital. The operational commitment on the part of trade investors also brings a transfer of technology and managerial skills, helps introduce new standards of product quality and operational efficiency, and can open access to new markets. Much still needs to be done by the host countries to create a more attractive environment for investment.

The difference between required and committed capital, which we term the 'financing gap' is thus very large indeed. So large, in fact, that it would be naive to depend solely on capital inflows to finance development in the region. One should not be too discouraged by such a clear conclusion. In the first place, in EESU one can *de facto* reject the assumption of constancy in domestic variables. Indeed, the expectation would be that transition involves, in the long term, a shift from a low-efficiency, command economy to a market economy. These efficiency effects are likely to be of much greater importance than the pure financial effects associated with capital inflows and they point to the importance of the *domestic* reform process for growth creation in the region. Indeed what falls out of this crude analysis is the finding that capital *will and will have to* come in large part from domestic sources.[4]

Another point to notice is that the current low contribution of private financing is largely a reflection of considerable political and economic uncertainty in the region and of the unpreparedness of the large bulk of domestic firms to absorb and effectively utilize foreign credit. Private flows, however, can be expected to increase significantly as uncertainty is reduced and firms become more creditworthy and responsive to market signals. These flows will heavily dominate official flows in the medium and long term. Much of the increased contribution of private flows will be effected through an expansion of East-West trade (see Aghion and Burgess, 1991). Indeed, the attraction of foreign direct investment to finance export expansion is considered to be critical for the development of the region. Export expansion will itself depend on access to foreign markets and this is an area where Western market economies can play a role in easing the financing constraint of EESU (see Messerlin, 1991). Another element is debt relief to encourage and support the restructuring efforts of the governments of EESU.

The above discussion suggests that a substantial financial gap will remain EESU for the next five to ten years. In this context, even though multilateral institutions like the World Bank or the EBRD can only provide a moderate financial contribution, they might still play a signficiant role in fostering investments and growth in EESU. First, the *high debt-rating (AAA)*[5] enjoyed by these institutions allow them to borrow on international credit markets at preferential rates of interest. This in turn would allow, say the EBRD, to make public or private loans at market rates of interest without imposing on its East-European counterpart as high a collateral requirement as private lenders would. The difference in terms of East-European enterprises' access to credit would be non-negligible. Second, both the reputational effect of the AAA rating and the *preferred creditor status* enjoyed by international financial institutions (EBRD, World Bank, IFC . . .) create a considerable scope for co-investments with private (Western) partners. In particular, the preferred creditor status,[6] which make IFIs the most senior creditors in any public loan to EESU institutions or enterprises, is automatically transmitted to the IFI's (private) co-lenders. Thus, directly and indirectly, multilateral institutions can both ease the EESU's access to international credit and also stimulate foreign direct investment in these countries.

The fact that multilateral institutions (IFIs) can mobilize considerable financial resources (e.g. through co-investment) and that these are targeted at critical bottlenecks to structural reform implies that the overall impact on EESU growth may be large relative to the original financial contribution of these institutions.

3   Privatization

The concentration of economic activity in the public sector under central planning is marked. For example, in 1986 in CSFR, 97 per cent of value added was in the state sector and in 1985 in the USSR the corresponding figure was 96 per cent (see Fischer, 1991). No country in EESU has a share of public sector in value added which falls below 60 per cent, whilst the OECD countries all have shares below 20 per cent. These observations have led to calls for rapid or immediate privatization of a large fraction of state-owned enterprises.

Aside from decreasing the size of the public sector, privatization was widely perceived as the most effective procedure to salvage and restructure state enterprises, and at the same time improve the efficiency of CEE economies (both in the sense of better resource allocation and also of a decoupling between production and political decision-making processes). This, in turn, motivated the setting-up of mass privatization programmes the scale and speed of which was well in excess of any historic privatization episode.

At the onset of transition the discussion of what to do with existing firms seemed clear cut. Non-viable firms would be declared bankrupt and eliminated. Viable firms would be privatized and this act would lead to the introduction of a correct set of incentives for market production. Both processes would be quick. In practice neither of these has occurred to any significant extent though there has been some success in the privatization of very small enterprises (less than 100 employees). A richer and broader theory and discussion has followed on the heels of these empirical observations where both the potential and importance of privatization in the short run is de-emphasized. The focus is being reoriented toward industrial restructuring with emphasis on incentives within the firm, management and technology transfers, vertical disintegration, demonopolization, containment of adjustment costs, finance and banking, infrastructure and the correction of market failures. These measures are increasingly seen as necessary to rationalize production, improve market functioning, facilitate privatization and contain the social costs of adjustments.

The emergence of a large and well functioning private sector is critical to a successful transition to a market economy.[7] If one examines the total population of firms in transition economies, four well defined and complementary sets of industrial polices suggest themselves. First, there is a lower strata of existing public firms which are non-viable in the long term and require policies to break them up or bankrupt them. Second, there is a large number of small enterprises and a smaller number of large viable state enterprises which can be quickly sold to domestic or foreign trade investors. Third, there is a large middle ground of large semi-viable public firms which require restructuring policies prior to their privatization, i.e. prior to finding potential purchasers for them. Finally, there is a fast-growing population of new private enterprises which would benefit from improved infastructures and also from institutional support including an improved access to credit. Our focus in this section is on the narrow issue of rapid mass-privatization; other aspects of industrial policy are covered in Section 4.

3.1 Implementation problems

Most countries in EESU have established or are in the process of establishing an administrative framework for privatization. The procedures adopted tend to be different for small and large enterprises.

Small enterprises and other small economic units can be privatized relatively quickly through a simple decentralized mechanism (e.g. auctions). The bulk of the task of restructuring and rationalizing production can be left to the new owners. In many cases profits can be expected within a relatively short period. Sales of small economic assets are also often attractive to the governments as they generate a short-term source of revenue and divest overstrained governments of responsibility for administration. These conditions set them apart from the situation in large enterprises and the experience reflects these differences. Newly privatized small enterprises and economic units along with new enterprises form the bed-rock of private initiative in transition economies.

The privatization of small public enterprises and state-owned economic units (e.g. retail networks, services) has to some extent been both rapid and successful. In Czechoslovakia over 15,000 small units were auctioned in 1991. In Poland approximately 60,000 small units were leased or sold to the private sector in 1990 and 1991 and 70 per cent of retail trade is now in the private sector. In Hungary a similar auction process is underway. Bulgaria is making some progress in privatization of small units in trade, services and tourism. In Romania the process for divesting small assets of commercial companies, such as small shops and restaurants, has been started under the supervision of the National Agency of Privatization. In Russia laws have been proposed for the auction of most small assets, and some auctions have taken place in St Petersburg. In Moscow the local authorities favour direct sales to minimize the displacement of the existing workforce; the situation with respect to the Russian authorities still requires clarification. Other nations and republics, including Latvia, Russia and Kazakhstan, are making progress in selling small assets.

The experience to date tends to argue in favour of sales auctions over other methods (e.g. direct sales or free distribution) for privatizing small enterprises. Auctions for small companies are best organized at a local level and they require simple and clear procedures set up by the state.[8] The particular auction mechanism that seems to perform most efficiently in a wide range of circumstances is the so-called English auction, whereby the price is publicly announced and then repeatedly raised by the auctioneer until only one bidder remains (see Maskin, 1992, for a formal analysis). In general, auctions have several advantages over other schemes. First, they are relatively simple to implement; second, they provide a rough valuation of the firm and can allocate assets in the absence of sound equity market institutions; third, they can be relatively fair in the sense that no particular interest need be *a priori* protected or favoured (e.g. if anyone can bid).

The absence of efficient financial markets in EESU may however qualify this last proposition: in the EESU context, indeed, initial wealth may override efficiency considerations in determining how the small privatized firms will be allocated among new private owners. As a way to reduce the extent to which limited access to borrowing could prevent the most efficient bidders from missing the auctions, a multi-part pricing scheme could be instituted whereby a bidder would be liable both to a down-payment at the auction stage and to a debt repayment out of future cash revenues.[9] The downpayment would constitute the bidder's initial equity share of the privatized firm, while the auctioneer's (government's) claim would constitute the firm's initial debt.[10] In the case where the government's claims were not met, the firm's ownership and control would be transferred back to the state agency which would then organize a second auction. The procedure just described can be reinterpreted as a variant of leasing-rights auctions where the successful bidder would have the option to acquire full ownership of the firm after a prespecified time-period and at a prespecified exercise price.[11]

The 'debt-equity' ratio in multi-part auctions should be set sufficiently high that initial wealth constraints do not prevent efficient bidders from participating in the auctions, but not too high for moral hazard reasons.[12] Too high a debt-equity ratio may indeed discourage successful bidders from investing the required effort or from choosing the adequate level of risks in managing the firm's assets.[13] (See Appendix B for the sketch of a formal proof).

The main problems in organizing auctions are, first, the lack of entre-preneurs able to run the newly privatized firms and second the lack of public agents to administer the process. This in turn explains why the auctioning of small firms is best accomplished at a local level but within a coherent national framework, and if possible with international advice. Their great strength is that they can effectively and quickly transfer activities (e.g. small scale production, retail, services) in which the state clearly has no comparative advantage to the private sector.

The privatization of large state-owned companies is proceeding more slowly than initially expected. Indeed in many industries, despite the existence of privatization plans, there is a virtual standstill in the implementation of these plans. This appears to be related, *inter alia*, to ill-defined property rights (including restitution); administrative bottle-necks (including uncertainty over areas of competence); high restructur-ing costs involving enterprise balance sheets, labour reorganization and operational restructuring; the low level of domestic savings; and a scarcity of management resources. The weaknesses which underlie many privati-zation plans are further compounded by legal and political complications which further delay privatization.

With the purpose of speeding up the privatization process for large and medium-size enterprises, a number of Western economists have advocated mass give away schemes working through voucher systems (see Blanchard *et al.*, 1991, Frydman and Rapaczynski, 1990).

Both the CSFR and Poland have adopted such schemes, with the CSFR using vouchers as a vehicle for direct distribution of enterprise shares to the popluation, whereas Poland is adopting a two-step approach whereby citizens can use their voucher endowments to acquire ownership in privatization funds managed by professional fund managers which in turn have the responsibility for restructuring and/or selling off the enterprises that have been allocated to them.[14] There are reasons to remain sceptical about these voucher schemes. One reason is that these schemes appear to be complicated and also costly to implement. For example in Poland we have estimated that the registration cost for voucher claims would amount to $2.50 to $4.00 per person (i.e. up to $80 million in total if we assume that half of the Polish population would be entitled to voucher endowment.)

More importantly, these schemes are not immune either from excessive transfers of enterprise ownership to wealthier or better organized private groups of individuals as is already the case in the CSFR,[15] or to governance problems associated with the high degree of ownership dispersion in the enterprises or, in the Polish case, in the privatization intermediaries. In particular the separation between ownership (by all Polish citizens) and management (entrusted to a limited number of fund managers) of the Polish privatization funds raises a serious incentive issue (see Frydman and Rapaczynski, 1991). On the other hand, the Polish 'solution' to this problem, which consists in the setting up of Supervisory Boards elected by the Fund's shareholders, is conducive to excessive and arbitrary state intervention as long as these new private shareholders remain dispersed.

More generally the excessive emphasis on building up an administrative machinery to operate grand schemes such as the Polish one has led to long and difficult legislative processes for each major transaction.

Potential buyers are often put off by the complexity and uncertainty of these legislative processes, which are due not only to administrative problems and bureaucratic difficulties, but also to the long rounds of mutual concessions and requests emanating from the various interested constituencies.

Efficient decentralized procedures might thus appear more appropriate. Such procedures would typically involve one of a small number of privatization agencies responsible for restructuring and selling off large state-owned enterprises. The first best seems to be state bodies such as the Trehandanstalt in Germany, operating on a decentralized basis with experts in the various sectors of industry, and managed by (or with) specialized Western fund managers whose reputation would be put at stake. Such agencies would encourage large privatizations to be initiated and processed by the enterprises themselves and by prospective trade investors. Efficient privatization agencies would require a large number of experts and also a substantial amount of financial capital to assist new investors in modernizing the enterprise they acquire and/or to protect the labour force against the adverse consequences of necessary restructuring and thereby avoid major social conflicts. A natural source for such financial capital should be the proceeds of the privatization itself. In the absence of appropriate taxation systems or of external financing sources such as that provided by West German citizens in Germany, (multi-part) auction mechanisms such as the one suggested above would substantially contribute to the finances of privatization agencies). Extending these mechanisms from small to large state-owned companies, however, involves a number of theoretical difficulties. In particular, the lack of domestic savings, together with the moral hazard problems involved in having too large debt-equity ratios, may constitute a case for piece-wise auctioning procedures. Similar procedures might also be recommended in the case where governments are relatively more risk-averse than private investors and the uncertainty about the future profitability of the company is to be resolved progressively over time. The flip-side of piecemeal auctioning procedures, however, is the risk that control rights be diluted over too large a number of successful bidders. Here is a trade-off that should be carefully evaluated. In any case, the need for governments to seek out 'stable cores' of investors is widely recognized as a priority in the privatization of large SOEs, even in the context of the various share distribution schemes where the governments would remain pivotal (minority) shareholders (see Fischer, 1991).

Having argued that voucher schemes are likely to be complicated, that they do not properly address valuation and restructuring issues, that they turn out to slow down the privatization process compared to more pragmatic and traditional approaches (such as direct sales and auctions), is there still a justification for this type of scheme? There may be one such justification, based essentially on political considerations and the reduction of incentive barriers to privatization. Free distribution of vouchers to employees or citizens can appeal to perceptions of wealth sharing and thus add to political popularity. Political and to some extent efficiency considerations (see Fischer, 1991) may also argue in favour of a conciliatory attitude towards incumbent managers (the so-called 'nomenklatura'); these managers need to be given some incentive to participate in privatization, otherwise they can act as a significant barrier to the process. However, the above requirements can be met through direct distribution to shares to managers and employees which should not affect more than 20 per cent and 30 per cent of total state ownership in large SOEs so as to preserve corporate governance.[16]

Shleifer and Vishny (1992) in the case of Russia suggest that a better compromise between stakeholder incentives, corporate governance and political considerations might be achieved through direct distribution of voting shares to incumbent managers and workers and of non-voting shares to local government.[17]

Should there be one or several privatization agencies operating in each country? Having one central privatization agency run by the state but decentralized both by regions and sectors has a number of advantages which become increasingly apparent in view of the German or the Hungarian experiences.[18] A single agency also has the advantage of being able to establish clear and coherent guidelines for privatization. In addition the managers or management funds in charge of a unique agency (or small number of agencies) are more visible and can be held responsible for the programme outcome. On the other hand, having a large number of agencies operate in parallel might improve incentives in each of them by having agencies' managers be rewarded on a *relative* performance basis. The performance criterion could be an aggregate indicator of consumer and producer surplus generated by privatizations rather than sales revenues alone. Indeed, using sales revenues as the unique managerial compensation criterion might deter the privatization agencies from engaging in the demonopolization of large SOEs before auctioning them.

As concerns the financing of the privatization process, as we have already argued above, significant financial resources will be needed. Part of these resources will be in the form of foreign direct investment (including the repurchasing of part of the enterprises' debt by foreign investors) but most of the resources for privatization will have to be generated domestically, through: (i) funding from domestic banks, (ii) debt-equity swaps by the creditors of state enterprises, including banks, to finance additional equity investments, (iii) the reform of enterprise taxation and the broadening of the tax system. Allocating shares in privatized enterprises to banks will also contribute to their recapitalization, whilst their bad loans to state enterprises will be written off – i.e. removed from their balance sheets.[19] Also, allocating shares to banks would increase their incentive to monitor the performance of the firm, even in a situation of solvency. Such a monitoring role may prove to be particularly important in the early stages of the transition process when, on the one hand, holding companies and their subsidiaries will not yet have acquired a self-sustaining reputation and, on the other hand, the disciplinary role of the stock market will not be substantial as it is nowadays in countries like the UK and US where, in any case, the efficiency of the take-over mechanism for this purpose is widely questioned.

3.2 Support by international institutions

What is the role of international institutions in supporting the privatization process in EESU? Two main areas of activity may be recognized: namely financial support and technical assistance.

As concerns viable enterprises, international institutions like the EBRD can act as a catalyst to privatization, either by helping arrange direct sales to a foreign trade partner, or by encouraging investment. These measures not only dilute state ownership and recapitalize enterprises; they also embody tranfers of technology and management ability which are essential for modernization and the rationalization of production. Co-investment by an international institution can also help to attract investment by domestic or foreign partners (see Appendix A) which may be instrumental in turning around semi-viable companies.

However, the main way in which international institutions can assist governments in organizing and implementing mass privatization programmes is through technical advice and assistance. Given empirical developments in EESU, this assistance should be based on experience at the firm level.

In the city of Moscow for example, the EBRD is assisting in the formulation and implementation of a privatization programme for roughly 16,000 small businesses and 700 medium to large enterprises, controlled by the city. The experience gained from the immediate processing of 'pilot transactions' is now being applied to designing an overall scheme that can deal with the large numbers of enterprises involved in a realistic and workable way. At the request of the Mayor of St Petersburg, a short-term technical assistance project based on a similar approach has been started there.

The European Bank and the World Bank Group are jointly organizing a large scale privatization advisory project for the Russian republic, and the European Bank has already been able to bring the Moscow and St Petersburg experience to bear on a better definition of various elements of the overall Russian programme. A project management unit, to be situated within the Russian State Committee for the Management of State Property, is currently being staffed to launch this project.

There is also increasing focus on restructuring to make firms attractive to investors and tenable for privatization. In Hungary, for example, the

European Bank is helping to assess the viability and define the business plan of a 'turnaround company', which will buy from the state potentially viable businesses which are in need of restructuring and investment in order to become attractive to buyers.

In EESU empirical developments relating to privatization have run ahead of the capability of policy or theory to address them. This led to the emergence of an 'empirical' or pragmatic approach to privatization amongst international institutions. This approach, based on experience, is the most realistic way in which to proceed. Four lessons emerge in this context.

(i)   For large enterprises restructuring cannot be divorced from privatization. Macro-reform and the act of privatization do not in themselves guarantee the existence of an appropriate set of incentives. Similarly, without proper attention for restructuring at the firm level, privatization may not itself proceed.

(ii)   Governments require advice on what needs to be done institutionally to facilitate implementation of the large volume of transactions inherent in mass privatization

(iii) Greater attention needs to be paid to the management structure within firms. Direct foreign assistance in this area can be helpful, but there is also a role for international institutions in attracting foreign investment which will serve a similar role.

(iv)   The multi-track approach to privatization which confronts the various boundaries for privatization is the most appropriate. Single elaborate plans for privatization are inappropriate and foreign assistance should address different economic levels and be based on the specifics of a given country.

4   Restructuring

The transformation of economic structure that is taking place in EESU is unprecedented in scope. It is generally acknowledged that the move from a command to a market economy will improve economic efficiency and welfare, in the long run; however, there is a great deal of debate on how such a transition should be accomplished and at what speed in order to keep close to what could be considered as a Pareto-improving path.[20]

4.1   Context

At least three distinct sets of arguments suggest that interventions to provide restructuring may be advisable and that complete reliance on privatization and the operation of market forces may be an untenable strategy.

(i) State enterprises are largely obsolete in terms of:

    (a) their trade structure which relied heavily on the command Comecon system;

    (b) their domestic markets which also relied on planned inter-firm trade flows;

    (c) technological processes; and finally

    (d) their management systems and management culture.

Most state managers are still unable to respond to consumer demand or rationalize production. Time is needed to turn these enterprises around to make them both viable and saleable.

(ii) Conflicting ownership and control claims of stakeholders in state enterprises need to be addressed. At present each stakeholder (e.g. government, managers, workers) has extensive veto power over changes and the standard way of resolving disagreements is to maintain the status-quo, thus blocking privatization and restructuring.

(iii) Trade and price liberalization, especially if implemented in a non-gradual way, will impose substantial adjustment costs in the East in the form of a rapid decumulation of capital in non-competitive (industrial) sectors. These sectors used to benefit from preferential market access mutually granted under CMEA rules, hence producing and exporting goods for which they had no or little comparative advantage (in particular in manufacturing, as shown by the large mismatch between Eastern European exports to OECD countries and to other Eastern European countries in the late 1980s). The large-scale phasing out of obsolete activities caused by trade liberalization can only be *gradually* offset by the emergence of new activities and sectors and the entry of new firms into these sectors. This 'stock-flow' problem, in turn, is bound to induce high rates of unemployment and therefore substantial wastes in human capital resources in the short (and medium) terms.[21] Containment of social costs associated with industrial reorganization is an essential part of restructuring and is critical to the transition process as a whole.

Industrial restructuring and the rationalization of production in the process of transition toward a market economy should involve three major elements: measures to bankrupt or break up non-viable state enterprises and to enforce hard budget constraints; measures to restructure semi-viable large state enterprises prior to privatization and measures to encourage the emergence of new private firms. In this section of the paper we will concentrate on some issues and principles underlying each of these important areas of restructuring policy and then turn to the role of multilateral institutions in supporting the overall process.

4.2   Bankruptcy

A number of enterprises and sectors in EESU have no competitive advantage and would be producing negative value added if input prices were fully costed. Despite strong macroeconomic pressures, the clear redundancy of some industries and the enaction of new bankruptcy law as in several EESU countries, very few bankruptcies have actually occurred.

Mitchell (1990) argues that a major part of the explanation for this phenomenon lies in the rapid expansion of inter-firm credits. This expansion has been based on the rational belief of creditors that the government would eventually bail out any debtor firm in financial distress. This belief has been found to be well founded and relies on the high costs to the government of dismantling large failing companies in EESU. As Mitchell points out, 'the extent of political costs entailed in liquidations is in part a function of inadequate development of capital markets that would facilitate the sale of a firm's assets. They are also likely attributable to the role of enterprises in providing social services to their employees. Housing, pensions, medical benefits and daycare are often provided through the workplace. Dissolving a firm may extinguish a worker's right to several of these benefits, especially housing'.[22] Other political costs include the increased burdens on safety-net systems and fiscal revenue generated by mass unemployment. In addition, there is the danger that the bankruptcy of one firm might prove contagious and spread to other firms, given the high degree of technical and financial interdependence across firms and sectors.

These considerations imply that no credible enforcement of bankruptcy laws and hard-budget constraints can seriously be expected in these countries until the political and social costs associated with liquidation have been substantially reduced, e.g. through the establishment of a generalized social security system, unemployment compensation and so on.

In addition, for bankruptcy and restructuring to be enforceable the industrial sector needs to be demonopolized and the branch ministries dismantled to avoid situations where the creditor-supplier would not insist on recovering its claims either because this supplier is controlled by the same branch ministry as the debtor firm or because the debtor firm is a monopsonist. It is necessary to increase the independence of banks *vis à vis* both the central government and the firms they invest in. This implies the commercialization or privatization of banks.

At a more fundamental level, how one ascertains the viability of a particular firm is problematic in the context of EESU countries. As long as prices are not market-determined, it is hard to evaluate which firms should survive and which should be liquidated. It is especially hard to distinguish between idiosyncratic and macroeconomic causes of financial distress. The absence of capital markets makes it difficult to determine the survival value of a firm in transition economies. Indeed, in a market economy, a standard way to determine whether a firm should survive or not is whether the firm's value is greater in continuation or in liquidation. Continuation value, however, is best estimated by the value of the out-standing equity and debt when secondary markets exist for both types of claim. In theory, the stock market price reflects the available information on a firm's future stream of income; however, the development of stock markets in EESU in the near future seems unlikely.[23]

In advising governments in EESU (in particular Russia) on bankruptcy reform one needs to take into account the risk of excessive (or too rapid) liquidation arising both from the high systemic risks inherent in the monopolistic structure of EESU production and from the high degree of capital market imperfections. Aside from complicating the asset valuation problem, these market imperfections may also prevent more junior creditors or shareholders (who would most favour reorganization over liquidation) from borrowing the required funds to buy out the more senior creditors for control of the firm's assets (in the case where the net present value of the firm exceeds its liquidation value).

4.3 Turnaround

There is a large middle ground of semi-viable state enterprises in transition economies which require restructuring to achieve financial viability and become privatizable. In this section we draw out some clear lessons about what can be done to this important class of firms. We structure the discussion around three themes:

(i)   vertical disintegraton;
(ii)   incentives and commercialization; and
(iii) management and technology transfers.

The basic premise of this section is that where markets cannot operate, institutions are needed that can organize transfers of control from the state to domestic residents.[24] The above discussions of the various legal, political, incentive and practical barriers to privatization made it clear indeed that in many countries in EESU there will be a prolonged interim period in which the state will continue to own a considerable part of the enterprise sector. Restructuring measures can achieve a certain degree of marketization of state enterprises, thus bringing them close to competitive functioning and privatization. This intermediate stage of industrial organization between central planning and private ownership which might be termed commercialization has so far received insufficient attention.

4.3.1 Vertical disintegration and financial restructuring

Enterprises under central planning pursue different objectives than those in capitalist economies. In particular many enterprises have a level of vertical integration which may imply excessive input costs in a market environment, and distraction of management from core economic activities.[25] Enterprise reform then must consist of concentrating resources on upgrading activities in areas where firms have a comparative advantage (i.e. production) and eliminating activities where the firm has no comparative advantage (e.g. social security, housing).

Vertical disintegration must consist first of breaking off and eliminating loss-making activities. This may arise at the instigation of managers seeking profits but this process may also be coordinated and facilitated by the involvement of government agencies. For example, the experience of East Germany has shown that the existing management is often pivotal in proposing reorganization plans to be implemented by the Treuhand. These involve plant closures, redundancies and the disposal of existing assets, as well as market expansion and the development of alliances with Western companies (Carlin and Mayer, 1992).

Second, there is a need to break up systems of integrated component supply. Inputs may continue to be provided through integrated systems only if these meet the criterion of being competitive relative to other sources.

Third, enterprises need to be absolved of their responsibilities to provide social services, in particular social security benefits and housing. These services will however have to be provided by an alternative source (e.g. local and/or central government), otherwise workers facing unemployment risks will display strong resistance to restructuring measures.

Fourth, it is important to try and break up highly integrated combinats which are not natural monopolies before privatization takes place in the corresponding sectors. It may indeed become harder to demonopolise and deconcentrate an industrial sector *after* such a sector has been privatized. New private monopolies will not indeed spontaneously engage in demonopolization because this would reduce their profits. 'As western experience shows, it would be much harder to rely on prospective anti-trust legislation and institutions to break-up private monopolies'.[26] The role of foreign competition in limiting monopolistic price distortions should not be over-emphasized either. The extent to which free trade can substitute for internal demonopolization of EESU economies depends first on the relative size of these economies compared to the rest of the world, second on the relative size of the tradeable goods sectors, and third on the average income level in any country in EESU as compared to other (Western) countries. In particular, if the average income per capita is low in a given EESU country, high quality producers in richer countries may prefer to sell at higher prices and concentrate on their domestic customers rather than penetrate EESU markets by lowering their price for their same products to take into account the lower purchasing power in the region.[27] In that case, the opening of EESU to free trade does not necessarily threaten the local monopoly power of (low quality) domestic producers in that country.

Another major impediment to the marketization and restructuring of state enterprises is the large amount of debt inherited from the socialist system. These debts are often of a magnitude sufficient to prevent enterprises from gaining a competitive footing in the domestic or world markets. It is clear that the restructuring of historic debt and current operational restructuring of enterprises should be kept separate. As the government is both the creditor (through state banks or state-owned enterprises) and the owner of the state enterprises, the writing-off of inherited debt is easy to accomplish while the company is in state hands. In this case indeed, writing-off debt involves shifting resources within the government budget. On the other hand, a complete writing-off of the debt may create serious moral hazard problems as regards future borrowing. Instead in most EESU countries a more gradual approach has been adopted whereby government buys up historic debt through the commercial banks, thus recapitalizing them. In both the case of the Treuhand in East Germany and in Czechoslovakia the necessary funds to do this were derived from the privatization funds so as not to threaten the normal tax-financed budget. These funds can be used both to write-off old enterprise debt and to provide a direct capital injection to the banks. Direct debt-equity swaps would recapitalize banks further and provide banks with a shareholding interest in enterprise. Also, allocating shares to banks would increase their incentive to monitor the performance of the firm, even in a situation of solvency. Such a monitoring role may prove to be particularly important in the early stages of the transition process when, on the one hand, holding companies and their subsidiaries will not yet have acquired a self-sustaining reputation and, on the other hand, the disciplinary role of the stock market will not be substantial as it is nowadays in countries like the UK and US where, in any case, the efficiency of the take-over mechanism for this purpose is widely questioned.

4.3.2 Incentives and commercialization

Different stakeholders in large public enterprises need to be provided with incentives to engage in restructuring and privatization. Many of the current stakeholders, such as incumbent managers and local government, may indeed be satisfied with the status quo as it grants them substantial control rights. Where managers do want to engage in reform their efforts may be blocked by Workers' Councils and unions whose priority is to maintain employment for their members. Restructuring may thus come to a standstill, as each of the stakeholders has sufficient effective control to veto any changes. This means no layoffs, no wage restraint, no plant closures, and no management changes until a way of resolving conflict between stakeholders is found. There are two complementary strategies that offer some solutions to these incentives and governance problems. First, stakeholders need to receive strong command and financial incentives (e.g. the form of stock options on the future privatized firm) to both preserve the assets of the corporations today and prepare for their privatization at a later date. Second, enterprises should be commercialized so that they are separated from the government and their formal governance structure becomes more clearly established (see Shleifer and Vishny, 1992).

Commercialization or corporatization of public enterprises is often seen as an intermediate and necessary step to turnaround and full marketization. In essence, the introduction of competition and market-oriented behaviour by management and worker is at this early stage of transition, more important than a nominal change in ownership. This problem has not yet been systematically addressed in any of the EESU countries.

Carlin and Mayer (1992) list the six central functions of the Treuhand as follows. It establishes the social value of firms; it disposes of uneconomic activities; it creates supervisory boards; it finds prospective buyers; it imposes investment and employment conditions; and it evaluates firms in a credit-worthy sense. These functions help firms to restructure and ready themselves for privatization but also help achieve social objectives concerning employment, regional and industrial policy.[28] The creation of supervisory boards and the training of East German managers is gradually permitting the evolution of self-sufficient enterprises that can raise debt finance externally while retaining control over operations.

For Russia, Shleifer and Vishny (1992) have advocated mandatory commercialization (or corporatization) of all enterprises. They suggest that, within six months, all large state enterprises should be converted into joint stock companies with publicly traded shares and boards of directors. Initially, all the shares would be held by the central government, but over time, as privatization proceeds, they would be given away or sold to the various stakeholders and investors in order to remove incentive barriers and solve the corporate governance problem. The board of directors would initially consist of representatives of the national privatization agency, the managers, representatives of the workers, bankers and others involved with the corporation. The idea is to realign intra-firm incentives and make the state companies resemble private companies from the start. Such mandatory extensive commercialization has also been advocated by Lipton and Sachs (1990) for Poland and by the IMF *et al.* (1991) for the (former) Soviet Union.

In the case of Hungary, the new Law on Economic Transformation transfers state-owned enterprises from the jurisdiction of enterprise councils to a company status, under the control of the State Property Agency (SPA). Corporatization involves such measures as the introduction of a board of directors and audited balance sheets. The state is made the legal owner, at least for the period up to privatization. Supervision of enterprise managements is partly sub-contracted to approved advisory agencies which act as the agents of the SPA.

In Poland, where managers have pushed strongly for restructuring, they often find themselves in a position of tension with the Workers' Councils. Commercialization is then envisaged as an important intermediate step to protect the manager from the control of the Workers' Council as it gives them some independence and a stronger profit incentive. Also the managers' emphasis on profitability would be best guaranteed by means of appropriate management compensation, involving long-term profit-sharing or stock options (see Tirole, 1991).

Based on the argument that only new owners know what is good for the firm, the Czechoslovak government seems to be taking the view that speedy privatization is the only solution to governance and control problems. As a result, no systematic thought has been given to the control of the middle stratum of semi-viable enterprises which may not be privatizable in the short term. Ignoring the problem, or leaving it to the market, is not helpful as regional unemployment problems and recession imply that there is mounting pressure to give subsidies or cheap credit to existing state enterprises.

In summary, the view that state enterprises which cannot be rapidly privatized should be eliminated is unlikely to make economic sense from a medium-term point of view, as a non-negligible fraction of industrial production could be made marketable after marginal investments in physical and human capital. A central question which remains open is how such investment should be coordinated and encouraged. Moreover, from a political view point, the huge potential unemployment problem would make the elimination solution unviable in the short term.

4.3.3 Management and technology transfers

The bulk of enterprises in EESU require technical assistance as regards management practice, pricing and costing, accounting, marketing, and research and development. Central privatization and restructuring agencies can have a pivotal role in coordinating transfers of technical assistance (e.g. Treuhand in East Germany – see Carlin and Mayer, 1992).

At this stage in the restructuring process, heavy emphasis should also be put on projects involving strong foreign strategic partners, whether in minority or majority positions. The significance of foreign partners lies in their ability to compensate for the physical and commercial obsolescence of many enterprises in EESU, and, through their commitment to provide technical, marketing and managerial know-how, to accelerate the transformation of these enterprises into modern businesses. These businesses will then be more able to attract capital.

Whilst in East Germany enterprises are able to draw upon both the expertise and resources of West German managers (Carlin and Mayer, 1992) the shortage of both foreign direct investment and technical assistance in other countries of Eastern Europe and in the former Soviet Union points to a significant role for multilateral institutions to act as foreign partners during the early stages of restructuring.

4.4   Labour allocation and the role of new private firms

Recent studies (e.g. Hare and Hughes, 1991 and Burda, 1991) have emphasized the extent to which the (potentially loss-making) heavy industries and agriculture have absorbed an excessive share of the labour force at the expense of the service and light industry sectors which are potentially more profitable in net present value terms. The expansion of employment in these disregarded sectors will have to take place within new small and medium-sized enterprises.

The implied employment reallocation that should take place in EESU is quite substantial. For example, *A Study of the Soviet Economy* (IMF *et al.*, 1991)[29] shows that if one only considers a downward readjustment of Soviet overmanned agriculture and manufacturing sectors, together with an upward readjustment of the undermanned wholesale-retail trade, financial and insurance sectors, (so as to coincide with the average Western shares of employment in those sectors), then this would already amount to a labour reallocation of over 21 million Soviet workers, which corresponds to over 14 per cent of the total labour force (assuming that the labour force remains stationary in the next few years).[30]

The natural sectors for expansion are consumer services, retail distribution,[31] construction and repair services, transportation and shipping activities and the financial sector, all of which are underdeveloped by Western standards. Although private employment has expanded rapidly in these areas, especially in countries like Poland, Hungary and, to a smaller extent, the Soviet Union, massive growth in new small (private) businesses is still necessary to absorb a significant share of the large scale layoffs from the traditional state industrial strongholds.

However, the scope for increasing the size and number of enterprises in these new sectors is limited by the current lack of financial resources and the unavailability of credit. In Czechoslovakia, for example, only 4.7 per cent of all outstanding credit is to the private sector and this credit tends to be provided on less favourable terms. More importantly, as a legacy of the central planning system, most of the (public) banks in the region are unable to operate on a commercial basis. In particular, they do not have a concept of credit risk and creditworthiness, their main functions having been for more than forty years to collect deposits and allocate funds within the overall state budget and without regard to the laws of supply and demand. In most EESU countries, local enterprises, private or public, find it nearly impossible to do such simple transactions as collect payments on exports, transfers funds, pay for imports, obtain letters of credit, open pay-roll accounts, pay local bills by cheque or wire or enquire about account balances. Borrowers, on the other hand, are unaccustomed to normal debt service and cooperation with their creditors. These represent serious constraints to the emergence of market activity. The strengthening of financial institutions and the development of private financial intermediaries represent an area where foreign expertise can be critical. The role of banks in transition economies needs to be completely redefined and they should be set up as institutions independent of government and run along commercial lines. Establishing a legislative framework in which property rights are well defined and contracts adhered to is another priority.

Another source of inertia in reallocating labour to light industry and service sectors is the inappropriate qualification and training of the labour force. Burda (1991) stresses that there is a mismatch between job vacancies and workers' skills. There is excess supply of university graduates on the one hand and of blue collar labour on the other hand.

Technical assistance to assist with training and labour reallocation becomes crucial at this stage.

A third, important source of inertia in employment reallocation is housing. Privatization of housing should, therefore, play a crucial role in speeding up the restructuring process in EESU countries. Unfortunately, as pointed out by Fischer (1991), little attention has been devoted to the problems involved in privatizing the housing sector, in particular, the unavailability of credit markets which is likely to substantially slow down the sale of housing process.

The implication then is that the growth of new small and medium-sized enterprises will be the major factor in the growth of a large private sector in EESU. This process will take time and during the period of labour reallocation complementary measures need to be designed to contain the number of liquidations and the ensuing flow of workers into unemployment to within 'reasonable' limits. These will be critical at least in the short run, so that the disbursal of unemployment benefits, necessary to prevent major social unrest, would not cause such a drain on fiscal resources so as to threaten macro-stability. Such measures include temporary employment subsidies (see Flemming, 1990) that would automatically accrue to firms or sectors that experienced negative quasi-rents as a consequence of dramatic changes in relative prices, for example, as a result of a rise in the price of inputs relative to that of output, opening of trade, or price liberalization. Such subsidies could be financed through the uniform profits tax or VAT. Temporary trade tariffs or state subsidies that would temporarily protect some sectors in the process of catching up in order that they become competitive with Western markets may also help (see Aghion and Burgess, 1991).

4.5   International institutional support

Market failures and missing markets characterize all EESU countries at the current stage of the transition process. Advice and essential investments are needed to provide an environment conducive to industrial restructuring and private enterprise. There is a substantial need for international institutional support to improve market functioning and foster private sector activity through helping to build infrastructure and provide a regulatory and legislative framework which allows competition to work effectively.

Market failure arguments are particularly persuasive as concerns infrastructural investment where increasing returns, public goods and externalities can all be of considerable importance. Investment to improve transport, energy usage and telecommunications can have large positive effects on market development for all types of firms. Infrastructural investment will also have a key role to play in the redevelopment of regions which have suffered extensive environmental contamination or which will suffer major contractions in employment. These projects may be coordinated through EESU government but should also attract foreign investment.

As we have shown, foreign direct investment and foreign partners can play a critical role in restructuring. However, the vast bulk of enterprises in Central and Eastern Europe will have to be restructured without the assistance of foreign strategic partners. International institutional support to assist this process should take a number of forms:

(i)   Support for investment funds, including restructuring funds;
(ii) Technical assistance for the restructuring of certain selected industries of enterprises, where this currently assists the management of key enterprises to take action;
(iii) Bridge-to-sale finance for enterprises which require restructuring in order to complement their privatization plan, and which can provide adequate security (which may include government guarantees).

Severe capital market imperfections impair the transactions of all types of firms but credit constraints act as a major barrier to entry for small and medium-sized enterprises. This type of market failure explains why institutions like EBRD concentrate on providing lines of credit or equity resources to financial intermediaries (like the Dutch bank NMB in Poland or the Czechoslovakia Investment Corporation Inc. in the CSFR) which, themselves, are dedicated to assisting small and medium-sized enterprises in these countries.

5   Concluding remarks

The subject of this paper has been microeconomic reform in EESU countries. A number of questions remain open, the answers to which are critical to the future course of transition. First, there is the issue of corporate governance and incentives. How should the various stakeholders in existing large state-owned companies be compensated so as to be amenable to and if possible promote restructuring and/or privatization policies, and what are the implications of this question for the design and efficient privatization methods? For example, what is the role of stock options and management buy-outs within the privatization process?

Another critical issue is the extent to which central institutions (e.g. Treuhand) can coordinate efforts to overcome the various governance and incentive patterns. There is also the question of the optimal design of such institutions given the specialities of different countries. The magnitude of the labour reallocation expected in EESU also raises the question as to what should be the trade-off of responsibilities between enterprises and the government for the social costs of transition.

A further issue is that of legal reform and enforcement, for example in the area of bankruptcy. In particular, what can be expected from the enactment of new laws in relation to the existing institutional framework as regards enforcement? For example, should bankruptcy laws be directly borrowed from Western economies or do they need to be progressively adapted as market structures and institutions emerge in EESU, or is there room for legal innovation?

Banking regulation is another area that has received very little attention. Yet the absence of a well-functioning commercial banking system in EESU remains a major barrier to the emergence of market activity. There is the question of what should be done with state banks in the interim period. For example, to what extent should government or state bank credit be maintained to public enterprises? More importantly, there is the issue of how to provide financial support for new small and medium-sized enterprises and to allow them to compete on an equal credit footing with firms within the public sector credit system.

Finally, there is the issue of how to design international financial institutions to best assist the transition process. More exactly, how should the operations and priorities of these institutions be structured and how should different institutions interact? The unique position and special needs of transition economies suggest that some rethinking in this area is required (see Appendix A). One might also ask how the financing policies of these multilateral institutions should reflect the structure of risks in the countries of operations. In this respect, as regards co-investment, the maintenance of creditworthiness (through conservative financial strategies) is of paramount importance.

Appendix A: The role and financing policy of the EBRD

1   The EBRD mandate

The European Bank's economic mandate is to foster the transition to market economies through the promotion of private sector investment, through its involvement in privatization, and through the creation and/or modernization of infrastructures and institutions (including financial intermediaries) necessary for private sector development. In short, the EBRD is primarily a market-based 'transition' Bank. This is in contrast to multilateral development banks (MDB) like IBRD and IFC, (or ADB, AfDB) whose charters emphasize growth and development as primary objectives but do not refer to the transition from one system to another or to the privatization of existing state-owned enterprises.[32]

To make the Bank's commitment to privatization credible, its founding charter imposes that 60 per cent of the Bank's committed loans and equity participations be devoted to private sector investments and privatization activities (this is the 'merchant bank' half of the Bank), with only 40 per cent of total commitment being devoted to public infrastructure (this is the 'development bank' branch).

The rationale for this dual approach (merchant bank/development bank) stems from the conviction that development banks (e.g. IBRD) over the last forty to fifty years have placed too much emphasis on public sector lending and planning. This tendency arose partly because of the observed efficiency of central planning during WWII, in particular in the US and the UK (see Little, 1982). In the World Bank group a shift in emphasis was signalled by these setting up a separate institution (the IFC) for operations with the private sector. However, the two entities have rarely moved along the same strategic path, thus making for a less effective use of total resources. By combining the two approaches under the same roof, the EBRD stresses the interdependence between private demand for and public supply of essential services and institutions necessary for the growth of private entrepreneurship in EESU. An example of this combination between 'bottom-up' (merchant banking) and 'top-down' (development banking) activities can be gleaned from the so-called 'pilot-privatization' programmes in Moscow and St Petersburg: where the European Bank uses detailed empirical studies of a small number of medium-sized 'pilot enterprises' (e.g. the plastic manufacturer 'Diapason' and the stone-processor 'MKK' in Moscow) to identify the various obstacles (financial and legal) that constrain the privatization process as a whole.

The 'top-down' (or development banking) activities of the Bank are then aimed at removing such obstacles whilst assisting in building up the legal, regulatory, physical and financial infrastructures needed by new private enterprises to operate under normal conditions. The 'bottom-up' (or merchant banking) activities of the Bank, in turn, *directly* support and assist enterprises in order to foster the growth of the private sector.

In summary, the role and concept of the EBRD differs significantly from other multilateral development banks. Unlike the IMF it is not involved in national monetary policy or macro stabilization. Unlike the IBRD and IMF its emphasis is not on the provision of direct financial assistance to governments and loans are restricted to viable projects, mainly in the private sector. It shares with the IFC a policy of making investments in the equity of private sector companies[33] both to absorb risk and ease credit constraints; however, it has a much stronger commitment to privatization. Technical assistance constitutes a significant part of EBRD activities and is normally provided directly to public and private sector firms and institutions as opposed to *via* government channels which has been the standard approach (e.g. IBRD). The concept is to assist and support the domestic reform process, as opposed to financing it.

The EBRD approach stems both from observations about the past problems and constraints of development banks,[34] and from the conviction that the transition problem is in many respects distinct from the classical economic development problem. The former involves a *change* in economic systems (involving a reduction in state ownership of physical assets and state control over economic activity), whereas classical development theory usually deals with growth and welfare improvements within a *given* economic system. This distinction helps explain the Bank's emphasis on restructuring and privatization. This is also in line with a change of thinking within development economics that emphasizes the role of the state not in planning or production but rather in the provision of infrastructure, social services and a legislative, financial and regulatory framework conducive to private enterprise (see Stern, 1991).[35] The main focus of EBRD is on private sector development; however, the development banking/merchant banking structure of the EBRD aims to capitalize on public–private complementarities such as these.

2   Financing policy of EBRD

Like the IFC and the IBRD, the Bank can make *loans* (but only *project loans*, i.e. not policy loans); like the IFC it can invest in the *equity capital* of private sector enterprises or public enterprises in the process of being privatized. Like the IBRD and the IFC, the EBRD can *guarantee* securities in which it has invested to facilitate their sale if enterprises have failed to sell them on the primary markets. It can also, unlike these other institutions, *underwrite* securities issued by (public or) private enterprise. In addition the Bank can provide *technical assistance* and training. The European Bank's total capital amounts to 10 billion Ecus ($12 billion), 30 per cent of which will be paid in within four years. The subscribed capital of IBRD is $140 billion, out of which 18.8 billion is paid-in. The total callable capital of IFC is $3.5 billion, out of which 2.5 billion is paid in.

Before examining the operations of the Bank, let us briefly describe its capital structure and financing policy. In doing this we will try to answer the question: how did the Bank obtain an AAA debt rating by *Standard*

Table 10A.1. *EBRD balance sheet*

Assets	Liabilities	
Equity investment	Paid in capital (30%)	
Loans and guarantee funds	Borrowings (70%)	Total liabilities equivalent to callable capital (10 bn Ecu – $12 bn)
Liquidity		

and Poor in spite of the high credit risk and sovereign risk concentrations in EESU countries?

Table 10A.1 shows the structure of EBRD assets and liabilities. Compared with other multilateral development banks (MDBs), EBRD benefits from a high proportion of paid-in capital and within both paid-in and callable capital there is a high proportion originating from AAA-rated countries; in the case of EBRD, the total share of AAA member countries is above 66 per cent (the figure for IBRD is about 55 per cent and for IFC, 61 per cent).

Lending by the European Bank is fully collateralized and therefore the Bank could only default on its borrowings if both its customers and shareholders defaulted.

It follows from the above that the total disbursed loans, equity investments, guarantees, and underwritings of the Bank cannot exceed the sum of callable capital and reserves. This brings us to the asset side of the Bank's balance sheet (Table 10A.1).

In theory (i.e. according to the *founding agreements*), we just split the 'asset' side of the balance sheet between our various ordinary operations (in disbursed terms rather than in committed terms).

The founding agreements limit total disbursed equity investments to paid-in capital and reserves. This in turn makes it less likely that the repayment of the Bank's credits will depend upon the uncalled capital of borrowing member countries.[36] The IFC has already introduced the same limit for similar reasons. This additional limit on equity investments implies roughly that the Bank's ordinary operations might eventually split according to 40 per cent, 30 per cent, 30 per cent: 40 per cent of public sector loans, 30 per cent of private sector loans, 30 per cent of private sector equity investments.

Also contributing to the Bank's management policy not to resort to uncalled callable capital is the *liquidity level* which, as in the World Bank, is set at a minimum level of 45 per cent of the next three years' cash requirements.[37] At this level the Bank expects to cover all committed but undisbursed lending and investment during the same time period.

As concerns the terms of the Bank's operations, they are meant to be profitable overall (although profit maximization is not the primary criterion of the Bank's investment policy) while covering the various risks, especially the *credit risk* and the *country risk*.[38]

There is a strict policy to ensure that the risk of the Bank's operations remain manageable.

(i)   By establishing specific *limits* on lending and equity financing by type of project, by country, and by industry (this is the so-called risk-management matrix).

(ii) By pricing loans according to the credit risk class.

(iii) Credit and country risks are diversified by imposing a maximum exposure to individual projects, and/or individual borrowers, and individual countries. For example, no single borrower can be eligible for more than 5 per cent of total paid-in capital plus reserves. Also, the maximum equity exposure in each individual project would be 3 per cent as in the IFC.

(iv) The EBRD share in any project financing should not exceed 50 per cent of total project cost, for public sector loans and 35 per cent of total project cost for private sector loans or equity participation. This in turn guarantees that the credit risks will be shared with co-financiers. The upper limit for public sector loans is relatively larger due to:

    (a) The *preferred creditor status* of the Bank regarding public sector loans (i.e. no debt obligations of the recipient country can be senior to those of the Bank).

    (b) The fact that (all) public sector loans are backed by a guarantee from the borrowing member country.

(v)   Defaulting borrowers will be submitted to similar sanctions as those imposed by IBRD: all further disbursements to a country will be suspended if a public borrower in that country is more than 30 days overdue on its repayments and no new commitment will be made when arrears exceed 60 days. For a private borrower, the suspension of disbursements will occur if the overdue period exceeds 60 days.

(vi) The Bank is exempt from any official action restricting the transferability of payments such as in the case of the repatriation of dividends. Any restriction such as foreign exchange control or remittance of capital gains on equity investments will be considered as a default by the country concerned.

All these precautionary provisions will clearly not completely eliminate the credit risks faced by the Bank. In order to meet its founding charter's requirements *without* having to resort to uncalled subscribed capital, the Bank is required to maintain adequate provisions against possible losses (on loans, equity investments, underwritings) and to charge such losses primarily to a *general loss provision fund* which for the moment covers only private sector activities.[39] This fund will be supplied automatically with 4 per cent of all new loans' disbursement and with 6 per cent of all equity disbursements at the time these disbursements are made. (The corresponding figures are 2.5 per cent for IBRD loans and 2 per cent for IFC loans or equity investments.) This loss provision fund will later be supplemented by transfers from retained earnings so as to eventually cover 10 per cent of disbursed loans and 25 per cent of disbursed equity. To be more precise, the Bank's founding charter requires that EBRD transfer *all* retained earnings to a *statutory reserve* until these targets are reached. Also, the statutory reserve must represent 10 per cent of the authorized capital before the Bank will be able to pay out dividends and/or make transfer to other special funds. These measures further enhance the credit-worthiness of the EBRD in the face of considerable EESU risk.

To be complete, we must indicate that 'special operations' such as technical assistance and training activities will be financed through a Special Fund which is both supplied and managed separately from the above. The supplies consist essentially of special grants from member countries' governments in addition to be callable capital of the Bank.

Appendix B: The trade-off between cash constraints and moral hazard in auctions: an example

We restrict our attention to first-price auctions, although the argument would clearly carry over to other types of auctions (e.g., second-price or English auctions).

The government chooses in advance the proportions $(a, 1 - a)$ for the firm it privatizes, where a (respectively $1 - a$) is the share of the bid price paid in period 1 – i.e. equity – (respectively in Period 2 – i.e. debt).

Then, if b_i and B_i denote period 1 and period 2 parts of bidder i's bid ($i \in \{1, \ldots, n\}$), we must have:

$$b_i = a(b_i + B_i), \quad \text{i.e.:} \quad b_i = \frac{aB_i}{1 - a} \qquad (1)$$

Let us first consider the simplest case without moral hazard or cash constraints. The revenue generated by bidder i is simply his valuation a_i

which is privately known by bidder i. From the point of view of the other bidders $j \neq i$, a_i is *uniformly* distributed on the interval $[0, 1]$, so that Probability $(a_i \leq a) = F(a) \equiv a, \forall a$.

Consider the decision of bidder i whose valuation is a_i. Given (1) above, his two-part bid (b_i, B_i) is entirely determined by its second-period bid B_i since the debt-equity ratio $(1 - a)/a$ is already fixed by the government.

The Nash equilibrium (or more precisely the Bayesian equilibrium) of the first-price auction, whereby the highest bidder gets the firm at his (highest) bid price, is defined as follows.

Bidder i predicts that all other bidders are bidding according to the same bidding function $B(a_j)$. Then, if bidder i bids a second-period price B_i, he will earn a surplus equal to

$$a_i - (b_i + B_i) = a_i - \frac{B_i}{1 - a}$$

if he wins, and a surplus of zero if he loses. The probability of winning with a bid B_i is the probability that all the other $(n - 1)$ bidders have valuations a_j such that $B(a_j) < a_i$ and this probability is equal to $[B^{-1}(B_i)]^{n-1}$.

Then, bidder i chooses his bid B_i to maximize his expected surplus:

$$\Pi_i = \left(a_i - \frac{B_i}{1 - a}\right) \cdot (B^{-1}(B_i))^{n-1}$$

Now the Nash requirement imposes that the rivals' use of the decision rule B be consistent with their own maximization behaviour.

Hence the symmetric Nash Equilibrium of the first-price auction is defined by the bidding function $B(a)$ such that:

$$B(a_i) = \arg \max \left[\left(a_i - \frac{B_i}{1 - a}\right)(B^{-1}(B_i)^{n-1} \right] \tag{2}$$

Then, one gets:

$$B(a_i) = (1 - a) \frac{n - 1}{n} a_i \tag{3}$$

Note that:

$$\frac{\partial \Pi_i}{\partial a_i} = \frac{d \Pi_i}{d a_i} = (B^{-1}(B_i))^{n-1} = a_i^{n-1}$$

(by the envelope theorem). Hence:

$$\Pi_i = \frac{a_i^n}{n} = \left(a_i - \frac{B_i}{1 - a}\right) a_i^{n-1}$$

This yields (3). $\square$

Therefore, in the absence of wealth constraints and moral hazard, the government obtains the same total payment $\forall a$, equal to:

$$\frac{B(\bar{a})}{1-a} = \frac{n-1}{n}\bar{a}, \quad \text{where} \quad \bar{a} = \max_i a_i$$

Introducing wealth constraints $b_i \leq m_i$, one gets:

$$B(a_i) = (1-a)\min\left(\frac{n-1}{n}a_i, \frac{m_i}{a}\right)$$

so that the government's revenue is given by:

$$\frac{\bar{B}}{1-a} = \min\left(\frac{n-1}{n}\bar{a}_i, \frac{m_i}{a}\right)$$

where i is the winning bidder defined by $\arg_j\max B(a_j) = i$. Clearly, the government's revenue is maximized when $a = 0$, that is when an 'all-debt' structure is first set up.

To obtain a 'trade-off', i.e. an interior solution in a, let us introduce moral hazard considerations by means of the following example.

We assume that bidder i can realize his valuation a_i only if the enterprise is successful, which in turn depends upon bidder i's effort once he has acquired the firm. Formally, if y_i denotes the revenue generated by bidder i in period 2 through his management of the privatized enterprise, we assume:

$$y_i = \begin{cases} a_i & \text{with probability } P \\ 0 & \text{with probability } 1 - P \end{cases}$$

where P is the effort and

$$C(P) = \frac{P^2}{2A}$$

is the quadratic cost of effort.

First, let us assume wealth constraints away. Then, given $(a, 1-a)$ chosen by the government, and given his winning bid offer B_i, bidder i chooses effort P so as to maximize

$$\max_P \{P(a_i - B_i) - C(P)\}$$

$$\Rightarrow f.o.c.: \quad a_i - B_i = \frac{P}{A} \Rightarrow P = A[a_i - B_i]$$

which we assume to be strictly less than 1;

(more generally, $P = \min(1, A(a_i - B_i))$.)

Anticipating this choice of effort, bidder i will choose B_i so as to maximize:

$$\max_{B_i}\left[(a_i - B_i)\left(a_i - \frac{B_i}{1 - a}\right)(B^{-1}(B_i))^{n-1} \right] = \max_{B_i} \Pi_i \tag{4}$$

First-order conditions are:

$$\frac{\partial \Pi_i}{\partial a_i} = \left(a_i - \frac{B_i}{1 - a} + a_i - B_i\right)a_i^{n-1} \tag{5}$$

Let $B_i = \hat{B}a_i$.

We have (integrating (4)):

$$\Pi_i = \frac{2a_i^{n+1}}{n + 1} - \frac{\hat{B}a_i^{n+1}}{(1 - a)(n + 1)} - \frac{\hat{B}a_i^{n+1}}{n + 1}$$

Equations (4) and (5) imply that $\hat{B}$ is a solution to the equation:

$$\frac{\hat{B}^2}{1 - a} - \frac{n}{n + 1}\left(1 + \frac{1}{1 - a}\right)\hat{B} + 1 - \frac{2}{n + 1} = 0$$

When $n \to +\infty$, the solution $\hat{B}$ converges to $1 - a$.

The corresponding effort level is given by:

$$P(a_i) = Aa_i(1 - (1 - a)) = aAa_i$$

In particular, *the higher a (i.e. the lower the debt-equity ratio), the higher the effort of bidder i.* We thus obtain the trade-off we were looking for once wealth constraints are reintroduced.

Assuming that the government chooses a *ex-ante* so as to maximize its expected sales revenue, one should generally end up with an interior solution a^*.

Remarks:

(1) The precise derivation of a^* requires further assumptions on the distribution of valuations and wealth endowments; under these assumptions, *ex-ante efficiency maximization* would also generally lead to an interior solution a^{**}.

(2) As mentioned in the text, if bankruptcy involved substantial costs for the bidder-manager, the optimal debt-equity ratio would correspond to $a^* = 0$.

NOTES

We are grateful to Chris Beauman, Patrick Bolton, John Flemming, Eric Maskin, Harry Sasson, Joe Stiglitz, Torsten Thiele, Jean Tirole, John Vickers and to our discussants Colin Mayer and Joan Pearce, for helpful comments and suggestions. Alberto Giovannini provided useful editorial suggestions. Information and financial support from the European Bank for Reconstruction and Development and the Centre for Economic Policy Research are gratefully acknowledged.

1 Appendix A provides a description of the role and financing policy of the EBRD.
2 Handler *et al.* (1991) independently and using a Harrod–Domar approach obtain a similar figure of US$1.0 to 1.1 trillion for the cumulated capital requirement of the EESU region in the year 2000.
3 EBRD estimates.
4 This is in keeping with the history of economic development in both industrial and developing nations. Mobilization of savings is critical – on this aspect in EESU see Tanzi (1991).
5 See Appendix A for a definition of these ratings.
6 Note that the preferred creditor status, which grants absolute seniority of debt-claims to the IFI which benefits from this status, may also have the negative second-order effect of crowding out subsequent loans to the public sector that would by definition be junior to the IFI's loans.
7 See Williamson (1991) for an interesting discussion of this issue.
8 Note that though the bulk of this discussion is couched in terms of enterprises, the arguments cited apply equally well to other types of small economic assets (e.g. retail outlets, services).
9 See Maskin (1992).
10 This idea was primarily suggested by Maskin (1992). Bolton and Roland (1992) develop this idea primarily from the point of view of sales revenue maximization.
11 The leasing-out of a state-enterprise's assets to new private companies, sometimes confusingly called 'liquidation', has proved to be very popular in Poland for the privatization of smaller companies. Of 143 liquidated as at June 1991, 48 were privatized through sale of assets and 95 through the leasing of assets. Leasing of small enterprises has also been an integral part of the industrial reforms in China.
12 This idea emerged from fruitful conversations with John Flemming and John Vickers. A similar multi-part auction approach is also developed by Bolton and Roland (1992).
13 However, as Grossman and Hart (1982) point out, if bankruptcy involved substantial (private) costs for the bidder-manager, then a higher debt-equity ratio would induce more effort from him.
14 Romania has developed a similar programme, but with a smaller number of funds and greater reliance on state-administered trade sales. Amongst the other CIS republics, the Ukraine and Kazakhstan are considering vouchers.
15 The emergence of 'funds' (e.g. the Harvard Fund) which offer a sum in excess of a voucher price in return for ownership of the voucher when it becomes tradeable is an example of this process.
16 For example, in Poland the Government conserves 30 per cent of the shares in

large SOE undergoing mass privatization. In Romania, where a voucher scheme is also being promoted, the government conserves 70 per cent of the shares of large SOE in the first stage of their privatization.

17 Giving *voting* shares to local governments 'would make them large shareholders with a substantial interest in active control. While workers' shares are dispersed, local government shares are concentrated. In many cases, local governments would use their ownership rights to deal with privatization and to continue managing the state firms . . .'

18 'Concentration of powers in a single agency responsible only to the highest level of government has made it easier to develop a privatization programme, particularly when the agency is given direct powers to divest assets. With such a centralization of powers, and because of the size of the privatization task, it has often been easier to implement privatizations if there is some decentralization of operations to local or regional branches, possibly coupled with a delegation of authority to enterprises for enterprise-led privatizations' (Sasson, 1991).

19 To recapitalize banks further, the state can also issue government bonds and exchange them against non-performing loans to enterprises. Shares received by state banks in the privatization of enterprises could later be sold to repay the government loans.

20 In particular, adherence to such a Pareto-improving path might not be achieved through a reform package that would involve industrial dislocation, mass unemployment and a deep recession in the short run.

21 Adjustment costs due to shut-downs and labour reallocation across firms and sectors are magnified by short-term factors affecting companies: reduced domestic demand, the collapse of intra-EESU trade, vertical disintegration and high debts, interest payments and taxes.

22 The same considerations become relevant when addressing the privatization issue: to prevent Workers' Councils councils from blocking privatizations (as they have already done in several EESU countries), social compensation for layoffs should be paid by the privatized company with financial help from the privatization agency.

23 See Aghion *et al.* (1992) for a bankruptcy procedure which overcomes this valuation issue.

24 In this context the experience of central privatization agencies such as the Treuhand in East Germany is of considerable interest (see Carlin and Mayer, 1992).

25 In addition, excessive vertical integration may induce inefficient (over)investment incentives and market foreclosure outcomes that would, in the EESU context, jeopardize the emergence and development of new private business.

26 Tirole (1991).

27 This type of argument may help to explain the empirical finding of a concentration of trade in high quality products amongst the rich, industrial nations. The argument can be formalized using a Shaked and Sutton (1982) type of model, see Aghion and Burgess (1991) for a technical discussion of trade and growth in the EESU setting.

28 Note that central government has a much greater ability to internalize social costs than private firms.

29 Prepared by the World Bank, the OECD, EBRD and IMF.

30 Given that the total Soviet labour force is around 148 million people, the

volume of total current employment in agriculture and manufacturing is about 64.8 million workers. This figure should be brought down to 47.4 million in order to meet the average Western proportions. On the other hand, total current employment in the wholesale-retail trade is about 9.8 million workers. This volume should increase to 38.5 million so as to meet Western standards. The corresponding aggregate turnover is at least equal to the minimum of these two labour flows, i.e. over 21 million workers (the maximum of the two flows is 27 million workers).

31 Although the existing state-owned retail shops are often considered as being overmanned by Western standards, in the sense that the productivity of labour on each individual transaction is much lower than in the West. There is nonetheless considerable scope for increasing the amount of retail transactions, both within existing retail units and through the multiplication of new retail shops and services throughout the countries. Such spreading out of retail units may involve some new inefficiency, e.g. of having unvisited shops during most of the working days; on the other hand, it eliminates the great economic inefficiency involved in the persistence of queues.

32 For example, the IFC's official mandate is to further economic development by encouraging the growth of private enterprises in member countries.

33 The provision of EBRD of lines of credit and equity investments in the Dutch bank NMB and in the Czechoslovakia Investment Corporation Inc. which provide critical financing for small and medium-sized enterprises in Poland and Czechoslovakia is a good example of this approach.

34 The poor financial and repayment performance of loans to the public sector in developing countries is a major consideration. The perceived inefficiency of the state in promoting private enterprise in these countries is another.

35 In a transition setting the implication is that the role of the state will change significantly; however, it will still remain important to the process. Indeed, given the great need for infrastructure, social support, coordination and the establishment of clear guidelines for economic activity, it would seem unwise to adopt a minimalist view of the state during transition.

36 The management policy of the Bank is also restricting the total volume of *committed* operations to less than 90 per cent of total callable capital and reserves, so that the repayment of the Bank's creditors should never depend on the callable capital of EESU countries.

37 The IFC has adopted a still more conservative policy with liquid assets covering over 90 per cent of the next three years' estimated cash requirements.

38 The latter embodies political risks, risks arising due to low foreign currency earnings and those related to foreign debt policy. There is also the *foreign exchange risk*, which the Bank will eliminate on its lending operations by imposing that its loans be repaid in the same hard currency (Ecu, US$, Yen . . .) as the one they are being billed in. Finally, *interest rate* risk will be issued by having interest rates set at the time of the loan disbursement, while the loan margin will be set at the time the loan is committed!

39 Losses on loans, equity investments and underwritings will be charged in the following order:
   – 'automatic' provisions against losses
   – statutory reserves (retained earnings)
   – paid-in capital
   – uncalled subscribed capital.

No provision is made regarding losses arising in 'special operations' such as technical assistance, which are covered by a Special Fund.

REFERENCES

Aghion, P. and R. Burgess (1991) 'Trade and Growth in Eastern Europe and the Soviet Union', Mimeo, European Bank for Reconstruction and Development.

Aghion, P., O. Hart and J. Moore (1992) 'The Economics of Bankruptcy Reform', paper presented at NBER conference on Transition in Eastern Europe.

Bolton, P. and G. Roland (1992) 'Privatization Policies in Central and Eastern Europe', *Economic Policy* 7, (15), 275–309.

Blanchard, O., R. Dornbusch, R. Layard and L. Summers (1991) *Reform in Eastern Europe*, MIT Press.

Burda, M. (1991) 'Labour and Product Markets in Czechoslovakia and the ex-GDR: A Twin Study', *European Economy*, Special Edition No. 2.

Carlin, W. and C. Mayer (1992) 'The Treuhandanstalt: Privatization by State and Market', paper presented at NBER conference on Transition in Eastern Europe, Cambridge, Mass.

Collins, S. and D. Rodrik (1991) 'Eastern Europe and the Soviet Union in the World Economy', Policy Analysis in *International Economics No. 32*, Institute for International Economics, Washington DC.

Economic Commission for Europe (1991) *Economic Survey of Europe, 1990–1*. New York: United Nations.

Fischer, S. (1991) 'Privatization in Eastern European Transformation', Working Paper, Institute for Policy Reform, Washington DC.

Flemming, J. (1990) 'Gradualism and Shock Treatment for Tax and Structural Reform', *Fiscal Studies* 11, 12–26.

Frydman, R. and A. Rapaczynski (1990) 'Markets and Institutions in Large Scale Privatizations', mimeo, New York University.

Grossman, S. and O. Hart (1982) 'Corporate Financial Structure and Managerial Incentives', in J.J. McCall (ed.), *The Economics of Information and Uncertainty*. Chicago: University of Chicago Press.

Handler, H., A. Kramer and J. Stanovsky (1991) 'Debt, Capital Requirements and Training of the Eastern Countries', Working Paper, Austrian Institute of Economic Research.

IMF, World Bank, OECD, EBRD (1991) *A Study of the Soviet Economy*.

Lipton, D. and J. Sachs (1990) 'Creating a Market Economy in Eastern Europe: The Case of Poland', *Brookings Papers on Economic Activity* No. 1.

Little, I.M.D. (1982) *Economic Development*, New York, Basic Books.

Maskin, E. (1992) 'Auctions and Privatization', Mimeo, Harvard.

Messerlin, P.A. (1991) *Trade Between OECD Countries and Central and Eastern European Countries*, Institut d'Etudes Politiques de Paris.

Mitchell, J. (1990) 'The Economics of Bankruptcy in Reforming Socialist Economies', Mimeo, Cornell University.

Sasson, H. (1991) 'The Privatization Experience in Western Europe', Mimeo, European Bank for Reconstruction and Development, London.

Shaked, A. and J. Sutton (1982) 'Relaxing Price Competition through Product Differentiation', *Review of Economic Studies* 49, 3–13.

Shleifer, A. and R.W. Vishny (1992) 'Privatization in Russia: First Steps', paper presented at NBER conference on Transition in Eastern Europe, Cambridge, Mass.

Stern, N. (1991) 'Public Policy and the Economics of Development', *European Economic Review* **35**, 241–71.

Tanzi, V. (1991) 'Mobilization of Savings in Eastern European Countries: The Role of the State', in A.B. Atkinson and R. Brunetta (Eds.), *Economics for the New Europe*, London: International Economic Association.

Tirole, J. (1991) 'Privatization in Eastern Europe: Incentives and the Economics of Transition', Mimeo, MIT.

Williamson, O. (1991) 'Private Ownership and the Capital Market', paper presented at a conference on 'Privatization' at the Kiel Institute of World Economics.

Discussion

COLIN MAYER

This paper provides an explanation for the importance of institutions in the transition of Eastern Europe. Initially, it was thought that all that the restructuring of the enterprise sectors of Eastern Europe would entail was privatization as rapidly as possible and the delegation of restructuring to the new private sector owners. In some quarters, this view is still held. However, as this paper clearly documents, the climate is changing. There is now an appreciation that privatization cannot be disassociated from restructuring and much of this can only occur over an extended period of time in the public sector.

The paper documents the market failures that undermine a simple privatization programme: absence of sound banking, inadequate infrastructure, inadequate management skills and in particular insufficient savings. Sales of equity are impeded by low levels of savings and poorly functioning credit markets which prevent potential bidders from being able to reveal their valuations. Attempts to overcome this by deferring payments that investors have to make are limited by the adverse effects that they have on incentives and the risks of default that extension of loans by governments to investors entail. Poorly functioning credit markets also undermine the operation of bankruptcy procedures since credit-constrained junior creditors are unable to reveal the values that they attach to acquiring control of enterprises; liquidations are therefore excessively high.

What is then required is less emphasis on privatization and more on restructuring, in particular the introduction of incentives into enterprises, the management of technology transfers and demonopolization and vertical disintegration of enterprises. Institutions, and in particular banks, are required to play a central function in organizing this. However, banks are seriously hampered by the huge loan loss hangovers that they inherited, poor staff and poor internal management systems. Aghion and Burgess therefore see an important role for foreign institutions and in particular international agencies, such as the European Bank for Reconstruction and Development (EBRD), in assisting in the reform process.

Appendix A to the paper provides an interesting description of the operation of the EBRD. This records the way in which the activities of the EBRD differ from those of other international agencies, such as the IFC. There is more emphasis in the EBRD on transition rather than development and a disillusionment with previous policies of channelling assistance through recipient governments. Instead, the EBRD emphasizes assistance with the development of institutional structures in Eastern Europe and a partnership with private and public sector institutions rather than governments in effecting change. The approach is a combination of a top-down (development banking) encouragement of the emergence of new institutions and a bottom-up (merchant banking) approach of providing direct assistance to individual enterprises.

The importance of this article stems from the clear and informative way in which it identifies the market failures that have undermined simple privatization programmes, establishes the need for institutional involvement and describes the role of international agencies, and in particular the EBRD, in this process.

The article displays a tension between on the one hand justifying the current approach taken by the EBRD and on the other documenting the limited progress that has been made to date. Why is there still so much uncertainty about what needs to be done? Why is there such a divergence in approaches taken by different countries? Why has progress been so slow? It is easy to respond that the problems are overwhelming, that the costs are formidable and that the reform process takes time. However, there is an alternative description of what is happening and that is that an appropriate solution to the problem of transition has not yet been identified.

The inadequacies of simple privatization have been recognized and the importance of institutional creation and restructuring has been correctly identified. However, that says nothing about the way in which these activities should be performed. How does one create an agency to oversee the privatization of enterprises? What form should it take? Should there be several of them or just one? How does one create a bank? What should be the structure of banks and what should be their relation with the enterprise sectors?

The reason why there is very little guidance on these points is clear: economics has virtually nothing to say about them. Economics has only rather grudgingly accepted the need for institutions over the past few years. It has little to contribute to why they exist, less on why there are differences between them and nothing on how to create them.

The reason why East European problems appear so formidable is that we do not possess the tools to address them. What the last few years have revealed is a yawning gap in our understanding of institutions. The rush by academics to fill that gap has begun and in ten years time we will unquestionably be much better placed to offer advice. Unfortunately, that is little consolation for the victims of our ignorance.

Instead, the best that can be done is to draw lessons from the experience of different countries in transition. There are two that are particularly pertinent. The first is Japan in the immediate post WW2 period and the second is East Germany now. Corbett (1992) argues that conscious government policy shifted the structure of the Japanese financial system from the pre-war period to the one that exists today. The current bank-oriented Japanese financial system stands in marked contrast to the much more market-oriented system of the 1910s and 1920s and the change was largely initiated by the Japanese government itself. A large shift in resources from military to industrial activities was accomplished with little reliance on freely operating capital markets. The highly concentrated ownership associated with zaibatsus was broken up by sales through public auctions and to employees. Company balance sheet restructurings were carried out centrally and balance sheets were restated to eliminate some of the debt overhang.

In East Germany, Carlin and Mayer (1992) document a similar role of the Treuhandanstalt in restructuring enterprises, writing off debt, creating balance sheets, installing supervisory and management boards and selling enterprises. Again securities markets are playing very little in this process and banks are central.

In both cases, the need for strong central coordination in the initial periods of reform was identified. Institutions existed or were created (for example, the long-term investment banks in Japan) that permitted the reform process to be implemented and financed. These above all appear to be the catalyst for successful development. There are two things that stand in the way of their establishment elsewhere in Eastern Europe. The first is there considerable cost and the second is their requirement for skilled employees. East Germany could draw on the financial and human resources of West Germany. The rest of Eastern Europe does not possess an equivalent benefactor; instead, it is dependent on the rest of the world to provide these resources.

This suggests that the 'top-down' approach of the EBRD and other international agencies will be particularly important in the reform process. The 'bottom-up' approach may be a useful adjunct but in many cases this is a role that can in large part be played by private institutions. It is the centralized creation of financial systems and financial institutions that only international agencies can manage and finance. What appears to have been lacking to date is a willingness to perform this function on the scale that Eastern Europe requires.

REFERENCES

Carlin, W. and Mayer, C. (1992) 'Restructuring Enterprises in Eastern Europe', *Economic Policy* 7, (15), 311–52.
Corbett, J. (1992) 'Structure and Behaviour in the Japanese Financial System: Lessons for Eastern Europe', mimeo.

11 Overview

JOSEPH E. STIGLITZ

I have been asked to provide a brief overview of the conference. Rather than discussing each of the individual papers, I want to focus my remarks on some general themes, into which many, perhaps most, of the papers can be placed.

1 Central questions

The central question motivating the conference is, what will be the effect of the formation of the European Monetary Union (EMU) on economic development and on the ability of governments to use monetary instruments to promote economic stabilization and development, both for their country as a whole, and for particular regions within their country. The longstanding presumption has been that with a unified currency, countries abandon the ability to use interest rate policies to promote either growth or economic stabilization: interest rates will be uniform within the currency area.

What is at stake, of course, is more than just the abandonment of an instrument. The very desirability of free trade – from the perspective of a particular country – may be thrown into question. While standard propositions in free trade (under perfect competition) assure us that there are gains from trade, they also point out that free trade may make particular factors of production worse off. The gainers can compensate the losers – though such compensation is seldom made. And if the losers happen to be concentrated disproportionately in a particular country, then that country may actually be worse off. The gainers within that country may not be able to compensate the losers. This would not be the case if there were flexible exchange rates: then the gainers within that country could compensate the losers.

Thus, the questions we wish to address are:

(1) To what extent will the formation of the EMU promote financial integration?

343

(2)   What will be the impact of increased financial integration on regional stabilization and development?

(3)   What are the *mechanisms* by which financial integration yields its effects?

(4)   Are there alternative instruments available to the government, which can be used as a substitute for any loss of ability to use monetary policy? Are these alternative instruments likely to be effective?

Most of the papers within the conference focused on the problems of economic development, and I will, accordingly focus my remarks there. What causes, or promotes, development is a long-studied question. Not surprisingly, we did not resolve these fundamental issues here: there will be plenty of opportunities for future conferences.

2   Perspectives on the growth process

While the question of development is well-studied, I do think there have been substantial increases in our understanding during the past fifteen years. Let me summarize these perspectives.

(1)   There have been some success stories, most notably the NICs (the Gang of Four, Taiwan, Korea, Hong Kong, and Singapore); but other countries, including Malaysia and Thailand have done remarkably well.

But while there have been some notable successes, for most countries, the gap between the developed and less developed countries remains unchanged. Thus, these non-success stories will dominate any cross-country regressions. We learn nothing from such regressions about successful development. Our attention should be focused on what distinguishes the success cases from the rest. Unfortunately, the number of success stories is sufficiently few that we hardly have a sufficient data set for making convincing statistical comparisons. Still, such studies may be useful, as I shall comment on later.

(2)   Success often seems episodic and localized. That is, it often seems to occur in spurts, and, at least initially, the spurts leave some regions within the country behind. Thus, in the United States, the South remained a relatively backward region until the 1930s. The gap between Sao Paulo and the northeast of Brazil is dramatic. Recent developments in China have been highly concentrated. This concentration of growth in time and space suggests the importance of several themes stressed in the earlier development literature: Rosenstein–Rodan's big push and Hirschman's linkages, or in modern

parlance, the importance of non-convexities and externalities, themes which have been taken up once again in the New Growth literature.[1]

Saying that there are non-convexities and externalities does not, however, take us very far. Both may be – and indeed are likely to be – localized, both geographically and by sector. (Indeed, another defect of much of the new growth literature is an unconvincing account of the 'units' over which the non-convexities and externalities arise. Countries consist of many regions. Is it the size of the region or the size of the country which determines the relevant 'scale'? Does it make a difference whether the goods produced are traded or not? Presumably, for many traded goods, full advantage of economies of scale can be attained even in a relatively small economy such as Singapore.)

Markets do not work well in the presence of externalities and non-convexities. There is a role for government intervention, or at least coordination. The difficulty arises in determining the nature of government intervention. As a first step, the particular nature and sources of the non-convexities and externalities have to be identified. This can be done – they loom larger, for instance, in some sectors than in others. And indeed, one can interpret the success cases of Korea and Japan as having involved precisely that – the identification of sectors where spillovers will be large and where coordination is particularly desirable.

To be sure, governments, like all humans and human institutions, are fallible. There will be mistakes. Advocates of free markets will always point to mistakes – such as MITI's attempt to discourage Honda from entering the car market. They will claim – without any supporting evidence – that but for MITI, Japan's growth would have been even more phenomenal.

Of course, MITI did not bar Honda from entering the market, and this illustrates, I suspect, an important part of a successful development programme: the recognition of the likelihood of error, and the maintenance of sufficient flexibility that the consequences of errors are limited.

The observation that successes have been episodic and localized has some further methodological implications, beyond those we have already noted. In particular, it suggests that the standard neoclassical model is likely to provide only limited insights into the growth process.

Arrow's Learning by Doing model, including the more recent elaborations of the New Growth theories, stresses one aspect of this: that there are positive feedbacks. Capital accumulation gives rise to productivity increases, which may in turn give rise to further growth. Diminishing returns do not set in, in the way envisaged by Solow's growth model.

Another aspect is that markets will be imperfectly competitive. As Dasgupta and Stiglitz (1980) have emphasized, economies with non-convexities, in particular the non-convexities associated with learning by doing, are naturally imperfectly competitive. Firms that get ahead have a competitive advantage; their costs are lower than their rivals; their cost advantage allows them to produce more, and thus their competitive advantage grows.

The older literature did stress one aspect of the relationship between investment and productivity increases which the New Growth literature has failed to emphasize: when technological change is embodied in new capital equipment, then in the short run productivity increases will be related to the rate of gross investment. This increased rate of productivity growth associated with increased rates of investment will offset the normal effects of diminishing returns, at least in the short run.

The single-sector neoclassical model also obscures one of the most important aspects of actual growth processes: the movement of labour from low-productivity sectors to higher-productivity sectors. In the standard neoclassical model, capital and labour are allocated efficiently, so that the (marginal) productivity of every factor in every sector is the same. In reality, there are marked discrepancies, and adjustments may take a long time. Thus agricultural labour typically has a much lower productivity than industrial labour; and the development process has been characterized by large movements of labour out of agriculture into industry. By the same token, there are marked differences in productivity of factors between one region of the economy and another. In both cases, there are large growth gains to be had from the reallocation of factors of production, rather than the increase in the supply of factors of production.

To put it another way, understanding the institutions and mechanisms which affect the efficiency with which resources get allocated is central to understanding growth process. Development is associated both with the reallocation of factors of production, and with the development of institutions which lead systematically to their more efficient allocation. Among those institutions are markets and, in the case of capital, banks.

While I have spoken so far of differences in factor productivities across sectors, we need to look at even a more micro-level, at the firm. Banks do not allocate capital blindly to sectors, but to particular firms. Capital does not flow freely across firms, for obvious reasons, having to do with imperfect information. This provides another important feedback mechanism in the growth process: *firms* that are more profitable can invest more; with their greater wealth, they can bear to undertake greater risks, to do more research; with their greater research and greater production, their costs decrease, enhancing their ability to grow. At the same time, limitations on capital may limit the ability of the low cost firm to expand in the short run, thereby limiting its ability to take full advantage of its cost advantage. Capital market imperfections may actually limit the extent of imperfections in the product market.

(3) Almost all successful development programmes have involved an important role for government. In the United States, government land grants facilitated the growth of railroads. Government research provided much of the impetus for the increase in productivity in agriculture. In Korea, Japan, and Taiwan, governments were hardly passive bystanders.

(4) Almost all successful growth programmes have been accompanied by rapid capital accumulation, though the links between growth and savings run both ways: we have already delineated several ways in which more rapid capital accumulation leads to more rapid growth; but it is also the case that when incomes are rising rapidly, consumption may not keep pace, so that savings – the residual between income and consumption – increases.

(5) But while rapid capital accumulation almost always accompanies rapid growth, it is not sufficient to ensure rapid growth. The most obvious examples to the contrary are provided by some of the socialist countries, where savings rates were extremely high. The high levels of capital accumulation simply served to offset the inefficiencies in its allocation.

Thus, what is relevant, as we noted earlier, is not only the aggregate supply of capital, but how it is utilized. And what is at stake is more than a matter of static allocative efficiency. Earlier, I spoke of embodied technological change and noted that there may be externalities and learning effects associated with investment. Some forms of capital may embody more new technology. And some forms of investment may have greater externalities and generate more learning than others.

(6) Capital, as we explain in our principles courses, is used in two senses: 'capital goods' and 'finance'. And just as the allocation of capital among capital goods makes a difference, so does the form in which capital is provided. This is the fundamental insight of the counter-Modigliani-Miller revolution in corporate finance. It does make a difference whether a firm is financed through debt or equity. They differ in their incentive and risk-sharing effects. Equity allows the firm to undertake greater risks.

The problem is that even in the more developed countries, a relatively small proportion of new capital is raised in equity markets. Equity is 'raised' through retained earnings. Thus low interest rates and low wages have an indirect effect on firms – they lead to higher profits, and thus more equity, inducing firms to invest more in riskier (higher return) activities.[2]

Equity is particularly important in banking. Without adequate 'equity' the kinds of moral hazard problems that plagued the S & L industry in the United States arise. There arises here a natural conflict between concerns about competition (both in the banking sector, and, more generally) and the growth and stability of the banking sector. Competition leads to lower profits and low bank equity, with the consequent moral hazard problems. These problems may be mitigated by appropriately designed regulations.

3   Financial market developments

This brings me to a central theme of the conference: the effect of improvements in financial markets and institutions on economic development. There seems little doubt that, in general, more developed countries have more developed financial institutions. The question is, what is the causal link?

Earlier discussions focused on the fact that financial intermediaries – when they were not repressed by government – allowed savers to earn higher real rates of return, and this encouraged savings. Yet most of the available evidence suggests a limited elasticity of savings with respect to the real interest rate; it may even be negative.

The US experience – the massive misallocation of capital by the S & Ls and banks (evidenced by the high rates of default) in the aftermath of the partial deregulation of the early 1980s suggests that 'freer' or 'more competitive' markets do not necessarily allocate resources more efficiently. Financial intermediaries *may* make a difference in leading to a more efficient allocation of resources; but for this to be the case, the financial intermediaries have to face the correct incentives; they cannot suffer from the kinds of moral hazard problems that characterized the banking sector in the United States (or in Chile).

This suggests an hypothesis that deserves further exploration: one of the central functions performed by the governments in most of the success stories was ensuring the viability of the banking system. A favourite question raised in discussions of banking in recent years has been: if banks monitor firms, who monitors banks? The answer, in the case of the United States, is, 'effectively no one'.

The appropriate form of monitoring raises subtle questions which I cannot go into in this overview: government monitoring may focus not so much on monitoring individual loans, as monitoring the banks' financial structure, to ensure that banks have the appropriate incentives.

While the problems of bank deregulation are by now almost well understood, the problems of other aspects of financial liberalization are not so transparent. Again, there often seems a confusion between secondary capital markets (on which claims are traded) and primary capital markets, where new capital is raised. Much of the discussion of financial market liberalization and development focuses on secondary capital markets. Most of the concern *should* focus on the impact on the ability of primary capital markets to perform their function, to raise new capital and to allocate it efficiently. Much of the primary capital market functions are mediated through banks, even in more developed countries; and this is likely to be particularly true in less developed countries. Improvements in secondary capital markets may even have adverse effects on primary capital markets, as funds are drawn away from domestic banks.

4   Regional development policies in integrated financial markets

While many LDCs thus may debate whether it is desirable to liberalize their secondary financial markets, that is no longer really a question within the Common Market. There, the issue is, what will be the consequences of financial market integration? Can there still be regional growth and stabilization policies? The answer is yes. I want to now discuss four such groups of policies that have been touched upon within the conference.

(1)   Monetary policy. Greenwald, Levinson and Stiglitz (1993) have, in effect, focused on the distinction between primary and secondary markets. Even with perfectly working markets for government securities, the markets for loans remains highly segmented. Information – and, consequently capital – does not flow freely throughout the EEC. Arbitrage is imperfect. Within the United States, where there have been no restrictions to the movement of capital, they show, for instance, that shocks to firms in one region of the economy get transmitted to banks in that region, and thereby to other firms in that region. (The United States has a fragmented banking system. These effects would, presumably, be at least partially mitigated if there were truly national banks.)

They argue that the monetary authorities can take advantage of these informational problems, by designing policies that have directed effects on the banks within a particular region. It is possible, for instance, to have different reserve requirements in different regions. Though the fact that capital is partially mobile means that there will be some arbitrage associated with any differential treatment, the arbitrage will be imperfect, and accordingly monetary policy can be effective. The government can, and should, take advantage of market imperfections.

Monetary policy has traditionally been concerned with the control of the stock of money or of money market interest rates through purchases and sales of securities in money markets. Monetary union would, almost necessarily, mean a loss of control over these market rates of interest (just as any form of market integration, by increasing the mobility of factors, gives rise to losses of instruments or reductions in the effectiveness of instruments). But what really affects economic activity is not so much interest rates on money markets (the rate of interest on government securities), but the availability of credit from banks and other financial institutions, and the terms on which credit is made available. These the government can affect, even with monetary integration.

(2) Regional development policies. Faini, Galli and Giannini (1993) show how these policies have been pursued in Italy, through targeted financial policies and subsidies. The evidence they present suggests that the incidence of the subsidies may have been markedly different than intended: interest rates have not decreased in the South. Banks in the South seemed to have appropriated much of the rent associated with the subsidies. In short, they have not succeeded in promoting growth.

This experience parallels government attempts in many LDCs to use subsidized rural credit to drive out high interest rate rural lenders, or at least, through competition, to induce them to lower their interest rates. Neither seems to have occurred. (See Hoff and Stiglitz, 1990.)

The lack of success in both cases may be related to the imperfect nature of lending markets, emphasized in the Greenwald, Levinson and Stiglitz paper. In imperfectly competitive markets, the incidence of credit subsidies may be markedly different from that in competitive markets.

(3) Subsidizing people. Rather than subsidizing industry in a region, one can subsidize people within a region. This is the tack taken in Spain, as explained by the paper by Cuadrado, de la Dehesa and Precedo. The failure of such a policy to promote growth is even less surprising than that of regional development policy. Indeed, by encouraging dependency, such policies may even hinder growth.

(4) Encouraging migration. If industry will not come to the unemployed workers, then the unemployed workers should go to where the jobs are. In a neoclassical model, with costless movement of capital and costly movement of labour, it makes sense for capital to move to

individuals. But if non-convexities are important, and if, because of costly and imperfect information, capital does not flow freely, then efficiency may entail workers migrating to jobs.

The question is, how important are the non-convexities? Switzerland is a small economy, and attained competitive advantages in certain industries (such as watch making.) This brings us back to the question I raised in the beginning of the discussion, concerning the relevant 'unit of analysis'.

Beyond these specific policies, the government may encourage the development of a region by enhancing the physical, human, institutional and legal infrastructure: improving transport systems, raising skill levels, facilitating the development of indigenous banks and other financial institutions, and ensuring that contracts are enforced, and that corruption, either within local governments or Mafia type, is limited. While there is no easy prescription for the latter, the existence of large rents caused by artificially imposed government constraints often aids and abets such corruption, and the deleterious effects of such corruption exceeds the potential gains had the loftiest objectives which might have motivated such constraints been attained.

Regardless of the policies being pursued, let me suggest three principles concerning the design of policies which, while not ensuring success, make success more likely. First, governments may be better at providing incentives than at actually managing economic activities. But the incentives they provide may be perverse: when there are excessive subsidies, incentives are directed at rent-seeking; when there are excessive constraints (such as on foreign exchange), incentives are directed at circumventing those constraints.

Second, there need to be 'checks' on the wisdom of government policies, some form of readily ascertainable external validation. Export-oriented policies have such checks: if the industry does not succeed in selling its goods abroad, it has failed the 'competitive test'. The failure of import-substitution policies may be largely attributed to this: the notion that there were some economies of scale and learning which, if production of the good became sufficiently large, would enable the industry to compete with foreigners may have considerable merit; but government's ability (or willingness, given the political pressures) to identify the relevant sectors and the absence of any external validation, as a check, meant that in many instances, protection and subsidies were misdirected.

(As an aside, it should be noted that the imperfections of information, and in particular, the imperfections of capital markets, to which I have referred several times in this overview, do provide a rationale for government intervention. The objection to the infant industry argument – that if the firm's costs would eventually be low enough to enable it to compete, it should go ahead and produce on its own, without a government subsidy – may not be valid, if the firm cannot finance the intervening losses.[4])

Third, there need to be sunset provisions, phasing out government subsidies. The governments' commitment to such phase-outs not only has positive incentive effects on the subsidized firms – they know that unless they reduce their costs, they will not be able to survive – it has negative incentive effects on rent-seeking – firms know that any rents they may collect from a government subsidy are only temporary, and may not be sufficient to offset the sunk costs associated with entry, unless the firm is, in fact, successful in the long run.

In concluding, let me return to a theme I noted in the beginning: that there have been relatively few success cases, and that we have more to learn by looking at these few success cases than at the myriad of other cases. There may, indeed, be many roads to success, but there are many more roads to failure. The success of Korea and other newly industrialized countries of East Asia have renewed our confidence that countries can make the Great Leap Forward, and that sensible government policies may facilitate that leap. If that is the case, we should be all the more confident that sensible policies can be found which will promote the growth of the lagging regions within Europe. Not everyone benefits from freeing trade, and not everyone is likely to benefit from financial integration. There are reasons to be concerned that the lagging regions of Europe may not only not be helped; they could actually be hurt. Yet there is also reason to believe that even under a European Monetary Union, there is a range of appropriately designed government policies (including those operating through financial markets) that can be used both to stimulate regional development and to promote regional stability.

The further analysis of these and other policies for regional growth and stability remain important questions for further research.

NOTES

1 Much of this literature, unfortunately, has not bothered to study the older growth literature. It is simply wrong to say (as advocates of this new growth literature claim) that the older growth literature took the rate of technological change as exogenous. Indeed, there were at least two strands of literature attempting to endogenize technological change (beyond the well known work of Arrow, 1962). The volume of essays edited by Shell (1967) represents perhaps the most well known set of studies undertaken by the students of Uzawa (see also Uzawa's own work, 1965), but there were others; the issues, both the economic problems and the modelling difficulties, were hotly discussed at all the major centres of research, including Chicago, Yale, and MIT. The second major strand was in Cambridge, represented most notably by the Kaldor and

Mirrlees (1962) article. My own earlier work on endogenous growth with Tony Atkinson (1969) was influenced by both of these strands.

Similarly, the importance of non-convexities was also recognized in the earlier literature. Not only did Nicky Kaldor stress the importance of increasing returns in manufacturing, he successfully advocated the introduction of the selective employment tax in Britain to take advantage of these returns to scale.

2 This provides an alternative reason to that suggested by Arthur Lewis for why having surplus labour may be conducive to growth. It is not so much that a 'shortage of labour' (whatever that might mean) inhibits growth, or that high wages lead to higher levels of consumption, and thus reduced the aggregate savings rate, but that high wages lead to low profits, and low *equity* formation.

3 Beyond this, there are imperfections of competition and externalities, both of which are frequently associated with the learning process, and to which I have referred earlier.

REFERENCES

Arrow, K.J. (1962) 'The Economic Implications of Learning by Doing', *Review of Economic Studies* **29**, 155–73.

Atkinson, A.B. and J.E. Stiglitz (1969) 'A New View of Technological Change', *Economic Journal* **69**, 573–78.

Dasgupta, P. and J.E. Stiglitz (1980) 'Uncertainty, Market Structure and the Speed of R & D', *Bell Journal of Economics* **11**, 1–28.

Faini, R., G. Galli, and C. Giannini (1993) 'Finance and Development: The Case of Italy', this volume.

Greenwald, B., A. Levinson, and J.E. Stiglitz (1993) 'Capital Market Imperfections and Regional Economic Development', this volume.

Hoff, K. and J.E. Stiglitz (1990) 'Imperfect Information and Rural Credit Markets: Puzzles and Policy Perspectives', *World Bank Editorial Review* **4**, 235–50.

Kaldor, N. and J.A. Mirrlees (1962) 'A New Model of Economic Growth', *Review of Economic Studies* **29**, 174–92.

Shell, K. (ed.) (1967) *Essays on the Theory of Optimal Economic Growth*, Cambridge, MA: MIT Press.

Uzawa, H. (1965) 'Optimal Technical Change in an Aggregative Model of Economic Growth', *International Economic Review* **6**, 18–31.

Index